CURIOCITY

CURIOCITY
IN PURSUIT OF LONDON

HENRY ELIOT & MATT LLOYD-ROSE

PARTICULAR
BOOKS

PARTICULAR BOOKS

UK | USA | Canada | Ireland | Australia
India | New Zealand | South Africa

Particular Books is part of the Penguin Random House group of companies
whose addresses can be found at global.penguinrandomhouse.com.

First published 2016
001

Copyright © Henry Eliot and Matt Lloyd-Rose

Designed by Here.

The moral right of the authors has been asserted

Colour reproduction by Rhapsody
Printed and bound in Italy by Printer Trento Srl

A CIP catalogue record for this book is available from the British Library
ISBN: 978–1–846–14867–5

Endpapers by Stanley Donwood, artist and author of
Catacombs of Terror!, a pulp fiction thriller set in Bath.

CONTENTS

NAVIGATION

MAP READING

Each of this book's 26 chapters explores a different aspect of London, and at the centre of each chapter is a map, drawn by one of 14 illustrators (see p.442). All of these maps preserve the city's geography, although they often bend and stretch it: some are clearly images of London, others transform the city and require more deciphering. A 'Map Reading' box explains the concept behind each map and provides guidance on how to interpret it. Texts on the tinted pages surrounding the maps are usually numbered (e.g. ⑧) and tell the stories contained on each map.

WHERE TO BEGIN

You could begin this A to Z at the beginning and read it through to the end, but you may wish to take a different approach.

1. DRIFT RANDOMLY

Explore this book as you would a big city and go where the mood takes you. Dip in and out.

2. FOLLOW THE FOOTNOTES

Umberto Eco draws a distinction between the dictionary and the encyclopaedia: a dictionary is a list, whereas an encyclopaedia is a network of connections. There are connections in many of the footnotes in this book, which will lead you across the chapters to related subjects.

3. START AT THE BACK

Use the book's indexes to hone in on specific places, people or events. There is a timeline; an index of people; an index of notable landmarks; an index of museums and galleries; an index of places to eat and drink; and a calendar of recurring events.

4. READ BETWEEN THE LINES

You can use this book to predict the future: write down the six digits of your birthday, add all four month and year digits, and turn to the corresponding chapter.[1] Then add the two day digits and turn to that page of the chapter.[2] Close your eyes and jab your finger at the page; wherever it lands may intimate future possibilities.

5. ESCAPE THE CITY

Andrew Norton[3] has sent in a number of picture postcards, which are scattered throughout the book. Follow his footsteps to escape from London.

> All practical information was accurate at the point of printing, but it will of course slide into the past tense as this book gradually changes from a functional guide into a historical record. When London eventually degenerates into toxic marshland, it will hopefully provide future inhabitants with an account of what people once got up to. It could also serve as a cudgel for beating off mutant rats.[4]

---

[1] If you were born on 13 April 1985 (13/04/85), you would add 0, 4, 8 and 5 = 17, and look up the 17th chapter = Q, 'Quarters'.

[2] i.e. add 1 + 3 = 4. Turn to the fourth page of 'Quarters'.

[3] Norton first appeared as the protagonist in Iain Sinclair's 1997 novel, *Slow Chocolate Autopsy*.

[4] See p.329

INTRODUCTION

'**FIND THE SEVEN NOSES OF SOHO,**' goes the legend, 'and you'll attain infinite wealth.' Stand at the corner of Meard Street and Dean Street, look up and you'll see a pale nose high on the brown brick wall. It's big – perhaps four times larger than life – with flared nostrils.' Walk left along Dean Street and you'll spot a similarly shaped black nose above Gino Gents Hairdressing and a third, indigo this time, outside the Sunset Strip striptease club. Scour the frontage of Quo Vadis (p.7) for a slim life-size schnoz and then look for a fifth outside Milkbar, just around the corner on Bateman Street. These noses tantalised us when we first heard about them. Easy to miss, but impossible to ignore once you know they're there, they set us wondering about the countless other signs, stories and mysteries half-hidden across the city.

When we first arrived in 2008, we were amazed by London and the parallel worlds it contains. In a single day you can swim with coots in the Hampstead bathing ponds (p.235), eyeball a mummified merman in Forest Hill (p.163), manhandle yams at Brixton Market (p.267), and witness laws being forged in the Supreme Court (p.280). By night, you can dine in a former squat kitchen in Vauxhall (p.136), spot comets from the Mill Hill observatory (p.208), and stay up late helping the homeless with a Street Rescue team (p.216). London is among the most vibrant, fascinating cities in the world, seemingly limitless in its variety, but it's also sprawling and cacophonous, making impossible demands on our time, attention and purse. And it's growing: in 2015 the population reached 8.6 million and the capital became more busy and crowded than it's ever been before (p.31).

How do you begin to get to know somewhere this complex and layered? On a walk through Oxleas Woods, southeast of Greenwich, we had an idea for a folded magazine where we could share lesser-known stories and places and, in so doing, get a firmer grip on London ourselves. At the centre would be a map of the city, looking at it from an unexpected point of view. We made eight editions of *Curiocity* magazine before embarking on this book-length exploration.

Curiocity is structured as an A to Z. Its twin inspirations are Samuel Johnson 'beating the track of the alphabet' as he compiled his famous dictionary in Gough Square (p.120), and Phyllis Pearsall, whose *London A–Z* is the definitive street map of the capital (p.13). For us, as for them, the alphabet provides a neat, limiting structure, but also hints at the limitless material that this kind of book could contain. As we pegged out the 26 chapters, we attempted to touch on every dimension of London life, down to the most functional and taboo, and to suggest ways of interacting with issues and subcultures that can seem inaccessible. We collected details that have brought the city to life for us, changing the way we see places and giving them a sudden and unexpected poignancy: the broom cupboard in the Houses of Parliament, for instance, where Emily Wilding Davison hid for the night (p.116); the ring of trees in Queen's Wood that hosts equinoctial pagan festivities (p.354); or the terraced houses in Croydon attempting to secede from the UK (p.135). We found that even something as bland as a row of railings can acquire significance when you know it's made of stretchers that carried the wounded during the Blitz (p.274).

With so much potential material, a major challenge in assembling this A to Z has been preventing the book becoming as unwieldy and overwhelming as the city it's attempting to map. In his story 'On Exactitude in Science', Jorge Luis Borges imagines a country of master cartographers, who create a perfectly precise map at a scale of 1:1. Their monumental chart is the same size as the territory it depicts and, therefore, completely pointless and unusable. In the late 18th century, Richard Horwood began work on the most detailed map ever made of London, 'shewing every house'. He died in poverty after spending nine years on a project that was supposed to take two. Horwood's tragic case is a reminder that the key to mapping and writing about London is omission, creating a likeness that's meaningful and functional by excluding all but the salient details.

A further difficulty is that writing about London is like publishing a biography while your subject is still in their prime: life outpaces you and your book is out of date before the ink has dried. Like the team of Horological Conservators at Buckingham Palace, who wind and rewind hundreds of clocks, only to begin afresh as soon as the last key is turned, when we completed this book we felt that we ought to start updating it immediately. London's greatest chronicler was the 16th-century historian John Stow, who spent most of his life writing a compendious *Survey of London*. Every three years, on or around the anniversary of his death (5 April), the Lord Mayor visits Stow's effigy in the church of St Andrew Undershaft and places a fresh quill in his hand so that he can continue his interminable undertaking.

While some people attempt to hold London still to map it and document it, everyone else is changing the city simply by being part of it, gradually altering its fabric and swelling its stock of stories. Some take the desire to leave their mark to extremes: in 1997, the artist Rick Buckley made a cast of his nose, and stuck replicas all over the centre of town. He didn't confess to his stunt until 2011 and, in the interim, more noses appeared and urban myths began to circulate, including the rumour that spotting seven noses in Soho would bring the finder untold riches.[2] As you pace London's highways and byways hunting for noses, why not add to the shifting city yourself? Leave your own trail of surreal clues for future chroniclers in pursuit of London.[3]

Henry Eliot & Matt Lloyd-Rose
2016

[1] The Meard Street nose is a replica of David's. Find the rest of him on p.69.

[2] Search for a sixth nose on Endell Street and a seventh on Great Windmill Street. Find an eighth on p.32.

[3] We've done just that: inspired by Buckley's nose, we've stuck six cryptic tiles up around the city for you to find. See p.449.

ATLAS

IN THE BATTLE FOR THE UNIVERSE, the primordial Titans fought against the younger upstart gods and lost. They were plunged into the dungeon of Tartarus, all except their strongest general. Atlas was banished to the westernmost edge of the world and charged with holding the sky and the earth, his father and mother, apart for ever more. There he stoops to this day, bearing the weight of the heavens on his shoulders.

Voyage to the westernmost edge of the classical world, to the capital city of an island in the Sea of Atlas,[1] to a place called King Street, and you will see Atlas kneeling outside a Grade II listed block of serviced offices, holding the celestial globe on his back. His eyes are cast down and he fixes you with a stony stare. When you tilt your head to meet his gaze, feel your spine flexing. Your tiny topmost vertebra, which supports the entire weight of your head, is known by anatomists as the 'atlas'.

Since the late 16th century, the celestial and terrestrial spheres, between which Atlas strains, have been squashed and squared and sliced into pages, so that now an 'atlas' is better known as a book of maps. Usually an atlas shows maps of different, contiguous geographies, but the book in your hands is an atlas in which all the maps cover the same geography. In this first chapter, we arrive, orientate ourselves and mark out the territory. As Karim, the narrator of Hanif Kureishi's *The Buddha of Suburbia* puts it, a first encounter with London can blow 'the windows of [your] brain wide open'.

ATLASES

The British Library's collection of over 4.5 million manuscript and printed maps spans the world and the universe, with maps that date back to 15 AD, embrace bird's-eye views and diagrams, and come in a wide variety of forms from globes to coins and posters.

— *Peter Barber*

❶ The Atlantic Ocean.

I

ARRIVALS

LONDON GATEWAY

The city sits at the hub of radiating roads that draw incomers from across the British Isles. The Romans paved six of these roads, which were later given Saxon names:

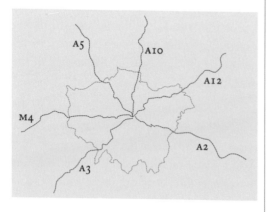

Ermine Street, from York to Bishopsgate (A10)

The Great Road, from Colchester to Aldgate (A12)

Watling Street, from Dover to London Bridge (A2)

Stane Street, from Chichester to London Bridge (A3)

The Devil's Highway, from Silchester to Newgate (M4)

Watling Street,[1] the other half of it, from Wroxeter to Newgate (A5)

When you enter the city today, consider refuelling at the George Inn on Borough High Street, London's last galleried coaching inn. Hand the ostler your panting post-horse and request a flagon of the house ale.[2] The modern equivalent of the coaching inn is the service station, where board and sometimes lodging can be purchased. The last station on the M1 is the 'London Gateway' services near Edgware. Gallop through the Gamezone and tuck into a limp toad in the hole.

LONDON TERMINUS

When the Eurostar first ran services from France, its London terminus was Waterloo Station, named after a humiliating French defeat.[3] Now the Eurostar runs into St Pancras, named after a murdered Italian teenager. St Pancras Station[4] is dominated by *The Meeting Place*, Paul Day's sculpture of a titanic couple embracing.[5] If you're feeling louche, quaff a flute of champagne at Searcys before descending to the streets of King's Cross.

CITY AIRPORT

There are six international airports that serve the city. London City is the most central. The runway requires a steep $5.5°$ glidepath, which affords breathtaking views across the capital.

PORT OF LONDON

Since the Royal Docks closed in 1981 there hasn't been a passenger terminal in central London and large ships have to stop at Tilbury Docks.[6] A new London City Cruise Port terminal at Greenwich is scheduled to open in 2017.

MATERNITY UNIT

A good way to arrive in London is to be born here and there's an excellent choice of venues across the city. If you'd like some entrance music, consider the Nightingale Ward at King's College Hospital, which lets you play your own power tracks; or if creature comforts are important, go for the private Lindo Wing of St Mary's Hospital, Paddington, where the Duchess of Cambridge has given birth twice.

---

[1] At the junction with Belsize Road a paving stone identifies Kilburn High Road as a section of Watling Street.
[2] George Ale (4%) brewed by Greene King.
[3] Florent Longuepée, a municipal councillor from Paris, wrote to Tony Blair to point out this cultural insensitivity.
[4] Meet the saviour of St Pancras Station on p.407.
[5] Examine the enigmatic frieze that Day added to the plinth in 2008, which features three-dimensional reflections, troubled skies and commuters who fix you with piercing stares.
[6] Berth your cruiser at Tilbury Docks on p.251 and p.407.

LINGUA LONDRA

Distinctive linguistic traits can act as a form of aural postcode. In the opening scene of *Pygmalion*, Eliza, the Covent Garden flower girl, says: 'Ow, eez ye-ooa san, is e? Wal, fewd dan y' de-ooty bawmz a mather should, eed now bettern to spawl a pore gel's flahrzn than ran awy atbaht pyin.' Professor Higgins overhears her and knows immediately that she was born in Lisson Grove, Marylebone.

Cockney Rhyming is the best-known variety of London slang, and has given the English language terms such as berk,[1] cobblers,[2] raspberry, Bristols[3] and taking the Mickey.[4] You translate Cockney Rhyming Slang by expanding the slang term, e.g. raspberry, to its longer form, raspberry tart. Then you find a word that rhymes with the second half.

[1] Berkeley Hunt
[2] Cobblers' awls
[3] Bristol Cities
[4] Mickey Bliss

NORTH OF THE RIVER

Traditionally, North London began at Hicks Hall, which stood on St John Street in Farringdon. Now Primrose Hill is the nucleus of North London celebrity bohemia. Don your smartest lally[1], stow the ankle-biter[2] and crash the loudest house hootenanny[3] you can find. London's Jewish community also centres on North London. You could go to Golders Green and nosh a kosher shawarma at Sami's, but avoid fressing[4] or you may grepse[5] or plotz.[6]

[1] Shirt
[2] Child
[3] Party
[4] Eating too quickly
[5] Belch
[6] Collapse with excitement

THE EAST END

Traditionally the East End begins at the corner of Fenchurch Street and Leadenhall Street: the Aldgate Pump, a defunct drinking fountain with a wolf's-head spout, marks the spot.[1] Nearby, on the Silicon Roundabout, you might well have a salmon day[2] if you're coding an angry garden salad[3], particularly if you have a seagull manager[4]. Among the hipsters of Dalston, things could get cray cray[5] if you bro-hug[6] a rando.[7]

[1] The pump commemorates the site where the last wolf was slain in London.
[2] A day swimming upstream
[3] A poorly designed website
[4] A boss who flies in, craps on everything, and leaves
[5] Crazy
[6] Embrace, in a manly way
[7] Creepy individual

THE WEST END

In the Middle Ages, the Church of St Peter was dubbed 'West Minster' Abbey to differentiate it from St Paul's. In Theatreland, use your mobile palare pipe[1] to remind your omi[2] to zhoosh[3] his riah[4] for the casting scouts, otherwise his eek[5] won't look bona[6] in those fantabulosa[7] new oglefakes.[8] Further west, maybs[9] you'll get on *MIC*[10] for totes[11] cheating with a fittie[12] in Juju? Among the more aristocratic circles of Kensington, however, you'll need to wait for a stiffie[13] to join the cockers-p[14] and get chateaued.[15]

[1] Phone
[2] Male friend
[3] Smarten
[4] Hair
[5] Face
[6] Good
[7] Wonderful
[8] Glasses
[9] Maybe
[10] The TV show *Made in Chelsea*
[11] Totally
[12] Attractive person
[13] Formal invitation
[14] Cocktail party
[15] Glamorously drunk

SOUTH OF THE RIVER

In 2013, Harris Academy in Upper Norwood banned slang. The school posted signs with lists of banned words, including 'coz', 'woz', 'bare', 'innit' and 'like'. 'Jafaican' is the most prominent South London patois: a hybrid London dialect that fuses elements of Caribbean, South Asian, African American and Cockney Rhyming Slang.[1] Oh my days! Man[2] bussed[3] these creps[4] outside the yard[5] and man looked peng,[6] bruv.[7] All the characters in the E4 TV series *Phone Shop* speak Jafaican; walk down Sutton High Street, where it was filmed, and make a blud.[8]

[1] Many linguists challenge the label 'Jafaican' and prefer the term Multicultural London English.
[2] I
[3] Wore
[4] Trainers
[5] At home
[6] Hot
[7] Brother, friend
[8] Friend

ESTABLISHING SHOTS

Find a vantage point with a panoramic view of London, and the centrepiece is likely to be St Paul's Cathedral. As Lord Byron put it in *Don Juan*, you locate that 'huge, dun cupola [...] – and there is London Town.'

This is no coincidence. Visit the Building Centre on Store Street and examine their 12-metre, 1:2,000-scale model of central London.[1] You can illuminate the city's 13 'protected views': invisible corridors around which city planners must arrange their projects.[2] Most of these views converge on St Paul's, ensuring that the cathedral remains plainly visible from afar.

HENRY'S MOUND
Stand on King Henry's Mound[3] in Richmond Park and use the telescope to look along 'The Way' to St Paul's, ten miles away. This is the oldest of London's protected views, created in 1710, a year before St Paul's was completed. Tall buildings are banned around Liverpool Street Station because they would spoil the backdrop.

HIGHGATE'S HEIGHT
The vista from Parliament Hill on Hampstead Heath is one of the most iconic London views; at dawn a bevy of lycra-clad joggers pause their running watches, and at dusk couples nestle in the meadow grass. Nearby, the view of St Paul's from the Kenwood House Viewing Gazebo is also legally protected.[4]

ALLY PALLY
Take a drink out on to the South Terrace of Alexandra Palace. The protected prospect from here intersects tightly with those from Highgate, prohibiting tall buildings in almost all of Southwark. The Shard is wedged into an implausibly tight gap between the lines, which is one of the reasons why it tapers so dramatically.

GENERAL WOLFE
Stand beside General Wolfe in Greenwich Park[5] for a spectacular protected panorama from the south, with a particularly fine view on to Canary Wharf.

WESTMINSTER PIER
As the view of St Paul's from Westminster Pier is protected, the curve of the London Eye had to be carefully calculated to avoid blocking the dome.

INSIDE OUT
For a completely uninterrupted view of the cathedral, go to see the Great Model[6] in the Trophy Room at St Paul's. This miniminster, one-twenty-fifth of the actual size, was commissioned by Wren as a guide for the builders before construction began.

BACK TO FRONT
Afterwards, climb to the Golden Gallery at the top of the dome, and look at all these protected views backwards. From the cathedral apex, Henry Mayhew thought the distant hills looked 'like some far-off shore'.

---

[1] Their model is updated quarterly with new landmark buildings.
[2] This awkward matrix is the reason for the peculiar clustering of London's new skyscrapers. See p.27.
[3] A Bronze Age tumulus where Henry VIII stood in 1536, watching for the flare from the Tower of London that signalled the execution of Anne Boleyn.
[4] Waterlow Park in Highgate also has an excellent view, and includes a sundial that is 'on a level with the top of the dome of St Paul's Cathedral'.
[5] Meet the woman who almost took Wolfe's place on p.342.
[6] Email admissions@stpaulscathedral.org.uk to book a free visit.

CLOSE-UPS

You've seen the city from above. Now spend the day racing around some of London's classic ground-level experiences.

9AM, *Breakfast at the Wolseley*
Breakfast at the opulent, airy Wolseley has quickly become a London institution, although the restaurant has only been open since 2003.[1] Enjoy immaculate eggs benedict at this Viennese-style grand cafe.

10AM, *Buy a Bowler*
Christys', on Shorts Gardens, make more than 6,000 fur-felt bowler hats every year.[2] If you're feeling flash, try their lightweight, scarlet 'fashion bowler'.

11AM, *Change the Guard*
Watch the Horse Guards pass up the Mall at 10.45, then dash to see the Old Guard and band leaving St James's Palace at 11.15, before sprinting over to Buckingham Palace for the Changing of the Guard at 11.30.

12PM, *Eat Pie and Mash*
To a Londoner, 'pie and mash' means a suet and short-pastry minced-beef pie and a mound of mashed potato slathered with liquor.[3] Order yours at M. Manze on Tower Bridge Road, which has been in business since 1902.

1PM, *Catch a Concert*
St Martin-in-the-Fields hosts free lunchtime concerts most Mondays, Tuesdays and Fridays. Gaze at the warped east window created by Iranian artist Shirazeh Houshiary.

2PM, *Climb Big Ben*
Contact your local MP in advance to arrange a free trip up the 334 stone spiral steps to the top of the Elizabeth Tower. Stand behind the 23-foot clock dials and hear the bells chime the *Westminster Quarters*.[4]

3PM, *Ogle the Crown Jewels*
Today a travelator keeps you moving past the Koh-i-Nur ('Mountain of Light') diamond in the Jewel Tower. In 1671, Colonel Blood successfully stole the crown jewels, but he bungled his escape, dropping the sceptre at St Catherine's Gate and King Edward's Crown on Tower Wharf.

4PM, *Take Tea at the Ritz*
Tuck into cucumber sandwiches and fresh scones in the Ritz Palm Court. There are 16 teas on the menu, but look no further than the Ritz Royal English: a malty blend of Kenyan, Assam and Ceylon leaves.

5PM, *Shop at Camden Market*
The complex of markets around Camden Lock are particularly buzzy at the weekend, when you can buy everything from goth gear to 20-sided dice and liquid nitrogen ice cream.

6PM, *Ride a Routemaster*
Curvaceous new Routemaster buses have hit London's streets, with a sweeping diagonal window along one side. You can still board via the traditional rear door and snuggle in the lover's seat on the staircase.

7PM, *Watch a West End Show*
West End theatres are famous for their Edwardian grandeur and cramped legroom. The ticket booth on Leicester Square sells cut-price same-day tickets; Boots on Piccadilly Circus sells painkillers.[5]

8PM, *Attend a Gallery Late*
The V&A kicked off a trend for after-hours museum 'lates'. They still host free drop-in lates on the last Friday of each month, with pop-up bars, catwalks, films, installations, debates and DJs.

---

[1] The Wolseley is located in the former Wolseley motor-car showroom on Piccadilly.
[2] They also made the Homburg worn by Don Corleone in *The Godfather* films.
[3] A green parsley sauce, traditionally made with stewed eel water.

[4] The words to the familiar chime are from Psalm 37: 'All through this hour / Lord be my guide / And by Thy power / No foot shall slide.'
[5] Alternatively, the Donmar Warehouse, the Royal Opera House and Shakespeare's Globe all offer standing tickets. More theatre on p.90.

UTOPIAN LONDON

The streets of London are paved with gold, or so Dick Whittington thought before he arrived in the city. In reality the streets are harsh, and young Richard initially works as a scullion in the pantomime story, relying heavily on the superior talents of his cat.

The Tudor statesman Thomas More was born in 1478 on Milk Street, adjacent to Honey Lane, but he too realised quickly that London is no land of milk and honey.[1] (1) In 1516, he wrote a satirical fiction describing an ideal society on a make-believe island called 'Utopia', a name that punningly combines the Greek construction *eu-topia*, 'happy place', with *ou-topia*, 'no place'. Utopia is a perfect place that can never exist.

It's still tempting to imagine London as a land of abundance. Some even claim that the word 'cockney' derives from the medieval Land of Cockaigne, a mythical place where the houses have sausage walls, salmon doors and grilled eels for roof beams.[2] Pastries rain from the sky and rivers flow with muscatel, claret and sherry. 'Those who longest sleep,' we learn from one account, 'earn the most.'[3]

London is not Cockaigne, however, and many new arrivals are sorely disappointed. Dick Whittington was so disillusioned he packed his bindle and trudged back up the Great North Road. (2) Nevertheless, sometimes there are glimpses of gold beneath the grime. Visit Highgate Hill and find the milestone[4] where Whittington is said to have stopped, hearing the optimistic chimes of the St Mary-le-Bow bells. He returned for a second crack at the capital, and famously made his fortune and became thrice Lord Mayor.

Over the page is a map of the hopes and dreams that drive people to London, and the reality of what greets them when they arrive. 'Paved with gold, no —' concludes Gilbert in Andrea Levy's *Small Island*, 'but, yes, diamonds appear on the ground in the rain'.

FAME & FORTUNE

Within moments of disembarking from the *Empire Windrush*, (4) the Calypso star Lord Kitchener was improvising the song *London is the place for me* for the news cameras. 'I have every comfort and every sport,' he sang in the version he later recorded, 'and my residence is Hampton Court'. (5) From Shakespeare to Freddie Mercury, many people come to London for a life of razzmatazz, glory and glamour. (6)

POP (7)

Budding artistes should keep a close eye on the ads in the industry papers. In 1994, *The Stage* placed an advert for 'streetwise, outgoing, ambitious' 18- to 23-year olds to form an all-female pop act. Four hundred women auditioned at Danceworks in Mayfair and the group that eventually emerged was the Spice Girls. Scour the brickwork on Frognal Rise in Hampstead, close to Mel C's residence, for tippex tributes from adoring fans. Then present your resumé at Danceworks.

---

[1] More was beheaded by Henry VIII in 1535. For more More, see p.110.

[2] Cockaigne was the inspiration for Edward Elgar's 'stout and steaky' overture of 1901, *Cockaigne (In London Town)*.

[3] The differences between Utopia and Cockaigne demonstrate that one person's paradisiacal sausage-house is another person's idea of hell. In More's Utopia, citizens do six hours of manual work a day; rule breakers are punished with slavery; and chamber pots are made of gold to foster a healthy disregard for material wealth.

[4] Today the milestone is topped by a statue of Dick's talented ratter; rub its nose for luck.

BAROQUE ⑧

Living near a historical musical icon can help you on your way to megastardom. Jimi Hendrix lived next door to George Frederick Handel on Brook Street in 1968, two centuries after the composer's death. Hendrix was unknown when he arrived in the capital, but he bought some Handel LPs for inspiration and by the time he left the flat he was a star. His rooms at No. 25 have recently been restored by the Handel House Museum.[1] Jimi later described the flat as the 'only home [he] ever had'.[2] Move in nearby or, if you're concerned that Hendrix has used up Handel's magic, rent a flat near 180 Ebury Street, where Mozart composed his first symphony at the age of eight. ⑨

PARK LIFE ③

In a world before petrol lawn mowers, there were opportunities aplenty for enterprising shepherds. In the 1920s and '30s, Hyde Park, Clapham Common and Hampstead Heath were all naturally shorn by sheep. The shepherd George Donald came all the way from Aberdeenshire for the purpose, creating an Arcadian paradise in the heart of the capital. Write to your local councillor and ask whether you can revive the tradition.

Clapham Common

FLIGHT

Carl Linnaeus had the idea of creating a giant clock using flowers that open at different times of day.[3] Thomas Carlyle adapted this idea for London, using refugees instead of flowers. 'In the great Revolutionary Horloge,' he wrote, 'one might mark the years and epochs by the successive kinds of exiles that walk London streets'.[4]

MARX

Go to Quo Vadis on Dean Street and read *The Communist Manifesto* over a Russian Standard vodka martini. In the rooms above you, Karl Marx lived as a political exile. During his sojourn in London, Marx wrote *Das Kapital* in the British Museum reading room. ⑩ Although his Soho accommodation was, in his words, 'an old hovel' so dirty 'that to sit down becomes a thoroughly dangerous business', it didn't deter him from producing a text that has inspired more real-life attempts at utopia than perhaps any other. Restaurant customers can ask to see his rooms.

LENIN

Just over 50 years later, Lenin was in London, reading Marx's works in the room where they were written. Some believe, without hard proof, that Lenin first met Stalin in the Crown Tavern on Clerkenwell Green. ⑪

MAP READING

Utopian London *is inspired by the circular, medieval world maps that chart myth and history as well as geography. Another reference is the frontispiece to Thomas More's* Utopia, *which shows vessels arriving at a fabulous island. More stands at the centre of our image holding a scroll with the word* UTOPIA *written in his invented Utopian language. The edible houses and eggs with legs were inspired by Bruegel's painting* The Land of Cockaigne.

KINDER ⑬

In the late 1930s, 10,000 Jewish children arrived at London Liverpool Street from Berlin and Prague. Look for a statue of five of them standing on a stretch of track outside the station

PADDINGTON ⑭

London's most cuddly refugee, Paddington Bear, was so determined to reach the English capital that he ventured across continents from darkest Peru with only a hatful of marmalade to sustain him. Think of the transcontinental teddy if you travel on the Eurostar from Paris to London. When the French and English stretches of the Channel Tunnel joined up beneath the seabed, a soft toy Paddington was the first item that English diggers passed through the opening to their Continental counterparts.

---

❶ To get a handle on Handel, see p.118.
❷ To commune with Jimi, listen to 'Purple Haze' on Woodgrange Road in Newham, next to the plaque commemorating the track's composition in the dressing room of the Upper Cut Club. You can also find him up a tree on p.129.

❸ Plant your own Flower Clock on p.311.
❹ Find more of the city's refugees on p.385.

WEYONOMON

A rippled granite boulder outside Southwark Cathedral commemorates Mahomet Weyonomon, an 18th-century Native American chieftain who came to England in 1735 to petition the king for the restoration of his tribelands. He died of smallpox before his case could be heard. A hundred years earlier, Pocahontas had arrived in London with her husband, John Rolfe, and shaman, Tomocomo. She too died of smallpox. There is now a statue of her at St George's Church, Gravesend. (16)

ZOG (12)

Zog, self-proclaimed King of Albania, fled to London when Mussolini invaded in 1939. He stole his country's gold, booked out the third floor of the Ritz and is purported to have paid in bullion. Go to the bar of the Ritz today, order a coffee and pay in slivers of gold leaf.

FULFILMENT

Although pilgrims have traditionally walked out of London to Canterbury and beyond, people have also treated the city as a spiritual destination.[1]

ADVENTURING (15)

'One foot up and one foot down, / That is the way to London Town' goes the old nursery rhyme. One long-range pedestrian was the 19-year-old Laurie Lee, who walked to London from the Cotswolds with his violin in 1934, before proceeding to walk through Spain. On 'the London road, I forgot everything but the way ahead,' he wrote. 'I was at that age which feels neither strain nor friction, when the body burns magic fuels'. Follow the six-mile Laurie Lee Wildlife Way in the Slad Valley and then continue to London in his footsteps.[2]

PROCESSING (17)

In 2011, Iain Sinclair and Andrew Kötting spent four weeks travelling from Hastings to Hackney in a swan-shaped pedalo called Edith. Their bizarre plastic pilgrimage was a counterpoint to the triumphalism they perceived in the 2012 Olympic torch procession. Over 160 hard miles they listened for 'the ambient echoes of British culture', finishing on the River Lea near the Olympic site and the 'vanishing landscape' of Hackney. Watch their film *Swandown* and then hire a swan-shaped pedalo on the Alexandra Park lake.

FASTING (18)

In 1888, when Gandhi arrived in London to study law at Inner Temple, he read Henry Salt's *Plea for Vegetarianism* and joined  the London Vegetarian Society.[3] Before coming to England, Gandhi had become vegetarian at his mother's request but, after reading Salt's book, he 'adopted vegetarianism on principle'. Go for a bowl of dahl in the canteen of the Indian YMCA restaurant on Fitzroy Square, which is open to non-guests. Then make a pilgrimage to Tavistock Square and leave flowers inside the hollow plinth below Gandhi's statue.[4]

HEALING (19)

Samuel Johnson first visited London as a two-year-old. He suffered from scrofula, the 'King's Evil', which was said to be curable with a royal touch. His mother conveyed him to Queen Anne at St James's Palace where, as tradition dictated, the queen touched him with a gold medallion. Ask to touch Dr Johnson's royal touch-piece (M.8007) in the Coins & Medals department of the British Museum.

LOVING (20)

On a summer Saturday in 1955, Philip Larkin got on a quiet train from Hull to King's Cross. As the stopping-service travelled south, a succession of newly-wed couples climbed aboard and he watched their marriages beginning.[5] Read the final lines of 'The Whitsun Weddings' on a slate plaque at King's Cross. Then travel to Hull's Paragon Station and find the opening lines next to a statue of the poet rushing for the train.

---

❶ Meet the city's saints on p.110.
❷ Lee describes his journey in *As I Walked Out One Midsummer Morning*.
❸ See p.44.
❹ In 2015, a new nine-foot sculpture was unveiled in Parliament Square to give Gandhi 'an eternal home in our country'.

❺ In an interview some years later, he recalled the sensation of being surrounded by so much 'fresh, open life', all 'aimed like a bullet – at the heart of things'.

FASCINATION

Do you love London so much that you 'shed tears in the motley Strand from fullness of joy'? The writer Charles Lamb did, and told William Wordsworth as much in a letter berating his friend for preferring 'dead nature'. Despite its imperfections, London can seem so glorious that people simply can't stay away.

MAGNETIC ㉑

'Fiction was my only data for London till I was nearly twenty', wrote the novelist Elizabeth Bowen. By the time she came from Ireland to London, Bowen knew the 'magnetic and dangerous' city so vividly through its stories[1] that it had 'gained on [her] something of the obsessive hold of a daydream'. Read the first chapter of *The Death of the Heart* on a bench by the boating lake in Regent's Park. Bowen lived at 2 Clarence Terrace, with a view over the park. She thought it 'among the most civilized scenes on earth' and set the openings of two of her novels there.

MISTY ㉒

The Japanese artist Yoshio Markino, who arrived in 1897, thought the city 'a paradise in this world', although he initially wore a respirator to avoid inhaling the smog. Ultimately it was the city's fog[2] that he came to love most. 'I think London without mists would be like a bride without a trousseau,' he wrote. 'The London mist attracts me so that I do not feel I could live any other place but London.' Look for his dusky painting *In the Rotten Row One Evening* in the Museum of London to see the murky metropolis through his eyes.

PROMISING ㉓

Although Mr Woodhouse announces in *Emma* that 'in London it is always a sickly season', Jane Austen herself seemed to be quite at home with the gritty glamour of the capital. She came to stay with her brother at 10 Henrietta Street in summer 1813 and described his lodgings as 'all dirt and confusion, but in a very promising way'. Find the house amidst the Covent Garden camping shops and then visit Austen's writing desk and spectacles in the British Library.

MAGNIFICENT ㉔

London 'is not a pleasant place,' wrote the novelist Henry James; 'it is not agreeable or cheerful or easy or exempt from reproach. It is only magnificent.' He came to live in this 'great grey Babylon' in 1869. Look for a portrait of James by his friend John Singer Sargent in room 4 of the National Portrait Gallery.[3]

ENCHANTING ㉕

Although she grew up in a fine house on Hyde Park Gate, Virginia Woolf described the move inwards from Kensington to Bloomsbury as crossing a gulf from 'respectable mummified humbug' to 'life crude and impertinent perhaps, but living'. Take the Piccadilly Line from Gloucester Road to Russell Square and contemplate the difference. 'London is enchanting', she later wrote in her diary. 'I step out upon a tawny coloured magic carpet, it seems, and get carried into beauty without raising a finger.'

---

❶ Find more city fictions on pp.412–413.
❷ See p.58.

❸ In 1914, this portrait was severely damaged by a suffragette attack. According to *The Times*, it was struck three times 'with a meat chopper' by Mrs Mary Wood, 'an elderly woman of distinctly peaceable appearance'. For more suffragettes, see p.79.

ARTS

'Drawing makes you see things clearer,' says David Hockney, 'and clearer and clearer still, until your eyes ache.' To bring London into focus, look at it with an artist's eyes. Before you begin scribbling, top up on fine papers and pastels at L. Cornelissen & Son on Great Russell Street, which has been catering to artists, from Turner to Tracey Emin, for more than 150 years.

CANALETTO'S GREENWICH

Set up your easel in Island Gardens, at the tip of the Isle of Dogs, and paint *A View of Greenwich from the River*. At the centre of the impeccably symmetrical Old Royal Naval College stands the statue of George II. Make him the focus of your canvas, with the Queen's House behind and the trees of Greenwich Hill rising in the distance. Fill the sky with gently scudding clouds and don't forget to capture any passing river traffic. When you finish, visit Tate Britain to compare your work with Canaletto's.

TURNER'S ROTHERHITHE

Set up on the Thames Path at Pacific Wharf when the sun is setting, and hope that a tug passes by, pulling a 98-gun warship. While you're waiting, work on the sky and the surface of the water. Use as little blue as you can: the sky should be moody and expansive, textured with browns, reds and yellows; the river should be flat as lacquer. If the tug doesn't appear, use your imagination. That's what Turner did.[1] If you can forgive his historical inaccuracies, visit room 34 of the National Gallery to see *The Fighting Temeraire tugged to her last berth to be broken up, 1838*.

CONSTABLE'S HAMPSTEAD

Ask nicely, and the residents of 2 Lower Terrace in Hampstead may let you set up in their front garden. Paint a *View of Lower Terrace*, paying particular attention to the pavement opposite and the foliage sprouting over the neighbours' walls. John Constable stayed at No. 2 in the summers of 1821 and 1822. Consult his version of the view in case 49 (shelf L) of the V&A Prints & Drawings Study Room.

PISSARRO'S LORDSHIP LANE

Set up on the overgrown footbridge in Sydenham Woods and sketch the view north-east along the abandoned railway line. Then visit the Courtauld Gallery to see Camille Pissarro's painting from the same footbridge, with a steam train approaching from Lordship Lane Station.

BEVAN'S WESTWAY

Perch on Stable Way below the roar of the A40.[2] Use dark, rusty tones to capture the sweeping underbelly of the concrete flyover and its elegant feeder roads. Then visit the Museum of London's Contemporary Gallery to admire Oliver Bevan's triptych of the same view.

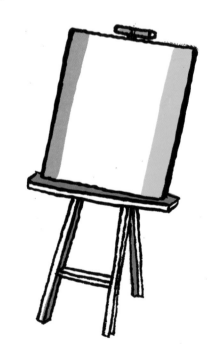

---

[1] In reality the *Temeraire* had its masts and rigging removed before it was pulled by two steam tugs to the Bull's Head Wharf at Rotherhithe in the early afternoon; in Turner's painting the sun is setting – in the east.

[2] See p.97.

CHARTS

In *Tristram Shandy*, Laurence Sterne writes a 'chapter upon chapters' in which Tristram makes unnecessary references to other authors (and includes long-winded French quotations *entre parenthèses*). He proclaims it 'the best chapter in [his] whole work'. Inspired by his success, we present here a London map of maps of London, the best page in this book.

FINCHLEY CENTRAL•

STANFORD'S • • 35 ST GEORGE ST
M&S VICTORIA •
•
GREENLAND DOCK

STANFORD

The travel bookshop Stanford's has been operating since Edward Stanford created his ground-breakingly accurate *Library Map of London* in 1862, still in print after 150 years. Today the shop has the world's largest stock of maps and travel books under one roof,[1] and its floors are laid out as a stack of maps: on the ground floor you walk around the world; on the first floor you trek across the Himalayas; and in the basement you stroll across a giant A–Z map of central London.[2]

BECK

Outside Marks and Spencer in Victoria Station, you can see old tiled maps of the London, Brighton and South Coast railway lines, meandering away from the station. The confusing 'Suburban Lines' map highlights the advantages of the sparse, schematic maps we use to navigate London's transport today. The tube map as we know it was designed by the visionary draftsman Harry Beck in 1931. You can see a faded copy of Beck's original map in Finchley Central, his local station.

PEARSALL

A sculpture of Phyllis Pearsall, creator of the *London A–Z*, stands behind a bench at Greenland Dock, next to Michael Caine. According to legend, Pearsall walked 3,000 miles along all of London's 23,000 streets to create her *A–Z*. When English Heritage investigated her story, however, they declined to award her a blue plaque, because in reality Pearsall based her atlas on maps made by her own cartographer father. Some feel her honour is unfairly besmirched, however. In her autobiography, *From Bedsitter to Household Name*, Pearsall openly acknowledges her reliance on her father's maps. Her truly extraordinary achievement was to combine meticulous research with on-foot corroboration, creating an essential London icon in the process. Pearsall does now have a blue plaque, at 3 Court Lane Gardens, awarded by Southwark Council.[3]

ROCQUE

Jean Rocque, a Swiss immigrant, created the greatest and most beautiful 18th-century map of London. Look at Rocque's 1746 map of the Environs of London: small settlements at crossroads in 1700 have now become the most vibrant communities of Greater London.[4] — *Peter Barber*

BLEEDING LONDON

Inspired by Geoff Nicholson's 1997 novel *Bleeding London*, in which the character Stuart London walks every street in the *London A–Z*, the Royal Photographic Society's Bleeding London Project is crowdsourcing photographs of every street in the city. Browse their collection of over 58,000 images as an alternative to the ubiquitous Google Maps Street View (bleedinglondon.co.uk).

> OTHER GREAT LONDON CARTOGRAPHERS
> *Charles Booth, see p.261*
> *Wenceslaus Hollar, see p.337*
> *John Snow, see p.54*

---

[1] Customers have included numerous adventurers such as Dr Livingstone, Captain Scott and Sherlock Holmes.
[2] In a similar vein, the walls of the Four Corners cafe on Lower Marsh are covered with maps, as is the ceiling of the Bonnington Cafe, see p.136.

[3] To arrange your own blue plaque, consult p.109.
[4] You can usually survey Rocque's map at the Altea Gallery on St George's Street.

BEATING THE BOUNDS

Is 'this grim necklace [...] the true perimeter fence?' asked Iain Sinclair, before walking around the M25 in 1999. Does this 'conceptual ha-ha mark the boundary of whatever could be called London?'[1]

The Beating of the Bounds takes place every year on Ascension Day.[2] It's a medieval 'gang-day', when clergymen, schoolchildren and notaries process the edges of a parish or ward and beat the boundary markers with green willow wands.[3] At each stop, the vicar says a short prayer and the children of the Beating Party thwack the pavement, shouting, 'Beat! Beat! Beat!'

Check whether your parish still beats its bounds. Otherwise, turn out to support All Hallows by the Tower, the oldest church in the City of London. The children of St Dunstan's College, Catford, join the clergy to beat the pavements outside office blocks, banks and sandwich shops. The southern boundary of the parish is in the middle of the Thames, so the party gets on a boat and thrashes the river.

But where are the boundaries of London? Here are some concentric suggestions for beating the bounds of the city.

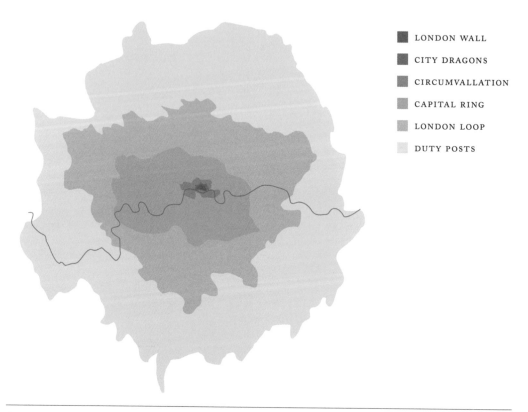

- ■ LONDON WALL
- ■ CITY DRAGONS
- ■ CIRCUMVALLATION
- ■ CAPITAL RING
- ■ LONDON LOOP
- ■ DUTY POSTS

---

❶ Sinclair recounts his walk in the book and film *London Orbital*.
❷ The 39th day after Easter.
❸ When the markers are trees themselves, they are known as 'Gospel Oaks'. Gospel Oak in Camden is named after a tree

that marked the parish boundary between Hampstead and St Pancras. It used to stand on the corner of Mansfield Road and Southampton Road.

LONDON WALL

For most of its existence, London was surrounded by an enormous 20-foot wall with seven gates: Lud, New, Alders, Cripple, Moor, Bishops, and Ald. The wall was built by the Romans in 200 AD and was maintained as a boundary line for a millennium and a half.

Take your willow wand and start at the Tower of London, beating the pavement periodically.[1] The tallest and most impressive remnant of London Wall stands outside Tower Hill tube station, overseen by an 18th-century statue of the Emperor Trajan. There is also a section of the wall built into the station platforms.

Walk along Cooper's Row, and pop through the Grange City Hotel to see another section in their courtyard.

A low section of the wall runs through the sunken garden that was once the churchyard of St Alphage on London Wall.

Continue into the Barbican Centre: this section of the wall was once the north-west tip of the Roman fort or 'barbican'. You can see the remains of a large tower at the far end, which doubled as a medieval hermitage.[2]

The section of the wall in Noble Street, which you can view from a raised platform, was exposed by bombing in 1940. This section covers the widest timespan of all the remnants, from 2nd-century Roman foundations to 19th-century bricks, used to patch up medieval portions.

Cut across to Old Bailey and follow Pilgrim Street and Pageantmaster Court to the Thames Path. Then walk back along the river to the Tower.

CITY DRAGONS

After beating the bounds of the Square Mile, spread your net wider and beat the 13 guardian dragons that encircle the City. These beasts were put up in the 1960s to mark the bounds of the City Corporation's jurisdiction: they have red tongues and stand on one leg holding the City's coat of arms. The two 7-foot originals are next to Temple Gardens on Victoria Embankment. The others are half-size replicas. Hunt them down at the south ends of Blackfriars Bridge and London Bridge, and on Aldgate High Street, Bishopsgate, Moorgate, Goswell Road, Farringdon Street and High Holborn. There is another, fiercer, black dragon who stands on the site of Temple Bar.[3]

CIRCUMVALLATION

In 1725, Daniel Defoe walked London's 'line of circumvallation', the boundary of the 'continued buildings that in the common acceptation are called London'. The line he walked was a tidemark on the eve of the Industrial Revolution: from Millbank through Westminster, Mayfair, Soho, Bloomsbury, Islington, Hackney, Whitechapel, Stepney, Mile End, Limehouse, Deptford, Rotherhithe, Bermondsey, Southwark and Lambeth. He describes the route meticulously in the second volume of his *Tour Thro' the Whole Island of Great Britain*. Walking it today gives you the measure of early-18th-century London.

CAPITAL RING

In 2005, the 78-mile Capital Ring was launched: a circular signed walk around the edge of Inner London, linking many of London's finest green spaces. Markers to beat along the way include the Thames Barrier, Eltham Palace, Richmond Park, the Wharncliffe Viaduct and Walthamstow Marshes.

LONDON LOOP

The 150-mile London Outer Orbital Path (LOOP), the 'M25 for walkers', traces the edges of Outer London and was completed in 2001. It runs round from Erith to Purfleet and crosses the river at Kingston. Get your wand out for some thwacking at Hall Place, Farthing Down, Enfield Lock and Rainham Marshes.

DUTY POSTS

Finally, try connecting all 218 surviving coal-duty posts, which form a large ring around London and mark the area within which taxes on coal were once payable to the City Corporation. Some are obelisks but most are white cast-iron posts, about a metre high, emblazoned with the city's crest. Feature posts, which shouldn't escape a beating, include the one next to Tattenham Corner at Epsom Downs racecourse; the one beside a footpath in the depths of Wormley Wood; and the one next to the Rose & Crown pillar box in Chelsfield. Martin Nail has plotted their coordinates (coaldutyposts.org.uk).

---

[1] In 1983, a 'Wall Walk' was set up along the route, but many of its tiled information panels have since disappeared.

[2] The first recorded hermit of Cripplegate was called Warin the Hermit; the last was John de Flytewyk, who resigned in 1341.

[3] For more on this dragon, known as 'The Griffin', see p.400.

BLOCKS

SINCE PLANTING THE GHERKIN and City Hall in central London, the architect Norman Foster has been commissioned to design a new city from scratch in the United Arab Emirates. Masdar City is springing up fully formed in the desert with one unified style and no past to contend with, the opposite of London's 2,000-year creep across a floodplain. In a city with roots as deep as London's, building anything new is demanding: there are remains and ruins underfoot, and, above ground, views to preserve and shadows not to cast.

Architecture is perhaps the most provocative art form because we're forced to interact with it. Whether you like the Shard or not, you can't ignore it: buildings indelibly affect how the city looks and how it makes us feel. Architects' drawings are always optimistic, but many new edifices never live out the sunlit fantasies displayed on the hoardings around their building sites. A prime example is Strata, the 43-storey tower block in Elephant and Castle, topped with three malfunctioning wind turbines. In 2010, it was awarded the Carbuncle Cup, an annual prize for the 'the ugliest building in the United Kingdom'.

Strata is visible for miles around, yet it's one of the few skyscrapers in the city not to have earned a diminutive nickname.[1] The gleaming new tower blocks that catch the public imagination – for better or worse – tend to be named after an object you can hold in your hand, as though this might bring these futuristic ziggurats down to a manageable human scale. Recent monikers include the comically banal Cheese Grater, Can of Ham and Walkie Talkie.

As well as providing the backdrop for our time in the city, at their best, buildings are the bones around which communities cohere. When they're not fit for purpose, people ridicule them, stop using them, or start abusing them. This chapter is a journey around some of the city's most striking and surprising structures, from London's building blocks to its newest tower blocks.

BODY BUILDING

Look for a rusting figure at the corner of Shoe Lane. As you approach, it pixelates before your eyes. 'Seen from afar it looks like a man,' says its creator Antony Gormley, 'from close up it looks like a city.' The sculpture is a human made of dozens of differently sized metal blocks.

---

❶ Despite bearing a close resemblance to an electric shaver.

BUILDING BLOCKS

NATURAL

ROMAN BRICKS
A strong contender for London's best brick is in the Roman Gallery of the Museum of London. While the clay was still soft a workman scratched a comment on to it, complaining about the work ethic of a lazy colleague. His irritable graffiti has probably endured well beyond his expectations.

WOODEN COBBLES
If you've ever wheeled a suitcase along a cobbled road you can begin to imagine how noisy London must have been when carts and horses filled the streets. To reduce noise, blocks of wood were often used instead of cobbles, even though they were far less hardy. Walk down one of the last stretches of timbered road on Chequer Street in Islington.

WEEPING MARBLE
The bust of Edward Cooke in St Bartholomew-the-Great used to astonish the congregation by weeping. In the damp days before central heating, drops of water would condense on the marble and trickle down Cooke's cheeks. Visit him now and you'll find a plaque encouraging you to bring your sorrows to Edward and 'unsluce yor briny floods'. If your tears won't come, the plaque continues, his statue will cry for you.

MOUNTING BLOCKS
One of London's premier trip hazards is a stone block outside the Athenaeum Club on Pall Mall. It was placed there to help the Duke of Wellington climb on to his horse.

BASALT FIGURES
The four craggy chunks of basalt on Exchange Square are actually a family: two parents, a child[1] and a dog. Compare their rough edges with the smooth lines of Hoa Hakananai'a, one of the magnificent basalt figures from Easter Island in the Living and Dying gallery of the British Museum.

OOLITHIC LIMESTONE
Go to the British Museum courtyard and see if you can spot the difference in colour between the recently rebuilt south portico and the older stone elsewhere. A mild scandal broke out during the portico's construction when it emerged that the wrong kind of oolithic limestone had been ordered.[2]

EGYPTIAN PEBBLES
The collection of individually labelled ancient pebbles in the Petrie Museum of Egyptian Archaeology may be London's most underwhelming museum exhibit. UC.36033 ('brown pebble') is a curvy highlight, but UC.9252 ('rough pebble') seems somewhat lacklustre.

BUILDERS' TEA

RIBA
Order a cup of builders' tea at the headquarters of the Royal Institute of British Architects at 66 Portland Place. You'd expect them to have a well-designed cafe and they do: a high-ceilinged art deco space full of glass and black marble.

AA
It's not clear from the outside that you're allowed into the Architectural Association on Bedford Square. Go to No. 36 for lunch in their basement canteen, take in their latest exhibition, then have a drink in their bar, open until 9pm on weekdays with a fine view across one of Bloomsbury's most handsome squares.

❶ Look at the base of the child-sized boulder and you'll see a pair of smart buckled shoes sticking out, giving the alarming impression that someone is stuck inside.
❷ Instead of traditional Portland stone, as stipulated, the builders used Anstrude Roche Claire limestone from France.

ARTIFICIAL

TESTING
If you'd like to test the quality of a material before you build with it, visit the Kirkaldy Testing Museum on Southwark Street. It houses a Universal Testing Machine, which assesses tensile strength, creep and fatigue. Carved above the door are the words FACTS NOT OPINIONS. The museum opens on the first Sunday of every month; goggles must be worn before entering the workshop.

PARKESINE
A plaque on Wallis Road in Hackney Wick announces that the 'first plastic in the world' was manufactured in a factory nearby. Parkesine, named after its creator Alexander Parkes, was a cheap substitute for ivory and was used to make jewellery and accessories. Its only flaw was its tendency to explode when heated. The Science Museum has a collection of knick-knacks, but Parkesine is degraded by light so they're only brought out for special exhibitions.

SUPER-FINE CONCRETE
Take a free tour of Somerset House on a Thursday or Saturday afternoon and walk up their new spiral staircase. Its wafer-thin white steps are made of ultra-high-performance concrete, which is a thousand times stronger than normal varieties.

ACRYLIC
London is home to the largest block of acrylic in the world. You can find it on the side wall of the Tower Hotel in St Katherine's Docks. This translucent 2-tonne cuboid was commissioned by Stanley Kubrick for the film *2001: A Space Odyssey*. It was meant to play the alien monolith that appears to a group of apes and kick-starts human evolution, but the acrylic failed its screen test and was replaced by a slab of black basalt.

PULHAMITE
Next time you're ogling the pelicans in St James's Park, examine the rocky outcrops in the lake. They look real enough, but they're made from Pulhamite, an artificial stone created by James Pulham. It was used in London's parks and gardens to create highly realistic grottoes, waterfalls, cliffs and rock formations, styled on local rocks so they didn't stand out. You can't make Pulhamite today: James Pulham took the secret recipe to his grave.

COADE STONE
The South Bank is a wonderland for artificial rock enthusiasts: today it's a brutalist love letter to reinforced concrete and two centuries ago it was home to Coade's Artificial Stone Manufactory. There were many fake stone makers in the 18th century but none as successful as Eleanor Coade, whose product could withstand the corrosive London air far better than natural rocks. The Coade stone lion at the south end of Westminster Bridge, not far from her old factory, still looks as good as new.[1] For a while, some thought the Coade stone formula was lost – or hidden inside the lion – but it still exists. To make your own, mix 70% clay with 10% grog, 5% flint, 5% quartz and 10% soda lime glass. Fire the concoction at 1110°C or microwave on high for 4 minutes.

DIY
Begin small with a game of giant jenga at the Ship pub in Mortlake. Once you've refined your technique, enrol with the LONDON SCHOOL OF DRY STONE WALLING [2] (londonschoolofdsw.co.uk). Sessions are held at the Hilldrop Community Centre in Holloway.

[1] Another Coade stone highlight are the caryatids propping up St Pancras New Church on Euston Road. They look a trifle petite because these eight women were made too large; part of their midriffs had to be removed so they would fit the space.
[2] The school oversaw the construction of the dry stone walls in the new Crossbones Graveyard Garden. See p.204.

BUILDING LONDON

In 1966, the cantankerous architecture critic Ian Nairn published 'Stop the Architects Now', an article denouncing the 'soggy, shoddy mass of half-digested clichés' springing up across Britain in the wake of the Second World War. 'The outstanding and appalling fact about modern architecture,' he wrote, 'is that it is not good enough.' The same year, his book *Nairn's London* appeared: one of the most strange and stirring books ever written about the city. He examines the built environment and creates 'a record of what has moved [him] between Uxbridge and Dagenham'.

Nairn sizes up both London's old stalwarts and its newer additions, and isn't afraid to deliver withering assessments of buildings that are 'not living up to their reputation'. He marks out places he dislikes by enclosing their entries in square brackets; rarely has punctuation carried such a weight of judgement. Nairn's subjects may be brick, stone and stucco, but the book is an expansive portrait of the whole city and a reflection on how places affect people. When he died in 1983, *Nairn's London* was long out of print. It only reappeared in 2014.

ST MARY WOOLNOTH, LOMBARD STREET ⑥
Nicholas Hawksmoor, 1714–30
Hawksmoor's St Mary Woolnoth is 'the one City church that you must go in', according to Ian Nairn. 'Space, here, is made so tangible', he writes, 'that you can experience, for the price of a bus ticket to the City, the super-reality of the mystics or mescalin'. Try it for yourself. [1] If you don't experience a spontaneous spatial high from your visit to the church, walk the short distance to St Mary Aldermary [2] where you can get a caffeine hit from Host, the cafe that trades in the nave.

[BRITISH MUSEUM, GREAT RUSSELL STREET]
Sir Robert Smirke, 1832–47
Sir Robert Smirke gets short shrift from Ian Nairn. Nairn didn't live to see them put a roof on the British Museum, but he was singly unimpressed by Sir Robert's Grecian design, which, he felt, 'never comes alive for a moment'. In 1994, after the British Library decamped from the central court, Foster and Partners installed an undulating glass roof. [3] This proved nightmarishly complex, as the Reading Room had been built slightly off centre. To make the roof fit around it and appear regular, all of the 3,312 panels are slightly different sizes. Visit on a sunny day and enjoy the fishnet shadows the frames cast on the museum walls.

ROYAL COLLEGE OF ARTS, KENSINGTON GORE ①
H.T. Cadbury-Brown, 1961
It defies comprehension that the robotic grey cuboid of the Royal College of Arts was approved for construction right next door to the Royal Albert Hall. But don't judge it too quickly. 'It smoulders through to your consciousness with quiet intensity', according to Nairn. Go to the annual graduation show of their architecture students to get a feel for the building, which, Nairn says, 'is meant to be used and worn and thumbed over and hugged, like the family's big woolly dog'.

---

[1] You'll need to remain above ground. The church had to sell off its crypt and dig up its bodies to make way for Bank Underground. Today the Baroque masterpiece sits directly on top of the station's lift shafts and stairs.

[2] Sir Christopher Wren rebuilt this church after the Great Fire, retaining its Gothic style although, in Nairn's words, he 'treated Gothic as though it were a cantankerous old aunt: with affectionate disrespect'.

[3] Before it was fitted, it was fritted: screenprinted with tiny dots that filter out ultraviolet rays.

[ROYAL FESTIVAL HALL, SOUTHBANK] ⑬
L.C.C. Architect's Department, Special Works Division, 1948–50 and 1963–4
The Royal Festival Hall's 'icy blind perfection is unforgivable', in Nairn's opinion. His comments have been borne out, and repeated attempts have been made to warm up the auditorium's glacial acoustics.[1] Take in a concert and assess for yourself; baroque chamber works apparently fare well in the space, epic symphonies less so.

JOHN SOANE'S HOUSE, LINCOLN'S INN FIELDS ⑤
Sir John Soane, 1812 onwards
For Nairn, John Soane's house[2] is 'worth travelling across a continent to see in the same way as the Sistine Chapel'. Soane gradually turned his house into a living architecture museum, filling it with casts and experimenting with every aspect of the building's design. It is the Breakfast Room, with its domed ceiling dotted with convex mirrors, which captures Nairn's attention. The 'human understanding of the nature of eating breakfast can only be caught here', he writes. Once you've deepened your understanding, walk around the square to the Fleet River Bakery for a plate of toast and eggs.

[VANBRUGH CASTLE, MAZE HILL]
Sir John Vanbrugh, 1717–c.1726
After designing Blenheim Palace and Castle Howard, John Vanbrugh built himself a curious home on the edge of Greenwich Park. 'For the very first time,' writes Nairn, 'medieval grimness was produced as a romantic fancy rather than sheer need.' Vanbrugh Castle sits on the top of Maze Hill and enjoys commanding views over London. For Nairn, it's 'an over-large Christmas parcel which you know is going to be a disappointment. But for all that, it ought to be seen.'

MICHELIN HOUSE, FULHAM ROAD ④
The Michelin Man's name is Bibendum,[3] although some just call him Bib. Bib's changed a great deal since he was dreamed up by the Michelin brothers in the late 19th century. He used to be spherically rotund, wear pince-nez and smoke cigars. You can see him enjoying a glass of wine and a cheroot in the stained glass[4] of Michelin House, built as the company's UK headquarters in 1911. The building is covered with white and green tiles and topped with white stone spheres, ribbed to look like Bib's body. It's now Terence Conran's restaurant Bibendum, and, for Nairn, this is 'one of the least likely buildings of an unlikely city'.

[EARLS COURT EXHIBITION CENTRE & EMPRESS STATE BUILDING]
New York has the Empire State Building. Its long-lost love, the Empress State Building, is next to West Brompton tube station. This 1961 tower block is now used by the Met Police, but it also contains the exclusive revolving restaurant Orbit[5] on the top floor. Until 2015, the Earls Court Exhibition Centre stood next to it, 'a hippopotamus in the water hole, rearing up above West London'. Together, Nairn writes, they are a 'visual joke, two monsters'. Big-game hunters have slain the Exhibition Centre to make way for 8,000 flats.

MAP READING
Building London presents the city as a perpetual building site and draws on the perspective of Pieter Breughel's *Tower of Babel* and the style of 1950s *Eagle* comics. The texts describing the 14 buildings on the map are numbered and spread out across the chapter.

---

[1] Great pains were taken to shield the auditorium from the rumbles of the Northern Line below. The architects elevated and padded it like 'an egg in a box'.

[2] You can visit by candlelight on the first Tuesday evening of every month.

[3] Cayce Pollard, the cool-hunting protagonist of William Gibson's novel *Pattern Recognition*, is so acutely sensitive to brands that she has an allergic reaction to certain logos. Bibendum is her kryptonite and is used against her by enemies when she visits a client in Soho.

[4] The current set are copies as the originals went missing after they were removed for storage during the Second World War. Michelin are still pursuing the lost windows: call their anonymous hotline (01782 402118) if you have any information.

[5] The restaurant has no website and it's not clear how to secure a reservation.

Building
London

BATTERSEA POWER STATION, NINE ELMS ⑭
Sir Giles Gilbert Scott, 1932–4
Although unimpressed by the 'timid fluting on brickwork and chimneys', Nairn acknowledges the brute power of Battersea Power Station. 'If there is such a thing as industrial melodrama,' he writes, 'this is it'. It closed down in 1983, the year of Nairn's death, and spent 30 years wondering what it would become. Proposals for theme parks, pleasure gardens and football stadia came and went. In 2015, work finally began on converting London's most prominent modern ruin into a hive of flats, shops and restaurants.[1] Before the refit, its four iconic chimneys were deemed unsafe and had to be dismantled and rebuilt from scratch. For full impact, Nairn recommends visiting the power station in 'mist or with the winter sun behind it'.

[ELEPHANT AND CASTLE SHOPPING CENTRE] ⑪
Boissevain & Osmond, 1964–5
The area from the South Bank down to Elephant and Castle was 'the place for huge gestures', wrote Nairn, but he was disheartened by the 'half-finished and mediocre work at the Elephant'. London County Council, on the other hand, had faith that their brutalist shopping centre, which opened in 1965, would make Elephant and Castle the 'Piccadilly Circus of South London'. Europe's first covered mall never fulfilled its promise and, on its 40th birthday, was voted the 'biggest eyesore in London' in a *Time Out* poll. Southwark Council flirted with redeveloping the complex, but eventually chose to demolish it

as they were 'less and less happy with how the scheme would fit in with the rest of the area's high-quality designs'. If you can, visit the mall and its pink elephant before it's too late.

GALA BINGO, MITCHAM ROAD
Cecil Macey, 1938
The Russian theatre director Theodore Komisarjevsky fled Russia in 1919 and travelled to London, where he staged productions of Shakespeare and designed the interior of a cinema in Tooting. The building's stark white façade gives way to a fantasia of vividly painted arches, alcoves, murals and chandeliers, trimmed in gold and more reminiscent of a Russian Orthodox cathedral than a South London picture house. It's now the city's best decorated bingo hall.[2] Nairn was dazzled by this otherworldly gem: 'Miss the Tower of London, if you have to, but don't miss this.'

BARBICAN ESTATE ⑧
City of London Planning Office, plus various architects, begun 1960
Nairn was tentatively excited about the Barbican Estate. It was still being constructed while he wrote his book, but 'make another date for the 1970s', he wrote. The divisive brutalist icon has succeeded on its own terms and become a much sought-after home in the City. Pack a map and explore the Barbican's lakes and winding uplands.[3] On Sundays, its large leafy conservatory is open to the public. Look for quails and terrapins.

---

[1] The surrounding area will be transformed by 2020, with outlandish new structures including Frank Gehry's scrunchy pink-and-orange Flower Building.

[2] And one of London's most unusual evenings out (galabingo.com/clubs/tooting).

[3] Or join a free tour, which will take you down into the boiler room. Find the centre of this concrete labyrinth on p.290.

RESVRGAM

ST PAUL'S CATHEDRAL ⑦
Sir Christopher Wren, 1677–87
'The way to come on St Paul's is along Fleet Street,' wrote Ian Nairn, 'and the way to go along Fleet Street is on top of a bus.' As you approach on the top deck of the No. 26, concentrate on the dome,[1] which Nairn particularly admires. 'The dome is an utter repose', he writes, '[…] it floats, serene but not detached'. St Paul's very consciously rises out of the ruins of its predecessor, which was destroyed in the Great Fire.[2] The floor plan of old St Paul's is etched on to the south churchyard and superimposed with the footprint of its replacement; and in the Lapidarium you can see stacks of stones from the old cathedral stored at the heart of the new.

In the Wren family memoirs, we learn that when the centre point of the new structure was decided a workman brought a 'flat stone from the Heaps of Rubbish […] to be laid for a Mark'. 'The Stone happened to be a Piece of Gravestone,' it continues, 'with nothing remaining of the Inscription but this simple word in large capitals, RESURGAM.' Look for that word, meaning 'I will rise again', carved beneath the feet of a phoenix on the building's exterior.

THE RED LION, DUKE OF YORK STREET
The Red Lion on Duke of York Street 'is not especially comfortable or especially atmospheric', wrote Nairn, 'but it strikes deeper than any other'.

He mentions numerous watering holes in his guide, but states that 'if [he] could keep only one pub out of the whole London galaxy, this would be [his] choice.' You can still order an ale in its mirrored interior today. Nairn's book ends with an unprompted postscript on London's beers, hinting at the preoccupation that would eventually lead to his alcoholism and early death at the age of 52. You can pay your respects in Hanwell Cemetery on Uxbridge Road.[3] Nairn was fond of Hanwell. 'From east or west along the Uxbridge Road,' he wrote, 'Hanwell is an apparition of meaning after miles of chaos.'

---

[1] St Paul's is better endowed with domes than appearances suggest. The main dome is actually three separate, ingeniously layered vaults: the outer hemisphere, the inner ceiling, and a supporting brick cone between the two.

[2] For Old St Paul's, see p.98, and for more on the fire's devastation, see p.342.

[3] His grave calls him 'A MAN WITHOUT A MASK'.

SKYSCRAPING

The polished skyscrapers around the globe, designed by superstar architects like Foster, Hadid, Gehry and Piano, are like the 'brilliant fragments of a splintered utopia' according to the theorist Marc Augé: signposts 'to a planetary society that is yet to materialize'.

CENTRE POINT, NEW OXFORD STREET ②

This slender slab, with its tight mesh of turquoise windows, was the tallest building in London when it was built in 1966. It then sat empty for its first decade because the landlord couldn't attract a tenant willing to match his extortionate rent. Centre Point became a symbol of developer greed and was seen by many as a product of council wheeler-dealing that ought never to have been built.[1] Its architect, Richard Seifert, constructed 400 towers in the capital and had, wrote Roy Porter, 'more influence over the London skyline than any man since Wren'.

LLOYDS, LIME STREET

Insurance behemoth Lloyd's of London began in Lloyd's Coffee House on Tower Street in 1688. And as business has grown, so have its premises. The company now insures priceless treasures, like the vocal cords of Celine Dion and Bob Dylan, and their headquarters are in Richard Rogers's black and silver skyscraper on Lime Street. This was Rogers's first major project after the Pompidou Centre and is one of the most starkly futuristic buildings in London. The inside-out design, with lifts, toilet pods and other services bolted on to the exterior, makes this a particularly satisfying building to examine from the street. It was completed in 1986 and Grade I listed in 2011: the youngest building ever to gain that level of protection.[2]

CHEESE GRATER, LEADENHALL STREET

Another Rogers project is the Cheese Grater opposite. Ordinarily architects would avoid a wedge shape like this as it cuts down on the amount of lucrative floor space towards the top of the building. The Cheese Grater tapers away to protect a view of St Paul's.[3]

GHERKIN, ST MARY AXE

After the trauma of the 1992 IRA bomb outside the Baltic Exchange, the building that rose from the devastation was Foster and Partners' 30 St Mary Axe, or the Gherkin as it's become known.[4] For such a curvaceous building, it's surprising to learn that all bar one of the glass panels are flat; the curved panel sits on the very top. If you don't work in the Gherkin, it's not straightforward to explore the building. Searcys, the restaurant on the top three floors, mainly holds events in its corporate crow's nest, but you can book to eat there on certain dates. Or, for a healthier option, sign up for the NSPCC's annual sponsored run up the 38-floor stairwell.

---

❶ Centre Point is now Grade II listed and in 2009 won the Concrete Society's prestigious 'Mature Structures Award'. For more on its centrality, see p.200.

❷ Enter Lloyd's strangest room on p.419.
❸ See p.4.
❹ To find out what's beneath the Gherkin, see p.397.

SHARD, LONDON BRIDGE STREET ⑩

Renzo Piano's Shard gives London a new spire that can be seen for miles around. There's an expensive viewing platform at the top, but if want to see the view from the Shard, it's cheaper to buy a drink in Oblix a few floors lower. Jones and Woodward, in their 2013 *Guide to the Architecture of London*, described the Shard as the kind of posturing structure 'rarely found in democracies', which 'represents nothing but itself'.

WALKIE TALKIE, FENCHURCH STREET ⑨

Grand projects can have unintended consequences. When the Walkie Talkie was built, its curved glass façade focused searing beams of sunlight on to the streets below, liquidating parked cars.[1] A vast sunshade was hastily erected to prevent further damage and the architect, Rafael Viñoly, was hauled before the public. Viñoly admitted that he'd been expecting the effect, but had 'judged the temperature was going to be about 36 degrees', rather than the 100-degree highs that were recorded. 'They are calling it the death ray,' he explained, 'because if you go there you might die.' The Walkie Talkie bulges on the way up to increase the amount of premium office space on the upper floors. It's easier to visit than many of London's towers, with a publically accessible 'Sky Garden' at its summit. It's free to visit, but you need to book in advance.

22 BISHOPSGATE

It's not clear what the new structure at 22 Bishopsgate will be called. Before building began it was excitedly known as the Helter Skelter, due to the twist at the top. Then, when the twist was snipped off the design, it was called the Pinnacle. Once seven storeys had been built and construction had stalled it was known as the Stump.[2] For the time being it is simply referred to by its address.

SHADOWS

With every new skyscraper comes a new patch of shadowed land – and as clusters of tall buildings shoot up, swathes of the city could be left sunless without careful planning. In early 2015, two shadowless skyscrapers were proposed for land next to the Millennium Dome in Greenwich. The mirrored surface of each building is designed to direct light downwards and illuminate the shadow cast by the other.

B ———

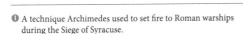
❶ A technique Archimedes used to set fire to Roman warships during the Siege of Syracuse.

❷ Find another half-built stump on p.346.

MATERIAL BENEFITS

When the pioneering Bromley by Bow Centre[1] was being built, its founder, Andrew Mawson, insisted on using expensive, high-quality materials even though money was tight. He later justified the decision in his book *The Social Entrepreneur*:

> *When we are careful about the way we create a physical environment, when we pay attention to every detail of it, people start to think about themselves and each other differently.*

Mawson isn't alone in this belief: here are three of the most compelling recent examples of high design in areas of high deprivation.

ACADEMY

'Children should experience well-made spaces,' writes critic Rowan Moore, 'just as they should experience art and music.' Walk along Brixton's Shakespeare Road, past Alice Walker Close and James Joyce Walk until you reach Zaha Hadid's extraordinary palace of pedagogy. Instead of the soft curves and primary colours of many modern schools, Evelyn Grace Academy has a slick black and grey exterior. The building is a long metal zigzag, covered with interlocking glass panels; at a glance, it could easily be mistaken for an airport. According to Hadid's team, this angular aesthetic is meant 'to translate a strong educational vision and ethos into a building that carries those aspirations'. A space-saving red running track cuts ingeniously under the middle of the school.

LIBRARY ⑫

If you like patinated copper, you'll love Peckham Library: a huge green tub on rickety stilts, every bit as ambitious and eccentric as Hadid's school. Its core is a vast reading room, presided over by three elevated plywood pods. Will Alsop's building has high windows, with panes the colour of highlighter pens and a view north to the City skyline. For critic Jonathan Glancey, bringing 'the best new architecture into such areas is to afford them status and inject them with the sort of urban adrenaline that encourages [...] financial investment'. Peckham Library is a stunning place to spend a few hours with a book. Request a copy of *Nairn's London*.[2]

DANCE CENTRE

The strange polycarbonate box casting multi-coloured lights on to Deptford Creek is the Laban Dance Centre. Pay a visit to dance, watch dance or have a coffee and a bun in the building's cafe. The flat roof is a hidden habitat specifically designed for the rare black redstart.

---

[1] See p.136.
[2] The shelfmark is LONDON 914.2104.

PROBLEM PLACES

APOLOGETIC

The Brunei Gallery in Russell Square is perhaps the only building in London that apologises for its existence. 'The University of London', reads a plaque outside, 'hereby records its sincere apologies that the plans of this building were settled without due consultation with the Russell family'. The family owns the land and retains the right to review university plans in certain locations. On this occasion, they neither saw the plans nor liked the result. The granite basin in the roof garden[1] further underlines the building's contrition: it's engraved with a single Japanese character meaning 'forgiveness'.

CONFUSED

Howard Carter discovered Tutankhamun's tomb just as the art deco movement was taking flight. Public enthusiasm for mummies spawned a peculiar mishmash of art deco and Ancient Egyptian styles. The finest example in London is the Carreras Cigarette Factory, whose sleek frontage is adorned with statues of the cat goddess Bubastis.[2] Take a tube to Mornington Crescent and admire the confused building from Harrington Square Gardens opposite.

FRAUDULENT

If you leave an incorrect plaque in place long enough, it begins to acquire a history and significance of its own. Anyone pausing by 49 Bankside, an early-18th-century house next to the Globe Theatre, would be forgiven for believing that this was where 'Sir Christopher Wren [lived] during the building of St Paul's Cathedral'. This isn't the case, and Gillian Tindall, who's studied the house, believes the ceramic plaque outside was put up as a hoax by the owner in 1945. The owner's prank may have been the building's salvation: while many neighbouring properties were pulled down after the war, Tindall believes that Southwark Council fell for the Wren connection and deliberately preserved 49 Bankside.

UNFIT FOR PURPOSE (3)

Cast your eye along the moulded terracotta animals on the façade of the Natural History Museum: extinct creatures are to the east of the entrance, the living are to the west.[3] The staggering main doorway itself was styled on the grandeur of the basalt columns at the mouth of Fingal's Cave in the Inner Hebrides. 'It is a magnificent building', wrote Bruce Frederick Cummings,[4] a young entomologist at the museum, but 'too magnificent to work there. A pious zoologist might go up to pray in it,' he continues, 'but not to earn his daily bread there.'

SUPERFICIAL

Inspect 23 and 24 Leinster Gardens and you'll see that they have no letterboxes or door handles. Look even closer and you'll notice that the windows are painted on. All becomes clear if you walk around to Porchester Terrace, the street directly behind them. They are just façades.[5] The original houses were demolished to make way for the Metropolitan Line and these lean replacements were built to maintain the character of the street and disguise the railway cutting below.

OPEN CITY

The London Open House weekend takes place each September, with hundreds of the city's most iconic and intriguing buildings open to the public for free. Visit spaces you might never otherwise access: homes and schools, waste facilities and factories, government buildings and corporate headquarters. Queues at the most sought-after venues can be off-putting, but if you volunteer as a steward for half a day, you receive a badge granting you immediate entry to any of the sites (openhouselondon.org.uk).

---

[1] This space for reflection and meditation is open to the public. See p.380.
[2] For more cats with a nicotine habit, see p.152 and p.254.
[3] Blackfriars Bridge has a similar design feature. The side of the bridge facing out to sea is decorated with marine birds; the inland side with freshwater birds.
[4] Meet Cummings and his wretched alter ego on p.123.
[5] Sherlock Holmes hides behind them in the recent BBC TV series. Visit Sherlock's homes on pp.410–411.

CONGESTION

EARLY ON SATURDAY 24 NOVEMBER 1810, a chimneysweep arrived at 54 Berners Street, the elegant townhouse of Mrs Tottenham, a widowed 'lady of fortune'.[1] Then another chimneysweep arrived, and another. Over the course of the day, multiple chimneysweeps, colliers, cakemakers, doctors, lawyers, vicars, fishmongers, upholsterers and shoemakers called at the address, all unrequested and unexpected. A dozen pianos were delivered, and a church organ. Accoucheurs, tooth-drawers, miniature-painters, artists, auctioneers, barbers, mantua-makers, grocers, post-chaises, poultry sellers, rabbit catchers and pigeon fanciers gathered outside, as well as the Governor of the Bank of England, the Duke of York, the Archbishop of Canterbury, the Lord Mayor of London, and an undertaker with a made-to-measure coffin. Thousands of people had received bogus letters requesting their presence, apparently from Mrs Tottenham. The surrounding streets were soon packed, Mayfair was brought to a standstill, and the Marlborough Street police officers couldn't clear the area until late that evening. The *Morning Post* called it 'the greatest hoax that ever has been heard of in this metropolis', and a reward was published for the apprehension of its author.[2]

Today London has more than twice the population of any other city in Western Europe, and crowdedness is one of its fundamental characteristics. The crowd, and the anonymity it offers, can be thrilling, threatening or simply irritating as roads jam and tube carriages overflow. Congestion not only hobbles London's infrastructure, it also takes its toll on the health of its inhabitants. The city's cramped living conditions enabled the devastating spread of the Great Plague of 1665, when red crosses were painted on the doors of stricken houses. Today city administrators mark Cs in red circles around the perimeter of the most congested zones, in an attempt to tourniquet affected areas, and mete out Congestion Charges to those who enter them. This chapter imagines London as a bloated human body, with A-roads for arteries, car park capillary beds and a one-way system of veins. Circulating inside it are nine million cellular citizens.

---

[1] Today the Sanderson Hotel.

[2] On the morning of the Berners Street Hoax, 22-year-old Theodore Hook took up position opposite No. 54, to watch the chaotic proceedings. He wasn't identified at the time and didn't own up for over 30 years. Hook is also credited with receiving the first picture postcard, which he sent to himself.

BODY PARTS

HEADS

Pat Eduardo Paolozzi's gigantic *Head of Invention* on Butler's Wharf in Shad Thames. This mechanical bust is cracked open by a Leonardo Da Vinci quotation.[1]

SHOULDERS

The M25 was the first motorway in Britain to lose its hard shoulder: in April 2014, an eight-mile section of the capital's Hertfordshire epaulette was converted into an extra lane for traffic.

KNEES

In 1968, the American artist Claes Oldenburg published 120 copies of *London Knees 1966*: a box containing plans for a colossal public sculpture of a pair of knees.[2] Oldenburg was inspired by London's columns, cigarette butts and miniskirts, which revealed to him 'the architectural and fetishistic functions of knees'. Claes's public monument was never built in London, but the knees have squeezed on to the Fantasy Piccadilly Line map by Nils Norman.[3]

& TOES

In the Members' Lobby of the Houses of Parliament, David Lloyd George and Winston Churchill flank the entrance to the House of Commons Chamber. Both statues are a dull bronze-brown, apart from their gleaming toes. Superstitious MPs give them a rub for luck before speaking in the chamber.

KNEES

The Grant Museum has several preserved bumblebees on display. Borrow a magnifying glass and examine the bees' knees.

& TOES

There is a prosthetic toe in the British Museum Egyptian Gallery 63, case 14. This big right toe was once appended to a mummy, and had an imitation toenail inserted. It appears to have been used by a living Egyptian, before its owner was mummified.

& EYES

London has been rolling its Eye since 31 December 1999. The giant ferris wheel on the South Bank is the setting for *The London Eye Mystery* by Siobhan Dowd: a young boy called Salim gets on to the Eye, and when his pod returns to the ground he has disappeared. His cousin Ted sets out to solve the mystery ...

& EARS

The walls have ears on Floral Street: look outside Ted Baker (9–10) and Agnès B (35–36). These protruding organs were cast from the artist Tim Fishlock's own lugholes. He installed about 50 ears across Covent Garden in 2000, but these are the only two still earwigging.

& MOUTH

'When the lions drink, London will sink.' Ferocious green felines line Bazalgette's Thames embankments[4] and hold mooring rings in their jaws. If the surface of the river reaches their mouths, run for the hills.

& NOSE

Ask a black cab driver to take you to the 'London Nose'. They will take you to a pink life-size nose that sticks out of Admiralty Arch. Some say it's Nelson's spare schnoz, others that it's a copy of the Duke of Wellington's nose and cavalrymen rubbed it for luck.[5]

---

[1] A reminder that human genius 'will never find an invention more beautiful or more simple or more direct than nature'.

[2] The box included a 39cm scale latex model. You can request to see a copy in the Prints and Drawings room of the British Museum (1979,0623.16).

[3] See p.414

[4] For more on Bazalgette's embankments, see p.55.

[5] For the truth, turn to p.x.

SKIN

At Cody Dock on the River Lea, you can see a giant anatomical cross-section of human skin. *Sensation* is a garishly painted bronze sculpture by Damien Hirst with bulbous follicles, capillaries and glands.

HAIR

It hasn't been necessary for barristers to wear wigs in court since 1995, but most of them still do. Get your itchy horse-hair toupée at Thresher & Glenny on Middle Temple Lane, which was founded in 1696. Pure white is the sign of a greenhorn; ask for yours to be fashionably soiled.

BRAIN

Half of Charles Babbage's brain is preserved at the Science Museum.[1] Look for it floating in the Maths and Computing Gallery, alongside his cerebral notebooks of calculations.

TONGUE

'I just stick my tongue out because I hate smiling in pictures,' says Miley Cyrus. In 2015 she entered Madame Tussaud's, tongue out, gingham hotpants on, straddling the massive tongue-slide that featured in her 2014 Bangerz Tour.

ARMS

If you're into breeding, visit the College of Arms on Queen Victoria Street and consult the Officer in Waiting about your heraldic heritage; if you're into brawn, join the London Armwrestling Team.[2]

C ——

CONGESTED LUNGS

London, the crouching monster, like every other monster has to breathe [...] Its vital oxygen is composed of suburban working men and women of all kinds, who every morning are sucked up through an infinitely complicated respiratory apparatus of trains and termini into the mighty congested lungs, held there for a number of hours, and then, in the evening, exhaled violently through the same channels. — *Patrick Hamilton*

HANDS

Take your newborn babe to Wrightson & Platt on Walton Street and have its hands cast in silver. Queen Victoria commissioned alabaster sculptures of her nine children's hands and feet, which inspired this 'baby life-casting service'.

HEART

Sign up to the next 'Hearts at Barts' workshop, where you'll learn the techniques of preserving human hearts in the Pathology Museum at St Bartholomew's Hospital. The museum's technical curator, Carla Valentine, will help you pot an animal heart over a glass of wine.[3]

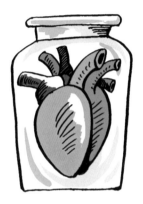

---

[1] The other half is at the Hunterian Museum. For more on Babbage, see p.160.

[2] See p.227.

[3] Perhaps she'll put on London's Heart FM while you work (106.2 FM).

CROWD FORMATIONS

A HUMORAL GUIDE TO URBAN HEALTH

Until the 19th century, the prevalent theory of medicine in London was humorism. This system, developed by the Ancient Greeks, views sickness as an imbalance of four bodily fluids: blood, yellow bile, black bile and phlegm. We all have a unique humoral cocktail, which determines our temperament, and sanguine, choleric, melancholic and phlegmatic constitutions require very different lifestyles.

To achieve *eucrasy* – perfect health – the four humours must be maintained in their correct proportions. If your leading humour starts to dominate, you may need to purge the excess through blood-letting, vomiting, or blistering. London deals with its imbalances in a similar way, by charging motorists, running more trains and creating pedestrianised zones. Despite these measures, there's no escaping other people in a metropolis. Deal with the city's excesses by joining the type of crowd that matches your temperament and avoiding those that don't.

CARNIVALS FOR THE SANGUINE

'Blood is a hot, sweet, temperate, red humour,' wrote Robert Burton in his 1621 masterpiece *The Anatomy of Melancholy*. That sweetness translates to the disposition too; sanguine types are often childlike in their optimism and playfulness, although one 19th-century academic described them as people of 'small brains and great activity'.

The crowd most suited to the sanguine temperament is the buoyant, carefree atmosphere of the carnival. In Georgian London, this spirit was characterised by a style of party known as a 'rout', which involved deliberately compressing a large number of revellers into a small space. 'Everyone complains of the pressure of the company,' wrote one rout attendee in 1802, 'yet all rejoice at being so divinely squeezed.'

London's best known contemporary rout is the Notting Hill Carnival, a fifty-year-old Caribbean street party that takes place at the end of August and which now attracts around a million people (thenottinghillcarnival.com). It grew out of the trauma of the Notting Hill Race Riots in 1959.[1] Read the story of the two women behind the carnival on plaques at the junction of Portobello and Tavistock Roads.

An even more chock-a-block affair is the Brixton Splash, which is held on the first Sunday of August and jams enormous sound systems and oil-barrel barbecues into a few heaving streets (brixtonsplash. org). The event began in 2006, the 25th anniversary of the Brixton riots, with the aim of 'making Brixton famous rather than infamous'.

Carnivals offer a vision of a different, more sanguine society. 'Carnival is not a spectacle seen by the people;' wrote the critic Mikhail Bakhtin, 'they live in it, and […] while carnival lasts, there is no other life outside it.' This is the spirit of the Pride in London LGBT[2] celebrations, which are held every June (prideinlondon. org). What began as a political rally in the 1970s has morphed into a colossal parade and street party promoting equality for all. Listen out for the Friends of Dorothy LGBT campanology society, who ring the bells of St Martin-in-the-Fields as the parade passes through Trafalgar Square.

---

[1] See p.89.   [2] Get proud on pp.74–75.

If these festivities overload your fragile frame, go to the Margaret Street Blood Bank and exsanguinate. You're not alone: the artist Marc Quinn is clearly a suffering sanguine too. Walk to the National Portrait Gallery and look for *Self*, a frozen cast of Quinn's head made from nine pints of his own blood.

C

CONGREGATIONS FOR THE CHOLERIC

Yellow bile, or choler, 'is hot and dry, bitter [...] and gathered to the gall', wrote Robert Burton. The choleric temper is similarly fiery; cholerics 'are witty and liberal, but wrathful and revengeful', according to a 17th-century *Compendium of Chirurgery*.

A delirious congregational atmosphere provides the ideal complement for cholerics, and the competitive frenzy of a football match is a particularly good way to expel some anger.[1] Eschew the sanitised stadia of the Premier League teams for the primal energy of the lesser-known Isthmian League, home to teams like the Cray Wanderers, Metropolitan Police FC and Corinthian-Casuals. Choose your favourite squad and roar at the opposing fans (isthmian.co.uk).

Once you've witnessed some soul-stirring soccer, make for the Wimbledon dog circuit, place some bets, and cheer on your chosen hounds from the rowdy trackside. Few activities stoke the choleric temper better than losing money on an underperforming canine.

Then turn your anger to a more political purpose and harangue the London Assembly at one of their People's Question Times (london.gov.uk/get-involved/events/peoples-question-time). 'Cholerics dream of thunder and of bright, dangerous things', wrote C. S. Lewis. Express your most baleful, bilious projections for humankind at Speakers' Corner,[2] at the north-east edge of Hyde Park.

Too much rage can be debilitating. Clammy comestibles like melon and lettuce are particularly recommended to rebalance a hot, dry constitution, so calm down by the soothing waters of Camden Lock and dine on moist, raw fare at the inSpiral Lounge on Camden High Street. This cafe began as a chill-out space on the green festival scene and its permanent base retains that vibe. Curmudgeonly cholerics will particularly benefit from the ambient electro music, the views out on to the canal and inSpiral's belief that 'every one of us can contribute in a meaningful way to a better future'.

---

❶ Play the beautiful game on p.224.　　❷ Explore the Corner on p.81.

COMMERCE FOR THE PHLEGMATIC

'Phlegm', writes Robert Burton, 'is a cold and moist humour', and generates the calmest, most stoic of the four temperaments. 'Pale, slow, inert' was Charlotte Brontë's judgement of phlegmatics. Nevertheless, they have a talent for patience and observation.

Phlegmatics are particularly comfortable at the centre of languorous crowds of window shoppers. They're natural flâneurs, 'drifting purposefully' through London's multitudes and 'noticing everything', as Iain Sinclair put it. Here are three fine flâneurial zones where you can experience the crowds at street level and then secure an aerial view.

1. BEGIN WITH A SATURDAY STROLL through Borough Market. Breathe in the aroma of coffee, hard cheese and raw fish as you merge with the dense glob of customers, then retreat to Roast, the restaurant in the glass-fronted Floral Hall above the market.

2. FROM THERE, TRAVEL TO OXFORD STREET and let the tide of shoppers carry you along. As Baudelaire wrote, 'it's an immense pleasure to take up residence in multiplicity, in whatever is seething, moving, evanescent and infinite'. Stop beneath Barbara Hepworth's *Winged Figure* on Holles Street, enter John Lewis and take the zigzag of white escalators to the fifth-floor cafe. As you sit by the window, 'you see everyone,' – in Baudelaire's words – 'you're at the centre of everything yet you remain hidden from everybody'.

3. FINALLY, VISIT WESTFIELD STRATFORD[1] and glide around the glimmering mall. Watch life spool past as you dine in unit 2003 on the balcony. Franco Manca has an unlikely outpost here amidst the bigger brands and serves fine sourdough pizzas.

Should you wish to put your perambulations to public use, apply to join the Mass Observation Project (massobs.org.uk). Mass Observation began in 1937 as a way of conducting 'the science of ourselves'. It's now active again and on the lookout for observers to gather 'descriptively rich material which can offer insights into everyday life'.

'Onyons ben gode for flemmatik men', advised one 15th-century nutritionist. Likewise, pigeon was believed to be particularly effective for correcting an excess of phlegm. Snare a London pigeon[2] and bake it with white onions to alleviate your malaise.

MAP READING
Crowd Formations *recalls the 13th-century* Ebstorf Map *(now destroyed) and Grayson Perry's* Map of Nowhere, *both of which fuse a circular map with a splayed human body. Here London's crowds bloat a human figure with a TfL circulatory system and the M25 for a girdle. The face is Robert Burton.*

---

1 For more on this monumental mall, see p.251.　　2 If you'd prefer a grey squirrel, see p.375.

CLAUSTROPHILIA

Nowhere does one feel more like a human sardine than in a lift, and yet we willingly pack ourselves into these constrictive canisters every day. Relish the squeeze in these premium elevators.

ASCENDER

Step into the Savoy Hotel's elegant red 'ascending room', which glides you to the Edwardian wing of the hotel amidst gleaming red-and-gold lacquer.[1] This was London's first electric lift; initially, nervous passengers were given a glass of brandy to steady their nerves. At the top you emerge into the realm of the Savoy's 'Personality Suites', inspired by famous former guests, including Noël Coward, Frank Sinatra, Claude Monet and Charlie Chaplin.

INCLINER

Ride the 'Millennium Bridge Inclined Lift' from the bottom of St Peter's Hill. This is London's only funicular railway, ideal for the louche lift-lover. Once at the top, you can stroll across the Millennium Bridge.

CYCLIC

Northwick Park Hospital in Harrow boasts London's only operational paternoster lift. This 19th-century design has chains of cubicles in constant motion: you step on as one arrives and step off as required. It's fraught with health and safety implications, not least because this particular paternoster was used as a location in the 1976 film *The Omen*.[2] Unfortunately it is in a restricted area of the hospital.

HARMONIC

Step into *Work No. 409* at the Royal Festival Hall, also known as the 'Singing Lift'.[3] As you travel up or down, you are accompanied by musical scales in four-part harmony, sung by the Southbank Centre's Voicelab choir. Floor six is A sharp; the ground floor is bottom E.

WEIGHTY

The Hospital Club on Endell Street is a members-only 'creatives' club in an 18th-century hospital building. Try to wangle a ride in their lift, which can take the weight of up to nine people. If they won't let you in, send a horse instead. If you don't have a horse, a sign explains that the lift can also accommodate 5,050 bananas, 6,666 hen's eggs, 2,941 pigeons, 88 haddock or 10,526 pound coins.

WEIGHTLESS

Step into deep space at the Sanderson Hotel on Berners Street.[4] The lights in the lift are low, there are stars in every direction, and there's a mesmeric galaxy far far away.

ONE NEW CHANGE

Take the glass elevator at One New Change for a spectacular ascending view of St Paul's. The open-air roof terrace has London's best public view of the cathedral from close quarters.[5] Admire it while sipping a 'Rooftop' cocktail from Madison's.

M&M WORLD

Everyone's favourite candy-themed megastore on Leicester Square has a kooky lift that looks like you're stepping into a red telephone box. You're not! It's a lift!

---

[1] This is the red lift; the hotel also has a blue lift. You take the blue lift, the story ends, you wake up in your bed and believe whatever you want to believe. You take the red lift, you stay in Wonderland.
[2] In the scene where Thorn and Jennings return to the hospital in Rome.
[3] The Singing Lift has its own Twitter following: @SingingLift.
[4] For more on this address, see p.31.
[5] For distant views of St Paul's, see p.4.

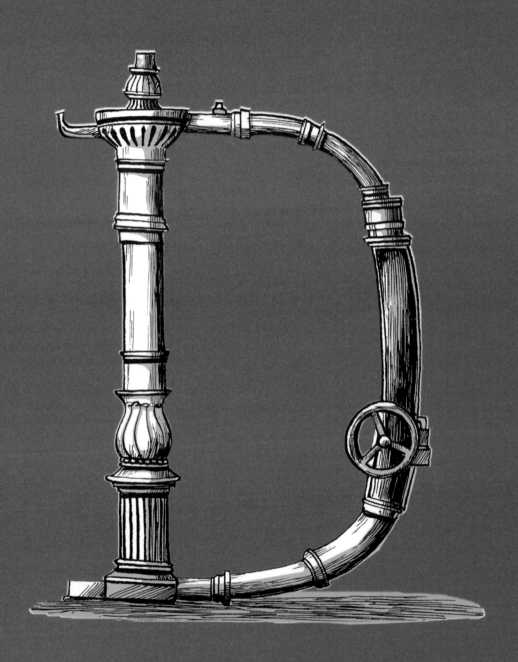

By the late 19th century, flushing toilets were a widespread phenomenon rather than a luxury. Experience one of the city's best preserved historic lavatories in the basement of John Wesley's Chapel on City Road: this set of **CRAPPER'S VALVELESS WASTE WATER PREVENTERS** was fitted in 1899.

At the Great Exhibition of 1851, George Jennings caused a sensation with his one-penny **MONKEY CLOSETS**: London's first flushing public toilets.[2] In 1852, public conveniences for men began to appear across the city. The Ladies Sanitary Association had to campaign for adequate facilities for women

Today London's flagship public convenience is the **JUBILOO**[3] on the South Bank, installed for the queen's Diamond Jubilee in 2012. There are Union Jack toilet seats and employees have shirts to match. Floors are washed and toilets flushed with rainwater collected on the roof or drawn from one of the Southbank Centre's bore holes.

There is currently a street urination crisis, with many London councils installing open-air urinals to deter desperate men from using doorways and bins. The most public of these is the **VAUXHALL OPEN-AIR URINAL** on the centre of a traffic island outside the train station.

Look for the unofficial blue plaque on White Post Lane in Hackney Wick, which states that the world's first **PERFORATED TOILET PAPER** was developed in London.

Designs have become increasingly ambitious over time. Currently, the city's most intriguing toilets are at the back of **SKETCH** on Conduit Street: a neon nest of gigantic egg-shaped pods, filled with the sound of belching bullfrogs.[1]

Today many of the city's old public premises are being sold off and converted. Visit the toilets in CellarDoor on Aldwych, a bar fashioned from an old public convenience. Their transparent cubicle doors only turn opaque on locking.

The Jubiloo offers a vision of things to come. Currently one-third of London's drinking water goes down the toilet, a habit that will become hard to sustain as pressure increases on the city's water supplies.[4]

MAP READING
In *A Flow Chart of London Sewage*,
the city is split open so that you can see the
journey of the sewage beneath the streets,
from the toilet to the Thames. South London
is on the left hand page and North London
on the right. Locations depicted on the map
are capitalised in the accompanying texts.
The creatures in the Thames are based on
William Heath's 19th-century cartoon
Monster Soup.

---

❶ If you find pond life off-putting, visit Maggie's nightclub on Fulham Road, which plays Margaret Thatcher's speeches in its latrines.
❷ One of the city's earliest public toilets was set up by Dick Whittington: a communal **HOUSE OF EASEMENT** that seated 128 people.

❸ To visit you need to spend 50 pennies.
❹ For more on London's water supply, see p.390.

D

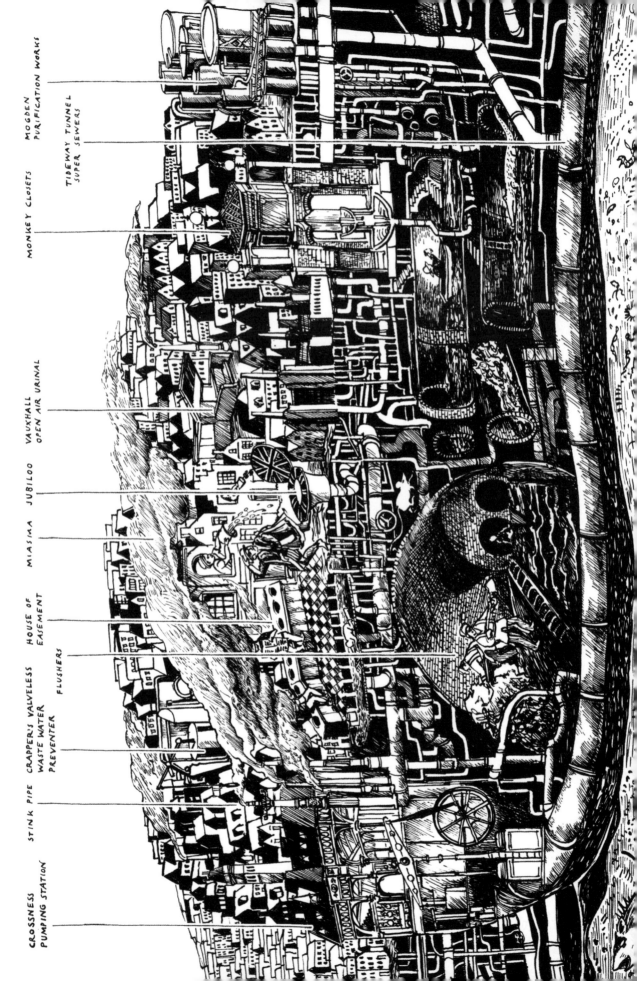

CROSSNESS PUMPING STATION

STINK PIPE

CRAPPER'S VALVELESS WASTE WATER PREVENTER

HOUSE OF EASEMENT

FLUSHERS

MIASMA

JUBILOO

VAUXHALL OPEN AIR URINAL

MONKEY CLOSETS

TIDEWAY TUNNEL SUPER SEWERS

MOGDEN PURIFICATION WORKS

A·D 1800

WILL.M BOUND, CHURCH
JOSEPH BIRD, WARDENS.

For the better accommodation
of the Neighbourhood,
this Pump was removed to
the Spot where it now
Stands.
The Spring by which it is
supplied is situated four
Feet eastward, and round
it, as History informs us,
the Parish Clerks of London
in remote Ages annually
performed sacred Plays.
That Custom caused it to be
denominated Clerks-Well,
and from which this Parish
derives its Name.
The Water was greatly
esteemed by the Prior and
Brethren of the Order of
S.t John of Jerusalem, and
the Benedictine Nuns
in the Neighbourhood.

Islington Libraries
Postcard Reprints
23

CLERKS' WELL IN 1822
Over 800 years old and still in existence

Produced by
Pamlin Prints
Croydon

---

17 Feb. 2015
BUNHILL FIELDS
(BURIAL GROUND).

Everything begins here. A reef of nonconformity running from WESLEY on
his plinth to the triangulation of
BLAKE - BUNYAN - DEFOE. All
English pilgrimages, quests, escapes.
        I followed the obelisks to the
east and failed.
        This afternoon, going west, I
discovered QUAKER GARDENS.
Enclosed by high flats. Reservoir
of silence in which to
contemplate the next move.
                Andrew NORTON.

HENRY ELIOT, MATT
        LLOYD - ROSE
                                ?
Flat 2,
HANLEY ROAD,
LONDON N4

PEA SOUPERS

FOG

'Fog everywhere,' wrote Dickens in the opening to *Bleak House*, '[...] it rolls defiled among the tiers of shipping and the waterside pollutions of a great (and dirty) city.' In the 19th and early 20th centuries, London fogs, or 'London Particulars', arrived in November and could be debilitating. Over New Year 1814, the Birmingham mail coach took seven hours to crawl as far as Uxbridge; and in 1918, Virginia Woolf described old gentlemen walking 'in numbers over the edge of platforms'. Today, you can imagine what a London Particular might have been like when the city is subsumed in low-lying cloud: stand on London Bridge and admire the Gherkin disappearing into the white sky, or the Shard three-quarters engulfed.

SMOG

What made London fog so particular was the grimy cocktail it created with the city's smoke. The longest smog lasted from November 1879 until March 1880; Londoners would travel with handkerchiefs over their mouths, navigating by gas lamps that were lit throughout the day. It came in a variety of colours: black, brown, grey, orange, dark chocolate or bottle green. This last, thickest variety of smog became known as the 'pea souper'.[1]

CLEAN AIR

In 1952, the Great Smog arrived. It was so thick that a Sadlers Wells performance of *La Traviata* was abandoned because the stage disappeared. The pollution was deadly and 4,000 Londoners died. The Great Smog led directly to the Clean Air Act in 1956. Smokeless fuel was introduced across London, and the city last saw thick fog in December 1962. Today there are a number of cosy pubs with open, smoke-free fires. Pass a wintry afternoon in the Holly Bush in Hampstead, with its dark wood panels, or the Old Red Lion in Kennington, which has intimate alcoves in its converted toilets.

POLLUTION

Before you breathe a sigh of relief, however, reflect on King's College London's research in 2014, which showed that Oxford Street has some of the highest levels of nitrogen dioxide pollution in the world. Don't try to escape underground: another 2002 study revealed that on average the air quality on the tube is 73 times worse than at street level, and that a 20-minute trip on the Northern Line has 'the same effect as smoking a cigarette'.

MIST

Evelyn Waugh thought London was 'designed [...] to be seen in a fog' and Giuseppe Mazzini[2] found the city's smog helped him to dream. 'One might believe the entire town subject to a sort of enchantment,' he wrote. If you feel nostalgic towards pea soupers, stand on Holborn Viaduct, the epicentre of fog in *Bleak House*, and imagine you are 'in a balloon, and hanging in the misty clouds'.

SMOKE

Seventy years ago criminals referred to London as 'The Smoke' and no wonder – coal dust, gas and the fumes of ten million cigarettes hung over the city in a permanent fog. Now the pea soupers have gone, and with them some of London's grimy, sinful old soul. London's dirt now is of the bland international variety seen in every great city: fast food wrappers blowing in the wind, discarded cans, piles of binliners standing patiently in the streets of Theatreland, like playgoers waiting for spare tickets.
— *Catharine Arnold*

---

[1] In an eccentric reverse etymology, the restaurant Simpson's-in-the-Strand christened their glaucous pea and ham soup the 'London Particular'. It's still occasionally on the menu.

[2] Mazzini had rooms at 187 Gower Street, next door to Sherlock's house in the recent BBC adaptation. During filming his blue plaque is covered with a lamp. See pp.410-11.

SUPER TREES

Trees inhale the polluted air of a city and breathe it out recycled and clean. When the Great Storm of 1987 felled dozens of trees in Hyde Park, Kew Gardens and the rest of the city, distraught Londoners were asked to nominate their favourite arboreal survivors, and today the charity Trees for Cities maintains a list of over 60 'Great Trees' in London.[1]

D ———

THE BATTERSEA PARK HYBRID STRAWBERRY TREE

This unusual species has red flaky bark and a gnarly, twisted trunk. Its lower portion has the largest girth of any strawberry tree in Britain. Visit in late autumn to catch its creamy white flowers and small, red, spherical fruits. Pick a punnet of bitter, but edible, hybrid strawberries and dowse them in cream.

THE GREENWICH PARK SHAGBARK HICKORY

Located in the Edwardian flower garden at Greenwich Park, this modest-looking tree is one of the oldest of its species in Britain. The shaggy bark wizens over the years into large wrinkled flakes. Its edible nuts are delicious when toasted: 'what the black truffle is to mushrooms', according to chef Odessa Piper.

THE HARDY ASH

One of London's strangest sights is in the graveyard of St Pancras Old Church. An otherwise unremarkable ash tree was surrounded in the 1860s by gravestones, moved to make space for the Midland Railway. They are arranged in tight concentric circles, and the trunk has gradually grown over and amongst the stones like biotic blubber. The young architectural apprentice who oversaw this artistic arrangement was the future poet and novelist Thomas Hardy.

THE MARYLEBONE ELM

The 150-year-old Huntingdon Elm on Marylebone High Street is a survivor. It once stood next to a church that was destroyed during the Blitz and, miraculously, it escaped the devastating Dutch elm disease that routed the species in the 1970s. It continues to flower every year.

THE RAVENSCOURT PARK TREE OF HEAVEN

This tree is considered a pest in America and Australia. It smells of rotting peanut butter and creates a toxic chemical that stunts the growth of surrounding foliage. It is admired in China, however, and this example descends from seeds that were posted from the Far East in the 18th century.

THE LONDON PLANE

The 'London plane'[2] was originally Spanish, and is the preferred tree for city planners because its peeling bark protects against sooty deposits and its roots are highly tolerant to compaction. The ancient plane in Barn Elms Park is knobbly and misshapen, with a very wide girth and wrinkled bark. It is a contender for the oldest plane tree in the city. The tallest plane tree in London is on the banks of the Thames at Richmond, towering over an Argentine steak house.

---

[1] A Great Tree must have historical significance, a landmark location and an endearing physical character (treesforcities.org).

[2] The novelist Richard Jefferies disliked plane trees, particularly the 'blotches where the bark peels, [and] the leaves which lie on the sward like brown leather'.

THE MAGNIFICENT SEVEN

Ashes to ashes, dust to dust: London has always been effective at swallowing its citizens. In the first half of the 19th century, seven large cemeteries were opened on the outskirts of London.[1] Today all seven are nature reserves, all have active groups of Friends, and several of them still accept burials.

KENSAL GREEN

Kensal Green Cemetery was completed in 1833. The garden layout, inspired by Père Lachaise in Paris, is home to Charles Babbage, Isambard Kingdom Brunel and Harold Pinter. Look for the eccentric tomb of circus stuntman Andrew Ducrow, with its motley assortment of Egyptian, Greek and Gothic motifs.

HIGHGATE

A 'Victorian Valhalla', as John Betjeman put it, Highgate Cemetery's star attractions are its eerie Egyptian Avenue and Circle of Lebanon. Wander the 37 acres and look for Karl Marx's giant beard, Harry Thornton's grand piano, the menagerist George Wombwell's sleeping lion and Douglas Adams's pot of pens.

ABNEY PARK

Enter Abney Park Cemetery through the overgrown Egyptian entrance[2] on Stoke Newington High Street. This cemetery doubles as an arboretum, with an alphabetical sequence of labelled trees around its perimeter, from *Acer* (maple) to *Zanthoxylum* (toothache tree). You can attend greenwood-working courses and learn to carve headstones.

TOWER HAMLETS

Ken Greenway, the park manager, is the resident batman at Tower Hamlets Cemetery Park. He leads evening bat walks[3] through the urban woodland, during which he serves up a three-course meal made from foraged food. Alternatively, wander the cemetery by day, listening to 'Meet Me at the Cemetery Gates',[4] an atmospheric compilation of local residents' memories, stories and field recordings.

NUNHEAD

The first burial in Nunhead Cemetery was Charles Abbot, a 101-year-old grocer from Ipswich.[5] On the third Sunday of every month you can volunteer to help with the Friends of Nunhead Cemetery's inscription recording programme. Report to the Friends hut in Linden Grove at 11am.

WEST NORWOOD

West Norwood was the first cemetery to be built in the Gothic Revival style. Celebrity residents include Mrs Beeton, Dr William Marsden[6] and Sir Henry Tate. There is a spectacular system of catacombs that extends into the hillside; you can book a subterranean tour with the Friends of West Norwood Cemetery (fownc.org).

BROMPTON

Beatrix Potter lived near Brompton Cemetery and based the names for many of her characters on its tombstones: Mr Nutkins, Mr McGregor, Mr Brock, Mr Tod, Jeremiah Fisher and Peter Rabbett are all buried here. Look out for John Keats's 'bright star' Fanny Brawne,[7] the suffragette Emmeline Pankhurst and the epidemiologist John Snow.

---

❶ Hugh Meller dubbed them 'The Magnificent Seven' in his book *London Cemeteries*.
❷ The hieroglyphics around the entrance translate as 'The Abode of the Mortal Part of Man'.
❸ For more bats see p.209.
❹ You can stream the audio file through the Shuffle Festival website (shufflefestival.com/at-the-cemetery-gates).
❺ Abbot was a Charterhouse brother. See p.136.
❻ For more on Marsden and his hospital, see p.43.
❼ For more Brawne, see p.105.

GREAT GRAVES

BEDOUIN

The adventurer Richard Francis Burton lies in a stone Bedouin tent in the graveyard of St Mary Magdalen, Mortlake. The tent was designed by his wife, Isabel, who shares it with him; you can see their coffins by climbing a metal ladder and looking through a small window at the back.

BIMMER

Steve Marsh, a BMW fanatic, was buried beneath a life-size granite replica of an M3 convertible in Manor Park Cemetery. At the funeral in 2010, a parking ticket was placed under the windscreen wiper.

TRAGEDIAN

The actor Charles Macklin had a strong temper: he once killed a fellow actor by jabbing him in the eye with his cane. His memorial plaque in St Paul's, Covent Garden, includes a relief sculpture of a tragedian's mask, with a dagger through its eye socket.

NECROPOLIS RAILWAY

Stand on Westminster Bridge Road, opposite the ornate red frontage of Westminster Bridge House. This was once the London terminus of the Necropolis Railway, which shuttled corpses from Waterloo to Brookwood in Surrey, at one time the largest cemetery in the world. There were three classes of coffin ticket, and the train was occasionally used by golfers, disguised as mourners, on their way to West Hill Golf Club. The cemetery is still worth a visit: catch a regular train from Waterloo to Brookwood Station.[1] Before you depart, make a detour to nearby Newnham Terrace: the elevated 'Make Space' artist studios run along what was the old Necropolis Railway platform.

DEADLOCK

In the crypt of St Bride's Church lies a 19th-century iron coffin, complete with rivets designed to deter body snatchers. A contemporary advert promises 'Safety for the Dead!'

GESTAPOOCH

A little stone on Carlton House Terrace marks the grave of Giro, the faithful terrier belonging to German ambassador Leopold von Hoesch. Giro was electrocuted whilst chewing through a cable and was given 'a full Nazi burial', according to *The Times*.[2]

NAVY SEALS

Joseph Woodward is remembered in the Golders Green Crematorium as the 'discoverer of the latent equilibrist powers given to the sea lion species'. Woodward trained sea lions to balance balls and juggle at the London Hippodrome. Later he taught them to track German U-boats during the First World War, although his flippered friends never actually saw active service.

---

[1] The Necropolis service left at 11:35 each day. Don't forget your golf clubs.

[2] Find more dead dogs on p.42, p.88, p.339 and p.350.

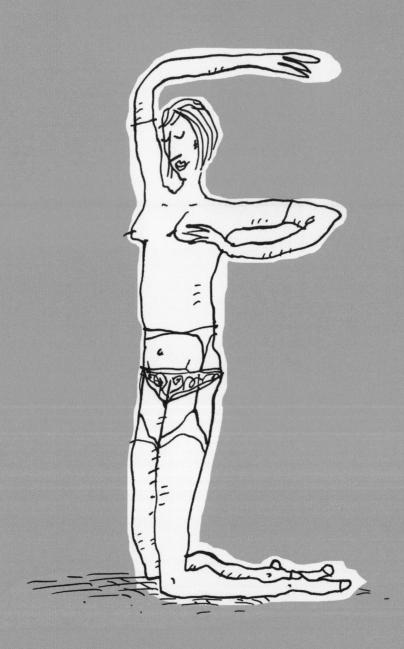

BURLESQUE

The emergent burlesque scene has recently strutted its frisky brand of fun out of the basement and into the mainstream, so here's a three-step programme for becoming the next Dream Bear or Immodesty Blaize.

E ———

1. GET DRESSED

What Katie Did on Portobello Road will sort you out with their vintage selection of torsolettes, waspies, bullet bras, girdles and Merry Widows.

With your underwiring in position, pop into the Fairy Gothmother on Commercial Street, who will adorn you with a handcrafted satin bustle, silk bloomers or taffeta dress, according to the style of your act.

If you need something closer-fitting, Atsuko Kudo on Holloway Road will vacuum-pack you into beautifully filigreed non-vulcanised rubber.

Men should apply to Fetish Freak in Oval, where you can squeeze into bespoke rubber chaps and a studded leather collar. Their innocuous shop front is next door to Mr Dandy's Fish and Chips on Bolton Crescent.

2. GET SEXY

Learn the daily grind at the House of Burlesque, which runs a variety of training courses from taster sessions to a six-week Performance Course, in which you rehearse a full solo showcase (houseofburlesque.co.uk).

Alternatively, The Cheek of It! specialises in tassel-twirling hen parties and femininity coaching[1] (cheekofit.co.uk).

CellarDoor, Zero Aldwych, is an excitingly grimy dive bar that has live events every night and 'the sexiest toilets in London'.[2] Vicious Delicious offers burlesque lessons before her live shows.

3. GET UNDRESSED

Now you've acquired skills, you can top the bill. The London Cabaret Society has recently taken over the opulent Bloomsbury Ballroom.[3] Join Anna the Hulagan, who strips with a fiery hoop, and the Cabaret Rouge dance troupe, who make putting clothes on look sexy.

Another option is Proud Cabaret, based in the 200-year-old Horse Hospital at Camden Stables Market: you'll join an array of performers including Ayesha the belly-dancer, Helen the glowing hula-hoop spinner and Dave the Bear.

Volupté off Chancery Lane is a basement world of decadence, where you can perform on a Saturday afternoon while the punters sip champagne and take afternoon tea. Be careful not to get clotted cream on your tassels.

Finally you'll be ready to compete in the World Burlesque Games (londonburlesquefest.com), in which hundreds of competitors perform teases and tricks around the capital. Categories include the Twisted, British and Newcomer Crowns, and the highly coveted Triple Crown, reserved for 'extra dance genres, hidden talents and special surprise gimmicks'.

---

[1] Watch the TED talk by founder Zoe Charles, aka Lady Cheek, on 'Respecting, Embracing and Celebrating Femininity on a Global Scale'.

[2] See p.51.

[3] An art deco sprung-floor hall with mirrors and swag curtains.

EROGENOUS ZONES

'In an expanding universe, time is on the side of the outcast', wrote London dandy Quentin Crisp. 'Those who once inhabited the suburbs of human contempt find that without changing their address they eventually live in the metropolis.'

Beliefs about appropriate sexualities and sexual behaviour are slippery; at any given moment, certain activities and inclinations seem off-limits, but the boundaries are in constant flux. For the last hundred years, the zone of acceptable behaviour has been expanding rapidly, bulldozing taboos and mirroring the sprawl of London itself.

'Anyone who has violated a taboo', wrote Freud, 'becomes taboo himself because he possesses the dangerous quality of tempting others to follow his example'. Through a process of erotic gentrification, the city's sexual vanguard moves into undesirable areas, improving their reputation and paving the way for others. And in these hinterlands of human behaviour, we find freedom and exploitation; openness and abuse; the best of human intentions and the worst. This a map of how morality shifts, of taboos old and new, of those who break them and those who reinforce them, of London stripping off and covering up.

WINDCHIME ENVY ①
It may be pure coincidence that the phallic wind chime in the British Museum is displayed in room 69. This Roman charm was designed to ward off evil spirits and hails from a culture with little of our present-day prudery.[1] The phallus at the centre of this handsome bronze chime has wings, feet and a tail. Replicas are not currently on sale in the museum shop.

LETTUCE SPRAY ②
Visitors to UCL's Petrie Museum often remark on the ithyphallic carving of Min, the ancient Egyptian fertility god. Min's striking member was fortunate to survive: many collectors simply chiselled off offending organs. As well as his famous erection, Min is frequently portrayed with a flail and a lettuce, a phallic symbol and aphrodisiac.

DIRTY BATHROOM ③
Go to the bathroom in Edward Linley Sambourne's Kensington townhouse at 18 Stafford Terrace.[2] Much of the interior is just as it was when the *Punch* cartoonist lived there with his family in the late 19th century. However, the collection of framed erotic photographs in the bathroom, taken by Edward of artists' models who came to his house while his wife wasn't in, was hung later. Kensington & Chelsea Council run regular costumed tours, some in the character of Mrs Sambourne.

LITTLE DEATH ④
Many thought that 2014 had sounded the death knell for London's last porn cinemas. The Abcat Cine Club and Oscars closed down, and then, finally, Mr B's. It seemed impossible that these outmoded onanistic darkrooms, with their quiet clientele and wipe-clean seats, could endure in the face of council crackdowns and competition from online outlets. But the obituaries proved premature; at the start of 2015, the family who ran Mr B's relocated from Islington to Deptford and reopened in the basement of a print shop at 487 New Cross Road.[3]

For map numbers 5–8 see p.76

---

[1] Where modern London has furtive cocks graffitied on cubicle doors, in Londinium the symbol of the phallus was a lucky emblem, painted in public places, carved on to furniture and popular in jewellery.

[2] See p.119

[3] The future of UK porn films is under threat after the government placed restrictions on which acts can be shown. In response, industry protestors staged a face-sitting demonstration in Parliament Square in December 2014.

STINKING BISHOP ⑨

The intriguingly named Clarice la Claterballock worked in the stews of medieval Southwark. Bankside's brothels were on the Bishop of Winchester's land and, because their presence was tolerated and they paid taxes to him, the prostitutes were known as 'Winchester Geese'. Henry Beaufort, Bishop of Winchester, was offered a cardinal's hat by the pope, but King Henry V prevented him accepting it, possibly because of his unseemly income. Cardinal Cap Alley off Bankside is an ironic memorial to the frustrated bishop.

COIN TOSS ⑩

Look for an unofficial blue plaque on Whitecross Street marking the home of Priss Fotheringham, who 'was ranked the second best whore in the city' in *The Wand'ring Whore*, a 1660 handbook to the city's prostitutes. Ms Fotheringham was particularly well known for reviving the Roman practice of 'chucking'.[1]

KALENDAR ⑪

Georgian Covent Garden was famous for its bawds, and each year from 1757 to 1795 *Harris's List of Covent-Garden Ladies Or Man of Pleasure's Kalendar* was published. This practical pocketbook offered detailed accounts of the area's prostitutes, who, we're told, had 'hearts as large and universal as their desires'. In the 1789 list, we learn that Miss W of 17 Goodge Street[2]

had a complexion 'beautifully contrasted by a pair of expressive dark eyes'. The reader is warned, however, that although 'she is naturally fond of a glass of wine' it 'must be administered in such a proportion only as to keep her merry, if it operates beyond that, she is rather a disagreeable bedfellow'.

MAP READING

Erogenous Zones presents London as an erotic territory, inspired in part by tantric maps of the 'subtle body' and its chakras.

HELL'S BELLES ⑫

Haymarket was a notorious hang-out for streetwalkers and became known as Hell Corner. James Boswell met a prostitute there and took her to Westminster Bridge where, he recorded in his diary, 'in armour complete did I engage her upon this noble edifice'.[3]

'TIS PITY HE'S A HORSLEY ⑬

The Soho dandy Sebastian Horsley[4] frequented prostitutes for years and even prostituted himself for a period. 'I wanted to […] turn myself into a slave and sell myself into freedom', he said. 'I saw it as a kind of sex rebate, having paid for sex all my life.' Look online for his short film about the experience, *Sebastian Horsley's Guide to Whoring*, and visit his former address at 7 Meard Street. A sign beneath the knocker reads, 'This is not a brothel. There are no prostitutes at this address.'

DOGGING ⑭

Sex in public places, or 'dogging' as it's more commonly known, has been revolutionised by the internet. The filmmaker Derek Jarman wrote affectionately in his diary about the gay scene on Hampstead Heath near Jack Straw's Castle. 'For those who know, the alfresco fuck is the original fuck', he wrote on 26 May 1989. 'Sex on the Heath is an idyll pre-fall.'

E —

RUDE MOVES ⑮

The most celebrated London nude show of the early 20th century was part of the 'Revudeville' at Soho's Windmill Theatre. The show's organisers outpaced censors by presenting nude *tableaux vivants*, following the guiding principle that 'if it moves, it's rude'. The venue, on Great Windmill Street, is now the Windmill International strip club.

---

❶ Chucking involved performing a headstand with 'naked breech and belly' and legs held apart, while 'four cully-rompers chuck'd in sixteen half-Crowns into her Commoditie'.

❷ Today this address is a Spaghetti House.

❸ 'The whim of doing it there with the Thames rolling below us amused me much,' wrote Boswell.

❹ More Horsley on p.111.

ANIMAL INSTINCTS ⑯

Go to Walker's Court in Soho, the former hub of the area's raunchy retailing, and look for a neon sign for Raymond's Revue Bar, set up by one-time comb salesman and mind reader Paul Raymond in 1958. When the Revue Bar proved successful, he took over the Whitehall Theatre (now Trafalgar Studios) and backed risqué farces such as *What, No Pyjamas?*, *Yes, We Have No Pyjamas* and *Let's Get Laid!* Raymond went on to build an immense erotic empire and later ran 'The Great International

Nude Show' in what is now the Peacock Theatre. In summer 1974, the show climaxed with the performer Lindy Salmon having her bikini removed by two dolphins called Pixie and Penny. Commenting on the show, Raymond said: 'We've got dolphins ripping knickers off girls. What's not to like?'[1]

SHOPOPHILIA ⑰

To be at the centre of your own striptease, go to Coco de Mer in Soho. The changing rooms have built-in peepholes so that your shopping companion can participate more fully in the experience.

PLAY ROOMS ⑱

'Sexual intercourse began / In nineteen sixty-three / (which was rather late for me)', wrote Philip Larkin in his poem 'Annus Mirabilis'. Casual sex has reached new heights since then, particularly with the advent of apps like Tinder, Grinder, Happn and Hinge. Some of London's clubs now allow sexual acts on the premises, often in designated booths or playrooms. This is particularly true of parts of the gay club scene. The Chariots chain of Roman spas around London are warrens of hot tubs, steam rooms and private booths, where men can convene and commune.

PRIVATE MEMBERS ⑲

The experience of social ostracism can lead to a high degree of inclusivity. Although members-only, Kinky Salon goes out of its way to be friendly and unintimidating, welcoming 'sexual or asexual, vanilla or kinky, queer, gay, bi, straight, pan, cis, trans […] whatever your body shape, disability status or age'. They run regular 'arty sexy parties' in a private venue and focus on creating a non-judgemental atmosphere. The centre of each party is a large padded playroom. Anything goes, but there are strict rules about safe sex and taking responsibility for riskier 'edgeplay' activities.

FEMDOM ⑳

BDSM is a compact formulation containing Bondage and Discipline, Dominance and Submission, Sadism and Masochism.[2] Club Pedestal, a BDSM night hosted by Fire in Vauxhall, is a female dominance event at which male attendees are required to wear collars and do what they're told.

TIES THAT BIND ㉑

Certain BDSM practices involve a high degree of skill, and none more so than Kinbaku, the art of Japanese rope bondage. Bound is a bi-monthly night at the Flying Dutchman in Camberwell. The dom ties up and suspends the sub with rope, creating intricate geometric patterns that correspond to pressure points on the body.

---

❶ The ethics of the show were broadly criticised and Pixie and Penny were retired and sold after 12 weeks.

❷ Some think that Shakespeare appreciated BDSM, quoting Cleopatra's line: 'The stroke of death is as a lover's pinch, / Which hurts and is desired.'

TITBITS

The politician Norman St John-Stevas pondered in 1971 whether 'after the public has gone through a certain number of vicarious sexual representations on the stage or in books, there is a reasonable chance that they will become bored by the whole thing'. It seems unlikely.

E ———

CROSS-DRESS
Transvestitism has a long history in London: John 'Eleanor' Rykener was a transvestite living near Cheapside in 1395; the singer Arabella Hunt accidentally married James 'Amy' Howard in 1680; and Ernest 'Stella' Boulton and Frederick 'Fanny' Park were a popular music hall double-act in the 1870s. Jessie the 'Clapham Tranny' has recently risen to fame through the Channel 4 TV show *Fried Chicken Shop*. Look out for his skimpy miniskirt and netted boob tube on Clapham High Street, then book a table at the Pale Blue Door restaurant: the front of house staff are transvestites and there are drag performances over dinner (tonyhornecker.com/work/the-pale-blue-door).

POSE ON A CHAIR
In the V&A museum you can see the chair on which Christine Keeler posed for her iconic nude photograph, taken in 1963 at the height of the Profumo Affair.[1] Inscribed under the seat you can see the names of several other celebrities who have sat on it, including Joe Orton and Dame Edna.

CROCODILE SMILE
In the Museum of Croydon you can admire a crocodile posing-pouch by Ann Summers. These were manufactured for sex parties in the 1990s: men would insert their genitalia into the two halves of the puppet, and an open red mouth was a signal that the man attached to the crocodile was ready for action.

TOOL UP
Sh!, an erotic emporium just off Hoxton Square, caters exclusively for women. Men enter by invitation only and the friendly staff offer tea and advice.

IMBIBE APHRODISIACS
Wander amidst the aphrodisiacal plants of the Chelsea Physic Garden. Float on wafts of musky ambrette and potency wood, caress Allah's Walking Stick and massage the bark of the yohimbe tree.

SPOT A PHALLUS
Look for a surprising feature in the ornate frosted windows of the Albert Tavern on Victoria Street. Large phalluses spout plumes of floral decoration.

CONSUMMATE
To consummate your relationship with London and swell its population, book an appointment at the Assisted Conception Unit at King's College Hospital, Denmark Hill, where you can donate your eggs or sperm.

DEFLATE
Stand on Broadway outside St James's Park tube station and find Jacob Epstein's sculpture *Day*: a frowning bearded figure with a young naked boy between his knees. The boy's prominent penis caused a scandal when it was unveiled in the 1920s, but the crisis deflated after Epstein snipped 1½ inches off the offending appendage.

POST COITUS
'I denounce the philistine's postcoital cigarette both as a doctor and an artist,' wrote Vladimir Nabokov in 1959. Unless you share Vladimir's qualms, après sex is the traditional moment for a toke. Stock up on quality cheroots from the walk-in humidor at Davidoff's on St James's Street, or, if you really want to impress your partner, visit the wonderfully archaic Segar & Snuff in Covent Garden Market and purchase a tin of their own-brand snuff. Their blends date back to Jacobean times; we recommend the Mature Crumbled. Where you sniff it from is up to you.

---

[1] The chair is a copy of an Arne Jacobsen '3107', an example of which is displayed alongside, as is the famous photograph.

FOLKMOOT

FEW PLACES FEEL MORE GLORIOUSLY REMOTE from modern London than the octagonal Chapter House in the East Cloister of Westminster Abbey. Its vaulted ceiling is held up by an implausibly slender marble stem, and high windows flood the space with coloured light. Go at opening time and stand in the centre of this 13th-century marvel, the room where modern parliament began. The King's Great Council met here from 1257 and the House of Commons sat here in the late 14th century.[1]

In 2013, a man went into the Chapter House and sprayed the word HELP across a portrait of the Queen. He was a member of the campaign group Fathers 4 Justice. A month earlier, the Peace Camp outside on Parliament Square ended after 12 years of continuous occupation. Its leader, Brian Haw, who died in 2011, lived opposite the Houses of Parliament for a decade and became such a powerful symbol of resistance that there is now a campaign to return him to the square permanently as a bronze statue.

The relationship between politicians and people has rarely been straightforward and, at times, groups of citizens have openly defied the ruling classes to achieve their ends. Among London's most revered dissidents are the suffragettes, and the movement's leaders are now honoured with memorials all over the city. One less well-known member of the sisterhood is commemorated by a plaque at 60 Thornhill Square in Islington. Edith Garrud, 'the suffragette who knew jiu-jitsu', was a martial arts instructor who trained the group's all-female bodyguard of 30 women.[2] 'Woman is exposed to many perils nowadays,' Garrud wrote in 1910, 'because so many who call themselves men are not worthy of that exalted title.'

London has a proud history of unrest and dissent: marches, protests and riots; anti-establishment balladry in left-wing folk clubs; politically-charged drama in music halls and theatres; and anarchic folk customs that turn the established hierarchy on its head. The business of government may centre on Westminster and City Hall, but the city's politics is also conducted in the push and pull of official authority and grassroots rebellion. Just as citizens once assembled for the Saxon Folkmoots, today people gather in pubs, theatres, commons and squares to scheme, debate and hold their leaders to account.

ACTIVISM
London's always been fertile ground for the most inspiring, creative community activism – determined campaigners coming together to battle for positive change. The Southall Black Sisters are a perfect example – they're a group of black and minority women who have been challenging domestic and gender-related violence for more than 30 years. — *Shami Chakrabarti*

---

[1] Parliament's roots do, in fact, go even deeper – to the Saxon Witenagemot ('Council of Wise Men') and the Folkmoots, when London's citizens would gather on the site of the old Roman amphitheatre, now the Guildhall. See p.397.

[2] Find other suffragettes on p.106 and pp. 116–17.

PROCESS

The machinery of state is surprisingly accessible. Here are some of the best places to brush shoulders with those in power and explore the political process.

VISIONS

Politics is about imagining and fashioning the future. Go to the Shaw Library of the London School of Economics and ask to see the Fabian Society stained-glass window. At its centre, two men with hammers are pounding a globe on an anvil, literally reshaping the earth with their new politics. Above them is the slogan: 'REMOULD IT NEARER TO THE HEART'S DESIRE'.

THEORIES

Not far from Jeremy Bentham, the mummified political visionary in the south cloisters,[1] UCL holds public politics lectures every Thursday evening in term time. Theorise with fellow enthusiasts at the free drinks reception afterwards.

ALLIES

Make friends with two old men on New Bond Street. Churchill and Roosevelt have been loafing on a bench there since 1995 and there's a gap between them where you can sit and seek their avuncular wisdom. The best place to rub elbows with living politicians is the Kennington Tandoori, a narrow Indian restaurant favoured by MPs.[2] It's conservative with its spicing, liberal with its portions and every dish on the menu is a labour of love. It has endorsements from eminent diners splashed across its menu.

MANIFESTOS

Hunker down in the former Labour Party Headquarters at 150 Walworth Road, which is now the Safestay backpacker hostel. Read Labour's 1983 manifesto, which was written there. It became known as 'the longest suicide note in history' after their catastrophic general election defeat.

ELECTIONS

Go to Sir John Soane's house[3] to inspect *The Humours of an Election* by William Hogarth, an excoriating series of four paintings that depicts the dirty business of electioneering. The candidates' tactics include plying wealthy constituents with wine and oysters, bribing undecided voters, and helping the old and infirm to complete their ballot papers.

DEBATES

The public are welcome to watch House of Commons debates from the viewing gallery. The liveliest session each week is Prime Minister's Questions on Wednesday lunchtimes, when the leader of the opposition goads the PM.[4]

VOTES

If a bell rings in the Red Lion on Parliament Street and you see someone jump to their feet, they're probably a Member of Parliament. This pub is fitted with a division bell, which gives MPs an eight-minute warning that their presence is required for a vote. The Westminster Arms, the St James' Court Hotel, the Marquis of Granby, the Cinnamon Club, St Stephen's Tavern, the Royal Horseguard Hotel and Green's Restaurant are also fitted with division bells. Race around all eight establishments, quaffing a quart of ale in each, before the bell stops ringing.

LEADERSHIP

Visit the prime minister at 10 Downing Street. If the armed police won't let you through, have a photo of yourself taken outside 10 Adam Street, which just happens to have an identical façade.[5] The similarity is so striking that it was used as the Downing Street stunt-double in the 2011 biopic of Margaret Thatcher, *The Iron Lady*.

---

[1] For more on the founder of Utilitarianism, see p.273 and p.349.
[2] The KT is one of the few curry houses to have been mentioned in the House of Commons, when raucous MPs received a stern rebuke from the Speaker: 'When you're eating curry in the Kennington Tandoori,' he said, 'you don't yell across the table.'
[3] See p.21.
[4] Book in advance as there's always a long queue for PMQs.
[5] Behind the door is the Royal Society of Arts, whose stated aim is '21st-century enlightenment'. The RSA holds free public events and prints an excellent free magazine.

PROTEST

If you're sceptical of the power-hungry, here are some ways to challenge their authority and hold them to account.

SPEAK OUT

Brush up your seditious arguments, grab a stepladder and head to Speakers' Corner at the north-east of Hyde Park. Public speaking by anyone, on any subject, has been allowed there since 1872 and the site remains well used to this day.[1] In 1866, this was the site of the Reform League's rallies. They burned down a tree and its charred stump became an unofficial rallying point until all men were given the vote in 1867. Look for a mosaic depicting the Reformers' Tree on the pavement nearby.

RABBLE-ROUSE

'You normally only get a blue plaque when you're dead', said the human rights campaigner Peter Tatchell, when he found himself in the unusual position of having a blue plaque attached to the address where he still lives.[2] Tatchell was a prominent member of the Gay Liberation Front, which organised Britain's first gay rights demonstration in Highbury Fields in 1970. Look for a commemorative plaque outside the Highbury Fields public toilets, where the sting operation that sparked the protest took place.

DEFY

'JAILED FOR SUPPORTING THE PEOPLE!' reads the Poplar Rates Rebellion mural on Hale Street in Tower Hamlets. In 1921, the Mayor of Poplar and 30 councillors[3] defied central government by refusing to collect certain taxes from impoverished local residents. They were sent to prison, but after six weeks of public uproar and other poor councils threatening to follow suit the rebels were released and a bill was passed to create a fairer split of taxes across rich and poor boroughs.

SCHEME

Discuss human rights on the stone bench in Bromley that marks the place where William Wilberforce and Pitt the Younger planned to abolish the slave trade in 1787. 'Just above the steep descent into the Vale of Keston', wrote Wilberforce in his diary, 'I resolved to give notice on a fit occasion in the House of Commons of my intention to bring forward the abolition of the slave trade.' Wilberforce was in the congregation of St Mary Woolnoth,[4] whose rector John Newton was the slave ship captain turned abolitionist who wrote 'Amazing Grace'. The hymn is now engraved in marble on the church wall.

VANDALISE

Looming over the locked lavatories opposite Bow Church[5] is a statue of Prime Minister William Gladstone with his hands painted red. The statue was a gift to the area from Theodore Bryant, of the Bryant & May match factory.[6] Legend has it that Bryant funded the statue by docking a shilling from his employees' pay and that, at its unveiling, the female workers slashed their hands and smeared them over the statue. Local vandals ensure that Gladstone's hands are always painted red in tribute to the women's stand.

F ——

---

❶ Listen to highlights from Speakers' Corner each week on Resonance 104.4 FM, a radical arts station that broadcasts from Borough High Street.

❷ 62 Arrol House in Southwark. The plaque has been worded in the past tense, in preparation for Tatchell's passage into the history books.

❸ Including the suffragette Nellie Cressall, who was six months pregnant at the time.

❹ For more on the church, see p.20.

❺ About 50 metres away, at 198 Bow Road, is the site of the bakery that became a suffragette base in 1912. The shop sign read 'VOTES FOR WOMEN' and Sylvia Pankhurst spoke from a raised platform outside.

❻ The site of the 1888 matchgirls' strike. See p.173.

ANTI-ESTABLISHMENTARIANISM

REBELS

In dimly lit backrooms and basements around the capital, folk singers belt out anti-authoritarian anthems. Here are some of their famous forebears.

FIREBRANDS

Upstairs at the Princess Louise pub in Holborn, the left-wing agitator Ewan MacColl held his Ballad and Blues Club in the 1950s. MacColl would sit on a chair backwards, cup his hand over his right ear and intone politically charged folk songs. Toast his memory and then sing a shanty[1] by the tree in Russell Square 'planted in recognition of the strength and singleness of purpose of this fighter for Peace and Socialism'.

TROUBADOURS

The window of the Troubadour on Old Brompton Road is full of rusting coffee pots, and its walls are lined with paintings and plaques celebrating the folk greats who've played there. In the early 1960s, a young Bob Dylan performed his scabrous protest songs here under the stage name Blind Boy Grunt.[2]

REVIVALISTS

Now a pounding cocktail bar, 49 Greek Street was home to the Les Cousins basement folk club in the 1960s, an incubator for upcoming artists in the British folk revival including Sandy Denny, Bert Jansch and Nick Drake.[3]

To listen to emerging folk music in the capital today:

1. Follow The Nest Collective, who run gigs around the capital.

2. Attend The Goose is Out sessions at the Ivy House in Nunhead, the city's first co-operatively owned pub.

3. Prepare a topical tune for one of the Singaround sessions in the Old Nun's Head.

REVELS

Folk traditions cock a snook at the authorities, crowning temporary rulers and unleashing bawdy energy on to the streets.

CHAIR LIFTING

Join the Blackheath Morris Men for a spot of Chair Lifting every Easter Monday. The raucous troupe move from pub to pub with a chair covered in flowers. At each stop, they perform a dance and heave local ladies high into the air on their floral throne. If you'd like to refine your own Morris Dancing skills, you can sign up for regular classes at Cecil Sharp House.[4]

GREEN MEN

Every May Day, you can follow the Fowlers Morris Troupe as they dance through the streets of Deptford with their Jack in the Green, a person encased in a 10-foot cone of flowers and leaves.

STRAW MEN

At the other end of summer, go to Carshalton to watch the Straw Jack being paraded through the streets for the Harvest Festival, accompanied by Sweepers, Corn Dollies and the Reaper Man. The Jack is torn apart and ritually burnt outside The Hope pub at the end of the day. Pieces are handed to the crowd to throw onto the blaze.

---

[1] Join a shanty choir on p.138.
[2] During his trip to London, Dylan heard Martin Carthy playing 'Scarborough Fair', which he later reworked as the song 'Girl from the North Country'.
[3] Whose 'shyness and awkwardness were almost transcendent', according to one audience member.

[4] The home of the English Folk Dance and Song Society also holds frequent gigs and ceilidhs, and an open session for musicians on the second Monday of each month. See p. 163.

THE RIGHT TO THE CITY

The impulse to own and enclose is at loggerheads with the desire to keep land common and open to all. Here are some of the city's most disputed territories.

> Inclosure, thou'rt a curse upon the land, / And tasteless was the wretch who thy existence plann'd. — *John Clare*

COMMON GROUND

Wander among the sedate flower beds of Kennington Park and consider that this used to be common ground, the site of the Chartists' 'monster rally' in 1848.[1] Four years later the common was enclosed and turned into a formal park. The site was reappropriated for political purposes in 1990, when the London Poll Tax March began there. Around 200,000 protesters assembled and forced open the park gates, which had been locked by police. The march ended as a riot in Trafalgar Square.

RECLAIM THE STREETS

In 1996, thousands of Reclaim the Streets protesters took over part of the M41[2] at Shepherd's Bush for a street party. Some of the dancers were on stilts, covered with floor-length skirts. Inside the fabric, and invisible to watching police, activists were drilling through the road and planting trees.[3] There are instructions online for holding your own illegal street party (rts.gn.apc.org/sortit.htm). To secure your position, they recommend setting up scaffolding tripods with people nested on top. If you'd like to reclaim public spaces more discreetly, follow the example of Space Hijackers, who staged midnight cricket matches in the City and organised parties on Circle Line trains.[4]

F

POP CULTURE

Granary Square, Paternoster Square, Bishops Square and Elephant Square[5] are all pleasant places to pause with a cheese roll and a copy of Henri Lefebvre's classic work *The Right to the City*. But they have something else in common: they're all privately owned public spaces (POPS)[6] and mark a creeping trend away from common ground. Richard Sennett calls them 'dead public spaces', because of the way private ownership limits how we can behave in them, and Bradley Garrett has pointed out that 'it's no longer possible to protest outside the headquarters of the Mayor and the Greater London Authority' because City Hall is on the private More London estate.

---

[1] The rally was organised by William Cuffay, the charismatic leader of the London Chartists and the son of a freed slave from St Kitts. Cuffay was eventually arrested and sent to Tasmania. There is no memorial to him in London.

[2] One of the few sections of the Ringways project that was completed. It has since been downgraded to an A Road. See p.93.

[3] For rogue planting that doesn't require a pneumatic drill, join London's guerrilla gardening community, whose local groups transform patches of unused or derelict land.

[4] See pp.330–331

[5] The site of the demolished Heygate Estate. See p.269.

[6] Canary Wharf is perhaps the most famous POPS in London, with its own security force dressed in pseudo police uniforms.

THE RIOT OF HIS MAJESTY KING MOB

O, then I see King Mob hath been with you.

The figure of King Mob gallops through the nightmares of London's authorities. From the Whitehall crowd that moaned ecstatically as Charles I was executed, to the Gordon Riots when 'King Mob' was daubed on the burning walls of Newgate prison, to the '60s anarchist group that took his name,[1] King Mob has held continuous court below the surface of the populace, flexing his royal prerogative at regular intervals.

Large-scale riots almost seem to be a natural phenomenon in London. They have taken place every 50 to 60 years since the Middle Ages. Riots are born of desperation and cramped living conditions, but they are sustained by a spirit of mischief, a carnivalesque hysteria that possesses Londoners with a hive mentality, so that they rampage as one body, blind to consequences, intoxicated by the newfound flimsiness of societal boundaries. Riots are a form of 'collective bargaining' with authority, as the historian Stephen Inwood puts it: they are Londoners' last and most powerful resort.

WILLIAM OF THE LONG BEARD ①

In the spring of 1196, the crusader William of the Long Beard[2] led an uprising to champion the rights of London's poor. He raised a large following and was planning an attack on the houses of the rich when the Archbishop of Canterbury's soldiers forced him to take refuge in the church of St Mary-le-Bow. Abandoned by the mob, William defended the church as a fortress until he was smoked out. He and his beard were then dragged naked behind a horse to Tyburn Brook, where he was hanged.[3] The chronicler William of Newburgh describes how supporters of William of the Long Beard declared him a martyr and gathered dirt from the spot where he died, forming 'a tolerably large ditch'. Scoop some of your own commemorative soil beneath the gigantic decapitated horse-head near Marble Arch.

MAP READING

The title of The Riot of His Majesty King Mob *is inspired by the fictional monarch of London riots. The central figure is a reference to the frontispiece to Thomas Hobbes's* Leviathan *(1651).*

THE WRESTLING RIOTS ②

In the summer of 1222, the City of London wrestling team trounced their Westminster counterparts in hand-to-hand combat on the site of what is now the church of St Giles-in-the-Fields. This defeat so enraged the Steward of Westminster Abbey that he offered another wrestling prize the following week, but secretly armed the Westminster pugilists with bludgeons, and they cruelly attacked the defending City team. The scandalised citizens, led by a wealthy burgher named Fitz-Arnulph, streamed from the City to Westminster. They destroyed several houses, including that of the perfidious steward, but in the process they raised the wrath of the child-king Henry III, who struck back fiercely: Fitz-Arnulph was hanged, many other rioters lost their hands and feet, and the City was fined the enormous sum of 5,000 marks.

---

[1] King Mob's best-known work was a massive graffiti slogan next to the tube line at Ladbroke Grove: 'Same thing day after day – Tube – Work – Dinner – Work – Tube – Armchair – TV – Sleep – Tube – Work – How much more can you take – One in ten go mad – one in five crack up'. The group visit Selfridges on p.143.

[2] William had commanding facial hair, which he 'cherished', in order to 'appear conspicuous in meetings', according to William of Newburgh.

[3] William's execution is the first recorded on this site, which later became infamous as the location of Tyburn Tree. See p.110 and p.281.

THE PEASANTS' REVOLT ③

When the people of Brentwood refused to pay their poll tax in May 1381, contagious rebellion broke out across south-east England. The radical cleric John Ball exhorted a crowd on Blackheath to 'cast off the yoke of bondage and recover liberty' and Jack Straw spoke to a group on Hampstead Heath from a hay wagon, dubbed 'Jack Straw's Castle'. On 13 June, Wat Tyler led a rebellious mob over London Bridge and Jack Straw led the Essex detachment through Aldgate, passing underneath the gatehouse rooms where Geoffrey Chaucer lived.[1] The rioters destroyed the Fleet Prison and the Savoy Palace, then stormed the Tower of London and beheaded the Lord High Treasurer and the Archbishop of Canterbury. When Richard II met the rebels at Smithfield, the Mayor of London, William Walworth, unexpectedly beheaded Wat Tyler.[2] The 14-year-old king then stepped forward and quelled the incensed crowd, agreeing to the rebels' demands and acknowledging the abolition of serfdom.

EVIL MAY DAY ④

By the early 16th century, London was home to many foreign merchants. According to *Hall's Chronicle*, the city's first race riot was ignited by a xenophobic sermon that encouraged Londoners to 'hurt and grieve aliens'. A group of apprentices ignored the curfew on May Day 1517 and gathered in the liberty of

READING THE RIOT ACT

In 1714, the Riot Act was passed, bringing in measures 'preventing tumults and riotous assemblies'. A proclamation had to be read aloud before any action could be taken, by which time the unlawful assembly had usually moved on. The wordy proclamation went as follows: 'Our Sovereign Lord the King chargeth and commandeth all persons, being assembled, immediately to disperse themselves, and peaceably to depart to their habitations, or to their lawful business, upon the pains contained in the act made in the first year of King George, for preventing tumults and riotous assemblies. God Save the King!'

St Martin's Le Grand;[3] frightened foreign residents showered them with bricks and boiling water, and the riot began.[4] Henry VIII was woken at his palace in Richmond with news of the disturbance and, even though nobody was killed in the short riot, 13 'poore younglings' were hanged as an example on 4 May. Today there is a workers' rally every May Day as part of International Workers Day, gathering on Clerkenwell Green near the Marx Memorial Library and marching to Trafalgar Square.

THE GIN RIOTS ⑤

On 28 September 1743, the day before a prohibitive rise in gin tax, crazed gin drinkers ignored the Riot Act and wrought havoc in the streets, desperate for the last drops of cheap liquor.

THE SPITALFIELDS WEAVERS' RIOTS ⑥

In the 1760s, there was a slump in British silk production due to smuggling and cheap foreign imports. Spitalfields was the centre of the silk-weaving industry, and the journeyman weavers joined forces to form a rudimentary, ruthless trade union and ensure minimum wages.[5] There were riots throughout the 1760s, including an attack by 5,000 weavers with pickaxes on the Duke of Bedford's house in Bloomsbury Square, after he opposed the introduction of a heavy import duty on Italian silk. You can get a sense of their desperate living conditions in the attic of Dennis Severs's House on Folgate Street.[6]

F ——

---

❶ A timber-frame replica of Chaucer's room, the 'Paleys upon Pilers', stood on stilts at Aldgate until 2015. It will be reconstructed in the forthcoming Minories development nearby.

❷ The site is marked by a slate memorial, and the sword used by William Walworth is on display in the Fishmongers' Hall. Some say it is the origin of the dagger on the City's coat of arms.

❸ Now Postman's Park. See p.109.

❹ A Venetian diplomat described, in a letter to his doge, how 2,000 bandits 'attacked the French and Flemish quarters, and sacked the houses'. For a different doge, see p.191.

❺ 'Cutters' would break into workshops and slash the work of any weaver accepting lower payment.

❻ For more on Severs, see p.309.

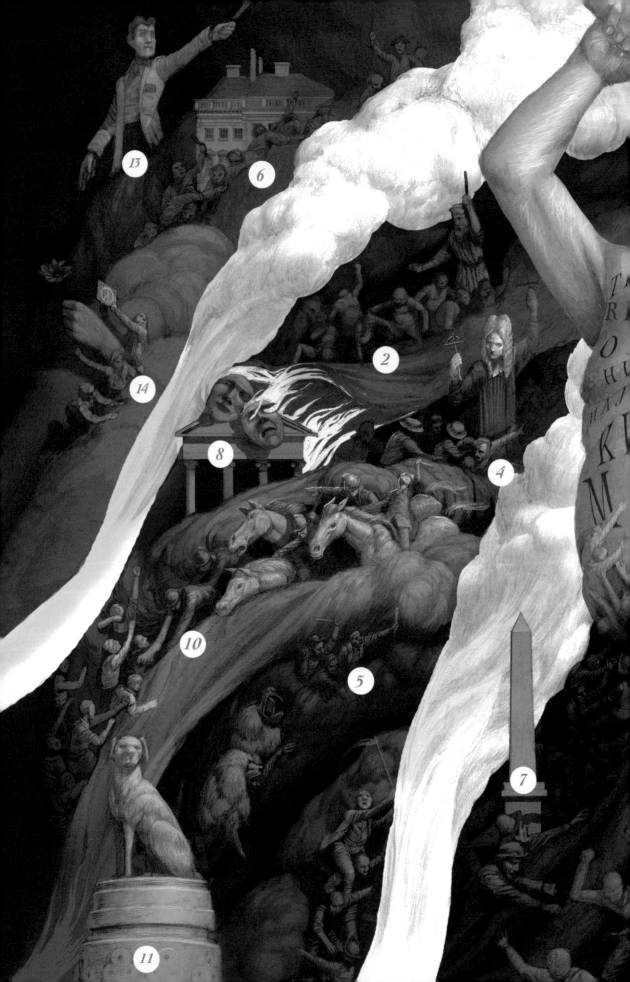

THE GORDON RIOTS ⑦

In 1780, the Gordon Riots shook London for six days and six nights. On 2 June, Lord George Gordon gathered a 50,000-strong crowd in St George's Fields,[1] Southwark, ostensibly as a protest against the relaxation of anti-Catholic Popery Laws. His mob surged towards the Houses of Parliament over Westminster, Blackfriars and London Bridge. Numbers swelled as they marched and the protest quickly degenerated into riots and looting. Politicians were assaulted, carriages vandalised, chapels attacked and embassies damaged; Irish houses were sacked and burned, and Newgate Prison was destroyed.[2] 'Gracious God! What's the matter now?' wrote the composer Ignatius Sancho in his diary as the crowd roared past. 'I was obliged to leave off', he continued later '– the shouts of the mob – the horrid clashing of swords – and the clutter of a multitude in swiftest motion – drew me to the door.'

OLD PRICE RIOTS ⑧

When the rebuilt Covent Garden Theatre raised its ticket prices by one shilling in 1809, riots broke out during the opening performance of *Macbeth* and continued on and off for three months, until the manager of the theatre made a public apology and lowered the cost. If the price of West End tickets seems prohibitive today, you could consider a similar tactic.

SPA FIELDS RIOTS ⑨

Thomas Spence wrote a six-point plan to abolish aristocracy and institute common ownership of land. His followers held two public meetings in Spa Fields, Islington, hoping to inspire rioting and use the commotion to seize control of the Tower of London and the Bank of England. They failed.

BLOODY SUNDAY ⑩

On 13 November 1887, William Morris and George Bernard Shaw joined a march to protest against unemployment in Ireland. The demonstration was well advertised, and a crowd of 30,000 spectators gathered to observe 10,000 protestors march into Trafalgar Square. Police attempted to disperse the protest and fighting broke out, involving 'iron bars, pokers, gaspipes and short sticks' according to the *London Daily News*. The *Pall Mall Gazette* accused the organisers of attempting to convert 'an English Sunday into a carnival of blood'.

THE BROWN DOG RIOTS ⑪

Down Battersea Park's leafy Woodland Walk, near the Old English Garden, a terrier cocks its ear atop a five-foot plinth. Modelled on Brock, the sculptress Nicola Hicks's own pet, the *Brown Dog* replaces an earlier sculpture, which was the focus of the inflammatory *Brown Dog* riots of November 1907. The Anti-Vivisection League erected the original Brown Dog in Latchmere Recreation Ground, 'In Memory of the Brown Terrier Dog Done to Death in the Laboratories of University College in February 1903'. Medical and veterinary students marched on the statue with a view to destroying it and riots erupted in Battersea. Following the riots, the statue required a constant police guard. The dog disappeared mysteriously overnight in 1910, perhaps spirited away by a nervous council, and was not replaced until 1985.

---

❶ Now the St George's Circus roundabout. The location is still marked by an obelisk erected nine years before the riots.

❷ William Blake was caught up in the surge towards Newgate Prison, the Bastille of London, and wrote later how 'millions sent up a howl of anguish.' For more on the prison, see pp.280-81.

THE BATTLE OF CABLE STREET (12)

Oswald Mosley led a march of the British Union of Fascists through the streets of London on 4 October 1936. The route was advertised beforehand, and a large group of anti-fascist demonstrators formed blockades across Cable Street, the long road in Limehouse originally used for laying and shackling ship's cables. The police attempted to clear the route, but the demonstrators fought back with improvised weapons,[1] chanting the anti-fascist slogan of the Spanish Civil War: *¡No pasarán!* – 'they shall not pass!' Eventually Mosley agreed to abandon the march, but by then the fracas had developed into a full-scale riot. In the end, 175 people were injured including police, women and children, making it one of the bloodiest street fights in London's history. There is a large mural depicting the battle on the wall of St George's Town Hall.

NOTTING HILL RACE RIOTS (13)

On 29 August 1958, Majbritt Morrison was arguing with her Jamaican husband, Raymond Morrison, outside Latimer Road tube station, and a small fight developed. The next day Majbritt was assaulted by a gang of white youths, calling her a 'black man's trollop', and the Notting Hill Race Riots kicked off. That night a mob of several hundred Teddy Boys attacked the houses of West Indian residents in the area, and the riots continued sporadically for several days.[2] On 30 January the following year, a 'Caribbean Carnival' was held in St Pancras

Town Hall as a response to the riots, an event that developed into the Notting Hill Carnival.[3]

ANTI-AMERICAN RIOT (14)

On 17 March 1968, a 20,000-strong anti-Vietnam War protest in Grosvenor Square led to violence with smoke bombs and marbles to rattle the police horses. A young woman offered a mounted policeman a flower and was truncheoned to the ground.

BRIXTON RIOTS (15)

On the side of Brixton Academy there is an enormous mural, which shows a multi-ethnic group of children smiling and playing in harmony. It was commissioned after the Brixton Riots the previous year. During the recession of 1981, relations between the police and Brixton's Afro-Caribbean community reached an all-time low, with accusations that the police were arresting black people on little or no pretext. On 11 April, Bloody Saturday, police stopped and searched a minicab on Railton Road. Riots erupted,[4] bricks were thrown at police cars, shops were looted and houses burned. It was the first time that petrol bombs were used in England, a technique imported from Northern Ireland. The riots led to a new code for police conduct.

THE BLACKBERRY RIOT (16)

On Thursday 4 August 2011, a police officer shot and killed 29-year-old Mark Duggan on the Ferry Lane bridge near Tottenham Hale Station. That Saturday, several hundred locals marched to Tottenham Police Station and demanded to speak

F

to a senior police officer. The crowd remained outside the station, becoming increasingly frustrated, until a girl threw a champagne bottle at the assembled officers. Violence broke out and news of the Tottenham disturbance sparked riots, looting and arson across the city that evening and on the nights that followed. The riots were partially coordinated through BlackBerry Messenger. One message circulating widely read: 'link up at enfield town station at 4 o clock sharp!!!! [...] Fuck da feds, bring your ballys and your bags trollys, cars vans, hammers the lot!!' There were a total of 3,443 crimes recorded across the capital, five deaths, sixteen injuries and an estimated £200 million worth of damage to property. Some commercial casualties have since risen from the ashes, including Party Superstore in Clapham Junction and Clarence Fresh Fruit and Veg in Hackney.

---

❶ One anti-fascist leader, Jack Spot, wielded a 'type of cosh shaped like the leg of a sofa but filled with lead at the end, which had been made for him by a cabinet-maker in Aldgate'.

❷ Local historian Tom Vague describes 'a crowd of a thousand white men and some women [...] tooled up with razors, knives, bricks and bottles'.

❸ See p.34.

❹ For a record of the riots, see p.309.

PUBLIC ASSEMBLY

One of the most provocative forms of public assembly in London is the theatre, bringing thousands of people together every night to watch the most political of all art forms.

MILITARY TAKEOVER
Until 1978, real Royal Guardsmen routinely performed non-singing military roles at the Royal Opera House, following a complaint from Queen Victoria about the slack discipline of actors playing guards in a performance of *Fidelio*.

OLD RED LENIN
Take in a show at the theatre upstairs in the Old Red Lion in Islington. The room used to be a bar favoured by local communists. Legend has it that Lenin would eavesdrop on their conversations through the lift shaft of the dumb waiter. The pub has a good political pedigree: Thomas Paine wrote *The Rights of Man* here in the 18th century.

CHAMPAGNE SOCIALISM
Wilton's Music Hall, where stars like Champagne Charlie walked the boards, was recently saved and restored, after stints as a Methodist church and a rag warehouse. Book a show and celebrate its return with a bottle of fizz in the Mahogany Bar.

WARTS & ALL
Visit the National Theatre in the daytime and examine the display of fake warts, beards and bloodstains on the Sherling High-Level Walkway. The walkway has a view down on to the backstage world of rehearsals, prop production and scene painting.

CLANDESTINE MEETINGS
The Bookshop Theatre on The Cut specialises in scripts and theatrical books, and has its own tiny, hidden theatre through the red drapes at the back of the shop.

> **AFTERSHOW GOSSIP**
> The Phoenix Artist Club just off Charing Cross Road is in the old dressing rooms of the Phoenix Theatre. This memorabilia-filled basement is members-only and fills up with thesps after the curtains fall on local shows. Non-members can enter if they arrive before 8pm.

CORRUPTION
Go to the old Victorian music hall on Hoxton Street for a show or a swing dancing class. The great Marie Lloyd performed there before she became famous. Lloyd was 'a mass of corruption' according to Virginia Woolf, 'and yet a born artist'.

BEEF & LIBERTY
Legend has it that John Rich, an 18th-century manager of the Royal Opera House, would grill the occasional steak in his private room. Friends began to join him, and before long they were meeting regularly and calling themselves the Sublime Society of Beef Steaks. Their motto was 'Beef and Liberty'. As you can't order a steak from your seat at the Opera House, go to Sarastro restaurant on Drury Lane, where your opera-singing waiter will serve you in a private box.

DRAMA QUEENS
Catch a 'Cockney Singsong' matinee, served with afternoon tea, at the Brick Lane Music Hall on North Woolwich Road. This converted church is the only permanent music hall venue in the world, with shows every day featuring Pearly Kings and Queens, flower-sellers, clowns and tap-dancing chimneysweeps.

HANDOUTS
Ensure you're in the cast at the Drury Lane Theatre on 6 January. On his death in 1794, the actor Robert Baddeley left a bequest to provide the theatre's performers with wine and cake every Twelfth Night.[1]

---

❶ If you're not an actor, you can celebrate Twelfth Night on p.205.

-ISMS

If you'd like to opt out of mainstream politics altogether, here are some alternative -isms you could consider.

ANARCHISM

To break free of authority, pick up some mind-expanding reading matter at the Anarchist Bookfair in October, which has been held annually in London since 1983 (anarchistbookfair.org.uk). You can also attend events and pick up radical literature from the Infoshop at 56a Crampton Street, a volunteer-run social centre and bookshop in a former Walworth squat (56a.org.uk).[1]

BAGISM

Resist being labelled by society by hiding inside a bag. In 1968, John Lennon and Yoko Ono sat inside a big white bag on the stage of the Albert Hall to demonstrate Bagism: a form of 'total communication' designed to stop people judging others on their appearance.

MADISM

Avoid the political classes at the Leigham Arms in Streatham. Angry plaques on the wall detail which officials are not permitted to drink there. 'KEN LIVINGSTON (sic) NEVER LIVED HERE', reads one, '(IN FACT HE IS BARRED) WITH THE REST OF HIS TAX COLLECTION, PARKING ATTENDANTS AND OTHER THIEVES.'

MARXISM

Plan the overthrow of the capitalist state in the Marx Memorial Library on Clerkenwell Green. Tip your cap to the bust of Lenin[2] in a replica of the room where he used to edit a radical newspaper, then hunker down in the Reading Room beneath a massive mural showing 'The Worker of the Future Clearing Away the Chaos of Capitalism'.

NATURISM

Assert your freedom with a skinny dip[3] in Brent Reservoir. In the 1930 Sun Bathing Riots, local residents attacked a group of naturists who regularly gathered there.

SQUATTERS

TOTTERS

Look outside the Brixton Bizness Cafe on Coldharbour Lane for an unofficial plaque to Julian Wall, 'TOTTER, SQUATTER / A TRUE INDIVIDUAL', who lived there from 1979–89. In 2014, after the residents were evicted, another plaque appeared commemorating the Carlton Housing Co-operative, who lived there from 1979–2014, 'Housing the homeless and many cats.'

MODEL CITIZENS

Ellingfort Road in Hackney was being squatted in the 1990s when the council mooted plans to demolish it and construct a chicken-freezing facility in its place. Tom Hunter, a local art student, decided to make a scale model as a record of his community. He took hundreds of photos of the area and collaged together a replica street. The result was astounding: a meticulous, fully peopled world that illuminated the life of the community, down to the pictures on people's walls, the bikes in their hallways, and the bins in their front gardens. The publicity that the model attracted led the council to reverse their decision. Visit Hunter's seven-foot squat in the Museum of London and then go for a walk along the real Ellingfort Road.

---

[1] It shares its premises with a radical supermarket. See p.245.
[2] Another revolutionary Communist leader, the Vietnamese president Ho Chi Minh, cut his teeth in London's hospitality industry: a plaque on Haymarket commemorates his time as a pastry chef at the Carlton Hotel.
[3] You can also swim naked on p. 229.

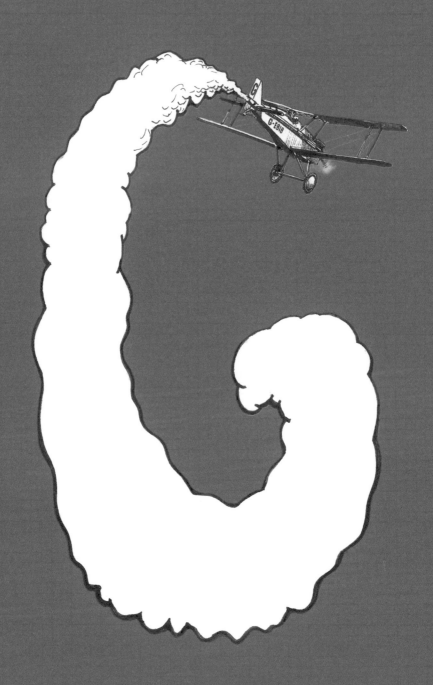

GRID

WHEN A SIX-LANE MOTORWAY was slated to cut through Brixton in the late 1960s, judicious architects designed a housing block with thick walls and tiny windows to shield residents from the pollution and noise. The road was never built, but Southwyck House – or the Barrier Block as it became known – was. You can still see this neo-brutalist fortress on Coldharbour Lane: its imposing design is now the only hint of the plans that almost devastated the neighbourhood. Brixton's motorway (Ringway 1) was part of an ambitious scheme to build a series of orbital roads, which would ripple out from the centre of London and give structure to a disorderly city.

For centuries, planners have bemoaned London's lack of coherence, believing that its 'straggling, confus'd growth', in Daniel Defoe's words, undermined its greatness and global status. It's little wonder, then, that planners have seized on moments of crisis to rationalise and remodel the capital. After the Blitz, the Head of the London County Council wrote that the 'war has given us a great opportunity, and by the bitter destruction of so many acres of buildings it has made easier the realisation of some of our dreams'.[1] In 1944, those dreams were set out by Patrick Abercrombie in the *Greater London Plan*, a comprehensive vision of a rebuilt, restructured city: London would be sliced into four concentric rings, served by five new orbital motorways. But although some of Abercrombie's ideas took root, his far-reaching plan proved unachievable in the straitened post-war years. Two decades later, his Ringways scheme was still being debated, and finally only one loop was built, the M25, which didn't open until 1986.

The Romans founded London as an orderly grid, but that structure is now long buried and the city has resisted subsequent attempts to impose order on to it.[2] With this in mind, some visionaries have focused on changing the way we perceive London, rather than trying to refashion the city itself. In his 1895 pamphlet *The Unification of London: The Need and the Remedy*, John Leighton proposed an entirely new system for imagining the capital. Instead of London's higgledy-piggledy borough boundaries, he drew the city as a honeycomb of perfectly regular hexagons.[3] Each hexagonal borough would be divided into six equilateral triangles, and each of those areas would be divided into a further sixteen equilateral triangles, marked out by 200 precisely positioned lamp posts, each bearing an arrow pointing north and a unique location code. 'Chaos is changed into Cosmos', boasted Leighton of his plan, confident that Londoners would be able to use his lamp posts to pinpoint their exact whereabouts at any time. His nightmarishly complex scheme wasn't adopted and London's baggy boroughs remain as they were. If you like the sound of Leighton's ideas, however, you could study his book at the British Library[4] and then enact his masterplan by spraying arrows and location codes on to all of London's lamp posts.

---

[1] John Betjeman despised what he called the 'Planster's Vision'.
[2] See p.337.
[3] Imagine London as a beehive on pp.176–7.

[4] It's also available online as a free e-book (access.bl.uk/item/pdf/ lsidyv3c0c937d).

BOLLARDS

Bollards perform an essential but under-celebrated role on London's streets. They mark out space in the city, guiding pedestrians and preventing vehicles straying where they shouldn't. Samuel Johnson reportedly touched bollards for luck. You're advised to do the same.

BOBBY
Look for the jolly blue bollard wearing a policeman's helmet outside the old Gerald Road Police Station on Sloane Square.[1]

ARTY
The rusty bollards on Peckham's Bellenden Road are high art, sculpted by Antony Gormley, whose studio is nearby. He made them in four different shapes: 'the oval, the snowman, the peg and the penis'.

MILITARY
The two bollards at the end of Boundary Passage in Shoreditch are French cannons from the Battle of Trafalgar. They each have a cannonball bunging their muzzle.

CROSSINGS

Walk down the main steps at Waterloo Station and use the ZEBRA to get to York Road. Zebra crossings were originally blue and yellow.

Turn left and use the raised walkway to cross the road. The first PANDA was installed on this spot in 1962. Panda crossings had triangular stripes and only lasted for five years.

Head towards the Eye and cross Westminster Bridge. Use the PELICAN to reach Portcullis House. Pelicans replaced pandas with red and green people.

You'll need to use another pelican to get to St James's Park, and two more to get to Buckingham Palace. Walk alongside Green Park and use the TOUCAN, designed for pedestrians and bicycles, to get to the traffic island. They're called toucans because two can cross together.

You're passing the site of the first pedestrian crossing in the world. Built on Bridge Street in 1868, it had police-operated semaphore arms.

Now take the PEGASUS, introduced in 2010, towards Hyde Park. It's a toucan-pelican for horses: the panel is 2 metres high for mounted riders.

Now you're only missing a PUFFIN. These intelligent sensor-controlled crossings are taking over our streets. See if you can find one. They display their red and green people on a small operating panel on the same side as waiting pedestrians. You always wait when you press a puffin.

---

❶ This is the personal favourite of bollard enthusiast John Kennedy, who founded the 'Bollards of London' blog (bollardsoflondon. blogspot.co.uk).

GRID LINES

WATTS

Stand outside Harrods at night and bask in the glow of the 11,500 bulbs on its façade. To keep the store gleaming, 300 of them have to be changed every week.[1] A lot of energy is required to fuel Harrods' bulb habit. Once London had its own local power plants, including Battersea and Bankside, but the city's electricity is now piped in from elsewhere on the National Grid. A ring of substations inside the M25 pull the power underground and spread its three-phase alternating current across the metropolis. But in some places the parade of pylons encroaches into the city: you can see them marching up to Falconwood in Bexley, the Greyhound Stadium in Wimbledon, Millfields Park in Clapton and Star Lane in Canning Town.

WIRES

Make a phone call in the lobby of Brown's Hotel on Albemarle Street, in homage to Alexander Graham Bell, the inventor of the telephone, who made the UK's first telephone call here in 1876. London's first telephone directory, published four years later, only contained 255 names. Nowadays, wires are optional. You can see a monument to mobile technology at the Three Mills complex on the River Lea: a bronze sculpture of a teenager in a puffa jacket checking his smartphone.

WATER

Admire the Wapping Hydraulic Power Station, which stands on Wapping Wall opposite the Prospect of Whitby pub. For almost 90 years, this station pumped Thames water at high pressure around a network of cast-iron pipes stretching from Wapping to Hyde Park. The pressure was used to power machinery, lifts and cranes; it was even strong enough to operate Tower Bridge.

WAVES

The BT Tower was declared an official secret on completion and did not appear on Ordnance Survey maps until 1993, despite being central London's most visible building. The tower was built in 1964[2] to transmit telephone and television data. Today, most TV and radio channels are fired across the city from the Crystal Palace and Croydon transmitters on the hills of South London.

WIFI

Big chunks of the internet are housed in London. LINX (the London Internet Exchange) is one of the biggest data hubs in the world. Its main site is Telehouse North,[3] a massive metal warehouse in East India Docks. To get inside the internet, you can request a facilities tour on their website – although you'll need to imply that you require end-to-end ICT solutions before they let you in.

G

---

[1] We don't know how many Harrods employees it takes to change a lightbulb.

[2] In Patrick Keiller's film *London*, Robinson notes that the BT Tower was built on the site of a house once occupied by the poets Rimbaud and Verlaine. He postulates that the tower was built as a 'monument to their tempestuous relationship'. See p.289.

[3] The city's most centrally located internet hub is the smaller Telehouse Metro site at 65 Clifton Street, an unassuming brick building on the edge of Shoreditch.

BIKES

VELODROMES

Herne Hill velodrome was used as a gun battery during the Second World War. A 1942 report described the extensive damage to the venue: the track was overrun with small trees and a grape vine of 'interesting proportions' had taken root on the back straight. Nevertheless, the velodrome recovered and is now the only 1948 Olympic[1] venue still in use. Sir Bradley Wiggins raced there as a child and the velodrome now runs cheap trial sessions for all ages and abilities. In the entrance hall of the Science Museum you can see bikes from across history suspended from the ceiling. The display is meant to look like 'a velodrome that has flown up into the sky'.

COFFEE STOPS

A new breed of coffee shops has sprung up to fuel the city's cyclists. Stop off at Look Mum No Hands! on Old Street, a handsome cafe with a workshop at the back.

BARE BACK RIDING

The music video for Queen's song 'Bicycle Race' was filmed in Wimbledon Greyhound Stadium and featured 65 women cycling naked around the arena. Although it was decried as crass and sexist by many, pedalling *au naturel* caught on and there's now a Naked Bike Ride in London every summer (wiki.worldnakedbikeride.org).[2]

LIFE CYCLE

Look for one of the city's best-used bikes in the London Transport Museum. Their Gentleman's Evans bicycle was manufactured in 1928 and did noble service until 2002 when it was retired by its 93-year-old owner, Mr W. F. Wagstaffe, a Post Office engineer.

RECUMBENTS

If you tire of traffic, recline on a banana bike and ride it around Dulwich Park. Hire one of these bright-yellow two-wheelers from London Recumbents (londonrecumbents.com), who've been in business for two decades and amassed a staggering range of recumbent bikes and trikes. They rent out individual and tandem vehicles that cater for children, families and a wide range of different needs.

MASS TRANSIT

Join the Critical Mass bike ride on the last Friday of every month. Participants meet under Waterloo Bridge at 6pm and pedal London together, aiming to outnumber cars and take over the roads. The event has no leader, no predefined route and describes itself as an 'unorganised coincidence' (criticalmasslondon.org.uk).

FRONT RUNNER

Pick up a Boris Bike[3] outside Waterloo Station, the largest docking point in the city. Each bike has a unique serial number and in 2015 Transport for London revealed that the most ridden is number 16191.[4] Unless you happen upon it straight away, keep switching bikes around the city until you find it. Don't rush: the bikes are heavy and low-geared to prevent you picking up speed.

---

[1] See p.223.
[2] For more naturism, see p.403.
[3] Although London's public bike-hire scheme was dreamed up by the mayor Ken Livingstone, the bikes have come to be associated with his successor Boris Johnson.
[4] Silver went to 15901 and bronze to 14630.

CARS

STRING THEORY

Look out for the bronze man on John Carpenter Street, near Blackfriars, frozen in the act of hailing a taxi. Hail one yourself and take it to 28 Sumner Place in South Kensington, where a blue plaque marks the former residence of the inventor of the hansom cab. Follow a map as you travel and stretch a string between the start and end points of your journey. Your driver will try to stay 'on the cotton', cabbie slang for taking the most direct route. When flagging down a cab, look out for fresh faces: if you're a cab driver's first-ever fare, you get the ride free.[1]

SPARE ARTS

If your motor overheats on the King's Road, stop off at the Saatchi Gallery and ask them to top up your oil. In the basement is a gallery flooded with recycled engine oil. Enjoy gazing into the mirrored black surface[2] before siphoning off a few litres.

TEMPLES

London is famous for the splendour of its parks, and the Debenhams car park on Welbeck Street is a particular highlight. Slow down as you approach this brutalist masterpiece and admire the interlocking concrete diamonds on its façade. For J. G. Ballard, multistorey car parks are 'the true temples of the automobile age'. 'Those canted decks', he eulogises, 'are trying to lead us to another dimension'. Next, drive to the Brewer Street Car Park in Soho. The original design of this sleek art deco structure featured a rooftop golf course.[3] Park up and visit the latest show by the Vinyl Factory (thevinylfactory.com), which has taken over part of the interior.

BEANMOBILE

At the London Motor Museum in Hayes you can see the 1966 Batmobile driven in the original *Batman* TV series, the Batmobile from the 1989 film, and Mr Bean's Mini.

JOY RIDE

Driving around London can be a delight, as the Clash observed in their song 'London's Burning': in this tirade against the boredom of London life, the pent-up punks weave along the Westway, pausing their invective for a moment to remark on the quality of this 'great traffic system.' Cruise along this iconic 3.5-mile flyover, which has chalked up numerous musical tributes in its short life.[4] Then visit its broody undercroft, where the cover photo of the Jam's album *This Is the Modern World* was taken.

DOUBLE PARKING

The new Francis Crick research institute at King's Cross is named after one of the co-discoverers of DNA. But the most impressive monument to the breakthrough is less than a mile away beneath Bloomsbury Square. Drive into the Bloomsbury Square underground car park and then, once you reach the bottom, drive back up, pay and leave. You have just travelled through a gigantic double helix, with ascending and descending spirals of cars woven around one another.

G

[1] Catch more cabs on p.157.
[2] Stare at another black mirror on p.361.
[3] Although it never got its golf course, the car park finally became a high-end destination when it was used as the official venue for London Fashion Week in 2015.
[4] Blur have also hymned the Westway: once in their 1993 song 'For Tomorrow', and again in their 2012 single 'Under the Westway'.

AIRSPACE

London reaches up into the sky in more ways than we might imagine, whether it's tennis balls flying above Centre Court at Wimbledon, (1) anti-aircraft rockets pointing upwards during the Olympic Games, or the beam of light shot into the sky to commemorate the centenary of the outbreak of the First World War. (2)

We're drawn to higher spheres. Kew Gardens installed a treetop walkway in 2008, allowing visitors to walk through the crowns of oaks, limes and sweet chestnuts, (3) and in 2014, a pop-up restaurant opened in the sky above Canary Wharf, with diners harnessed to a 'sky table' 100 feet in the air. One simple way to feel the exhilaration of the sky is to go to Streatham Common on a sunny day and fly a kite.[1] (4) 'With your feet on the ground / you're a bird in a flight,' rhapsodises Mr Banks in the Disney film of *Mary Poppins*, 'with your fist holding tight / to the string of your kite.'[2]

HIGHLANDS (5)

Unlike Rome or Sheffield, London is not known for its hills. At first glance, it appears to be a vast flat floodplain, yet in truth there are plenty of places within the Thames basin where you can get closer to heaven. At 804 feet above sea level, Westerham Heights in Bromley is the highest ground in Greater London. The highest point near the centre is the village of North End on the edge of Hampstead Heath (440 feet), closely followed by Shooter's Hill in Greenwich (433 feet). Try and bag all the city summits, including Sanderstead Plantation in Croydon (574 feet), the Clockhouse Recreation Ground in Sutton (482 feet) and Highwood Hill in Barnet (476 feet).

SPIRES (6)

In the 1200s, the tallest building in the world was Old St Paul's Cathedral. At 489 feet, it was taller than any building had ever been before, 8 feet taller than the Great Pyramid of Giza, and a third taller than St Paul's today. The spire caught fire in 1561, proclaimed at the time as a heavenly judgement on hubris: it fell through into the nave and was never reconstructed.

MAP READING

Airspace is a map of the sky above London, with the four Heathrow holding stacks in each corner. It is inspired by a map of the seven Zeppelin raids on London, which appeared in Sphere magazine in 1919.

The height of Old St Paul's was not surpassed in London until the Crystal Palace Transmitter was built in 1950, partly thanks to Queen Victoria, who was offended when a 14-storey tower blocked her view of the Houses of Parliament from Buckingham Palace. Her lack of amusement led to the 1894 London Building Act, which capped all new structures at 80 feet. The act was not relaxed until the 1950s.

TOWERS (7)

You can climb to the top of several London towers. At 202 feet, the Monument was once the tallest structure in the city. It was designed with an underground laboratory at its base, for use in early experiments into gravity. If you can't face the 311 steps, a panoramic 360° photograph of the view is streamed live to a screen at the bottom. Alternatively, a lift will take you to the top of the Westminster Cathedral campanile. (8)

(1) Streatham Common Kite Day takes place every June. (2) Meet Mary Poppins on p.141

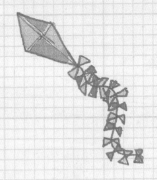

SKYLINES

London boasts several ways to get airborne without actually flying. Catch the Air Line from the Royal Docks to the Greenwich Peninsula. You'll soar to 300 feet and have a superb view of Antony Gormley's *Quantum Cloud*.[1] Alternatively, traverse the Tower Bridge walkways, high above the river. The transparent floor allows you to look past your feet at the traffic below. In 2013, Norman Foster revealed designs for SkyCycle, a 136-mile network of cycle routes built above existing train lines. The plan has the backing of National Rail and Transport for London, and the developers are currently raising funds for a feasibility study.

FLY-LINES (9)

Some Londoners can reach 6,000 feet under their own steam. Feral pigeons are the most familiar of London's birds. They are the mongrel siblings of European rock doves, descended from medieval dovecote escapees. Urban pigeons still yearn for the cliff crevices and rocky caves where their ancestors nested; today they settle for window ledges and railway arches. Before the ban on feeding pigeons was introduced in 2000, the Trafalgar Square flock comprised 35,000 birds; now they are systematically eliminated by Harris hawks, flown daily by an environmental pest control company. Take a moment to watch those that remain. Peter Ackroyd has remarked on their habitual 'fly-lines' over London, citing a route from Lincoln's Inn Fields via Trafalgar Square to Battersea. A careful observer will perceive a sky cross-hatched with pigeon leys, invisible thoroughfares connecting green spaces. If you fancy pigeons, and want to get more involved, consider joining the Kingsland Racing Pigeon Club, based in Hackney, an area once famous for its pigeon-hutches and pigeon-traps.

SONGLINES (10)

Sparrows were once a common sight across the city, and a 'cock-sparrer' was a cockney term of endearment, but numbers dwindled significantly when the insects associated with horses disappeared. More recent additions to the London aviary are gulls,[2] which first appeared in 1891 and caused a popular sensation: crowds would gather on their lunch breaks to feed them minnows and watch them dive for fish in the Thames. More recent still is London's colony of over 10,000 rose-ringed parakeets. Visit Hither Green Cemetery at dusk to witness one of the largest parakeet roosting sites in London. Some say the exotic green birds escaped from the set of *The African Queen*, filmed at Isleworth Studios in 1951; others that a breeding pair was released by Jimi Hendrix in the 1960s. If you can't tell your tit from your wagtail, unmuddle your warbles by booking a London Wetland Centre workshop, where you'll learn to recognise the most common birdsongs in the city.

BUTTERFLIES

Of course, birds aren't the only airborne creatures in London; look out for bats, bees and butterflies as well. London Zoo created the world's first Butterfly House in 1981, and its current 'Butterfly Paradise' exhibit is housed within an enormous, walk-through caterpillar. Alternatively, you can encounter wild specimens on a stroll through the Roding Valley water meadows in summertime.

G

❶ Taller than the *Angel of the North*, this sculpture's random tetrahedral units trace a gigantic outline of Gormley's body.   ❷ See p.125.

AIRSPACE

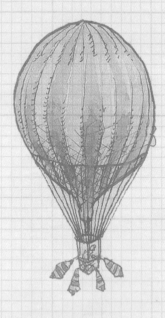

HOT-AIR BALLOONS ⑪

In Old Change Court, Michael Ayrton's sculpture of Icarus [1] launches into the sky with upstretched wings. Ever since Icarus flew out of the labyrinth, people have longed to join the birds on the wing. Vincent Lunardi achieved the country's first manned balloon flight in September 1784, taking off from Moorfields Artillery Ground in an impressive red-and-white silk balloon. The public reaction was effusive and Lunardi was lauded as the 'idol of the whole nation'. The actress Mrs Laetitia Sage was the first British woman to fly, also in a Lunardi balloon. She flew from St George's Fields to Harrow, where she came down in an angry farmer's field and had to be rescued by boys from Harrow School. Soon balloons became a fashionable addition to most of London's pleasure gardens; Charles Green's party trick was to ascend from Vauxhall Gardens on horseback.

ZEPPELINS ⑫

During the First World War, between May 1915 and October 1917, seven slow-moving, cigar-shaped Zeppelins glided over the city and dropped incendiary bombs. The first Zeppelin attack, on 31 May 1915, approached from the north-east. The first bomb landed at 16 Alkham Road in Stoke Newington, and the second at Cowper Road in Newington Green, killing three-year-old Elsie Leggatt, London's first fatality from aerial bombing. Several websites map the route; try walking it, imagining the vast balloon above you, bigger than an upended Gherkin.

BARRAGE BALLOONS ⑬

In the Second World War, British Balloon Command used balloons defensively: by 1940, 1,400 barrage balloons were floating over London. Their purpose was to force enemy dive-bombers up to heights of 5,000 feet, and into range of anti-aircraft guns.

FLYING PIGS ⑭

Today, Adventure Balloons run hot-air balloon flights over London at dawn. As you drift above the capital in a wicker basket, picture the 40-foot floating pig which broke free from Battersea Power Station in December 1976. The pig had been strung between the chimneys for the cover shoot of the Pink Floyd album *Animals*. When it broke its moorings and floated away, all planes at Heathrow were grounded and the RAF was scrambled to chase it to the ground in Kent.

VAPOUR TRAILS ⑮

Plane contrails are a familiar sight across the London sky, white streams of artificial cloud created by water vapour from aircraft exhausts. These ephemeral trails mark flight paths that crisscross the city and form a web across its six international airports. The routes that planes take into, out of and across London are designed to cause the least disturbance to the fewest number of people. Heathrow has four holding stacks on the outskirts of London, above Bovingdon, Ockham, Biggin and Lambourne. Incoming planes circle above navigation beacons until they get the green light from air traffic control and begin their final approach. [2]

---

❶ Hunt for Ayrton's Minotaur on p.290.

❷ A good place to watch incoming planes is outside Hatton Cross Station, located at the end of the Heathrow runways.

OFF GRID

If the National Grid collapses, here are some ways to keep the lights on.

1. Ask if you can shelter in the new American Embassy in Nine Elms, which can survive off grid for 'an extended period', according to official sources.

2. Go to Marylebone's Sunday Farmers' Market and buy a sack of spuds at the Potato Shop. Satisfy your energy needs by sticking electrodes into your Jersey Royals.[1]

3. Take shelter in Blackfriars Station, which was recently rebuilt on a rail bridge over the Thames. The station is roofed with solar panels that provide around half of its power.[2]

4. Power up he old Brixton Windmill[3] and harness the gusts that sweep down Brixton Hill. If that's not enough to fire your kettle, tap into London's first three wind turbines on the Ford estate in Dagenham.

5. Consider lending your roof or your money to one of the Community Energy Schemes springing up across London, funding and installing solar panels. Investors receive an annual return (communityenergyengland.org).

G —

ODD GRID

PNEUMATIC MISMATCH
The London Pneumatic Dispatch Company believed it could move mail around the city faster than the Post Office by using compressed air to fire it through pipes at 'very nearly the pressure of a hurricane'. Although they dug a stretch of pipeline to demonstrate the 'irresistible velocity' of their system and won a contract to build the complete network, the Post Office decided that the time savings weren't significant enough and the company was liquidated in 1875. Walk the 500-metre route of the defunct pipeline from Euston Station to the delivery office on Eversholt St, and commemorate this near miss by visiting one of the pneumatic dispatch carts in the Museum of London. The Post Office ran their own underground mail train from 1927 to 2003. From 2020 the public will be able to ride along a stretch of the line.

ELECTRO SUBSTATION
The dimpled steel box at the centre of the Elephant and Castle traffic island looks like it might just be an electricity substation. In fact, it is an electricity substation, but its grander purpose is to serve as a memorial to Michael Faraday, who was born nearby and conducted pioneering research into electricity. It's also rumoured that the electronic music pioneer Aphex Twin lives there in an underground bunker.[4] Go to the substation at night and listen to his spacey debut EP *Analogue Bubblebath* beneath the flashing multi-coloured lights.

FRANKEN-POSSUM
On noticing a 'a yellow coloured growth' on their pickled opossum, the Grant Museum opened it up and discovered that a Duracell D battery had been implanted in its abdomen. They don't yet know who tried to create the battery-powered opossum or why. Inspect it in the museum and ask staff for the latest updates on their investigation.

---

[1] For more potato power, see p.315.
[2] 900,000 kWh per year. See p.343.
[3] Built in 1816, it opens to visitors once a month.

[4] He lives nearby. Aphex Twin also performs under the names Blue Calx, Caustic Window, GAK, Karen Tregaskin, Polygon Window, Q-Chastic, Smojphace, Soit – P.P., Tuss, user18081971, and user4873635300.

HAGIOLATRY

IN AN ATTEMPT TO LEAVE HIS MARK, George Villiers, Duke of Buckingham, named five streets after himself in 1672: George Street, Villiers Street, Duke Street, Of Alley and Buckingham Street. Villiers was a rakish poet and statesman who was, in his own estimation, 'possessed of uncommon qualifications', but the profligate duke failed to make a lasting impression, and is now all but forgotten. His monuments are his streets, which still exist off the Strand.[1]

The city actively commemorates many individuals: saints and celebrities who continue to assert their influence from beyond the grave. Since 1866, London has venerated its secular saints by marking the places where they lived or worked with blue plaques.[2] If you know of someone who ought to be celebrated, you can propose them to English Heritage (english-heritage.org.uk/visit/blue-plaques). If they're selected, their gently domed, stoneware plaque will be hand-fired by Frank and Sue Ashworth in their Cornish workshop, the lettering will be hand-piped, and the finished plaque will be bedded and pointed flush into the face of London. If your proposal is rejected, make your own memorial instead. Spot the unofficial blue plaque to 'Joe ("You're All F***ing Barred") Jenkins' outside the Newman Arms on Rathbone Street, commemorating a former proprietor who was a 'Poet, Bon Viveur & Old Git'.

Many extraordinary lives and courageous deeds never make it on to a plaque. The artist G. F. Watts set out to remedy this in 1887 by establishing a Memorial to Heroic Self-Sacrifice in Postman's Park: a wall of plaques dedicated to the city's humbler heroes. The rescue attempts described on these touching ceramics frequently involve inflammable clothes, train accidents, quicksand and broken ice. One of the plaques, and a story that particularly inspired Watts in his endeavour, commemorates Alice Ayres:[3]

DAUGHTER OF A BRICKLAYER'S LABOURER,
WHO BY INTREPID CONDUCT SAVED THREE CHILDREN
FROM A BURNING HOUSE IN UNION STREET, BOROUGH,
AT THE COST OF HER OWN YOUNG LIFE. APRIL 24, 1885.

The project dwindled in the 1930s and the first new plaque for almost 80 years was put up in 2009, in memory of Leigh Pitt:

REPROGRAPHIC OPERATOR, AGED 30,
SAVED A DROWNING BOY FROM THE CANAL
AT THAMESMEAD, BUT SADLY WAS UNABLE
TO SAVE HIMSELF. JUNE 7, 2007.

Others will no doubt be added in due course: there is space for at least 66 more.

---

[1] George Street is now called York Buildings, and Of Alley has been renamed York Place. Villiers was a companion of John Wilmot: see p.76.
[2] Start plaque-hunting at 16 Eaton Place, where you can tick off William Ewart MP, the man who devised the scheme in the first place. Plaques haven't always been blue: look out for brown, sage and terracotta examples.
[3] Postman's Park is a key location in Patrick Marber's play *Closer*, in which one of the characters is called Alice Ayres.

SAINTS

London is a reliquary, a shrine to many saints. Make a pilgrimage to these holy body parts.

ST ETHELDREDA ⑱
In the 7th century, Princess Etheldreda of East Anglia renounced her wealth and position to become a nun. Despite this act of self-effacement, she eventually died of a tumour on her neck, which she saw as divine punishment for having worn a precious necklace in her youth. Nowadays a piece of her hand lies in a closed casket next to the altar of St Etheldreda's church on Ely Place; visitors can ask to see it. On St Blaise's Day (3 February) the church hosts the 'Blessing of Sore Throats', at which you can be anointed beneath the chin with a pair of lit candles.

AUTO ICON ⑲
The philosopher Jeremy Bentham transformed himself into a relic. In his will, he asked to be embalmed after death and you can visit his Auto Icon in UCL. See p.285 and p.349.

ST EDWARD THE CONFESSOR
The only saint buried in Westminster Abbey is St Edward the Confessor, King of the English from 1042 until 1066. Join the national pilgrimage to his incorrupt body every 13 October, when the abbey celebrates 'Edwardtide'.

ST THOMAS MORE
St Thomas More was beheaded by Henry VIII because he refused to recognise Henry as the Supreme Head of the Church of England. More's head was boiled and displayed on London Bridge, and then thrown into the Thames. His daughter Meg rescued it, however, and it may now be buried in the family tomb he commissioned at Chelsea Old Church.[1]

ST JOHN SOUTHWORTH
St John Southworth was hanged, drawn and quartered in 1654 for being a Catholic. You can find his body, encased in a silver effigy and dressed in red vestments, in a crystal coffin in Westminster Cathedral.

THE TYBURN MARTYRS
The Shrine of the Martyrs at Tyburn Convent on Hyde Park Place is a replica of Tyburn Tree.[2] Pilgrims are escorted to the shrine three times daily by the Crypt Sister. The crypt contains several relics, including the fingernail of Blessed Thomas Holland. 'If I had

MODERN MARTYRS
The niches above the great west door of Westminster Abbey had always been empty until 1998, when they were filled with life-size statues of 20th-century martyrs from across the world, including St Maximilian Kolbe, killed by the Nazis in 1941; civil rights campaigner Martin Luther King, assassinated in 1969; and Archbishop Janani Luwum, murdered in Uganda in 1976.

ARTY MARTYRS
Damien Hirst's gilded *Exquisite Pain* depicts St Bartholomew, holding his own flayed skin and a scalpel, and is occasionally on display in St Bartholomew-the-Great. In the South Quire Aisle of St Paul's Cathedral, Bill Viola's permanent video installation *Martyrs (Earth, Air, Fire, Water)* shows four individuals being martyred by the four elements on a seven-minute loop.[3]

as many lives as there are hairs on my head, drops of water in the ocean, or stars in the firmament,' Blessed Thomas said at his hanging, 'I would most willingly sacrifice them all.'

---

❶ There is a 1969 statue of Thomas More with a gold face outside the church, facing the river.

❷ For more on the three-sided gibbet, see p.84 and p.281.

❸ For more on the elements, see pp.390–91.

CELEBRITIES

AMY ⑬

The singer Amy Winehouse joined the '27 Club'[1] in 2011 when she died 'by misadventure' at her home on Camden Square. Fans write messages on the street sign; add yours, unless the sign has been stolen, as several have before. Then visit the life-size statue of Amy in Camden Stables. Her bronze beehive hair is constructed so that you can push the stem of a flower into it. Finally, go for a drink at the Dublin Castle pub on Parkway, where Amy often played. On the wall is a gigantic signed photo: 'Peggy – Thanks for letting me behind the bar – I need the tips! Lotsa love, Amy x'.

DIANA

Between two sphinxes in the basement of Harrods is a shrine to Diana, Princess of Wales, and Dodi Al Fayed. Flickering candles flank photographs of the couple, and inside a crystal pyramid is a diamond engagement ring, purchased by Dodi the day they died, and a wine glass from their hotel suite with traces of Diana's lipstick.[2]

MARC ⑭

The sycamore tree on Queens Ride in Barnes is owned and looked after by TAG: the T-Rex Action Group. The elfin hippy turned glam rock star Marc Bolan[3] died in a car accident there in September 1977, when the purple Mini driven by his girlfriend collided with a fence post next to the tree. Listen to Bolan's

breakthrough single 'Ride a White Swan' at the site and leave a feather boa on his statue. Below his bust are the words: 'Sad to see them mourning you when you are here within the flowers and the trees.'

SEBASTIAN ⑰

In 2000, the Soho dandy Sebastian Horsley had himself crucified. He then exhibited a series of paintings and a film of his crucifixion in a gallery on Crucifix Lane. His crucifixion was both real and entirely staged, embodying his belief that 'glamour is a far greater asset than spirituality'. Take a copy of Horsley's autobiography, *Dandy in the Underworld*,[4] and read it on your way to Viktor Wynd's Museum of Curiosities, where you can see his red sequinned suit and the nails with which he was crucified.[5] 'The dandy recognises', said Horsley, 'that given that all character is manufactured […] you might as well manufacture an interesting one.' He died of an overdose in 2010.

WAXWORKS ⑳

These days, there are no barriers at Madame Tussaud's and visitors can rub shoulders with their icons: Brad Pitt even has a purpose-built squeezable posterior. One figure you might not recognise immediately is Marie Tussaud herself. Before coming to London and setting up her exhibition, Tussaud moulded wax death masks for guillotine victims during the French Revolution. Look for her self-portrait at the entrance to the museum and then rush inside for quality time with Brad.

---

① Many notable musicians have died at the age of 27, from the blues musician Robert Johnson, to Jim Morrison, Kurt Cobain and Jimi Hendrix. Hendrix died in 1970 at 22 Lansdowne Crescent in Notting Hill.

② On the other side of Kensington Gardens, Café Diana on Wellington Terrace is decorated exclusively with images of the princess.

③ Born Mark Feld and brought up at 25 Stoke Newington Common, marked by a plaque today.

④ Named after T-Rex's final album, released in March 1977.

⑤ On 25 July 1968, Hungarian interior decorator Joseph de Havilland was found crucified on Hampstead Heath. He had convinced three friends from Maida Vale to pin him up, 'to make the world a happier place'. He survived.

BEYOND BELIEF

A sure-fire way to be remembered is to found your own belief system. Nonconformity in the capital reached its peak during the 17th-century Interregnum, when state religion was temporarily abolished and Londoners were free to dissent. Here are ten commandments for initiating your own religious cult.

I. WAIT FOR GUIDANCE
'There's a new world somewhere / They call the promised land,' sang the Seekers in 1965. Their early-17th-century namesakes believed that the promised land could only be achieved once Christ returned to Earth. The SEEKERS held silent gatherings with no hierarchy or priests, and spoke only when God inspired them.

2. CHAMPION EQUALITY
Have a drink at the Rosemary Branch in Islington. This was the office of the LEVELLERS, who wore sprigs of rosemary in their caps and preached religious tolerance.

3. PLANT VEGETABLES
Gerrard Winstanley founded the DIGGERS, or the 'True Levellers', in 1649. They advocated turning London into an agrarian community. They started on St George's Hill in Weybridge, planting vegetables on common land. Today the hill is a private residential estate, but land rights campaigners reoccupied the summit in 1999, to mark the Diggers' 350th anniversary.

4. ORDINATE EVERYONE
Attend a meeting at the Friends House on Euston Road and listen to the spirit of love in equitable silence: QUAKERS profess the priesthood of all believers. The Religious Society of Friends took their popular name from the advice of a judge, who commanded them in 1650 to 'tremble before the Lord'. Traditionally Quakers wear plain clothes and don't swear, drink or fight. Luckily, they can indulge in confectionary: Cadbury's, Rowntree and Fry's are all Quaker businesses.

5. WORSHIP EVERYTHING
The RANTERS believed that God was in every living creature. They had scant respect for authority and used nudity as a form of social protest.[1] Attend one of the World Pantheist Movement's occasional meet-ups on Hampstead Heath to learn more (pantheism.net).

6. CREATE A NEW COSMOLOGY
In 1651, a London tailor named Lodowicke Muggleton revealed that he was the last prophet foretold in the Book of Revelation. The MUGGLETONIANS, who grew out of the Ranters, scrapped rational science and based their cosmology on scripture. Kentish fruit farmer Philip Noakes was the last Muggletonian: he died in 1979 and left the movement's archive to the British Library (MSS. 60168-60256).

---

[1] In the 1640s, the Adamites believed they could regain the innocence of Adam by dispensing with clothes. For other reasons to bare all, see p.403.

7. ANNOUNCE THE END OF THE WORLD

During the Interregnum, the FIFTH MONARCHISTS believed the end was nigh. In 1661, fifty of them attempted to take over London and launch the 'Fifth Monarchy of King Jesus'. They broke into St Paul's Cathedral and made their last violent stand against the authorities in a pub on Bishopsgate.

8. CONFER WITH ANGELS

Emanuel Swedenborg was a Swedish scientist and mystic who spoke to angels. After he died in 1772, a SWEDENBORGIAN church was established off Eastcheap; today you can attend the Sunday morning service at the Swedenborgian church in West Wickham, and midweek lectures at Swedenborg House on Bloomsbury Way.

9. DANCE IN THE STREET

Hop up and down below the railway lines on Sutherland Walk, off Walworth Road. This is where Mary Ann Girling held mass meetings in 1871, at which she announced her own divinity and the imminent advent of the Second Coming. Her delirious devotees jumped and danced ecstatically and became known as the WALWORTH JUMPERS.

> ### CATHEDRALS
> Once your cult is fully established, why not build a cathedral? There are already sixteen in London. The Anglicans have St Paul's and Southwark; Catholics have Westminster and St George's; there are ten Orthodox cathedrals (two Russian, seven Greek and one Ukrainian); and there's a Ukrainian Catholic cathedral in Mayfair and an Antiochian cathedral in Camden.

10. ACHIEVE ECSTASY

The Georgian Orthodox Church on Rookwood Street, Upper Clapton, has two weathervanes: a fiery chariot of desire and a sheaf of phallic arrows. The church was built as an 'Abode of Love' in 1892 by the AGAPEMONITES, a religious love cult. Adherents were wealthy, unmarried women of all ages who enjoyed spiritual (and corporeal) sex with their leader, John Hugh Smyth-Pigott, the self-declared reincarnation of Christ.[1]

H ——

MAP READING
London Icons references religious icon paintings and altarpieces such as the Wilton Diptych (c.1395, now in the National Gallery). The luminous style of the cityscape was inspired by Macdonald Gill's *Wonderground Map of London Town* (1914). The texts describing the figures on this map are numbered and spread across the whole chapter.

---

❶ In his film *Metro-Land,* John Betjeman pauses outside Smyth-Pigott's 'helmeted house' on Langford Place and remarks that it has an 'uncanny atmosphere: threatening and restless'. The house is now occupied by the broadcaster Vanessa Feltz.

London

FLORIOGRAPHY

Floriography is the art of using flowers symbolically.[1] Londoners commemorated for symbolic reasons are often remembered with flowers, such as the Unknown Soldier in Westminster Abbey, whose tomb is fringed with poppies.

WHITE ROSES (9)

'All women together ought to let flowers fall upon the tomb of APHRA BEHN,' wrote Virginia Woolf, '[...] for it was she who earned them the right to speak their minds.' Behn is considered by many to be the first British woman who made her living from writing. However, this 17th-century playwright is something of a cipher. She seems to have deliberately obscured the details of her background, her early life and her work as a spy in Belgium. She was a woman, writes her biographer Janet Todd, who wore 'an unending combination of masks'.[2] Visit her grave in the East Cloister of Westminster Abbey and leave white roses, symbol of secrecy and silence.

GERANIUMS & DAFFODILS (16)

The decision to honour MARY SEACOLE, the enterprising mixed-race Crimean War nurse, with a large statue outside St Thomas's Hospital was met with outrage by the Nightingale Society, champions of the better-known Crimean War nurse, FLORENCE NIGHTINGALE, who founded the nursing school at St Thomas's that still exists today. The society believes that Seacole, who set up her own hospital in the Crimea and had little formal training, is a less significant figure in the history of nursing and should not encroach on Nightingale's patch. This spat over the reputation of the woman voted the 'Greatest Black Briton' in a 2004 survey has stirred up bigger questions about how and where Londoners from different ethnic backgrounds

are commemorated.[3] For their part, Nightingale and Seacole met several times and had no quarrel with one another in life; visit both of their statues at St Thomas's Hospital, and leave geraniums and daffodils, symbols of determination and respect respectively.

NASTURTIUMS (11)

Naoroji Street is a stubby residential road in Finsbury with an unofficial blue plaque to DADABHAI NAOROJI, 'the first Asian elected to the House of Commons'. Naoroji, an Indian living in London, became MP for Finsbury Central in 1892. He advocated fiercely for the rights of Indians under British imperial rule and later wrote *Poverty and Un-British Rule in India*. In 1894, Gandhi wrote a letter telling Naoroji that the 'Indians look up to you as children to the father'. Leave nasturtiums, symbol of patriotism, outside the old town hall on Rosebery Avenue, where another plaque celebrates his achievements.

GLADIOLI (10)

'I have put up several plaques – quite illegally, without permission,' explained Tony Benn to the House of Commons in 2001. 'I screwed them up myself. One was in the broom cupboard to commemorate EMILY WILDING DAVISON'. Arrange a tour of parliament and ask to visit the cupboard in the Chapel of St Mary Undercroft, where the suffragette spent the night before the 1911 census so that she could give her address as the House of Commons.[4] Two years

---

[1] Flirtatious Victorians exchanged tussie-mussies, or 'talking bouquets', to be decoded with trembling floriographical dictionaries.

[2] Behn sometimes wrote under the name Astrea and was known as Agent 160 while on His Majesty's Secret Service.

[3] There is a blue plaque to Mary Seacole ('Jamaican Nurse, Heroine of the Crimean War') on her former home at 14 Soho Square.

[4] The census form recorded her postal address as: 'Found hiding in crypt of Westminster Hall.'

later, Wilding Davison was fatally injured beneath the hooves of the king's horse at Epsom. Fresh analysis of the race footage in 2013 suggested that she was attempting to attach a sash to the horse and not, as was generally believed, deliberately martyring herself.[1] Look for the flag in the Museum of London that fellow suffragettes hung behind her hospital bed, and leave gladioli, symbol of conviction and strength of character.

OLIVE ⑧

In 1969, the Nigerian diplomat Clement Gomwalk was arrested in Brixton on suspicion of being in possession of a stolen vehicle, which was actually his black diplomatic Mercedes. It's said that a 17-year-old OLIVE MORRIS attempted to intervene, but was arrested herself and beaten up. Morris went on to become an influential activist, squatter and community organiser. She inspired many, but died of Hodgkin's Lymphoma aged only 27. Seven years later, Lambeth Council named an administrative building after her, but Morris began to slide into obscurity. In 2006, the Brixton artist Ana Laura Lopez de la Torre came across a photo of a young woman with a wry expression, holding a sign reading: 'BLACK SUFFERER FIGHT POLICE PIG BRUTALITY'. She started to piece Olive Morris's life back together and launched the 'Do you remember Olive Morris?' project (rememberolivemorris.wordpress.com), which gathered documents and oral histories before they were lost forever. Visit the Olive Morris Collection in the Lambeth Archives to peruse the materials they gathered, and leave an olive branch, symbol of peace.[2]

SUNFLOWERS ⑮

There is a tug of war over ADA LOVELACE's reputation. Many claim her as the 'first computer programmer' because of a series of algorithms she published and her prescient understanding of the potential of the machines we now call computers. Others see her as a colourful character whose role in Charles Babbage's work has been significantly overstated. Find the blue plaque to this 'Pioneer of Computing' at 12 St James's Square and then look at a trial model of the Analytical Engine, on which she collaborated with Babbage, in the Computing Gallery of the Science Museum.[3] Visit on 13 October, Ada Lovelace Day, which celebrates 'the achievements of women in science, technology, engineering and maths', and leave sunflowers, symbol of pure and lofty thoughts.

H ——

DAFFODILS ⑫

In 1993, 18-year-old STEPHEN LAWRENCE was stabbed to death by a group of white men while waiting at a bus stop. The marble plaque that marks the spot where he died on Well Hall Road in Eltham has been vandalised on numerous occasions: a reminder that the racism that motivated his murder is still a force in London today. The brutal senselessness of the crime, the appalling police response (which ultimately led to the Met being declared 'institutionally racist' in the 1999 Macpherson Report), and the relentless campaigning of his parents have all meant that Stephen has become an iconic figure in debates about racism and equality. Lay daffodils, symbol of hope, on his plaque and then visit the Stephen Lawrence Gallery in Greenwich, a space dedicated to work by young artists.

---

❶ The return rail ticket in her purse, now in the Women's Library at the LSE, also indicates that she was expecting to survive.
❷ You can find Olive Morris on the Brixton One Pound note. See p.191.

❸ Babbage called her 'the enchantress of numbers'. For more on the Analytical Engine, see p.160.

HOUSES OF THE MUSES

London has many house museums, whose former residents were inspired by one or other of the nine classical muses.

THE BEAUTIFUL OF SPEECH
Charles Dickens lived at 48 Doughty Street from 1837 until 1839; it's now the Charles Dickens Museum. Stand in the study where he completed his first three novels, inspired by CALLIOPE, muse of epic literature. Above the fireplace is the portrait *Dickens' Dream* by Robert William Buss, which shows Dickens surrounded by a vision of his fictional creations. In the kitchen is a stuffed hedgehog called Bill Spikes.

THE FAME MAKER
At the top of Thomas Carlyle's House on Cheyne Row is his soundproofed study and the desk where he wrote his ground-breaking history of the French Revolution. CLIO, the muse of history, was no doubt floating near the retractable skylight at the time. The house was opened to the public just 14 years after Carlyle's death in 1881 and is still open today, almost exactly as Carlyle left it.

THE AMOROUS
You can sense ERATO, the muse of love poetry, in bosky Keats Grove as you approach his house in Hampstead. It was here that John Keats fell increasingly in love with Fanny Brawne,[1] whose ripening breast was immortalised in the poem 'Bright Star'. When you visit, look for the lyre brooch made with Keats's hair.[2]

THE WELL-PLEASING
Stand in the Composition Room in Handel House on Brook Street, where George Frederick Handel was visited by EUTERPE, the muse of song. Afterwards, attend a recital in the Rehearsal Room; or book ahead to rehearse on the harpsichord yourself. If Euterpe speaks to you while you're there, join in with the annual *Messiah* sing-along at the Albert Hall (trbc.co.uk).

THE MELODIOUS
Horace Walpole cultivated what he called 'gloomth', pleasure in gloomy things, at Strawberry Hill, perhaps under the influence of MELPOMENE, the muse of tragedy. Visit the modest cottage in Twickenham that he transformed into a gleaming white fairy-tale Gothic castle. The only tragedy today is that his eccentric collection of antiquarian objects has dispersed. Luckily it has been painstakingly recreated online by the Lewis Walpole Library at Yale University (images.library.yale.edu/strawberryhill).

THE SINGER OF HYMNS
John Wesley and his brother Charles were prolific hymnodists, inspired no doubt by POLYMNIA, the muse of hymns. Visit Wesley's House on City Road, next to the Museum of Methodism.[3] Hum a hymn as you stand in his small, bare-boarded Prayer Room, revered by Wesleyans worldwide as the 'Power House of Methodism'. Look out for his bouncy Chamber Horse (for stimulating the liver)[4] and his 'electrical machine', with which he administered uplifting blasts of electroshock therapy to his parishioners.

THE DANCER
Many of Britain's greatest ballet dancers began their training at the Royal Ballet School in the White Lodge in Richmond Park. TERPSICHORE, the muse of dance, infuses this building, and one of the old dormitories has been converted into a ballet museum, which researchers can visit by appointment; others can explore the collection online (royalballetschool.org.uk/the-school/museum). Read Darcey Bussell's school report: 'Darcey tends to overwork and be overkeen'.

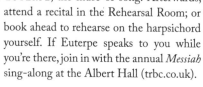

---

[1] For more on their love affair, see p.105.
[2] When Keats died in Rome, his friend Joseph Severn cut a lock of his hair, 'To make a Broach in form of my Greek Lyre – and make the strings of poor Keats's hair'. See more mourning brooches on p.339.

[3] Nearby, on Aldersgate, a black plaque marks the spot where John Wesley first 'felt his heart strangely warmed' and the Methodism movement began.
[4] More livers on p.172.

THE JOYOUS

William Hogarth, the print-maker and satirist, was guided by THALIA, the muse of comedy. Today you can invoke his witty spirit by visiting his country retreat in Chiswick. The house was restored by the enthusiastic Lieutenant-Colonel Robert Shipway, who bought it in 1901, formed a collection of Hogarth's works and commissioned replica furniture based on Hogarth's prints. He opened the house to visitors in 1904. The top floor has a research room, accessible by appointment.

THE CELESTIAL

Over the course of 30 years, the artist Frederic Leighton created one of London's most spectacular houses with the aid of URANIA, muse of star-gazing. The house appears modest from its exterior on Holland Park Road, but as you enter you step into a 'private palace of art' with golden domes, intricate mosaics, Islamic tiles and silken wall-hangings. The two-storey 'Arab Hall', with its centrepiece fountain, was created to display Leighton's collection of Middle Eastern tiles, but the most magnificent room is the vast upstairs studio, lit by a giant north-facing window.

THE HOUSE OF DREAMS

Stephen Wright created his own group of muses in the House of Dreams on Melbourne Grove in East Dulwich. The *Bride* is a white elephant-like figure in a blood-stained wedding dress, representing the loss of Donald, Wright's long-term partner.[1] *The Messenger of Lost Souls* is a composite ebony goddess, a 'wise and comforting' sculpture inspired by a dream. Wright's extraordinary abode is open to the public on six days of the year and by appointment. Every inch is covered with a mosaic of discarded objects, including milk bottle tops, deformed dolls, false teeth, used hair rollers, bleach bottles and pen lids. Wright has bequeathed the House of Dreams to the National Trust.

HALLOWED HOUSES

DARWIN

Darwin lived at Down House in Bromley[2] for 40 years, with his wife, Emma, and their ten children. Look for the slide he commissioned so that his children could skitter down the stairs.

FREUD

In 1938, Dali visited Freud at home and painted him with a head shaped like a spiral, exclaiming, 'Freud's cranium is a snail! His brain is in the form of a spiral – to be extracted with a needle!' Look for the painting on the landing of the Freud Museum.[3]

SAMBOURNE

After the *Punch* cartoonist Edward Linley Sambourne died, his son Roy preserved the house at 18 Stafford Terrace as a Victorian time capsule, with its original William Morris wallpaper, indoor water garden and monogrammed stained glass.[4]

SOSEKI

The Japanese novelist Natsume Soseki lodged at 81 The Chase in Clapham from 1900 until 1902. The translator Sammy Tsunematsu was inspired to turn the apartment opposite (80b) into a shrine (soseki.intlcafe.info). Visit and read extracts from *Wagahai-wa Neko-de aru* ('I Am a Cat'), the novel that turned Soseki into an overnight celebrity.

STEPHENS

Dip a quill in Stephens ink in the house that once belonged to Henry 'Inky' Stephens. Inky built his fortune on his father's indelible 'blue-black writing fluid', and bequeathed his house and gardens[5] on East End Road to the people of Finchley when he died.

H ———

---

[1] The *Bride* shares Donald's rare skin condition, which Stephen treated with camomile lotion.
[2] Find Darwin in his garden on p.160.
[3] Find Freud's baboon god on p.167.

[4] Enter his bathroom on p.68.
[5] Sit on a fantastical bench in the grounds, next to a statue of Spike Milligan.

LITERARY GIANTS

PEPYS ④

Samuel Pepys thought he'd made it into the atlas when he heard that a newly discovered island had been named after him in 1683. Alas, he was a victim of a hapless navigator who claimed the already-discovered Falkland Islands as a new territory. Instead, Pepys's enduring fame was secured by the candid diaries in which he embalmed his life and times. He wrote for ten years, a period spanning the Great Plague and the Great Fire, stopping at the age of 36 when his eyesight began to fail. The diary, which was never intended for publication, veers between the mundane and the monumental, and exhibits a contagious lust for life. Due to their popularity, since losing his island, Pepys has gained a Street, a Road, a Crescent, a Court and a Walk in London, as well as several pubs and a launderette.

JOHNSON ⑦

'Had his other friends been as diligent and ardent as I was,' wrote Boswell in his *Life of Samuel Johnson*, 'he might have been almost entirely preserved.' Nevertheless, Boswell felt certain he had captured his friend's likeness 'more completely than any man who has ever yet lived'. Boswell shaped the way we think about biography; he freely discussed Johnson's private life and used poignant, trivial details to conjure up his personality (including, for example, a bizarre conversation about why Johnson refuses to throw away orange peel).[1] 'Some say that Boswell resurrected Johnson,' wrote Michael Holroyd, 'others that Johnson lies imprisoned in Boswell's book'. For Thomas Carlyle, 'the babbling Bozzy' was 'inspired only by love' and created a 'free, perfect, sunlit' likeness.

Dry some orange peels and leave them outside 8 Russell Street in Covent Garden, now Balthazar's Boulangerie, where Boswell and Johnson first met in 1763.

WOOLF ⑤

Virginia Woolf disliked being depicted by others, generally only agreeing to paintings or photos by those she knew well. In Room 31 of the National Portrait Gallery you can see a 1931 bust by Stephen Tomlin, carved from life and cast in lead.[2] While he was sculpting Virginia, her sister Vanessa painted her. 'Nessa and Tommy', she wrote, 'pinn[ed] me there from 2 to 4 on six afternoons, to be looked at; and I felt like a piece of whalebone bent.' The best depiction of Virginia Woolf is in her diary, which she kept from 1915 until her death in 1941. She wanted it to be 'so elastic that it will embrace anything, solemn, slight or beautiful that comes into my mind'.

SHAKESPEARE[3]

There are still places like St John's Gate or Southwark Cathedral or the Great Hall at Middle Temple, where you can enter the same airspace as Shakespeare. From the river bank outside The Globe, you'll see cormorants on the buoys, and Shakespeare writes about cormorants a lot: he compares cormorants to Time, devouring everything. You can stand there today and watch a cormorant dislocate its beak to swallow a whole fish right down, and you *know* — it's wonderful to *know* — that Shakespeare saw that too.
— *The Gentle Author*

---

[1] 'JOHNSON. "I have a great love for them." BOSWELL. "And pray, Sir, what do you do with them? [...]" JOHNSON. "I let them dry, Sir." BOSWELL. "And what next?" JOHNSON. "Nay, Sir, you shall know their fate no further."'

[2] There is a bronze copy of the sculpture in Tavistock Square. See p.412

[3] Visit Garrick's Temple to Shakespeare on the banks of the Thames in Hampton. On May Day, the celebrity actor David Garrick would sit in the temple dispensing 'a shilling and a piece of plum-cake' to poor children. Today the temple is a shrine to Garrick, and opens on summer Sundays.

PINTERESQUE

Harold Pinter, the Nobel Prize-winning poet and playwright, died in 2008. He is best known for the menacing world of his plays, in which pauses distend taut dialogue. The world of Pinter's youth was Hackney, and the streets of East London stalk his writing.

Pinter was born at 19 Thistlewaite Road on 10 October 1930. A plaque was unveiled in September 2012 by his second wife, Lady Antonia Fraser. The site of Hackney's first synagogue is marked by a plaque three doors away.

Pinter's local Kenninghall Cinema was built in 1896. Aged 14, he wrote a love letter to the older girl who ran it. 'Crabbed age and youth cannot live together,' she replied. Today, the cinema is an Ethiopian Orthodox Church.

The Dwarfs, Pinter's only novel, is set in Hackney. At Clapton Pond, the sexual rivalry between Mark (a cipher for Pinter) and Pete (Ron Percival, Pinter's school friend) reaches its climax.

In 1963, *The Caretaker* was filmed at 31 Downs Road, now demolished. It starred Alan Bates and Donald Pleasance, and was funded by private investors, including Elizabeth Taylor, Noël Coward and Peter Sellers.

Pinter used to walk across Hackney Downs with his inspirational English teacher, Joe Brierley, whom he commemorated in the poem 'Dear Joe'. They would pause to talk by the old bandstand.

KENNINGHALL CINEMA • • 19 THISTLEWAITE ROAD
31 DOWNS ROAD • • CLAPTON POND
HACKNEY DOWNS • • MOSSBOURNE COMMUNITY ACADEMY
RIDLEY ROAD MARKET • • HASH E8
HACKNEY PICTUREHOUSE • • HACKNEY EMPIRE

H

LONDON BOROUGH
OF HACKNEY

The site of Pinter's grammar school, where he edited the school magazine and first acted, has been revamped as the Mossbourne Community.

Ridley Road is still a bustling food market.[1] On this corner, an anti-Semitic gang threw an onion at Pinter and surrounded him, wielding bike chains and broken milk bottles. His friend Jimmy Law came to his aid and they managed to escape on a passing trolleybus. Pinter's memory of Hackney was that it 'brimmed over with milk bars, Italian cafés, Fifty Shilling tailors and barber shops'. Hash E8 is a substitute for the Swan in *The Dwarfs*, where the friends discuss *Hamlet*. Try the corned beef.

Pinter escaped to Hackney Library for comfort; he called it a 'fountain of life'. The building he knew is now the Hackney Picturehouse. When he died, a stolen library copy[2] of a Samuel Beckett novel was found on his shelves and returned. The current library has Pinter's plays shelved alongside Beckett's.

Pinter's first theatre was the Hackney Empire, which is still thriving. Charlie Chaplin once walked the boards here. There is a studio space called the 'Harold Pinter Room'.

❶ See p.373.   ❷ Find another book-thieving playwright on p.275.

NATIONAL TREASURES

Certain towering figures are commemorated on an industrial scale, with multiple memorials or mammoth monuments.

SIR CHRISTOPHER WREN

The words *Lector, si monumentum requiris circumspice*[1] are engraved on a circle of black marble in St Paul's Cathedral, directly below the centre of the dome. The building itself is the great architect's memorial.

ELIZABETH FRY ①

There is no finer publicity than appearing on a banknote. In early 2015 there were 320,000,000 five-pound notes in circulation, all displaying an image of Elizabeth Fry, the Victorian prison reformer.[2] Look at her reading to the inmates of Newgate Prison before exchanging your crumpled fiver for a bar of Fry's Turkish Delight.[3] Enjoy it on Elizabeth Fry Place, a residential cul-de-sac in Greenwich, or Elizabeth Fry Road in Hackney, a short graffitied backstreet lined with high walls and skips.

QUEEN VICTORIA ②

George Bernard Shaw railed against the 'pure plastic calumny' committed by many sculptors when they portrayed Queen Victoria as a 'huge heap of a woman' instead of 'a little woman with great decision of manner'. Look for one of the statues Shaw detested at the centre of the gigantic Victoria Memorial outside Buckingham Palace, and then find a less libellous sculpture, showing the young queen at the start of her reign, in nearby Victoria Square.

ALBERT WETTIN ③

For all Shaw's protestations, Queen Victoria still tends to be portrayed as rather stout and austere. To experience the monarch at her most relaxed, read her diary on the 11 February 1840, the day after her marriage to Albert Wettin:[4] 'When day dawned (for we did not sleep much) and I beheld that beautiful angelic face by my side, it was more than I can express!' Albert died aged 42 and Victoria outlived him by 40 years. The queen's passion never dimmed: she wore black for the rest of her life and set about constructing a series of extraordinary monuments to her husband, culminating in the immense, gilded Albert Memorial in Hyde Park.[5] Albert is also remembered by Prince Albert Road at the base of Primrose Hill, the Albert Embankment at Vauxhall, and the raucous Prince Albert pub on Brixton's Coldharbour Lane.

GUY THE GORILLA ㉑

The binomial name for a western gorilla is *Gorilla gorilla*. The western lowland gorilla, by contrast, is known as *Gorilla gorilla gorilla*. Guy, a much-loved resident of London Zoo until his death in 1982, was a western lowland gorilla. He could be cantankerous, but zoo visitors fell for his gentleness: when sparrows flew into his enclosure, he would pick them up, eye them affectionately and then let them go. Daniel Richter, the principal ape-man and ape-choreographer for Kubrick's *2001: A Space Odyssey*, spent many hours in the zoo observing Guy while designing and rehearsing the film's famous opening sequence.[6] Today Guy's admirers have a choice of three memorials: a black marble statue, erected in 1961 while Guy was still alive, stands in Crystal Palace Park; a bronze sculpture of Guy was unveiled in the zoo to mark his passing; and, on his death, Guy was carefully stuffed and given to the Natural History Museum. Meet him there in the Cadogan Gallery.

---

❶ 'Reader, if you seek his monument look around you.'
❷ Elizabeth's visibility was significantly reduced when Winston Churchill took her place on the new five-pound note.
❸ Manufactured by J. S. Fry & Sons, Quaker relations of Elizabeth. See p.112.
❹ Queen Victoria didn't know Albert's surname and researched it after his death to establish the surname of her heirs. His branch of the family had the name Wettin; it was never adopted by the British royal family.
❺ So thoroughly mourned was Albert that Dickens wrote to a friend asking whether he knew of 'an inaccessible cave […] to which a hermit could retire from the memory of Prince Albert'.
❻ Encounter an alien monolith that failed its audition for Kubrick's film on p.19.

FORGETTING

Sometimes fame can be a burden. Try these strategies for being consigned to oblivion.

BE BURIED AT SEA (22)

Charles Byrne wanted to be forgotten. The 7'7" 'Irish giant', a perpetual novelty in life, asked to be buried at sea in a lead casket, to avoid becoming an object of morbid curiosity in death. The casket was buried at sea as planned, but without its intended inhabitant, after the surgeon John Hunter bribed the undertaker and purchased the body. You can still gawk at Byrne in the Hunterian Museum on Lincoln's Inn Fields. He's now been standing there for over two centuries, although there are growing calls for his burial wishes to be respected.

HIDE IN PLAIN SIGHT

In 2000, Mayor Ken Livingstone suggested that the statues of the 'two generals that no one has ever heard of' should be moved from Trafalgar Square and replaced with better-known figures. Generals Havelock and Napier have faded from popular memory despite their prime position at the heart of London.

CHOOSE AN UNMARKED GRAVE

Somewhere at St Leonard's Church, Shoreditch, two forgotten fools are buried in unmarked graves: William Somers, jester to Henry VIII, and Elizabeth I's favourite comic actor, Richard Tarlton.[1]

USE DIVERSION TACTICS

Commission a fake blue plaque to deflect attention from yourself. Apply to the Fake Blue Plaque Company in Crouch End, who will produce a bogus memorial to your specifications. You can see an example at 118 Hillfield Avenue, which commemorates 'Carswell Prentice,[2] 1891–1964, inventor of the supermarket trolley'. Likewise, at 312 Kew Road a self-effacing square plaque states that 'on this site, September 5 1782, nothing happened'.

H ——

INDESTRUCTIBLE (6)

Bruce Frederick Cummings worked as a junior entomologist in the National History Museum and wrote a study called *The Louse and its Relation to Disease*.[3] This résumé would not normally guarantee a place in the canon of great Londoners, but Cummings kept a diary and, when he found out that he was dying of multiple sclerosis, he filled it with a searingly honest account of his decline. It was published in 1919, six months before his death, as *The Journal of a Disappointed Man* under the pseudonym Wilhelm Nero Pilate Barbellion.[4]

Cummings's diary charts a staggering journey from teenage enthusiasm ('Am writing an essay on the life-history of insects and have abandoned for the time being the idea of writing on "How Cats Spend Their Time"') to his confrontation with death as a 28-year-old: 'nothing can alter the fact that I have lived; I have been I, if for ever so short a time. And when I am dead, the matter which composes my body is indestructible – and eternal, so that come what may to my "Soul," my dust will always be going on, each separate atom of me playing its separate part – I shall still have some sort of a finger in the pie.'

Sit in the Wildlife Garden of the Natural History Museum reading *The Journal of a Disappointed Man* and think of Cummings's atoms swirling around you. An unidentifiable new insect appeared in the garden in 2007 and is now the most numerous creature in there. Look for the red-and-black 'almond-shaped bug' on the plane trees.

---

[1] Tarlton's skull has in fact earned posthumous fame, because he's thought to be the model for the dead jester Yorick in *Hamlet*.

[2] Carswell Prentice never existed.

[3] 'I probably know more about Lice than was ever before stored together within the compass of a single human mind!' he boasted.

[4] The forenames reference three of the most wretched figures from history; the surname was lifted from a cake shop at 79 New Bond Street (now an outlet of Hermés).

QUIET

If you tire of crowds and company, here are some fine spots to be alone.

FLOTATION TANK

For total solitude and sensory deprivation, few things can match an hour in a flotation tank. You step into a plastic pod the shape of a giant clog, turn off the lights and lie down on ten inches of warm concentrated brine. It's perhaps the closest thing in London to returning to the womb. There are several centres around town, including Floatworks, Floatopia and the London Float Centre.

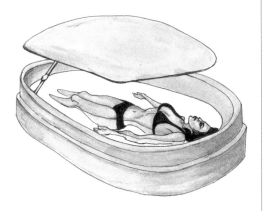

BEANSTALK

Lose yourself in the branches of a tall beech tree on Hampstead Heath that Jimi Hendrix liked to climb to get high above the city. To find it, stray off the path between the central sports ground and the red brick viaduct. The tree is still scalable and is known to climbers as 'the beanstalk' because of its regular, reliable handholds.[1] At the top you're unlikely to be disturbed and can enjoy a commanding view of the Heath while you strum 'Voodoo Chile' on a ukulele.

RIVERBANK

There is a fine riverside nook on Montague Close, behind Southwark Cathedral, with a row of carved stone seats. If you arrive there early, you're likely to have the place to yourself. Head to Borough Market for 7.30am, when Monmouth Coffee opens, grab a warming brew, then take a pew by the river and watch the City come to life. Engraved on the wall are words from Sir Walter Raleigh:

'THERE ARE TWO THINGS SCARCE MATCHED IN THE UNIVERSE / THE SUN IN HEAVEN AND THE THAMES ON EARTH.'

RED ROOM

Attracting five million visitors a year, the Tate Modern is hardly a solitary spot. But go at opening time on a weekday morning, if you can, and go straight up to the Rothko Room.[2] The paintings are bruise coloured, made of plummy red and black rectangles that fur at the edges. Sit on a bench in the centre of the dimly lit gallery and you can imagine how it might feel to be in the belly of a whale. Rothko said he wanted viewers to have 'the feeling of being caught in a room with the doors and windows walled-in shut'.

PIER

London is a city of abandoned piers: as you walk along the Thames look out for the mouldering poles and struts left in the river to rot.[3] The best, and longest, remaining pier is at Erith. To avoid taking up too much of the Thames, this 100-metre concrete walkway is boomerang-shaped: shooting straight out before bending sharply back on itself. Enjoy the solitude by the hut at the end, where you can fish for flounder, sole and silver eels.

---

[1] The main challenge is reaching the first branch, which is about seven feet from the ground. Prop a log at the base of a tree if the jump proves tricky.

[2] Mark Rothko had been commissioned by the Seagram beverage company to create a series of murals but became uncomfortable with the commission and ultimately donated several of the pictures to the Tate, on the condition that they be displayed in a room on their own.

[3] Find the city's oldest rotting pier on p.393.

THE THAMES ARCHIPELAGO

'The day-dream of being marooned on a desert island still has enormous appeal', wrote J. G. Ballard in the introduction to *Concrete Island*, his 20th-century retelling of *Robinson Crusoe*.[1] The book is the story of a man whose car crashes off the edge of the elevated A40 trunk road on the way into West London. There are no witnesses and he finds himself marooned on a patch of scrubby ground, invisible to the traffic above and unable to scale the steep gravel embankment back to the road. He must survive on his wits and the natural bounty of the motorway undercroft. His castaway life is fraught with challenges but he comes to relish the struggle, just as Alexander Selkirk, the real-life inspiration for Robinson Crusoe, found contentment[2] during his time on Mas a Tierra off the coast of Chile, since renamed Robinson Crusoe Island by the Chilean government.[3]

There's an undeniable romance to the idea of building a new life for ourselves with only the contents of a sea chest or car boot to get us started. As Ballard demonstrated, today's Robinsons don't need to sail the world in search of strange shores. If you secretly dream of being cast away, look no further than the Thames Archipelago. The dark ocean of the Thames is strewn with ancient aits, and the great Island of London contains still stranger territories at its interior. This is a chart of rugged outposts and forgotten worlds, disputed territories and micronations, islands real and reclaimed.

THAMES ISLANDS

CHISWICK EYOT

There are only 43 tidal islands in Britain. Alternately joined with and divorced from the mainland, they're often considered sacred places. Chiswick Eyot is London's holy island.[4] Go at low tide, and you can plodge out across the river bottom to explore it. At high tide, the Thames floods it entirely, leaving only the treetops exposed. In 2010, Chiswick Eyot acquired its own ascetic: a pensioner called Nick, who lived there for six months, cooking on an open fire and sleeping in an improvised mesh hammock suspended above the water. 'I've achieved freedom,' he told a BBC reporter. 'If most people had to choose between being here on an island and being in a bank or government office, they would say: "Oh, give me the island!"' On a fair night, pack a flint and a hammock and follow his example.

ISLEWORTH AIT

Isleworth Ait is most famous for being the site of the Mogden Sewage Works outfall.[5] However, the island is also an important wildlife reserve and one of the last places in the UK where you can find the two-lipped door snail and the German hairy snail. The two-lipped door snail is a beautiful air-breathing mollusc with a tightly wound, high-spired shell. The hairs on the shell of its less elegant compatriot, the German hairy snail, allow it to sweat and generate more glutinous slime. This long island is only accessible by boat, but visits can be arranged through the London Wildlife Trust (wildlondon.org.uk/reserves/isleworth-ait). Call them to schedule a meeting with the molluscs, or volunteer with their Hounslow Branch to support conservation work on the island.

---

[1] The figure of Robinson has stalked London since Defoe invented him, reincarnated in Ballard's novel and, most recently, as the unseen narrator of Patrick Keiller's films *London*, *Robinson in Space* and *Robinson in Ruins*. See p.289

[2] 'His Nights were untroubled, and his Days joyous, from the Practice of Temperance and Exercise', wrote Richard Steele after conversations with Selkirk. Selkirk got back to London eight years after leaving England; instead of settling down, he shipped out again on anti-piracy patrols along the West African coast.

[3] To confuse matters, a neighbouring island, which Selkirk never visited, has been renamed Alejandro Selkirk Island.

[4] In the 7th century, St Cuthbert would wade off the coast of Holy Island in Northumberland and pray all night in the biting North Sea. According to the Venerable Bede, otters would then dry Cuthbert's feet with their breath and fur.

[5] See p.56.

EEL PIE ISLAND

It is high time to revive the 'Landing the Pie' ceremony, a tradition that began in the 16th century when Henry VIII acquired a taste for the eel pies of one Mistress Mayo. He commandeered the first pie of each season from her island kitchen and tasked the Senior Waterman of Twickenham with conveying the pie along the river to him. Over time, monarchs ceased to claim this royal privilege and by the early 19th century the ceremony had vanished. Nowadays, the island is home to a community of artists.[1] You can visit their studios on open weekends and you can reach the island at all times by boat or footbridge. When you visit, take an eel pie[2] with you. Then catch the boat from Richmond to Westminster, land the pie and convey it in state to Buckingham Palace.

OLIVER'S ISLAND

Order an ale at the Bull's Head pub on the Chiswick riverbank and look for the underground tunnel connecting it to neighbouring Oliver's Island, named after Cromwell, who was once believed to have sheltered there. Few people believe this now, or that Cromwell briefly ran his operations out of the conveniently located Bull's Head. The pub claims that there is no tunnel on its premises.

MONKEY ISLAND

This island just beyond Eton is named after an ancient colony of monks, not apes. Nevertheless, the third Duke of Marlborough couldn't resist a few simian touches in the pavilion he built in the early 18th century. Take tea and banana cake on the terrace of what is now the Monkey Island Hotel and ask to see the Monkey Room. Its charming murals show monkeys fishing, hunting and smoking. H. G. Wells and Rebecca West[3] were frequent visitors.

RAVEN'S AIT

If you're planning a secluded, exclusive event, look no further than Raven's Ait. You can hire the entire island for high-end boozing and schmoozing. Alternatively, you could attempt a peaceful takeover and reclaim the island for the people, as a group of squatters did in 2009. Their attempts to establish a community centre on the island were thwarted by a police eviction. If you'd prefer to stay beneath the radar, take over one of the other 150 uninhabited islands along the Thames.

FROG ISLAND

Frog Island is not a haven for amphibians. It got its name after being used as an internment camp for French prisoners during the Napoleonic Wars; now it's home to a Waste Management Facility.[4] You can find real pond life on nearby Rainham Marshes. Formerly used as army firing ranges, this medieval marshland is now owned by the RSPB and is riddled with trails and cycle paths. Look for plovers, peregrine and lapwings and then visit Rainham's most prominent water-dweller, clearly visible from the car park by the Tilda rice factory on the edge of the marsh. Presiding over the shipping lanes like an industrial wicker man is *The Diver*: a hollow metal effigy of an early-20th-century dock diver, sporting a cycloptic metal diving helmet. This 15-foot sculpture was self-initiated, and initially self-funded, by John Kaufman, as a tribute to those little-known frogmen who toiled beneath the Thames in copper helmets, canvas suits and weighted boots clearing the river bottom of obstacles and inspecting the underbellies of clippers and frigates.

---

[1] In the 1960s, Eel Pie Island shot to prominence once more when it became the unlikely hub of London's rhythm and blues scene. Davie Jones played there before he was Bowie, and the Rolling Stones had a residency on the island in 1963.
[2] For eel vendors, see p.181, or fish for them on p.129.
[3] They began a passionate affair after West wrote a scathing article about Wells.
[4] The Frog Island facility transforms refuse into fuel. See also p.47.

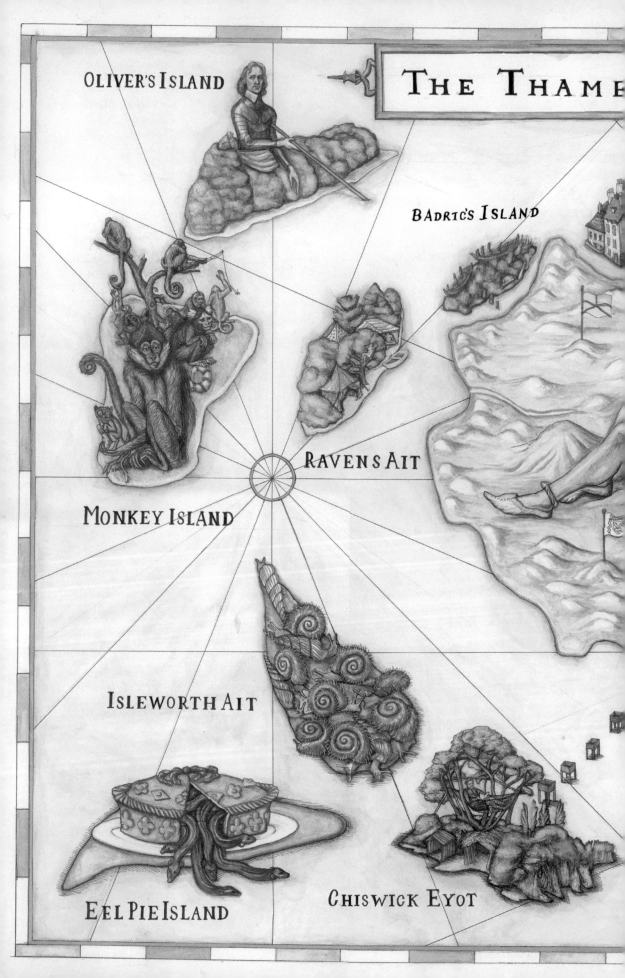

OLIVER'S ISLAND

BADRIC'S ISLAND

THE THAME

MONKEY ISLAND

RAVENS AIT

ISLEWORTH AIT

EEL PIE ISLAND

CHISWICK EYOT

RCHIPELAGO

BEORMUND'S ISLAND

FROG ISLAND

ISLE OF DOGS

PRINCIPALITY OF SEALAND

NEY ISLAND

RECLAIMED ISLANDS

THORNEY ISLAND

Built up and bound back into the city, Thorney Island is no more. The Palace of Westminster and its Abbey were both constructed on this sacred isle, and some chroniclers claim that it was here that King Cnut humbled himself before his courtiers[1] by sitting on his throne at the water's edge and demonstrating that he could not command the tides. Now the island's memory is preserved only in the name of Thorney Street, an austere alley behind MI5. Enjoy a commanding view of the lost island from the deck of the Tamesis Dock, a multi-coloured boat pub near MI6 on the opposite shore.

BEORMUND'S ISLAND

Although Bermondsey's name (Beormund's Eyot) suggests that it may once have been an island in the Thames, many archaeologists believe that it was never entirely disconnected from the mainland. The area did, however, contain a notorious isle of its own. Jacob's Island, moated by Folly Ditch, was an infamous slum, used by Dickens as the site of Bill Sikes's demise. Walk through the warehouse conversions of Shad Thames and stop to read the end of *Oliver Twist* at the mouth of the River Neckinger,[2] the site of Jacob's Island. From there, you have a view over the houseboats of Reed's Wharf, connected to the shore by a long narrow jetty. This long-standing river community is famous for its spectacular barge-top gardens, but is threatened with eviction by the council.

BADRIC'S ISLAND

The Americans are opening a moated embassy on Badric's Island, better known as Battersea. Driftwood, bladderwrack, treasure and wrecks wash up on the blasted shores of Badric. Locals trade this booty from their cars every Sunday morning.[3] Join them and stock up on ships' chests, cracked leather and the horns of rare beasts.

ISLE OF DOGS

Whether London's Isle of Dogs is a real island or a peninsula is a matter of some debate. 'Pen-insula' literally means 'almost-island': somewhere that can't quite make up its mind. Today South Dock very nearly severs the Isle of Dogs from the mainland. Walk the Thames Path on the south bank from Rotherhithe to the Millennium Dome to enjoy a three-sided view of the Isle and its skyscrapers. Canary Wharf, which dominates the Isle of Dogs, is so called because of the fruit trade between the UK and the Canary Islands.[4]

MAP READING

The Thames Archipelago turns London inside out. The north shore of this London island is the south bank of the Thames, and the south shore is the north bank. London is an island; its suburbs have become its centre and the Thames has become an encircling sea with an idiosyncratic archipelago. The Middlesex escarpment and the Surrey Hills, the rims of the city, now meet in a central mountain range. The style was inspired by early nautical charts and the map in Treasure Island. *In the centre sits Robinson Crusoe.*

---

[1] Find Cnut on p.398.
[2] The River Neckinger is named after the 'Devil's Neckcloth', a reference to the riverside gibbet where pirates used to swing.
[3] The Battersea Car Boot Sale is held in the playground of the Harris Academy (batterseaboot.com).
[4] Coincidentally, the name of the Spanish archipelago comes from the Latin, *Canariae Insulae*, which means 'Isles of Dogs'.

FROM: NORTON,
MOLE MAN'S HOUSE,
MORTIMER ROAD, N.1.

16 MARCH 2015

The first duty of any true Londoner is to secure
the means of escape. Cultivate an exit
strategy.

I infiltrated the eccentric system of
burrows beneath the Mole Man's house,
hoping to find the Hackney Brook. To float
out. Tunnels were blocked. My cabinets of
subterranea literature. Mental travelling.
Books w maps.

Henry Eliot &
Matt Lloyd-Rose,
Flat 2,
395 HANLEY ROAD,
LONDON N.4

JUVENALIA

LONDON'S ELVES ARE RARELY SIGHTED and notoriously hard to catch. The only colony in captivity is in a cage in the north-west corner of Kensington Gardens. Go and watch them scrambling around on their gnarled oak stump;[1] Groodles and Grumples are generally the easiest to spot as they spend most of their time asleep. Kensington Gardens is one of the most enchanted places in London. As well as its elves, the park is the home turf of Peter Pan. Before flying to Neverland, Peter appeared in J. M. Barrie's book *Peter Pan in Kensington Gardens*, about a little boy who runs away to live with birds. You can see a statue of him in the park today and, next to the Elfin Oak, there's a Peter Pan playground containing a pirate ship, wigwams and hoards of whooping whippersnappers.

Peter is determined not to grow up and he's still active in London today. In 1929, Barrie transferred the rights to *Peter Pan* to Great Ormond Street Hospital,[2] which has received royalties from the films and plays of the story ever since. The hospital now has a statue of Peter and Tinker Bell outside the entrance, and you can book a tour of its Peter Pan memorabilia.

Unlike Peter, most of us grow up whether we like it or not. But that doesn't have to be such a bad thing – the practically perfect nanny Mary Poppins shows us how to recapture the joy of childhood at any age. 'We have no idea where childhood ends and maturity begins,' said her creator, P. L. Travers, 'it is one unending thread.' Travers lived at 50 Smith Street in Chelsea, the model for Cherry Tree Lane. Nearby, Mary met Bert the Match Man[3] sketching chalk landscapes on the pavement. As a treat on her day out, Bert drew Mary right into the pictures, and you can do the same. Find your inner child – or a real one – and a box of chalks. Draw a picture on the pavement and step through it into the imaginary London of your dreams.

HOUSES OF WONDER

Children should be brought to museums by pied pipers and shown how marvellous everything is. The Museum is a House of Wonder.
— *Irving Finkel*

---

[1] In the 1990s, Spike Milligan led a campaign to restore the Elfin Oak, a 900-year-old oak stump, which was carved with fairy folk in the 1920s. It appears inside the cover of Pink Floyd's *Ummagumma* album.

[2] The hospital's first patient was three-year-old Eliza Armstrong. She had consumption and was successfully treated with milk, wine and beef tea.

[3] Bert had a career change before appearing in the Disney film.

UNREAL CITY

Children are more open than adults to the impossible and absurd. Here are some surreal spots suited to a child's elastic perspective.

BELIEVE IN FAIRIES

'Children know such a lot now,' wrote J. M. Barrie, 'they soon don't believe in fairies'. Believers should go to the shop with no sign at 7 Mansfield Road, opposite Gospel Oak Station. On the door, next to a drawing of a fairy, are the words: 'WE DO NOT EXIST, BUT IF YOU THINK WE DO, PLEASE KNOCK'. Knock and wait for Kristin Baybars[1] to let you into her toyshop, which specialises in all things magical and miniature. Browse through the tiny costumes, button-sized cakes and microscopic jigsaws, and pick up anything you need to accommodate visiting fairy folk.

WALK ON THE CEILING

Mary Poppins's Uncle Albert laughed so hard that he floated up to the ceiling and had to make himself think sad thoughts to come back down. Look for the bronze man[2] standing on the ceiling of the Wellcome Collection lobby. Start giggling and fly up to join him.

SHAKE HANDS WITH A GIANT

When the BFG visits Buckingham Palace, he's so out of proportion with his surroundings that a chest of drawers has to be stacked on top of a grand piano to make him a seat. Shake the metre-long hand suspended above the garden gate in Vauxhall's Bonnington Square,[3] then go in and play on the swings next to a wagon wheel as tall as a house.[4]

GOLF WITH DINOSAURS

Recently, dinosaurs have begun materialising on otherwise unremarkable mini-golf courses around the city. It's not clear what sparked this sporting trend, but you can now putt with predators at Jurassic Encounter in New Malden, Lost Island Encounter in Sidcup, Dinosaur Safari in Arkley and Dinosaur Escape in Northolt.

PLODGING[5]

ACCOUNTANT SEA

The artificial stream that runs past PwC on the More London estate is a serious trip hazard for the management accountants rushing to work. For the under-threes, often seen splashing along it, it's a challenging white water torrent that leads to dozens of shimmering water jets.

LEMON AID

Inhale deeply as you wade across the elegant oval pool in the central courtyard of the V&A museum. In the summer, the planters around it are filled with fragrant young lemon trees.

WATER WALLS

The fountains on the terrace outside the Royal Festival Hall throw up solid walls of water that create constantly changing rooms. Quick reactions are needed to avoid getting boxed in.

JET SETTERS

While the children are jumping through the 1,080 water jets on Granary Square, you can control a line of jets with your phone by downloading the Granary Squirt app (kingscross.co.uk/granarysquirt).

---

[1] 'It's so lovely the way a child looks at things,' says Baybars, 'so different from blooming grown-ups who are terribly conventional and so boring.'
[2] A cast of the sculptor Antony Gormley.
[3] Find out more about this former squat on p.136.
[4] According to official accounts it's a Victorian water wheel.
[5] Plodging is an energetic form of paddling.

TOYS

ANTIQUITOYS

Fans of vintage toys should visit the Ancient Egyptian clay mouse in Pollock's Toy Museum. This weathered plaything, which looks suspiciously like a lump of coal, claims to have been made in 2000 BC.

FREE GIFTS

This Christmas, visit Santa in the Selfridges toy department and see if he'll give you some freebies. That was the experience of children in December 1968, when a member of the radical situationist group King Mob entered the shop dressed as Father Christmas and began handing out the shop's toys to delighted youngsters.[1]

MODEL FAMILY

You can stock up on dungaree-wearing rabbits at the world's only Sylvanian Families shop on Mountgrove Road in Highbury. They sell rolls of miniature wallpaper; buy up several hundred thousand to decorate your house.

TOY BY TOY

In the event of torrential rain, seek refuge in Hamleys toyshop on Regent Street, which was named Noah's Ark when it was founded in 1760. The entry policy for this ark is rather slacker than Noah's and preferential treatment is given to bears.

WARREN STREET

Leave the Leicester Square crowds and follow a white rabbit down Cecil Court. The rabbit is called Harley and he lives in the window of Alice Through the Looking Glass, a shop dedicated to *Alice in Wonderland* curios. Admire the chessboard on the back wall decorated by Sir John Tenniel,[2] the original illustrator of Carroll's books.

FINNISHING SCHOOL

If you like Hemulens and Hattifatteners, you'll enjoy mincing through the small replica of Tove Jansson's Moomin Valley in the Moomin Shop in Covent Garden.

J

TALES

MAGIC CARPETS

Every Sunday the National Gallery unrolls a magic carpet in front of a different painting and tells its story to two- to five-year-olds. Around the corner, the National Portrait Gallery runs a monthly session for children telling the tale of one of the people on its walls.

UNICORNS

The Unicorn Theatre began as a mobile theatre troupe, touring Britain to perform for children after the Second World War. Go and see a play in its permanent home on Tooley Street. Watch out for the enormous bucking unicorn in its lobby.

MARIONETTES

Book tickets for a show at the tiny Puppet Barge in Little Venice; all of the performers are marionettes. If you're inspired, attend a puppet making class at the Little Angel Theatre in Islington, which carves its own characters in a workshop next door.

ALLIGATORS

'A book is like an alligator's mouth', said Lemony Snicket, 'if you see one open you often end up disappearing inside.' Disappear into The Alligator's Mouth bookshop in Richmond for their themed storytimes on Mondays and Tuesdays.

---

[1] The police intervened and forced the children to return the toys. For more on King Mob, see pp.86–87.

[2] Replicas are available for £3,500.

CHILDHOOD DREAMS

London is a wonderland for young pirates, princesses, inventors and explorers. So buckle your swash, dust off your compass and polish your glass slippers: the make-believe metropolis is waiting…

PIRATES

Avast, me shipmates! Do ye long for a life of plunder on the seven seas? Then climb aboard the Pirate Castle[1] off Oval Road for some scourging of the Regent's Canal in kayaks and narrowboats, or show off your rigging skills in the lofty Pirate's Playhouse on Green Lanes.

Keep your eyes peeled for treasure. In 1912, workmen found a chest buried on the corner of Cheapside and Friday Street, which contained jewellery, gemstones, gold, rings and brooches. You can survey the Cheapside booty for yourself at the Museum of London.

As you're marauding, pay your respects to our former colleagues at Execution Dock off Wapping High Street, and give Roger a grin at the St Nicholas Church gateposts in Deptford, still jolly after 500 years.

If you're a little longer in your one tooth, try volunteering with the Hackney Pirates children's charity on Kingsland High Street, or simply buy ye some peanuts and Cracker Jack and settle down to watch a ballgame with the South London Pirates, Croydon's premier baseball team.

Either way, get back to the *Golden Hinde*, the piratical galleon on Pickford Wharf, in time for a Tudor 'living history experience' and a restful night's sleep on the gun deck.

INVENTORS

Eureka! It's time to iron your labcoat and crazy your hair with a static balloon. Many great inventors have lived in London, and you can be next! Your first stop is the Science Museum in South Kensington for some inspiration. Their Launchpad area is full of whiz-popping physics experiments, from chatting with your own echo to making water stretchy. Collect your thoughts as you glide across the Serpentine on the Solarshuttle, powered entirely by the sun; you can even try your hand at steering.

Budding biologists should drop into the Centre of the Cell, at the Blizard Institute on Newark Street: you can step into a giant organic cell with interactive games in the nucleus and a view of real scientists working in a vast subterranean laboratory.

No need to stop inventing over lunch: in Drink, Shop & Do on Caledonian Road you can use the tabletop Lego to start developing your designs while you tank up on brain food.

Then get some final tips at the Royal Institution on Albemarle Street, which hosts regular child-friendly events, before creating your working prototype and booking yourself into the British Invention Show, held every October. The awards jury will judge your invention alongside mobile sun-seeking plant pots, glow-in-the-dark dog food and wrinkle-reducing headgear.

---

[1] Designed, somewhat unexpectedly, by high-rise specialist Richard Seifert, the architect of Centre Point. See p.26.

PRINCESSES

If you wish upon a star, maybe your Fairy Godmother will arrange a £1,000 Royal Princess experience at the Bibbidi Bobbidi Boutique at Harrods.

With your certificate, sash, crystal slipper and luxury travel case under your arm, tinkle down to the Tantrum Salon on the King's Road, and choose whether to sit in a sports car or jet plane to have your hair styled. Each has a private flat-screen TV.

No time to waste! Pre-order a gingerbread version of your own house from Georgia's Cakes (a fairy-tale snip at £49,750)[1] and then get down to the London Porridge Championships in Rude Health on Fulham High Street. On World Porridge Day, 10 October, you can throw your goldilock into the ring and try to beat the big bears. Your recipe will need some coconut cream and an elaborate fruity garnish to be in with a whistle.

Finally, climb the spiral staircase to the highest room in the tallest Monument on Fish Street Hill, and waft your tresses towards Princes Street, before going to Hamleys for a well-earned princess-themed beauty sleepover in the party room.

NATURALISTS

London is teeming with animals, but to spot them you'll need a sharp pair of eyes. To get into training, start with a farm or a zoo. Spitalfields has one of the most central city farms, where you can get up close to Bayleaf the donkey and Bentley the goat.[2]

There are also animals on the streets. The nine City of London Mounted Police horses live in stables on Wood Street, and have frequent holidays to Bushy Park in Hampton; St James's Park has a colony of five pelicans;[3] and the city is home to twenty-four pairs of breeding peregrine falcons, the fastest animal on earth. One pair lives at the Tate Modern; in summer there's a viewpoint manned by volunteers with telescopes.

You're getting your eye in, so stop for a quick break at Lady Dinah's on Bethnal Green Road, where you can have tea with cake in a cafe full of cats[4] before stalking some bigger beasts.

If you ask at the Savoy Hotel, they will introduce you to Kaspar, their metre-tall black wooden cat who joins dinner parties when there's an unlucky 13 at the table; and in Tobacco Dock in Wapping there's a statue of a Bengal tiger confronting a nine-year old boy.[5]

J

MAP READING

Childhood Dreams shows the city as imagined by a group of children with different passions and fascinations. The layout was inspired by the children's song 'There Were Ten in the Bed'.

When you went down to Wimbledon, you used to be sure of a big surprise: a museum devoted entirely to teddy bears, in the Polka Theatre. This was the personal collection of Giles Brandreth, but Sooty, Winnie and friends migrated to Yorkshire in 2015. Today the best place to spot bears is the V&A Museum of Childhood. Look for Little Tommy Tittlemouse, whose owner James sent him a birthday card for twenty years after donating him to the museum. James died in 1986, but every year many children keep up his tradition: send Tommy a card on 24 November.

Finally, as darkness falls, peer through the railings at the sinister pet cemetery on the north edge of Hyde Park, described by George Orwell as 'perhaps the most horrid spectacle in Britain'.

---

[1] Includes real pearls.
[2] Or try Battersea Park Children's Zoo, where you can feed short-clawed otters and pot-bellied pigs and go wild in their outdoor play area.
[3] Feeding time is between 2.30 and 3pm daily. For more of London's pelicans, see p.375.
[4] Snuggle up with Mue, Biscuit, Indiana, Romeo, Donnie, Artemis, Carbonelle, Petra, Wookie, Alice and Lizzie.
[5] Read the full story on p.153.

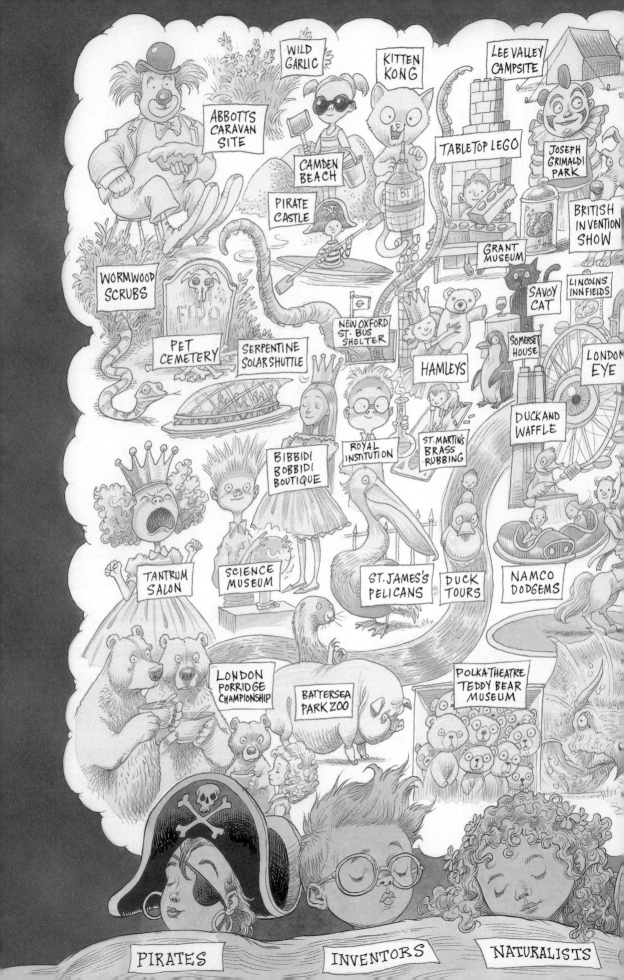

DAREDEVILS

Big thrills don't come bigger than this. Start by fuelling up on a toffee apple waffle in Duck & Waffle, at the summit of Heron Tower, the third-tallest building in London. To get there, you'll need to zoom up in their great glass elevator. [1]

Plummet back to earth, then jump on the Docklands Light Rollercoaster at Tower Gateway. Sit at the front and hold on as you rattle up and down the twisting tracks to Royal Victoria.

From there you can take the hair-raising cable car to the other side of the theme park, 90 metres above the river and swaying in the breeze.

When you touch down in North Greenwich, clip on and clamber right over the Dome with the Up at the O2 experience; you'll need to negotiate ascents and descents of 30 degrees.

The fun's not over! Go to the South Bank and show off your reverse spin skills on the Namco dodgems below County Hall, then wait at the Duck Stop for the Duck Tours log flume, the amphibian vehicle that launches in and out of the Thames.

Finally wind things down by hopping on the London Eye ferris wheel, for a relaxing spin at 0.6 mph.

CLOWNS

If you're planning to run away with the circus, a good place to start is the Vale of Health, Hampstead Heath. The caravan site on the edge of the Vale has been owned by the Abbotts family for 150 years and travelling fairground folk often stop here when they're performing in town.

To hone your circus skills beforehand, try a youth experience day of trapeze and tightrope-walking at the National Centre for Circus Arts off Hoxton Square.

Once you're a trained artiste, you'll want to attend the annual Clowns Service in Holy Trinity Church, Dalston, on the first Sunday in February. Come in make-up, wig and baggy trousers and honour the memory of Joseph Grimaldi,[2] father of clowning. While you're at the church, drop into their Clowns Museum, which has a collection of eggshells painted with clown faces to ensure that no two clowns ever use the same make-up.

Grimaldi was born on 18 December 1778 and became famous as the clown with the upside-down smile. Charles Dickens wrote his biography, and reports him saying, at his farewell performance, '[I've] jumped my last jump—filched my last oyster—boiled my last sausage and set in for retirement.'

Circuses were invented in London by Philip Astley, who used to perform with his horse in a field near Waterloo. He rode in a tight circle, which was nicknamed a 'circus', and the act became so popular he introduced jugglers and clowns and eventually set up Astley's Amphitheatre on Westminster Bridge Road.[3] Today you can aspire to perform in Zippo's, London's largest touring circus.

[1] Don't miss the country's largest private aquarium behind the reception desk.

[2] You can also honour his memory on p.339.

[3] Read about an ill-fated owner of Astley's on p.343.

EXPLORERS

Calling all explorers! Pack your rucksack and grab your compass. First you must navigate some tough terrain: hack your way through the hidden jungle of the Barbican Conservatory,[1] which is home to over 2,000 species of plants and pools of exotic fish; struggle across the sprawling desert of Camden Beach, the dunes that form on the roof of the Roundhouse in summertime; affix your crampons and claw your way up the 528 stairs to the Golden Gallery of St Paul's Cathedral; and finally, set a course for the pack ice at Somerset House in winter and traverse the arctic wastes with skates and a fibreglass penguin.

You'll need to forage for food. In May, rummage for wild garlic on Mill Hill; in September, there's good blackberrying in Wormwood Scrubs Park. Beware though, the name Wormwood Scrubs means 'snake-infested thicket'.

After lunch, Young Indiana Joneses[2] can look for archaeological clues at the London Brass Rubbing Centre in the crypt of St Martin-in-the-Fields, or you could put on your trusty marigolds and join the Thames and Field Mudlarking and Metal Detecting Society for some mudlarking on the Thames beaches at low tide (thamesandfield.com). If you're lucky, you might unearth an old coin, a pilgrim's badge or even a Roman sandal.

After a long day's exploring, you'll need to set up camp. The best family-friendly camping spot is the Lee Valley campsite near Chingford.

MONSTERS

Why are you lurking under the bed? It's time to get scary! If you're shy, stock up on monster equipment at Hoxton Street Monster Supplies, who will kit you out with boxes of cubed earwax, fang floss, tinned fear and the salt from angry tears.[3]

You're not the first monster in London. In 1959 *The Giant Behemoth*[4] emerged from the sea and destroyed large tracts of the city with its radioactive breath, and in 1970 the cute but deadly Kitten Kong flattened the BT Tower in an episode of *The Goodies*. On New Oxford Street in 2014, an augmented-reality bus shelter showed passers-by being grabbed by sewer swamp tentacles.

Why not make some new monster friends in Crystal Palace Park? Track down the life-size dinosaurs, which are marooned on their own lake island.[5]

Finally, if your creator was Dr Frankenstein, look for the brain collection in the Grant Museum on University Street and choose yourself a new one. The scientific experiment that inspired *Frankenstein* took place in Lincoln's Inn Fields, not far away: in 1803 Giovanni Aldini ran electric current through a murderer's corpse, causing it to kick its legs, punch the air and open one eye.

J

---

[1] It contains terrapins. See p.24.
[2] Older Indy fans can hunt for the Holy Grail on p.399.

[3] Monster Supplies belongs to the Ministry of Stories, who run writing and mentoring programmes for local children.
[4] This film contains the same stock screams used in *King Kong*.
[5] See p.163.

BEACONS

London can be a risky place for the poorest, most vulnerable children. But over the centuries, in the face of abandonment, child labour and uncertain futures, certain institutions have been looking out for them.

FOUNDLINGS

When a mother in dire straits gave up her child at the Foundling Hospital she was asked to leave a token – a badge, a button or a scrap of fabric – so that it would be possible to match parent to child again one day. Thomas Coram set up the institution in response to the high numbers of 'exposed and deserted young children' on London's streets. When you visit the Foundling Museum,[1] look at the display of tokens, still in the museum's possession because the families were never reunited.

BLUECOATS

The little statues of children dressed in blue on Scandrett Street in Wapping mark the separate girls and boys entrances to a charity school founded in 1695. There were bluecoat schools for poor children across the city and you can see more scholarly statuettes nearby on Raine Street and elsewhere.

LIGHTHOUSES

Looking out across London from a train window, Holmes directed Watson's attention to the tall red-brick schools. 'Lighthouses, my boy!' he declared. 'Beacons of the future! Capsules, with hundreds of bright little seeds in each, out of which will spring the wiser, better England of the future.' Today London's schools are again seen as beacons of the future after a decade of meteoric, unanticipated improvement. From 2002 to 2012, children's results shot up and there was a dramatic narrowing of the achievement gap between rich and poor. London became an unexpected success story, with researchers scrambling to understand what happened and replicate it elsewhere.

RAGGED SCHOOLS

Brush up on your grammar at the Ragged School Museum in Tower Hamlets. Primary education didn't become free and compulsory until 1891, so for much of the 19th century charity-run 'ragged schools' were the best on offer for those who, in Charles Dickens's words, were 'too ragged, wretched, filthy, and forlorn, to enter any other place'.[2] The museum is in the building that housed Dr Barnardo's ragged school. There's a recreated classroom where family lessons are held in fancy dress on the first Sunday of each month.

---

[1] There is a playground with a city farm in nearby Coram's Fields that adults may enter only if they're accompanied by children.

[2] Dickens was a vocal critic of 'the frightful neglect by the State of those whom it punishes so constantly, and whom it might, as easily and less expensively, instruct and save'.

BORRIBLES

Like Peter Pan and the Lost Boys, Borribles are children who don't age and have a disregard for adult authority. But unlike Pan and his gang, they have no Neverland to retreat to. Borribles are the runaways who never went home; they live in tribes in central London, a law unto themselves.[1] They wear woolly hats so that the police can't spot their distinctive pointed ears. If they're caught, their ears are clipped and they grow up into adults. 'It is better to die young than to be caught', goes an old Borrible saying.

Despite their fantastic premise, Michael de Larrabeiti's books are perhaps the most controversial of London's children's stories. 'Borribles are outcasts', he wrote, 'but unlike most outcasts they enjoy themselves and wouldn't be anything else'. The stories revel in the wild, self-sufficient life of these tearaway children, and celebrate their courage and loyalty. When the third Borrible book was due to appear in 1985, Collins refused to publish it, worried that it could be seen to glorify the kind of youth violence the city had just experienced in the Brixton and Tottenham riots.[2]

J

The Borribles are uncomfortably close to real life. They may have pixie ears and eternal youth, but they also have a lot in common with London's real street gangs, tight-knit groups with a powerful sense of belonging. Today London's gangs are going strong. In a parallel universe, just a few metres from the everyday lives of most other Londoners, children are selling drugs, carrying knives, and, with reasonable frequency, killing one another. The Cafe of Good Hope in Lewisham was set up as a tribute to murdered teenager Jimmy Mizen. As well as being a cafe, it serves as one of the city's designated safe havens for young people who feel in danger.[3]

Gang members live on high alert in a high-risk city, abiding by codes and boundaries other people can't see. Many gangs are named after their area (the E3 Bloods, the Kennington Crips, the Brick Lane Massive), but some names give a sense of the machismo and mystique groups want to convey: Guns and Shanks, Tell No 1, Ghetto Boys, Murderzone, All Bout Money, Dont Say Nothin, Loyal Soldiers, Easy Cash, Shankstarz. A notable exception is the now defunct PDC gang: PDC originally stood for Peel Dem Crew, but changed to Poverty Driven Children when the group converted itself into a legitimate entertainment business.

Names and numbers change all the time and nobody really knows how many people are seriously involved. The vast majority of London's young people never have anything to do with gangs,[4] but the few who do have a powerful impact on the city. Children in gangs cause real harm and are harmed in turn by their experiences. The Borribles, lurking beneath the civilised veneer of the city, provide a perfect image for the distance that exists between adults and some groups of lost children in London today.

---

[1] China Miéville calls Borribles 'tribes of children who don't need us, punky urban elves who've gone their own way'.
[2] 'The battle between the law and lawlessness is glamourised and given a status, which we cannot appear to condone [...] now that Britain has entered a new era in which this battle is a daily reality', reads a leaked letter. The book was published by Pan in 1986.
[3] There are over 600 safe havens for young people across London (citysafe.org.uk/map).
[4] Linton Kwesi Johnson blasts the tendency to generalise about young people in his poem 'It Noh Funny'. 'People sayin' dis / People sayin' dat / 'Bout di yout' af today', he writes, 'How dem causin' affray / An' it noh funny / It noh funny'.

LONDON ZOO

The city's wild side is never far away. We're going to the zoo. How about you?

SETT DESIGN

Kew Gardens is a badger stronghold and contains over 20 setts. Badgers are private, nocturnal beasts so you're unlikely to spot any. Instead you can forage for earthworms in their human-sized replica sett.

TRUNK & DISORDERLY

Stagger up the shallow steps in the basement bar of Octave on Endell Street. They were made that way for Victorian stage elephants, because this building was the animal depot for West End theatres. One day, two bulls broke loose and smashed the other pens, liberating a host of wild animals on to the streets of Soho. Go to Waterloo Station and look for a life-size chicken-wire elephant bursting through the brick wall by the entrance to the Jubilee Line.

HIPPO REPLACEMENT

In 1850, a hippo called Obasych was delivered from the Ottoman Viceroy of Egypt in exchange for a greyhound. He lived in London Zoo and inspired nationwide hippomania.[1] You can still visit an Egyptian hippo in the capital: go to the British Museum and look for a miniature blue hippo made in 1850 BC. Boost the native population by modelling a replica out of Blu-tack and leaving it nearby.

GOAT GHOST

In a little Thames-side garden at Ballast Quay, a spectral goat stands upright above a simple gravestone. He's made of beach detritus, old U-bends and bones. He commemorates the animals that died in 2001 'not of foot and mouth but of the cure for foot and mouth': those that were slaughtered by the army and burned.

TOP CAT & TAILS

While you're admiring the trilbies in Bates the Hatter[2] on Jermyn Street, doff your cap to Binks the top hat-wearing shop cat. Binks is now stuffed and smokes a cigar.

LLAMA FARM

A hop, spit and a jump from the world of high finance is the city's largest farm at Mudchute. Sheep graze in the shadow of Canary Wharf skyscrapers. Make sure you meet Boxer the llama, who can spit like a fizzing gross profit margin, and don't miss the mid-afternoon duck walk.

EX-PARROT

There's a parrot lying on its back on a plinth at the corner of King William Walk and Romney Road in Greenwich. Its head is lolling off the edge and it's not clear whether the bird is deceased, resting or pining for the fjords. This *Monument for a Dead Parrot*[3] was installed in 2009.

---

[1] The popular 'Hippopotamus Polka' was written in his honour.
[2] Find out about Bates's beaver hats on p.275.

[3] Monty Python's 'Dead Parrot' sketch was filmed in a pet shop on Caledonian Road.

URBAN BIRDING

Take the trouble out of twitching by spotting birds that can't move. Track down the rooftop vulture at the junction of Tyers Street and Laud Street in Vauxhall and the pigeon-deterring owl behind the flats on Concert Hall Approach in Waterloo.

HOLY HORSES

Saddle your steed and ride to the Horseman's Sunday ceremony, held every September at St John's Church in Hyde Park. After the morning service, the vicar jumps on a horse and leads a crowd of riders to the church, where he blesses their horses. The tradition began in 1967 to protest against the proposed closure of the Hyde Park stables.

THE RIGHT STUFF

Walruses have loose wrinkly skin. The taxidermists who prepared the walrus[1] in the Horniman Museum had never seen a live specimen so they just kept stuffing until the creature was completely full. The bloated mammal has a surprised expression and is now the museum's most popular exhibit.

ONE HUMP OR TWO

For a budget camel ride, trek to Orientalist Carpets and Rugs on Highgate Road. Outside sits a noble ungulate, glorious in its faded concrete. Hop over the railing for a quick perch.

A WHOPPING TIGER

Enter Tobacco Dock[2] by Porter's Walk and look for a snarling Bengali beast, reared up with a raised paw. On this spot in 1857, a little boy stroked an escaped tiger and was promptly knocked down and carried off in the big cat's maw. Charles Jamrach, the German menagerie-owner, gave chase and pulled the boy from the jaws of death.

J

---

[1] Hands off. See p.276.   [2] For more on Tobacco Dock, see p.256.

GROWING UP

Even the Lost Boys eventually returned from Neverland and grew up: Curly, Nibs and the twins took office jobs; Tootles became a judge. If childhood is dragging and you can't wait for adulthood, here are some ways to accelerate the process.

ENTER THE WORKPLACE

It's not fair that grown-ups get all the fun of going to work. Leave London and move to Kidzania, a hyper-realistic child-sized city at the heart of the Westfield White City shopping centre. You'll be electronically tagged[1] and unleashed on a mini-metropolis where you'll experience the thrills of working life. You change career every 20 minutes, choosing between being a surgeon, a department store manager, a chocolatier and an air conditioning technician, among others. Payment is in kidZos, the district's currency, which you can splash in the gift shop.[2] Kidzania would make the perfect setting for a dystopian children's story; its slightly sinister slogan is 'get ready for a better world'.

GIVE AWAY YOUR TOYS

When the time comes to put away childish things, consider donating your toys to the Museum of Childhood in Bethnal Green, which is constantly on the lookout for present-day playthings that will interest future generations. At the moment they're particularly interested in 'computer games and digital technology; nursery and childcare equipment; and school uniforms'. In fact the museum updates its displays so frequently that by the time you turn 18 you'll be able to visit and see the toys of your youth displayed as historical curiosities. Outside the cabinets, there are activity stations where children and nostalgic adults can play with toys from across time, including stickle bricks, rocking horses and Lego. Toy lovers should also attend the museum's free summer festival.

BECOME AN ART SNOB

Tired of being patronised with finger paints and fuzzy felt? If you're a sophisticated sprog, indulge your taste for contemporary art at the Abbey Leisure Centre in Barking and Dagenham. You can climb all over a monochrome soft play area created by Turner Prize-nominated artist Marvin Gaye Chetwynd. Her design was inspired by an ancient wooden idol found in Dagenham in 1922. According to Chetwynd, 'he's not that bling as idols go', so she decided to wallpaper the room with cosmic symbols and transform the idol into a robot.

GEOFFREY CHAUCER

AGED 4
For mo Chaucerie, seken page 246

ELIZABETH I.

AGED 7
Find good Queen Bess on page 178

IGNATIUS SANCHO

AGED 8
Ignatius is disturbed by a riot on page 88

---

[1] Adults can track your location in the Parents Room, which has a bar.

[2] 'Outside KidZania London, kidZos have no value', the website warns.

REGRESSING

Growing up has its perks, but it's not always all it's cracked up to be. If you're an adult bored of age and responsibility, here are some ways to regress.

ADA LOVELACE

AGED 10
The Enchantress of Numbers is on page 117

MARIE LLOYD

AGED 6
Get your knees up with Marie on page 90

JOHN BETJEMAN

AGED 5
Join the poet on a train to the suburbs
on pages 406–7

SLIDE DOWN THE SLIPPERY SLOPE

Although the slide inside Anish Kapoor's *Orbit* tower is being billed as a 'major new art installation', there's no disguising the fact that this controversial sculpture is simply being converted into a massive adult helter-skelter. Modern-art connoisseurs will zip around 12 polished metal loops at 15 mph.

BE READ TO

Pin Drop's evening story sessions began as a reaction to the fact that we cease to be read aloud to when we become adults. Pin Drop invites authors to read their own, and their favourite, short stories in handsome rooms around the city (pindropstudio.com).

PLAY POOH STICKS

Few games are as gloriously childish and skill-free as Pooh Sticks. Grab your favourite twig and head to the white bridge in Morden Hall Park, a National Trust property at the southern end of the Northern Line. This low bridge over the Wandle was recently voted the second-best Pooh Sticks location in the UK.[1]

WATCH KIDS TV

Put on your tweediest jacket and drop in to the BFI Mediatheque[2] where, among the archival footage and art films, they have an impressive range of classic children's television programmes. Take a seat among the film studies students and adopt a serious expression as you work your way through the back catalogues of *Blue Peter*, *Knightmare* and *Grange Hill*.

FORMER CHILDREN

Lean down to look at the child-height graffiti scratched on to the brickwork of the Boundary Estate[3] on Navarre Street. From the 1940s to the 1960s, local children carved their names and ages on to the walls. Some even proudly inscribed the time of the crime. 'RICHARD MILLS THURSDAY 19TH APRIL 1950 3:30PM', reads one. The mark makers have long since grown up, but a fragment of their childhood remains on an East London side street.

J

---

[1] If you're feeling competitive, attend the World Pooh Stick Championships, which are held annually up the Thames in Oxfordshire. The best Pooh Sticks location is Sheepwash Bridge in Derbyshire.

[2] See p.169.
[3] See p.268.

DEAD ENDS

Not every horse can be a winner, however, and there have been as many dead ends as discoveries.

PERPETUAL MOTION

In the early 17th century, Robert Fludd designed several perpetual motion machines while living on Fenchurch Street. Most of his designs involve water tanks emptying and powering Archimedes screws that carry the water back to the tank. Although it violates the first and second Laws of Thermodynamics, the dream of perpetual motion is still alive in London: in 2007, an Irish technology company called Steorn unveiled a device called the 'Orbo' at the London Kinetica Museum in Hackney. They claimed it would generate 'free, clean, and constant energy'. It didn't.[1] Visit the museum to see other exhibits that contribute to 'evolutionary processes and universal exploration'.

HOLLOW EARTH

The astronomer Edmund Halley is best known for correctly predicting the reappearance of Halley's Comet in 1759.[2] He was also an exponent of the 'Hollow Earth Theory', which imagines the earth as a set of concentric shells, separated by luminous atmospheres. The best place to envisage this theory is in the lobby of Deutsche Bank on Great Winchester Street, which houses a hollowed-out stainless steel sphere. The reflections inside the sphere flip the foyer on its head; Deutsche Bank says that Anish Kapoor's sculpture, called *Turning the World Upside Down III*, stands as 'a warning of the fragility of ideas'.

PHLOGISTON

Drop into the Grand Connaught Rooms on Great Queen Street. This was once the location of the Freemasons Tavern, where the scientist Joseph Priestley

attempted to prove the existence of 'phlogiston'. Phlogiston was a hypothetical fire element thought to be present in combustible materials, but Priestley's demonstration failed when some phosphorous caught light and exploded his glass lamp.[3] Phlogiston has since been discredited.[4]

MIASMA

'All smell is disease', stated social reformer Edwin Chadwick in 1846. Until the 1880s, it was widely believed that diseases were spread through the smells in noxious air, or 'miasma'.[5] An increased understanding of germs superseded this theory of disease, but if you do notice a nasty niff you can call your local council. Since the Environmental Protection Act of 1990 they are obliged to investigate 'complaints about odour'.

K

PHRENOLOGY

Labelled ceramic heads are a common sight in London's antique markets. Phrenology was a pseudoscience propounded by the German physiologist Franz Josef Gall, who claimed that brain qualities could be assessed through external examination. The Science Museum has a phrenological bust of Gall himself in its collection.

RELATIVITY

Albert Einstein is famous for his theory of general relativity, published in 1915.[6] Next time you pass Imperial College in South Kensington, spare a thought for Professor Alfred Whitehead. In 1922, he published *The Principle of Relativity with Applications to Physical Science* proposing an alternative theory of relativity. It has not been adopted.

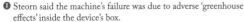

[1] Steorn said the machine's failure was due to adverse 'greenhouse effects' inside the device's box.
[2] The comet's next appearance will be 28 July 2061.
[3] William Blake satirised this incident in *An Island in the Moon*, in which a scientist called Inflammable Gas accidentally cracks a flask of boghouse fart and releases its pestilence.
[4] Find something that was invented in the Freemasons Tavern on p.224.
[5] Robert Boyle formulated the theory in his *Suspicions about the Hidden Realities of the Air*. For more noxious air, see p.58.
[6] Einstein visited London in 1921 and laid flowers on the grave of Isaac Newton in Westminster Abbey.

A COLLECTION OF COLLECTIONS

'Knowledge does not keep any better than fish,' wrote Professor Alfred Whitehead. In 2009, University College London's museums held an exhibition called 'Disposal?', which explored the tension between growing a collection and culling items to keep it manageable. The exhibition featured an assortment of borderline specimens, including a set of plastic dinosaurs, a chunk of rock used in a Nobel Prize-winning experiment, and a picnic hamper loosely connected to Agatha Christie. Visitors were invited to vote on which of the five objects should go and which deserved to stay.[1]

London is a constantly swelling *Wunderkammer*; its museums and archives are testimony to the hoarding impulse of collectors. As well as objects of undisputable importance, each collection contains artefacts whose charm derives from their oddity or banality. In 2011, the curator of the Grant Museum discovered a plum in the museum store, preserved in a jar with a very narrow neck. The plum's scientific significance, and why it was added to UCL's zoology collection, is a mystery.

THE ARK ①

The contents of the Tradescant family's 'Ark' in South Lambeth were bequeathed to Elias Ashmole[2] and taken to Oxford, where the collection forms the basis of the Ashmolean Museum. A cabinet of curiosities with encyclopaedic ambitions, the Ark was the first public museum in London. In 1634 one visitor described the Ark as a place 'where a Man might in one daye behold and collecte into one place more curiosities than hee should see if hee spent all his life in Travell'. Another described notable artefacts

---

CABINET OF CURIOSITY

There are very few labels in the British Museum's Enlightenment Gallery. You can see shells and rocks and rare minerals and ivories and statues and strange inscriptions and peculiar early tools and early scientific apparatus, and mermaids and wonderful things that were collected by scientists as the disciplines of archaeology and anthropology were beginning.

— *Irving Finkel*

including a 'squirrel like a fish', a cheese 'changed into stone' and 'the passion of Christ carved very daintily on a plumstone'. In 2017, the lost Ark is scheduled to return to Lambeth: a new Tradescant Ark gallery will open in the Garden Museum[3] with artefacts from the original collection.

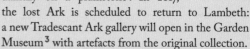

THE HOLOPHUSIKON ②

The Holophusikon,[4] which opened on Leicester Square in 1775, has been lost forever. Sir Ashton Lever spent years gathering 27,000 items, acquiring many from Captain Cook's voyages around the world. Visitors were particularly struck by the room full of 'curious monkies and monsters', stuffed and arranged 'in human attitudes'. Lever's museum was highly popular, but his expenditure on new items outstripped takings on the door and he came close to ruin. He offered the collection for sale to the British Museum; they declined, and he disposed of the museum by lottery in 1784. The lucky winner ran the Holophusikon until 1806, when it was auctioned off. Richard Cuming was present at every day of the 13-week sale and bought 58 items, including a tabooing wand brought back from Haiti by Captain Cook. Cuming eventually built up his own eccentric collection of 100,000 artefacts, which was bequeathed to the people of Southwark. The Cuming Museum opened in 1906 but closed after a severe fire in 2013. Most of the collection survived unharmed but the museum is not due to reopen for several years.

---

① The toy dinosaurs now have their own shelf in the Grant Museum.

② For more Ashmole, see p.361; for moles see p.324.

③ The Garden Museum is housed in the deconsecrated church of St Mary-at-Lambeth. The Ashmole and Tradescant tombs are in the former churchyard.

④ Meaning all (*holo*) nature (*phusikon*).

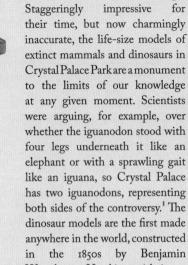

UNKNOWN CREATURES ③

Staggeringly impressive for their time, but now charmingly inaccurate, the life-size models of extinct mammals and dinosaurs in Crystal Palace Park are a monument to the limits of our knowledge at any given moment. Scientists were arguing, for example, over whether the iguanodon stood with four legs underneath it like an elephant or with a sprawling gait like an iguana, so Crystal Palace has two iguanodons, representing both sides of the controversy.[1] The dinosaur models are the first made anywhere in the world, constructed in the 1850s by Benjamin Waterhouse Hawkins, with input from Sir Richard Owen, the man who came up with the name 'dinosaurs', meaning 'terrible lizards'. To celebrate Hawkins's creations, Owen hosted a dinner party inside the massive mould of the straight-legged iguanodon.

DISTANT TREASURES ④

To this day, pilgrims with scallop shells walk for weeks to reach the Cathedral of Santiago de Compostela in the north-west corner of Spain. Less energetic supplicants can visit the cathedral's Portico de la Gloria in South Kensington: an enormous replica of the structure stands at one end of the V&A Museum's Cast Courts, among other plaster copies of great works of European sculpture. The casts are marvellous recreations of the originals, but are also astounding in their own right: examine the 1866 cast of the Portico and consider the technical ingenuity required to execute such a copy. Walter Benjamin wrote that 'in even the most perfect reproduction, one thing is lacking: the here and now of the work of art'. As they age, these meticulous imitations quietly refute his claim.

PERISHABLE SPECIMENS ⑤

Marine invertebrates are notoriously hard to preserve. Their saggy structures make them difficult to display in jars and they quickly lose their colour. In the 19th century, a Czech glass-eye manufacturer developed an ingenious solution. Go to the Grant Museum and look for the Blaschka glass model collection: perfect facsimiles of sea cucumbers, cephalopods and sea anemones made out of glass. The models were used for teaching in schools of zoology and were considered 'an artistic marvel in the field of science and a scientific marvel in the field of art'. The Blaschkas did not pass on their techniques and, with the advent of underwater photography, their approach has not been replicated.

MYTHICAL TAXIDERMY ⑥

Frederick Horniman used profits from the family tea business to build his collection and founded the Horniman Museum in Forest Hill in 1901. It is particularly well known for its taxidermy and ethnographic collections. Look for the golden, seated figure of Buddha on a lotus flower in the Centenary Gallery, and the Japanese Monkey Fish: a homemade merman made from papier mâché and fish bits.

K ——

DYING VOICES ⑦

Cecil Sharp collected his first folk song at a friend's house in Somerset in 1903 and dedicated the rest of his life to transcribing hundreds more before they vanished from the cultural memory of the places he travelled. Root through the vast folk music and dance archive in the library of Cecil Sharp House. Search for Sharp's first song, 'Seeds of Love', and then learn it on your hurdy-gurdy, lute or shawm.

MAP READING

A Collection of Collections *presents London as a cabinet of curiosities. Each item represents a different collection or museum in the city. Spilled water indicates the route of the Thames.*

---

❶ In fact paleobiologists now think iguanodons walked on their two back feet.

A COLLECTION
of collections

MUSEUM OF MAN (8)

Pharmaceuticals magnate Henry Wellcome assembled the most tantalising of London's collections. His aim for the 1.5 million objects he amassed was to create a 'Museum of Man' that would illuminate humanity's development and allow 'the study of the roots and foundations of things'. The sheer quantity of items, the breadth of their scope, and the fact that Wellcome didn't filter out incomplete, duplicate or unexceptional pieces meant that the task was ultimately unrealised and much of Wellcome's collection went to existing museums after his death in 1936. Visit the Medicine Man exhibition at the Wellcome Collection on Euston Road for a flavour of his extraordinary hoard. Look for Wellcome's life mask, a plaster cast of his face made in the early 1900s, flecked with hairs from his substantial moustache.

ANTIQUITIES (9)

Those with an interest in vintage fashion should visit the Tarkhan dress in the Petrie Museum of Egyptian Archaeology. The garment is thought to be around 5,000 years old. It was unearthed by Flinders Petrie in 1913 at the Tarkhan cemetery south of Cairo. The tattered frock was overlooked until 1977 when it was found in a pile of linen and identified as one of the oldest dresses in the world. A detailed sewing pattern is available on the Petrie Museum website for those who wish to stitch their own.[1]

MECHANICAL CABARET (10)

Visit Novelty Automation on Princeton Street and bring a pocketful of 10p pieces. This collection of eccentric, homemade arcade machines was assembled by Tim Hunkin.[2] Take a magic carpet holiday, race your partner to a divorce or pay a sinister puppet to massage your foot.

KAMMER CHAMELEON (11)

'No attempt is made at classification and comprehensiveness' in Viktor Wynd's Museum of Curiosities, a Hackney basement that wilfully offers 'an incoherent vision of the world'. Look for dodo bones, Happy Meal Toys, an eight-legged lamb, a furby, and a sealed box containing 'some of the darkness that Moses brought upon the Egyptians'. A pop-up menagerie makes regular appearances, at which you can pet a python, fondle a frog and cuddle Gizmo, the Veiled Chameleon.[3]

BABEL (12)

If London is the Modern Babylon,[4] its hanging gardens are in Kew. The Royal Botanic Gardens is the collection in present-day London with the most Babelian ambitions, seeking to become a comprehensive repository of all the plant life on earth. Visit their titan arum in the Princess of Wales conservatory. Known to some as the 'corpse flower', because it emits such a hideous smell, this mammoth plant can go years without blooming. When it does, its single flower grows over 2.5 metres tall and lasts for just two days.[5]

---

[1] The dress is joined selvedge to selvedge down the left-hand side with a weft fringe.

[2] See Hunkin's timepiece on p.314.

[3] For more Wynd, see p.111 and p.338.

[4] As Prime Minister Benjamin Disraeli called it, in his novel *Tancred*.

[5] The last flowering was in 2009.

SPECTACLES (13)

Pop along to the MusEYEum at the Royal College of Optometrists, Craven Street. Entrance is free, but you need to book in advance. Amongst their collection of scissor spectacles, folding eyeglasses, pince-nez, lorgnettes, magnifiers, quizzing glasses and monocles, you'll discover spectacles belonging to Samuel Johnson and Ronnie Corbett, and a dazzling selection of porcelain eyebaths.

MATERIALS (14)

Muscle wire, fish-scale plastic, deranged sticky tape, self-healing concrete, breathable chocolate and yellow quantum dots are just a few of the items in the Materials Library on Malet Place. Visit on one of their monthly open days.

TEETH (15)

Walrus ivory makes mediocre dentures. The finest synthetic gnashers in 19th-century London contained real human teeth, some gleaned from soldiers who died at the Battle of Waterloo. Find a set of Waterloo Teeth in the British Dental Association Museum on Wimpole Street.

BUTTERFLIES (16)

Butterfly collecting in London has a baleful past. The first Society of Aurelians (lepidopterists) emerged in the early 18th century and met weekly at the Swan Tavern on Exchange Alley until the Great Cornhill Fire obliterated their collection. The members were so downcast that the group dissolved. The second Society of Aurelians was instituted in 1762, before disbanding 'owing to dissension among its members'. In 1801, the third Society of Aurelians was founded. They broke up in 1806 due to the unwillingness of members to donate personal specimens to the society's collections. Grab a net and consider founding a fourth Society of Aurelians.[1]

SHIPS (17)

James Henry Pullen was known as 'the genius of Earlswood Asylum' and is believed to have had savant syndrome. He became a master carpenter while at the institution and created extraordinary scale models of ships. In 1862, he built a 40-gun man-of-war inspired by a picture on a handkerchief, and in 1872 he completed a replica of Brunel's *Great Eastern*[2] paddle steamer. You can visit the collection of Pullen's ships in the Langdon Down Museum of Learning Difficulty in Teddington. Most intriguing are his fantastical vessels: look for the 'Mystic representation of the World as a Ship', an ebony-hulled State Barge he designed as an imperial craft for Queen Victoria.

SPURS (18)

Horace Walpole's eccentric antiquarian collection included several royal mementoes, including James I's gloves, King William's spurs and a lock of Edward IV's hair.[3]

DOGS (19)

The Kennel Club on Clarges Street contains the largest collection of canine portraiture in Europe. Visit on weekdays by appointment and look for Sir Edwin Landseer's painting of Bob, the shipwrecked dog who lived on the Thames Waterfront and saved 23 people from drowning.

TOTEMS (20)

Sigmund Freud acquired an impressive personal collection of ancient figurines, fragments and amulets. You can see them around the study in his house museum on Maresfield Gardens. Examine the inspirational Baboon of Thoth on his desk: Freud would stroke this marble monkey god while he was thinking.

SEWING MACHINES (21)

The London Sewing Machine Museum contains 600 appliances, from the very first Singer onwards. The museum is a labour of love, assembled by Ray Rushton over 50 years, and contains a replica of his father's second-hand sewing-machine shop front. This free museum is situated above the Wimbledon Sewing Machine Company on Balham High Road and opens on the first Saturday of each month.

SELF-PLAYING INSTRUMENTS (22)

An orchestrion is a single machine that generates the sound of an entire orchestra. Hear orchestrions, player pianos, whirlitzers, music boxes and self-playing violins at the Musical Museum, a collection of self-playing instruments and music rolls on Brentford High Street.

K

---

❶ Catch butterflies on p.99.
❷ See p.183.

❸ Admire Walpole's dispersed *Wunderkabinett* on p.118.

BIBLIO-TREK

The British Library on Euston Road is the largest in the world, with over 170 million catalogue items. It adds six miles of shelving every year to cope with its ever-expanding collection. Other libraries, however, cater for research topics that are more niche.

WELLCOME
In the Wellcome Library's Reading Room you can relax on Freud's couch while wearing a straitjacket. The room is a library-gallery hybrid, with objects, books and activities designed to spark the imagination. The Library's collection includes a sinister 16th-century tome on virginity bound in a 'portion of female skin'.

DR WILLIAMS
A Gothic entrance on Gordon Square leads to the dark wooden interior of Dr Williams's Library. Leaf through Roger Morrice's *Entring Book*, a lively diary from the late 17th century, which describes coffee houses, stage plays and the expansion of London.

WARBURG
The Warburg Institute library on Woburn Square specialises in the 'History of Ideas', and its books are organised under the categories Image, Word, Orientation and Action. Stroll the open-access shelves past sections labelled 'Magic Mirrors', 'Amulets' and 'The Evil Eye'.

WIENER
Among the one million items in the Holocaust archive at the Wiener Library on Russell Square is a terrifying board game called *Juden Raus!* ('Jews Out!'). This is the world's oldest library of material relating to the Holocaust.

WOMEN
The Women's Library, inside the LSE Library on Portfolio Street, archives women's histories. Download their Women's Walks app, which geolocates archive materials as you walk around London.

ST BRIDE
The St Bride printing and graphic arts library on Bride Lane hosts regular letterpress printing workshops.[1]

LONDON METROPOLITAN ARCHIVE
Ask to see the 'hairy book' at the London Metropolitan Archive in Clerkenwell, the City of London's trove of texts, images, maps and films relating to the history of London. This volume of ecclesiastical manuscripts was bound in the 13th century with untanned deerskin and is still covered with long, silky hair.

SENATE HOUSE
My favourite location in London is the Goldsmiths Reading Room in the Senate House Library. I wrote most of my PhD there and I used to love the way the wind would whistle through the glass above us as the readers shivered and typed furiously together.
— *Bradley Garrett*

ST PAUL'S
The hidden library of St Paul's Cathedral is on the triforium level behind the south-west tower.[2] Carved in stone outside are the words *Faciendi plures libros nullus est finis* ('Of making many books there is no end').

---

[1] See p.159.

[2] Access to the wood-panelled sanctuary is by prior appointment only on Mondays, Tuesdays and Friday afternoons.

168

BISHOPSGATE

The Bishopsgate Institute was founded in 1895 as a home for 'ideas and debate', and its library has books on socialism, cooperation and protest. It also houses Irving Finkel's Great Diary Project, which is currently collecting as many diaries as possible in order to preserve the 'ups and downs of human existence' (thegreatdiaryproject.co.uk).[1]

PICTURE RESEARCH

The Rotherhithe Picture Research Library on St Marychurch Street is a collection of scrapbooks, arranged by subject and filled with eclectic visual material clipped from postcards, magazine illustrations, bookplates and photographs. This free-access collection is housed in a low-ceilinged room built from the reclaimed timbers of 18th-century ships.[2]

K

BEYOND BOOKS

BLOOMS

Queen Mary's Rose Garden in Regent's Park is London's largest collection of roses. There are more than 12,000, with examples of nearly every rose variety. Try to spot 'Royal Parks', a strain unique to this garden.

FILM

You can access the entire British Film Institute National Archive in the Mediatheque at the BFI Southbank. Try *Borderline* (2005), an Escher-inspired experimental film, in which cars travel vertically around London and iconic architecture shape-shifts.[3]

LIQUOR

Soho has two superior liquor libraries: Gerry's and Milroy's. Gerry's Wines and Spirits on Old Compton Street is crammed to the gunnels with hand-labelled bottles of all colours and shapes. You are welcome to sample before you buy. Milroy's on Greek Street is London's comprehensive whisky emporium: drop in for a dram of Jura or Talisker.

MUSIC

The Westminster Music Library on Buckingham Palace Road has orchestral sets and soloist's scores available for loan. There is a digital piano so you can test unusual bassoon parts.

FANS

Touch your finger to the tip of your fan, and your message will be clear to your prospective amour: 'I wish to speak with you.' If someone touches their fan at you while you're visiting the Fan Museum in Greenwich, you could respond either by holding yours over your left ear ('I wish to get rid of you') or slowly drawing it across your cheek ('I want you').

---

❶ You can bequeath your own diary to the project and specify a privacy period during which public access will be forbidden.

❷ There is also a free cinema club on Tuesday evenings.
❸ Watch something more juvenile on p.155.

LIVERY

SINCE THE MIDDLE AGES, Londoners have sought to protect the 'art and mystery' of their professions by banding together in unions and professional networks. In the Middle Ages, some of these associations were formalised as guilds, and these in turn developed into 'livery companies' with royal charters.

Today there are 110 livery companies in the City of London. Many of them have fallen by the wayside over the years: the Woodmongers, Silkthrowers, Maltmen, Silkmen, Shivers and Pursers have all been disbanded, as have the Combmakers, Hatband Makers, Longbow String Makers and Horse Rubbers. In their wake have come a new breed of worshipful companies: the Information Technologists, International Bankers, Tax Advisors and Security Professionals.

Liverymen[1] are still responsible for electing the sheriffs and the Lord Mayor of the City of London Corporation. In 1130, a hundred years before the Magna Carta was sealed, King Henry I granted the City of London a charter confirming that 'all the men of London shall be quit and free [...] from all toll and passage and lestage, and all other customs'. In effect, the City of London became an offshore tax haven at the heart of the capital.

The City's status is the result of a 'simple formula', in the words of journalist Nicholas Shaxson: 'over centuries, sovereigns and governments have sought City loans, and in exchange the City has extracted privileges and freedoms from rules and laws'. Despite frequent calls for reform, the Lord Mayor, the Guildhall and the livery companies continue to thrive, as they have done for almost a thousand years.

If a livery company doesn't already exist for your profession, you could campaign to create a new one.[2] You may end up wielding extraordinary powers.

LORD MAYOR

When I was elected an alderman for the Ward of Candlewick in 2007 I knew the role went back to Saxon times, but I was even more conscious of the weight of history when I was elected the 686th Lord Mayor, a role that began in 1189.[3] I was also conscious that as one of the four great global financial centres, London owes a great deal to its history. I loved to explain that our deep pools of capital and primary and secondary markets began by people getting together in coffee shops like Lloyds of London. — *Dame Fiona Woolf*

---

[1] This term is used to refer to both men and women.
[2] The latest addition, the Worshipful Company of Arts Scholars, was constituted in 2014.

[3] Dame Fiona was the second woman ever to be elected Lord Mayor.

THE LIVERY

Liveries are exclusive uniforms that denote a rank or position in society.

BEARSKINS

Foot Guards from the Household Division stand to attention outside Buckingham Palace, wearing their tall bearskin caps.[1] Despite considerable opposition from animal-welfare groups, the caps are still made by Patey Hats on Connaught Street from the skins of Canadian bears. Regular bearskins are made from the fur of the black bear; officers' hats are made from the more lustrous fur of the female brown bear, dyed black.

BEEFEATERS

The Yeoman Warders at the Tower of London usually wear an 'undress' dark-blue uniform with red trimmings. On state occasions they wear 'Tudor State Dress', an extremely uncomfortable red-and-gold livery.

PENSIONERS

Within the Royal Hospital Chelsea, Chelsea Pensioners are encouraged to wear a blue uniform with a peaked 'shako' hat. Outside the Hospital they wear a scarlet coat, and a tricorn hat for official occasions. Just inside the London Gate of the Royal Hospital you can see a model pensioner sitting on a bench in his scarlet uniform.

THE LIVER

PRESERVED

Go to the Hunterian Museum on Lincoln's Inn Fields and examine the collection of 18th-century human livers in the Crystal Gallery, bay 104, prepared by John Hunter himself.

PLUCKED

Find Prometheus enchained in the V&A Museum.[2] The Titan was punished for stealing fire from the gods by being bound to Mount Kazbeck and having his liver torn out every day by an eagle.[3]

PROPHETIC

Memorise the clay liver tablet in the British Museum.[4] This is a diagram for prospective haruspices learning the art of hepatomancy: liver divination. Once you have the basics, buy a pack of fresh lambs' livers and scan them for omens

PASSIONATE

Call your lover liver. In late Greek physiology, the liver was thought to generate dark emotions such as anger, jealousy and greed, but in Iranian slang, liver (*jigar*) means sexy, and in Zulu the word for liver is the same as the word for courage (*isibindi*). Plato thought the liver was the seat of the soul.

PAN-FRIED

Try the calf's liver at Vasco & Piero's Pavilion Restaurant on Poland Street, prepared with sage and sautéed cabbage; alternatively, supplement your diet with iron-rich Norwegian cod liver oil from Planet Organic on Tottenham Court Road.

PISSED

The liver doesn't cope well with drink: the chemistry required to break down alcohol damages its tissue, and sustained drinking prevents it repairing itself. The London Liver Centre on Tooley Street deals with all liver afflictions.

---

[1] A bearskin should not be confused with a busby. The smaller busby is worn by the Royal Horse Artillery.

[2] Sculpture room 22, case FS.

[3] The liver is the only human organ that can regenerate naturally. For another Titan, see p.1.

[4] Ancient Mesopotamia gallery 56, case 22.

THE JOB LADDER

WORKHOUSES

The Cinema Museum is housed in the former administration block of the Lambeth Workhouse on Dugard Way in Kennington. Stand in front of the cabinet of Charlie Chaplin memorabilia and imagine Chaplin as a seven-year-old boy, arriving at this very workhouse in 1896 with a feeling of 'forlorn bewilderment', separated from his mother and having his hair shaved off.[1] Workhouses were, in Roy Porter's words, the 'favoured official weapon for reinforcing social discipline', from 1601, when parishes were made responsible for those unable to work, until their abolition in 1930.

THE DOLE

Today every child in the UK is presented with a National Insurance number when they turn 16, and regular payments 'insure' a citizen of working age against unemployment. But the dole only assists with the financial side of unemployment. If you have time, you could volunteer for Community Links, an East London charity (community-links. org), which has six cross-generational community hubs designed to build the confidence and skills of those who are unemployed: the garden at Play, Sow and Grow on Gay Road, for instance, has vegetable plots to maintain and chickens to care for.

JOBCENTRES

If you're looking for a job, a good place to start would be one of the 93 jobcentres across London. Alternatively, the Princes Trust offers 'Get Into' courses across London that guide you through the process of beginning a specific career path (princes-trust.org.uk). Women Like Us supports women to continue working after they've had children (womenlikeus.org.uk).

THE APPRENTICE

Can you pitch, sell and blag? Work for a stallholder at the Chatsworth Road Sunday Market in Clapton. This is where Lord Alan Sugar cut his teeth selling shampoo, before he began giving entrepreneurial exhibitionists the finger. Budding apprentices may wish to consider some of London's more unusual apprenticeships, including ballet-shoe apprentice at the Royal Opera House, jewellery apprentice at the Goldsmiths' Centre and apprentice gardener with the Royal Parks. The Camden Society manages six social enterprise cafes that offer apprenticeships specifically for the disabled (thecamdensociety. co.uk).

INDUSTRIAL ACTION

Each year the Living Wage Foundation calculates an hourly cost of living: the London Living Wage in 2015 was £9.15, but the minimum wage was actually just £6.50. Next time you pass the old Bryant & May match factory in Bow,[2] think of the 1888 Matchgirls' Strike, when the entire workforce of women and teenage girls protested against their slim wages and exposure to dangerous chemicals.[3] The 'Spirit of Brotherhood' sculpture outside the Trades Union Congress HQ on Great Russell Street symbolises the power of solidarity and industrial action.

[1] Charlie and his half-brother Sydney were allowed to see their mother once a week; at their first visit she brought coconut candy and stroked the boys' cropped heads.

[2] Now a gated community. See p.135.

[3] The white phosphorous in matches caused 'phossy jaw', gangrene of the jawbone.

HIVE OF INDUSTRY

The beehive has often been used as an economic metaphor. If you stand in Change Alley and look upwards, for example, you'll see a large masonry beehive that was once the symbol of Lloyds Bank.[1]

In Bernard Mandeville's poem *The Grumbling Hive* (1705), a spacious beehive 'well stock'd with Bees' is greedy and prosperous. When the bees become thrifty, however, the hive fails and thousands of bees die. Mandeville's moral anticipates Adam Smith's *Wealth of Nations* by 70 years: 'Bare Virtue' is a disastrous economic policy; society must consume to prosper.[2]

THE WORSHIPFUL COMPANY OF BARBERS (17)[3]

The Worshipful Barbers had many talents in the Middle Ages. As well as cutting, dressing and shaving hair, they also performed surgery, removed earwax, lanced boils, leeched wounds, cupped fire and extracted teeth. The red-and-white striped barber's pole still symbolises their twin profession: red for surgery, white for barbering. They haven't stopped diversifying today: The Pet Spa, on Fulham Road, is London's premier pooch pampering salon, where your hound can have her nails trimmed, ears cleansed and hair shampooed.

THE WORSHIPFUL COMPANY OF BLACKSMITHS (40)

'By Hammer and Hand All Arts Do Stand' goes the Blacksmiths' Company motto, and you can still hear the clink and hiss of hot metal in Ravenscourt Park. Will Barker runs his own smithy there. Book a one-day course and he'll have you bending, punching and welding, and you'll walk away with a handmade fire poker.

THE WORSHIPFUL COMPANY OF BREWERS (14)

The patron saint of the Brewers is St Thomas à Becket. The story goes that St Thomas's father was taken prisoner by pirates while trading off the North African coast. A Moorish maiden fell in love with him and helped him escape, then followed him to London and married him. This tale explains why the Company's coat of arms is topped by a black woman with flowing blonde hair and sheaves of barley in each hand. Today London's breweries are still hopping. Meantime of Greenwich has recently become a mainstay of the capital's pumps, and is best sampled in the Tasting Rooms at their brewery off Blackwall Lane.

THE WORSHIPFUL COMPANY OF BRODERERS (48)

The Broderers' Company, specialists in embroidery, is the only livery company to have a 'Master's Song', sung solo at each dinner. The chorus goes: 'So give us your plain dealing fellows, / Who never from honesty shrink, / Not thinking of all they shall tell us, / But telling us all that they think.' For your own hand-embroidery needs, apply to Hawthorne & Heaney, who will monogram just about anything. Or do it yourself in their beginners' classes at their Islington studio on Cobble Lane.

BRODERERS

MAP READING

Hive of Industry *takes the beehive as a metaphor for the professions of London, depicting a mixture of real and imagined livery companies. The livery companies observe a strict order of precedence (indicated here by the numbers in brackets after the name of each company). The design was inspired by George Cruikshank's* British Bee Hive *(1840) and John Leighton's hexagonal plans for the city.[4] Look for the Queen Bee in Buckingham Palace and the flock of hybrid pigeon-bees.*

---

❶ Before the bank adopted the black horse. The headquarters of Lloyds Bank were located here until 2003.
❷ Maynard Keynes ponders this issue on p.198.

❸ The number after each guild's name denotes its position in the companies' order of precedence, which is roughly based on the order in which they were founded.
❹ See p.93.

THE WORSHIPFUL COMPANY OF COOKS (35)

The Cooks' Company is the smallest livery company with only 75 liverymen, and they are unusual in having welcomed freemaiden members since their inception. Today, as celebrity chefs experiment with molecular gastronomy, spare a thought for the flame-grilled renaissance roasting team at Hampton Court Palace. The Tudor palace serves authentic roasts every day of the summer months, prepared over roaring fires in Henry VIII's enormous kitchens. Watch the roasters turning massive joints on back-breaking spits before tearing off a hot haunch for yourself.

THE WORSHIPFUL COMPANY OF CORDWAINERS (27)

Cordwainers worked white *cordovan* leather from Spain, specialising in fine footwear. You can find a sculpture of a cordwainer bending over a boot on Watling Street in the City. Not far away, in her Shoreditch studio on Christina Street, Áine Hanson makes a range of soft-leather goods, from handbags to whippet collars.

THE WORSHIPFUL COMPANY OF CUTLERS (18)

Cutlers produce knives, swords, razors and scissors; their 19th-century livery hall on Newgate Street has an external terracotta frieze illustrating the knife-making process. The tradition is kept alive today by the Blenheim Forge, based in the railway arches below Peckham Rye Station. The forge specialises in Damascus steel cooking knifes, with handles made from locally foraged wood. Blunter but just as beautiful are Barn the Spoon's spoons, on display in his Spitalfields shop on Hackney Road. Barn runs regular carving days in his East End woodworking school at Stepney City Farm.

THE WORSHIPFUL COMPANY OF DISTILLERS (69)

Bunter's Tea, Kill-Cobbler, Meat-Drink-Washing-and-Lodging, Needle and Pin, Geneva, and Mother's Ruin are all names Londoners have given to gin. Today 'London Gin' is a legal term that refers to a pure, dry, distilled version of the liquor. There are currently several active distilleries in the city: the largest is Beefeater on Montford Place in Kennington, which has a gin museum on site; more recent is Sipsmith on Cranbrook Road in Turnham Green, the home of Prudence, the first new copper still in the city for 200 years. Book a session at the Ginstitute at The Portobello Star, where you can distil your own bottle of botanicals.

THE WORSHIPFUL COMPANY OF FISHMONGERS (4)

Until the late 14th century, the Fishmongers convened the *Leyhalmode*, their own court of law that settled disputes over fish.[1] Two of London's finest fishmongers are F. C. Soper's in Nunhead and Steve Hatt on Essex Road.

L ——

THE WORSHIPFUL COMPANY OF FOUNDERS (33)

Founders pour molten metal into casts, rather than shaping it in a forge. The oldest manufacturing company in Great Britain is the Whitechapel Bell Foundry on Whitechapel Road, which was itself founded in 1570, and has occupied its current premises since 1739. The Liberty Bell, the bells of St Paul's and Westminster Abbey and the 2012 Olympic Bell were all founded here.[2] On the other side of town, New Pro Foundries of West Drayton specialise in metalwork for films, and since 1975 they have cast all the BAFTA Award masks.

---

[1] Go to Teddington Lock and settle your disputes with a fish, as demonstrated by Monty Python's 'Fish-slapping Dance', which took place on the site.

[2] A profile template of Big Ben, the largest bell ever cast at Whitechapel, stands inside the door to the foundry's free foyer museum.

BRODERERS

VINTNERS

TATTOO ARTISTS

MANNEQUIN COLOURISTS

MERCHANT TAYLORS

FOUNDERS

MYSTERY DINERS

LAUGHTER THERAPISTS

COOKS

BARBERS

BLACKSMITHS

SPECTACLE MAKERS

SHIPWRIGHTS

TAXIDERMISTS

HIVE OF

GIRDLERS

Until 1960, the Crown received excise duty on all packs of playing cards. Each playing-card-maker printed a distinctive symbol on the Ace of Spades, to confirm that their taxes had been paid. Since 1882, the company has produced a double pack of playing cards each year, with the new Master's face on the Ace of Spades,[1] and on the first Monday of March each year the company organises an inter-livery bridge tournament. Today, Games & Print Services on Canvey Island will create a bespoke deck of cards for you.

THE WORSHIPFUL COMPANY OF GIRDLERS (23)

Girdlers are beltmakers, and at the coronation of each British sovereign the company still presents the belt for the new monarch's Sword of State. Tura is a family business on Amhurst Terrace near Hackney Downs that has been producing hand-finished leather belts since 1991. Tura supplies big brands, but you can order a bespoke girdle for yourself.

THE WORSHIPFUL COMPANY OF GROCERS (2)

The Grocers' Company is second only in precedence to the Mercers. There's a legend that the Grocers used to be first in the order, until Elizabeth I, as Honorary Master of the Mercers' Company, found herself behind the Grocers' flatulent camel at her coronation procession. There are many great greengrocers in London, including the cornucopian Newington Green Fruit and Vegetables, where purslane, peppercress, galangal and rambutans spill out of the shop across rows of upturned crates.

MAKERS OF PLAYING CARDS

THE WORSHIPFUL COMPANY OF MERCHANT TAYLORS (6/7)

The Merchant Taylors' Company is either number six or seven in the order of precedence, alternating each year with the Skinners.[2] Saville Row has been synonymous with bespoke tailoring since the late 18th century, and a stroll along the Mayfair street today is a journey through sartorial history. Lord Nelson, Winston Churchill and Jude Law have all been measured in these hallowed fitting rooms. The oldest tailor on the street is Henry Poole & Co., founded in 1846 by the creator of the dinner jacket.

THE WORSHIPFUL COMPANY OF PLUMBERS (31)

In 2013, Ché Richard and his Hampstead & Highgate Heating & Plumbing Company were named the best plumbers in Britain after he won the *Which?* Local Business of the Year award. Every November, Pimlico Plumbers cover their building on Sail Street with a bombastic Christmas lights display, visible from trains approaching Waterloo.

GROCERS

---

[1] They also have a vast collection of historic playing cards, which you can examine in the London Metropolitan Archives.

[2] This tradition follows an ancient Tudor dispute, and may be the origin of the expression 'at sixes and sevens'.

THE WORSHIPFUL COMPANY OF SHIPWRIGHTS (59)

Raise a glass to seafarers in the Shipwrights' Arms on Tooley Street and admire the tiled mural of shipwrights at work. If you want a vessel of your own, go to John's Boat Works on Lot's Ait, the Thames island between Kew and Brentford. As well as maintenance and repairs, John Watson also specialises in boatbuilding, and will craft you a dinghy to your specifications.

THE WORSHIPFUL COMPANY OF SPECTACLE MAKERS (60)

If spectacles did not meet this company's standards in the 17th century, they were seized forcibly, taken to London Stone and 'with a hammer broken all to pieces'. The Algha Works Factory, based on Fish Island in Hackney Wick,[1] is the only spectacle-frame-maker still operating in Britain. They manufacture the iconic 'round-eye' glasses made famous by John Lennon.[2] Although their frames may look simple, they are the product of 130 operations, including swaging, notching, crimping and pressing.

THE WORSHIPFUL COMPANY OF STATIONERS (47)

You can observe every stage of the bookbinding process through the windows of the Wyvern Bindery on Clerkenwell Road, which Mark Winstanley has been running since 1990. Take along a battered book and give it a new lease of life.

THE WORSHIPFUL COMPANY OF VINTNERS (11)

The Vintners collaborate with the Dyers in one of London's oddest annual rituals: swan upping. In the third week of July, liverymen from both companies row up the Thames in skiffs, rounding up mute swans, ringing their feet and releasing them again. Any swans caught by the queen's Swan Uppers, however, are left unmarked as the property of the queen, the 'Seigneur of the Swans'. This medieval tradition is now a way of checking the birds' health. When not upping swans, vintners sell wine. If you're struggling to choose a vintage, call in to Vagabond on Charlotte Street, where the walls are lined with wine bottles rigged up to tubes and taps. This isn't a mad scientist's laboratory, it's a blue-chip *enoteca*, where you can sample 100 different wines through high-tech dispensing machines.

THE WORSHIPFUL COMPANY OF WAX CHANDLERS (20)

The Worshipful Wax Chandlers produced fine beeswax candles, a luxury compared with tallow candles made from animal fat.[3] The beekeeper Steve Benbow maintains hives across the capital, including those on the roofs of Fortnum & Mason, the Tate Modern and the National Portrait Gallery, and sells honey and beeswax candles (thelondonhoneycompany.co.uk). If you want to get busy yourself, Barnes & Webb will rent you a hive, install it in your garden, maintain it and leave you the honey (barnesandwebb.com).

---

[1] See p.125.
[2] And sported by Daniel Radcliffe in the *Harry Potter* films. Algha also made the heart-shaped frames in Stanley Kubrick's *Lolita*.

[3] These drab, everyday candles are the purview of the Worshipful Company of Tallow Chandlers.

CONTEMPORARY WORSHIP

Here are our predictions for the next generation of Worshipful Companies.

THE WORSHIPFUL COMPANY OF BARISTAS

Watch the city's baristas battle for the coveted title of Coffee Master at the London Coffee Festival.[1] Disciplines including cupping, brewing, blending and latte art.

THE BLESSED COMPANY OF CHEESEMAKERS

Philip Wilton founded Wildes Cheese on Queen Street in Haringey in 2012. Philip offers one-day cheese making courses: you'll bring home a trio of cheeses and a starter pack for turning your kitchen into a dairy.

THE WORSHIPFUL COMPANY OF GLOBE MAKERS

After founding Bloomsbury Bowling Lanes, Peter Bellerby decided to build globes. Bellerby & Co. in Stoke Newington make globes ranging from the desktop Albion (22.9 cm diameter) to the monumental Churchill (1.27 m). You can visit their studio by appointment.

THE WORSHIPFUL COMPANY OF LAUGHTER THERAPISTS

Attend a course with a laughter therapist at the London Waterloo Academy to reduce your stress, boost your immune system and tone your muscles. The body can't distinguish between real and forced laughter, so faking it has the same beneficial effect.

THE WORSHIPFUL COMPANY OF MANNEQUIN COLOURISTS

Every morning at Madame Tussaud's,[2] teams touch up the waxworks to remove all traces of yesterday's star struck fans. There's usually lipstick on the faces of the One Direction boys, and sometimes underwear in their pockets. If you visit, twirl Dickens's beard, plant a smacker on ET and sneak a pair of Y-fronts under Chaplin's bowler.

THE WORSHIPFUL COMPANY OF MYSTERY DINERS

Sign up with Mystery Dining (mysterydining.net) and you and a friend can critique chic eateries and swanky hotels across London, while someone else picks up the bill.

THE WORSHIPFUL COMPANY OF TATTOO ARTISTS

If you're thinking of inking, seek out one of the capital's tat Picassos. A zen-like calm pervades Good Times on Curtain Road, where Nikole Lowe will cover your back with a samurai warrior; or for cult noir, try Into You on St John Street, where Duncan X will etch occult fantasies on to your limbs.

THE WORSHIPFUL COMPANY OF TAXIDERMISTS

The shop window of Get Stuffed on Essex Road is crammed with an exotic frozen menagerie: baboons and giraffes rub snouts with crocodiles and a great white shark.[3] To learn the craft yourself, book a London Taxidermy Academy two-day squirrel workshop in London Bridge (londontaxidermy academy.co.uk).

THE WORSHIPFUL COMPANY OF WINDOW CLEANERS

Advance Cleaning Services, based in Epping, are one of the UK's leading rope-access cleaners, abseiling from dizzying heights with suds and a squeegee, or climbing up to buff the nub of the Gherkin.

THE WORSHIPFUL COMPANY OF ZOMBIES

The London Bridge Experience had so many applicants for the role of zombie in 2009 that they had to hold open auditions. The role requirements are a willingness to work in undead make-up and the ability to terrify passers-by on Tooley Street with a lolloping walk and a craving for brains.

---

[1] Every early May bank holiday in the Old Truman Brewery on Brick Lane (londoncoffeefestival.com).
[2] For more Tussaud, see p.111.

[3] Buy with caution: the owner, Robert Sclare, was jailed for six months in 2000 for forging licences allowing him to import rare animals.

THE FAMILY BUSINESS

There are over 350,000 family businesses in London.

BANKERS

Samuel Pepys banked with Sir Richard Hoare, at the 'Sign of the Golden Bottle' in Cheapside. Founded in 1672, Hoare & Co. is still thriving after 350 years, and is still owned and directed by 11th-generation members of the family. Hoare's have just two branches, one of which has been on the same site in Fleet Street since 1690. When you visit, don't worry about the rain. The bank keeps giveaway umbrellas in the entrance hall for its customers.

EEL-JELLIERS

There is a jellied eel stall on the corner of Goulston Street and Whitechapel High Street. It has been called Rose Seafood since 2013, but for 94 years this was the site of Tubby Isaac's jellied eels, a fourth-generation family business. When fresh eels are boiled, they exude their own jelly, a useful natural preservative.[1]

VINTNERS

Visit the Boot and Flogger on Redcross Way. Until 2000 it was the only bar in the country that didn't require an alcohol licence, after James I granted a dispensation to vintners in 1611. The bar is run by Davy's, a fifth-generation family firm of vintners.[2] Order a glass of Boot & Flogger Red No. 1 and sink into one of the deep leather armchairs.

COFFEE SHOP

The legendary Bar Italia on Frith Street has been run by three generations of the Polledri family since 1949. It never closes. The ceiling is adorned with football memorabilia and the floor is paved with 65-year-old stones laid by Uncle Torina Polledri, a 'terrazzo mosaic specialist'.

L

THE GENTLE AUTHOR

'I love shopkeepers and small shops. Most shopkeepers do what they do because they want to earn the respect of their customers, and they love the idea of being able to give people good service.

'Gardners Market Sundriesmen in Commercial Street is London's oldest paper bag shop, opened in 1870 by James Gardner, then run by Bertie Gardner, next Ray Gardner, and today Paul Gardner. It's where all the market traders and stallholders buy their paper bags. To pay a visit is rather like going to a pub because everybody's in there telling stories about the market – it's a completely magical place.

'Undoubtedly my favourite place to have breakfast is E. Pellicci's restaurant in Bethnal Green Road, still run by Maria Pellicci and her son Nevio and daughter Anna. The family started this cafe in 1900 and it's still thriving. It has the most wonderful 1940s marquetry interior. You will meet people who have their grandchildren with them and they'll tell you that their grandparents first took them there.

'Both my parents died at exactly the same age, and one day I sat down and I worked out how many days I had until I reached that age, and I calculated it was 10,000 days. Then I decided that I had to make a choice of what I was going to do with those 10,000 days, and my decision was to write a story every day. The plan is to carry on until I literally drop, and to do a self-portrait revealing the identity of The Gentle Author as the last one so, when that comes up, it's all over.'

The anonymous Gentle Author has been writing daily about the culture and characters of the East End of London at spitalfieldslife.com since 2009 and plans to continue until at least 2037.

---

[1] Tubby's only resorted to refrigeration in the 1990s.

[2] The are 24 Davy's wine bars across London with memorable names including Bangers, Crusting Pipe, Gyngleboy and Truckles of Pied Bull Yard.

THE DOCKLANDS

At the top of Stave Hill, on the Rotherhithe Peninsula, there is a tactile map showing the surrounding area as it was in its heyday. The map is designed to be seen in the rain: its three-dimensional pools, channels and docks flood with water, so you can imagine the area around you as the industrial water world it once was.

The Docklands have been London's powerhouse of industry and employment since the 19th century: first as an international port,[1] then as the centre of the manufacturing industry, and now as a global financial centre. The Docklands Light Railway is the most relaxing way to tour the area. It glides above ground between stations with exotic, evocative names, such as Cyprus, East India and West Silvertown. If you want to explore the working life of the docks, however, you should set out on foot.

SAILOR'S ALPHABET

Take the DLR to Prince Regent Station. Before you leave the platform, walk along Brian Yale's stainless-steel frieze of Docklands history. You'll see elephants, tea served at Mr Brewster's mobile canteen and barrels of tobacco and spice. Recite 'The Sailor's Alphabet', a song that lists A for anchor, B for bowsprits, C for capstan and so on, with a chorus after every verse: 'Sing high, sing low, wherever you go / Give a sailor his tot and there's nothing goes wrong.'

Take the footpath below Connaught Bridge, passing London City Airport[2] on your left. Turn right on to the North Woolwich Road and left into the Thames Barrier Park.

GREEN DOCK

The Thames Barrier Park was built on the toxic wasteland of a demolished petrochemical plant. Today the centrepiece is the Green Dock, a long trench of topiary yews clipped into the shape of waves. On the other side of the river you can see the aerial conveyor belts of the Angerstein and Murphy wharves, London's last major import dock. You also get a spectacular view of the Thames Barrier's gleaming conches.

Turn left along North Woolwich Road.

TNT

This area between the road and the river was once the site of the Brunnor Mond factory, which manufactured explosives during the First World War. On the night of Friday 19 January 1917, a fire broke out and triggered the catastrophic 'Silvertown Explosion': 50 tonnes of TNT detonated at once and obliterated the surrounding area. The flames were visible for 30 miles.

Turn left down Knight's Road to spot the world's largest tin of syrup.

GOLDEN SYRUP

The Tate & Lyle factory produces a million tins of golden syrup each week. It is the oldest branded product in the world.

Double back and turn down Mill Road, towards a slender, isolated chimney.

HOVIS MILL

Once the centre of London's flour-milling industry, this chimney is all that remains of the Rank's Empire Mills, which milled the flour for Hovis.

Cross the Royal Victoria Dock Bridge.[3]

ROYAL VICTORIA

As you stand above Royal Victoria Dock, imagine the three miles of warehouses that once surrounded it. There was an acre of storage space for oranges, and the banana berth processed over a million bananas every week. The Excel Exhibition Centre dominates the north side of the dock today. When you descend from the bridge, look for the sculpture near the main entrance: two dockworkers, modelled on real-life stevedores, labour under the watchful eye of their foreman.

Make your way west to East India Dock.

---

[1] See p.251.
[2] The airport is built on top of the former King George V dry dock, which is still underneath the terminal building, boxed in with steel girders.

[3] This 40-foot-high pedestrian bridge has spectacular views. Plans to sling a suspended 'transporter car' beneath it never materialised.

EAST INDIA

This dock has mostly been filled in, but the street names evoke the goods that were once offloaded here by the East India Company:[1] Saffron Avenue, Clove Crescent, Oregano Drive and Nutmeg Lane.[2]

Walk towards Canary Wharf.

DOCK LANDS

The hundred acres of the private Canary Wharf Estate are unlike any other part of London. The old docks have been in-filled with underground, luxury shopping malls, while on the surface, the shining towers form a mirror maze of manicured pavements and green lawns. Visit the Museum of London Docklands, which traces the history of the port of London, including a recreation of 19th-century Wapping. Then follow Emma Biggs's 'Wharf Walk' through Jubilee Place shopping mall: a string of 17 mosaics that evoke the trades that once flourished on the site.

Cross South Dock on the S-shaped footbridge and walk left along Marsh Wall.

RIVER MAN

Find the 'London River Man' sculpture: a charismatic seafarer in oilskins and a sou'wester, pointing seaward and saluting 'all London river workers — toshers — bargees — dockers — ale tasters — coalheavers — ferrymen'.

Bear south and cross Inner Dock over the bascule bridge.

INNER DOCK

At the south end of Inner Dock, look into the water beside Clippers Quay. This section used to be a dry dock, and under the surface you can still see the first of a series of steps or 'altars' where wooden stanchions supported ships during repairs.

Cross into Millwall Park.

MILL WALL

This area has been called Mudchute since the excavation of docks in the 1860s, when it was smothered in liquid mud. At the south end of the park is an unusual sculpture of a naked woman handling a giant fish.

Turn right along Westferry Road.[3]

PINK PIGEONS

Running alongside the river is Blasker Walk, once famous for its pink pigeons. The Burrell & Co. factory stood here and manufactured paints and dyes. The smoke from the chimneys was often red, so the local pigeons were rose-tinted.

Finish on Burrell's Wharf Square.

GREAT EASTERN

This is where the *Great Eastern* was built, the monstrous ship[4] that killed Isambard Kingdom Brunel: after the stress of overseeing the tortuous construction, he had a stroke just before the *Great Eastern* made her first voyage to America. In a sunken garden you can see the original wooden cross-braces from which the ship was launched in 1858, and the massive chains that lowered it down the slipway.

Now catch the RB1 riverboat from Masthouse Terrace back to central London.

L

---

[1] For more on the East India Company, see p.247.
[2] These roads still surround a very important warehouse. See p.95.
[3] Look out for the plaque on the old Millwall Fire Station, which commemorates two women firefighters, Joan Bartlett (18) and

Violet Pengelly (19), who died during an air raid in 1940. The building now houses a Turkish restaurant called the Old Millwall Fire Station.
[4] The *Great Eastern* was initially going to be named the *Leviathan*.

WORKING LUNCH

Opposite the Big Easy Lobster Shack in Covent Garden is Rules, the oldest restaurant in London. This designation is slightly misleading, as it's actually younger than many inns and taverns that serve food. Here are some of the antique eateries that are still serving.

OYSTER TOP-UP

Rules was set up as an oyster bar in 1798 and is still serving them on Maiden Lane today. Rules also specialises in game: if you order a guinea fowl, be careful not to break a tooth on a piece of lead shot.

LAWYERS WHO LUNCH

Dress up and go to lunch in Middle Temple, one of the city's Inns of Court. During term time, you can mingle with London's lawyers and eat in the hall where Elizabeth I watched the first production of Shakespeare's *Twelfth Night* in 1602.

SMALL & STOUT

London's first Irish pub is the Tipperary, a corridor-width alehouse on Fleet Street. It was built in 1605 with stone from the White Friars monastery and survived the Great Fire, unlike its wooden neighbour Ye Olde Cheshire Cheese,[1] which had to be rebuilt. The Tipperary claims to be the first pub in the city to serve Guinness. Order stew and a stout.

LIFE INNSURANCE

The George Inn on Borough High Street, the last 17th-century galleried coaching inn in London, gets the briefest of mentions in *Little Dorrit*.[2] The menu is decidedly un-Dickensian these days: Charles would probably have baulked at the quinoa and squash parcel. For a whiff of the bearded genius, go in to the Middle Bar and look for his life insurance certificate on the wall.

SIMPSON'S SAUSAGE

When you get to Simpson's Tavern, stow your bowler on the brass hat-rail above your booth. This City institution, tucked away on Ball Court, has been feeding London's money men[3] since 1757. All meat dishes are served with an unrequested sausage. Try the 'famous stewed cheese' for dessert.

CULTURE VULTURES

Another George Inn opened on Castle Court in 1748 and used to share its premises with a wine merchant who kept a live vulture outside on a perch. When the bird moved on, the inn remembered it in its new name, the George and Vulture. In *The Pickwick Papers*, Samuel Pickwick makes the pub his centre of operations. Visit for traditional pub fare; if you're lucky, you'll coincide with a meeting of the City Pickwick Society, who gather there regularly under Dickensian nicknames.[4]

WASHING UP

While I was researching *In the Kitchen*, I spent six months hanging out in hotel kitchens, sometimes just talking and observing, sometimes chopping onions because it was easier to get people to talk to you that way. I never go out for dinner without wondering who might be washing the pots that night.
— *Monica Ali*

MAIDS OF HONOUR

Stop for a tea break in the Original Maids of Honour on Kew Road. This bakery specialises in 'maids of honour', a type of Tudor custard tart much loved by Henry VIII. The king apparently encountered Anne Boleyn and her maids eating them and became so infatuated with the pastries that he confiscated the recipe and kept it locked up at Richmond Palace.[5]

---

[1] See p.219.
[2] Tip Dorritt 'goes into the George and writes a letter'.
[3] Quite literally. Women weren't allowed to dine at Simpson's until 1916.
[4] Or go on Christmas Day to join the Swedish Bankers of London, who hold their festive lunch there.
[5] Find another of Henry's favourite pastries on p.131.

BEER O'CLOCK

In 1751, William Hogarth published *Gin Lane* and *Beer Street*. Gin Lane depicts a scene of depravity stalked by the evil juniper berry. Beer Street, however, shows a cheerful tableau of portly merchants and buxom fishwives going about their business in a thriving district. Beer is deeply embedded in the culture of London. During the 18th and 19th centuries the city was home to the biggest breweries in the world. Today the focus is on quality not quantity.

BROWN

Brown ale, the oldest style of British beer, was traditionally sweet and malty. Try the Stokey Brown by Pressure Drop, served in the Cock Tavern on Mare Street.

PORTER

Porter was invented in the Old Blue Last on Curtain Road in 1730. It's made with roasted brown malts  and matured for four or five months to develop its smoky tang.[1] It was initially popular with labourers and porters, who drank it for breakfast. Strong porter, known as 'stout', eventually overtook the original in popularity, but old-style porter is now making a comeback. Buy Brockley Porter directly from the Brockley Brewery on Harcourt Road and compare it with a Dark Matter stout, made at the George and Dragon in Acton.

PALE

Pale ale relies on carefully controlling the temperature of the hops, which was only possible after the invention of coke fuel in the 1640s. The East India Company started shipping pale ale to India, and discovered that the turbulent tropical voyage matured the beer perfectly. India Pale Ale, or IPA, became hugely popular, first in India and then in London. Try the Five Points Pale, available from Clapton Craft in Hackney; the Notting Hill Amber by Moncada, served in the Mall Tavern, Notting Hill; or Kernel's Mosaic IPA at the Craft Beer Co. in Brixton.

BITTER

The signature British cask-conditioned beer is 'bitter'. Like IPA, bitters evolved from hoppy pale ales in the late 18th century, and now they are the most popular and most brewed  ales in London. Traditionally, London breweries made three bitters of increasing strength: ordinary, best and special.[2] Try the Wandle by Sambrook's, available directly from their brewery on Yelverton Road, Battersea; the Runner by Truman's, served in Williams Ale and Cider House on Artillery Lane; or the dark Urban Dusk by Redemption, served in the Antwerp Arms, Tottenham.

MILD

Mild ale[3] was developed in the 1830s as an alternative to porter. Mild was cheaper and sometimes considered an inferior brew, but CAMRA (The Campaign for Real Ale) are currently promoting it through initiatives such as 'Mild Month in May'. It is a fruity, biscuity ale with caramel malt. Try the East End Mild by Tap East in Westfield Stratford.[4]

LAGER

Lagers have been brewed in Britain since the 1870s, but until recently most commercial British lagers were poor imitations of the crisp Pilsner beers of Germany and the Czech Republic. Today the best craft lagers produced in London include Hells by Camden Town, served in the Horseshoe in Hampstead, and the Fourpure Pils from the Fourpure Taproom in South Bermondsey.

L ——

---

[1] Visit the old brewery on Chiswell Street, now a corporate events space, and ask to see their Porter Tun room. This gaping chamber once held Whitbread's vats of porter. Huge tubs like these could be dangerous: see p.340.

[2] Fuller's retain this model with their Chiswick, London Pride and ESB (Extra Special Bitter).

[3] In the context of beer, 'mild' means 'fresh' rather than weak.

[4] See p.251.

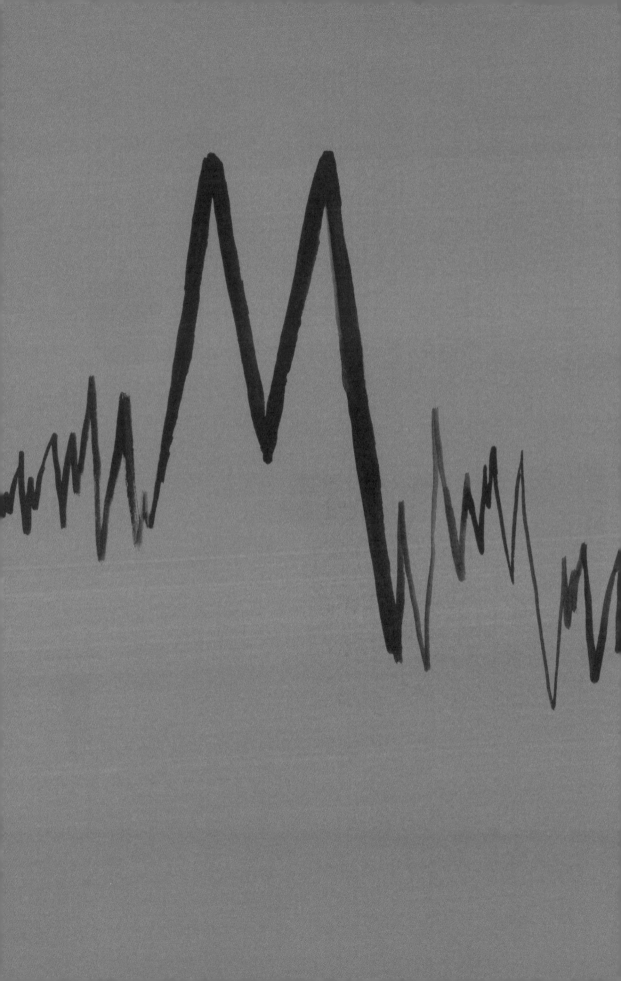

NEW MONEY

BRIXTON POUNDS

Although Brixton hasn't seceded from the rest of London,[1] it does have its own currency. Take a wad of notes to Cheques for Cash on Atlantic Road and swap them for Brixton Pounds (B£).[2] The B£ launched in 2009 to encourage residents to support independent businesses and keep money circulating within the local area. Some shops and cafes offer a discount if you pay with it. Notes feature local heroes, including David Bowie and the activist Olive Morris.[3] If paper money feels passé, you can also set up a pay-by-text account and make B£ payments through your phone.

DOGITAL CURRENCY

You can also convert your bitcoin into other cryptocurrencies. The most charming is dogecoin, which uses the unthreatening image of a Shiba Inu dog (the Doge) as its logo (dogecoin.com). The dogecoin community is characterised by its naive dialect[5] and spontaneous acts of generosity. The gentle spirit of the Doge has infiltrated Camden Market and several vendors now accept the currency. Offerings are suitably carnivorous: you can buy a burger steamed in bourbon at Bitburgers or a pulled pork roll at La Porca.

M

DIGITAL CURRENCY

Visit the UK's first bitcoin ATM inside the Old Shoreditch Station Coffee Bar on Kingsland Road. You feed in sterling notes and out pops a code for the equivalent amount in bitcoin (₿), the world's best-used cryptocurrency.[4] When you've withdrawn your bitcoin, you can use it to buy a pastry and a cappuccino. Digest your crypto-croissant, then purchase a pint at the Pembury Tavern in Hackney, which is run by a computer scientist with a souped-up till. If you want to get out of bitcoin, either trade your digital cash for good old-fashioned pounds in the two-way Robocoin ATM in Rathbone News, an off-licence near Tottenham Court Road, or you can swap bitcoin for gold bullion at Clerkenwell-based AU Trading.

---

❶ Travel to some of London's actual micronations on p.135.
❷ You can also acquire the currency at the menswear counter of Morleys department store.
❸ For more Morris, see p.117.
❹ To delve deeper into London's cryptocurrency scene, attend one of the regular CoinScrum meetups in Shoreditch's Vape Lab: (coinscrum.com).
❺ Around the edge of the dogecoin logo run the words: 'much coin how money so crypto plz mine v rich very currency wow'.

DR JOHNSON'S FINANCIAL DICTIONARY

Those who make money from money have rarely been popular. Samuel Johnson compares them to 'pestiferous animals', who, 'however detested or scorned, long continue to add heap upon heap'. Johnson's scorn made it into his dictionary: nestled among the usually sage and objective entries are a clutch of scathing definitions aimed squarely at the occupants of the money world. A STOCKJOBBER is a 'low wretch who gets money by buying and selling shares in the funds'. EXCISE is a 'hateful tax' administered by 'wretches hired by those to whom excise is paid'.

Johnson had no time for those who MUCKER. 'The peace of life is destroyed', he wrote, 'by a general and incessant struggle for riches.' The contempt that Johnson expressed is alive and well in the city today, fuelled in part by the opacity of high finance and its impenetrable jargon, which drives a wedge between those inside and outside the industry. By way of a remedy, on this map around London's financial sector we provide a Johnsonian LEXICOGRAPHY of the language of FUTURES, HEDGES, OPEN-OUTCRY and SWAPS, using a mixture of his definitions and those provided by the sector itself. [1]

Start at Dr Johnson's House ① on Gough Square. You can gaze out over the City from the garret window where he compiled his dictionary.

STOCKJOBBERS

BEAN COUNTING

Change Alley is actually several narrow thoroughfares shaped a bit like a TV aerial. STRAGGLE around looking for a plaque that marks the site of Jonathan's Coffee-house, ② where the first generation of London's stockjobbers assembled from 1680. The City has become a coffee destination again in recent years, with demand for fine brews from office workers provoking an influx of independent cafes. Order a cup in the artfully industrial interior of Association Coffee, tucked down Creechurch Lane. They use beans supplied by nearby Square Mile Coffee Roasters.

STILL LIFFE

Come face to face with a stockjobber a few streets away inside the entrance of the City's Guildhall: a 1996 sculpture of an open-outcry trader, ③ portrayed mid-action at LIFFE (the London International Financial

Futures and Options Exchange). He epitomises the spirit of the boom years: hair slick, tie loose, an ID badge on each lapel, and a chunky mobile phone pressed to his ear. Although it's disconcerting to see the recent past cast in bronze, this young hopeful is already a historic curiosity. Open-outcry, with its yelling and one-handed financial sign language, all but disappeared after the BIG BANG [2] of 1986. To experience the buzz of playing the stock market, go to the Reserve Bar Stock Exchange on Gresham Street. The bar uses an algorithm that prices drinks according to demand: a ticker shows the latest prices in the beer, spirits and alternative markets.

---

❶ Drawn, for the most part, from J. P. Morgan's jargon buster.　　❷ For another Big Bang, see p.389.

192

AUDIT. *n.s.* A final account; a professional examination and verification of a company's accounting data.

BEAR. *n.s.* A rough savage animal; an investor who has a negative view of the market.

BELLYGOD. *n.s.* A glutton; one who makes a god of his belly.

BIBBER. *n.s.* A tippler; a man that drinks often.

BIG BANG. *n.s.* A sudden and complex change to trading practices; specifically, the deregulation of the London Stock Exchange on 27 October 1986.

BULGE BRACKET. *n.s.* The largest and most prestigious firms.

BULL. *n.s.* In the scriptural sense, an enemy powerful, fierce, and violent; an investor who has a positive view of the market.

CASH FLOW. *n.s.* The flow of ready money, as receipts and payments into and out of a business.

CHAFFERY. *n.s.* Traffick; the practice of buying and selling.

COUNTERCASTER. *n.s.* A word of contempt for an arithmetician; a book-keeper; a caster of accounts.

DRIBLET. *n.s.* A small sum; odd money in a sum.

EXCISE. *n.s.* A hateful tax levied upon commodities, and adjudged not by the common judges of property, but by wretches hired by those to whom excise is paid.

FUTURE. *n.s.* That which will be hereafter; the right and the obligation to enter into a security transaction at a date in the future and at a price fixed now.

GOLDFINDER *n.s.* One who finds gold. A term ludicrously applied to those that empty jakes.

GOLD STANDARD. *n.s.* A monetary system in which a country's government allows its currency unit to be freely converted into fixed amounts of gold and vice versa.

HEDGE. *v.n.* To shift; to hide the head; to hold two contrary positions in two or more financial instruments in order to offset a loss in one by a gain in the other.

HEDGE FUND. *n.s.* A largely unregulated investment fund formed as a private limited partnership.

HIGGLER. *n.s.* One who sells provisions by retail.

INCOME STREAM. *n.s.* A flow of money into a business.

IRONY. *adj.* Made of iron, partaking of iron.

JAKES. *n.s.* A house of office.

LEXICOGRAPHER. *n.s.* A writer of dictionaries; a harmless drudge, that busies himself in tracing the original, and detailing the signification of words.

MONEYSCRIVENER. *n.s.* One who raises money for others.

MUCKER. *v.n.* To scramble for money; to hoard up; to get or save meanly.

NEPOTISM. *n.s.* Fondness for nephews.

OPEN-OUTCRY. *n.s.* A system of financial trading in which the dealers shout out their bids and contracts.

OPTION. *n.s.* The right, but not the obligation, to buy or sell a given stock, security or commodity at a fixed price on a specified date in the future.

PHILOMOT. *adj.* Coloured like a dead leaf.

PONTAGE. *n.s.* Duty paid for the reparation of bridges.

PORKLING. *n.s.* A young pig.

PRIVATE EQUITY. *n.s.* Private equity firms buy companies and restructure them, and look to resell them for more than they bought them for.

PROG. *v.n.* To rob; to steal.

SAMLET. *n.s.* A little salmon.

SHARE. *n.s.* Part; allotment; a certificate issued by a company for general purchase entitling the holder to dividends from any profits the company may make.

SLUBBERDEGULLION. *n.s.* A paltry, dirty, sorry wretch.

SMELLFEAST. *n.s.* A parasite; one who haunts good tables.

SPATTERDASHES. *n.s.* Coverings for the legs by which the wet is kept off.

STIRIOUS. *adj.* Resembling icicles.

STOCKJOBBER. *n.s.* A low wretch who gets money by buying and selling shares in the funds.

STRAGGLE. *v.a.* To wander without any certain direction.

SWAP. *n.s.* A contract between two parties to make a cash flow exchange now or at a point in the future.

TOMBSTONE. *n.s.* Advertisements announcing the issuance of a new security.

DR JOHNSON'S FINANCIAL DICTIONARY

Algorithm

Straggle

Big Bang

T_

Higgler

Goldfinder

Slubberdegullions

Audit

Philomot

1.

Mucker

Hedge Fund

BERKELEY
SQUARE W1

7.

MAYFAIR

Bibber

Lexicographe

THE BANKER

14.

Pontage

8.

10.

private Equity

NIKON CORP

-100.00

Option

Open Outcry

Spatterdashes
11.

Future

Chaffery

Swap

13.

12.

4.

STSP
1.34 ▲

2.

3.

PTS
923 ▲ 121

Equities
6.

Stockjobbers 15.

Stirious

ENRON
LEHMAN
JP MORGAN

STSP
1281 ▲ 721

CANARY WHARF

TESCO 0.05
623 ▲ 121

FTSYT

LOMP
11.2 ▼ 0.15

Bulge Bracket

5.

Moneyscriveners

SA 0.15

EMM ▲ 1.2
621.3 ▼ 7729

MUG HOUSE

Cash flow

ALCODA
63.1 ▼ 9.2

Income
Stream

9.
Countercasters

SHOCK & ORE

The City's only remaining open-outcry floor is at the London Metal Exchange on Leadenhall Street. ④ If you're sitting on hefty steel billet holdings, nip over for some raucous hedging at the epicentre of the global metal market. London is the irony capital of the world: the LME sets prices and trades precious rocks from zinc and copper to obscure ores like cobalt and molybdenum. Until recently, the public were admitted to the viewing gallery, but security fears have sealed it off. For a sense of the pace and animality of the trading floor, look up a clip of Marc Isaacs's film *Men of the City*, shot at the LME and overdubbed with big-game howls and roars.

VAULTS

One metal exchange you can visit is hidden beneath Chancery Lane. London's Silver Vaults are a complex of silver HIGGLERS, most of them old family businesses. From the formal doorway at street level, it's not immediately apparent that this warren of strong rooms is open to the public, but walk downstairs and through the giant vault door to discover legions of shimmering sugar bowls and snuff boxes.

SHARED INTERESTS

If you have a DRIBLET to spare, become part owner of a major multi-national corporation. Keep an eye on the TOMBSTONES, select a company and purchase a single SHARE. With your share, you're eligible to attend the company's AGM and vote on the organisation's future. To keep track of your investment, go to Canary Wharf and camp out next to the LED stock ticker on the Thomson Reuters building. ⑤

MONEYSCRIVENERS

WHITE ELEPHANT

The Canary Wharf development 'looks like being a white elephant' wrote Roy Porter in the mid-1990s. His pessimistic prediction was not borne out and Canary Wharf is now home to several BULGE BRACKET investment banks who employ many of London's sharpest MONEYSCRIVENERS. Canary Wharf is not insensible to Porter's warning, however, and hosts an annual ritual at the base of its STIRIOUS towers to contemplate its own impermanence: the London Ice Sculpting Festival takes place each January.

PIER TO PIER LENDING

The financial sector often employs natural imagery to talk about itself. Investors are BULLISH when confident, BEARISH when reticent. Ideas come from blue-sky thinking and brain storms. Information cascades, CASH FLOWS and INCOME STREAMS. Reconnect corporate finance with the natural world with a walk along the most untamed stretch of the Thames Path in central London, between Maritime

Greenwich and the Millennium Dome. Near the old Victoria Deep Water Terminal ⑥ there's a nature reserve pier, covered in wild flowers, with an extraordinary prospect over the river to Canary Wharf.

PRIVET EQUITY

HEDGE FUNDS and PRIVATE EQUITY firms tend to operate out of the PHILOMOT townhouses in Mayfair. There are no swaggering skyscrapers here; the only sign of the businesses around Berkeley Square ⑦ are elegantly simple gold plaques. Hedge funds take high risks, and, unless you're an accredited investor with gargantuan personal wealth, you can't invest in them. Instead, visit some well-funded hedges outside the Dorchester hotel on Park Lane.[1] ⑧ This venerable institution frequently boasts lavish topiary in the courtyard outside its front entrance.

BERKELEY
SQUARE W1

---

❶ The Dorchester claims to have the deepest baths in London.

COUNTERCASTERS

CORPORATE HOSPITALITY

Johnson didn't include specific terms for accountants and AUDITORS in his dictionary. Those not directly involved in CHAFFERY were all COUNTERCASTERS, 'a word of contempt', he notes, 'for an arithmetician; a book-keeper; a caster of accounts'. Today they're often found in professional services firms. There are no public viewing galleries from which to watch them filling out their spreadsheets; the closest you can get is to mingle with them in their lofty office atria. Deck yourself out in corporate finery and go undercover to Ernst and Young at 1 More London. ⑨ Push through the revolving doors and sashay to the sleek subsidised coffee shop. Enjoy the privacy of the high-backed booths.

COMMUTED SENTENCE

The Bloomsbury Group were appalled that T. S. Eliot spent his days banking instead of penning modernist poetry. To liberate him, some of them offered to set up an 'Eliot Fellowship Fund', through which subscribers would provide him with an income. Eliot, who enjoyed the nine to five, rejected the offer and included the crowds of City workers flowing over London Bridge in *The Waste Land.*[1] ⑩ Scrum across it at the end of the working day and look for another artistically rendered rush hour in Finsbury Avenue Square: six bronze commuters in macs and SPATTERDASHES, ⑪ which were cast from live models.

M —

GOLDFINDERS

BARBELL

Johnson was frustrated by the way the word GOLDFINDER was used. The word means 'one who finds gold', but it is also 'ludicrously applied' he complained 'to those that empty JAKES'. Isaac Newton's actions as head of the Royal Mint ⑫ ultimately led to Britain adopting a GOLD STANDARD. Britain sold off the majority of its reserves in 1999 and there isn't much bullion stashed in the capital these days. Visit one of the remaining gold bars in the Bank of England Museum. ⑬ It weighs 400 Troy ounces and there is a hole in its glass case so that you can reach in and attempt to lift it one-handed.

MAP READING

Dr Johnson's Financial Dictionary *uses the orderly grid lines of financial charts and graphs as a backdrop for watercolours of the three main zones of London's financial sector: Mayfair, the City and Canary Wharf.*

HUB

London is a routing and coordinating hub for enormous global money flows, steered through a myriad of offshore structures and fibre-optic cables. You can sit in a Canary Wharf bar and overhear gossip about huge merger deals, or look over someone's shoulder in the train and see emails from an Arab prince on their Blackberry.
— Brett Scott

❶ See p.300.

BELLYGODS & BIBBERS

GROWTH RATE

The word banking conjures up a whole lifestyle, neatly encapsulated by the term BELLYGOD in Johnson's dictionary. But the heyday of the boozy lunch is long past and breakfast is now the meal where deals are sealed and careers are made. To breakfast like a bellygod, order a PORKLING bap and a SAMLET bagel among the bankers in Gordon Ramsay's Bread Street Kitchen, which opens at 7am.

BRIDGING LOAN

The simplest way to insert yourself into banker culture is to drink at a City pub of an evening, when the BIBBERS are out in force. Buy a pint in the Banker, ⑭ beneath the north end of Blackfriars Bridge, and find a seat by the windows that look down on to the river. The after-work crowd can be rowdy, and disorderly behaviour may result in PONTAGE.

SLUBBERDEGULLIONS

CRISIS

The course of true finance never did run smooth: the pengo, one of the world's most charmingly named currencies, met a bitter end when Hungary suffered the worst case of hyperinflation on record after the Second World War. Look in the money gallery of the British Museum for a 100,000,000,000,000,000,000 pengo note. In 2008, another financial crisis struck and bankers were roundly denounced as SLUBBERDEGULLIONS and accused of everything from PROGGING to NEPOTISM. In their defence, bankers argued that the public are SMELLFEASTS, happy to enjoy the fruits of business when it booms and all too ready to blame the financial sector in harder times.

BANKRUPTCY

Go and stand at the foot of 25 Bank Street in Canary Wharf, ⑮ a tower block that now houses the London offices of J.P. Morgan. This ill-fated building had been earmarked for a subsidiary of Enron before the company's fraud was uncovered and it went bankrupt

in 2001. Lehman Brothers subsequently moved in and remained there until they filed for bankruptcy in 2008, the moment that heralded the onset of the financial crisis. There is no commemorative plaque to mark this historic location; in fact, when the building was cleared out, the Lehman Brothers sign was auctioned as a piece of memorabilia for £42,050.

FAIR IS FOUL

Bloomsbury Grouper Maynard Keynes saw the rampant acquisitiveness of the financial sector as a necessary evil. In 1930, he looked forward to the day when 'the economic problem' would be resolved and we could concentrate on living 'wisely, agreeably, and well'. But for another hundred years, he warned, 'we must pretend to ourselves and to everyone that fair is foul and foul is fair; for foul is useful and fair is not. Avarice and usury and precaution', he said, 'must be our gods for a little longer still.'

CASHLESS

'Money doesn't mind if we say it's evil,' wrote Martin Amis, 'it goes from strength to strength. It's a fiction, an addiction, and a tacit conspiracy.' If you're frustrated by filthy lucre, scrap it and find another mode of exchange.

REPURPOSING MONEY

Defacing or destroying banknotes is a striking anti-establishment statement, but it's also a criminal offence and an expensive habit. Repurposing copper coinage is a more low-cost act of rebellion.

LOOSE CHANGE
Currency is the perfect vehicle for spreading subversive messages. The suffragettes[1] stamped 'VOTES FOR WOMEN' across the king's face on copper coins and released them back into circulation. You can see a Suffragette penny in room 68 of the British Museum.

TOKEN AMOUNT
In the same room is a defaced coin not designed to circulate: a shilling turned into a love token by a soldier in the First World War. He filed

away the pattern on one side and replaced it with the words: 'FROM FRED TO NELLIE. FRANCE 1916.'

POULTRY SUM
Devalue some money at the London Wetland Centre, which has a coin press machine that will flatten your pennies and print ducks on to them. Or, for something more personal, visit the Parasol Unit art gallery in Islington. They have a coin press designed by artist Navid Nuur, which elongates pennies and stamps them with his fingerprint.

M ——

RECIPROCITY

Money is just a way of encoding reciprocity. Why not experiment with some simpler forms of mutual credit?

TIME BANKS
In 1832, the utopian socialist Robert Owen set up the National Equitable Labour Exchange in London and invented a new currency, the labour note, based on hours of work. Producers would swap their goods for labour notes and then use them to buy products from other workers at the exchange. As the system rewarded neither quality nor efficiency, it was ripe for exploitation and only lasted two years. Nevertheless, the concept lives on in London's Time Banks. You offer a service to a local network, perform it as requested, and then claim the same amount of time from somebody else. Everyone's time is worth the same, regardless of the skill they provide (timebanking.org).

STREET BANKS
Streetbank provides an online hub through which neighbours can share things like fondue sets and electric sanders that often languish in cupboards, and, in the process, get to know one another and become a stronger community (streetbank.com).

FREE BANKS
Freecycle is a massive online network that exists to help people rehome unwanted items and reduce waste going to landfill. From bubble wrap and building materials to beds, fabrics and plant cuttings, the listings are varied and fast-moving. Look online to join a local group. It's free but you have to list something of your own before you can begin hoovering up offerings from others (uk.freecycle.org/region/London).

❶ See p.79.

CITY CENTRE

Many cartographers have attempted to identify the centre of the city, but it's tricky to pin down.

POLE OF INACCESSIBILITY
51°30'47.2" N 0°08'03.0" W

An alternative method for calculating the geographical centre is to find the 'pole of inaccessibility': the point that is furthest from all borders. Oliver O'Brien at CASA has identified this desolate location as the narrow Tyler's Court off Wardour Street.[1]

CENTRE POINT
51°30'58.3" N 0°07'47.1" W

The controversial concrete icon Centre Point[2] is in an area that has come to be known as 'Midtown', a name concocted by hoteliers, restaurateurs and estate agents for the cluster of businesses that lie between Tottenham Court Road and Farringdon stations. 'The front door to London is moving east' says Inmidtown (inmidtown. org), the umbrella organisation promoting the district.

CENTRE OF GRAVITY
51°30'1.81" N 0°06'33.5" W

To find the geometric centre of Greater London, print a map of the city and mount it on cardboard. Cut it out and balance it on the point of a needle: your cardboard's centre of gravity will be the centre of the city. You'll find the centre of Greater London is Greet House, part of the Tanswell Estate in Southwark.[3]

---

❶ London's pole of inaccessibility is not far from Piccadilly Circus. In Sam Selvon's *The Lonely Londoners*, Galahad feels that 'that circus have a magnet for him, that circus represent life, that circus is the beginning and the ending of the world'.

❷ See p.26.

❸ The centre of gravity is not far away from Elephant and Castle, which taxi driver John Kennedy calls 'the true centre of London', because most of London's taxi routes converge at the Elephant and Castle road junction.

BENCHMARK
51°30'37.6" N 0°06'56.3" W

In May 2014, the estate agent Knight Frank revealed a new geographical centroid, the 'bullseye of the bullseye': a pavement bench on Victoria Embankment, opposite the King's College Strand campus.[1] In fact the bench is the centre of an arbitrary area enclosed by what Knight Frank defines as London's 'inner ring road'.

MILLIARIUM
51°30'26.4" N 0°07'39.5" W

Stand on the small traffic island on the south side of Trafalgar Square, next to the bronze equestrian statue of Charles I, and you will be standing at the centre of London,[2] from which all mileages to the city are measured.[3]

WEIGHTED CENTROID
51°30'16.0" N 0°06'57.6" W

Adam Dennett, a researcher at UCL's Centre of Advanced Spatial Awareness (CASA), has used London's population distribution to produce a population-weighted centroid, which lies in the Shell Centre next to the Hungerford Bridge train lines.

OMPHALOS
51°29'33.6" N 0°00'49.7" W

Enter the north-west corner of Mudchute Park from East Ferry Road. You'll pass through an ivy-girt portal and ascend a set of stone steps to a raised, cobbled circle. This is the omphalos, the navel of London, where Dr John Dee[4] once performed a shamanic ritual with Christopher Marlowe in 1593, which invoked, blessed and laid the spiritual foundations for the British Empire. This omphalos is the city's, and the country's, 'spiritual centre', according to a 1993 article by the London Psychogeographical Association, entitled 'Nazi Occultists Seize Omphalos'.

---

[1] The *Evening Standard* warned that 'thousands of roadside signs' might need their mileages adjusted.

[2] Charles I's horse stands on the site of the original Eleanor Cross. When Queen Eleanor of Castile died in 1290 near Lincoln, her body was conveyed to Westminster Abbey over the course of two weeks. Edward I commissioned an elaborate 'Eleanor Cross' to be built at each of the 12 locations where her corpse rested overnight.

The final cross was erected at La Charryng, the bend in the Thames. Three and a half centuries later it was destroyed during the Civil War and an ornate Victorian replica now stands outside Charing Cross Station.

[3] Some think London's original milliarium is London Stone on Cannon Street. See p.402.

[4] See p.361.

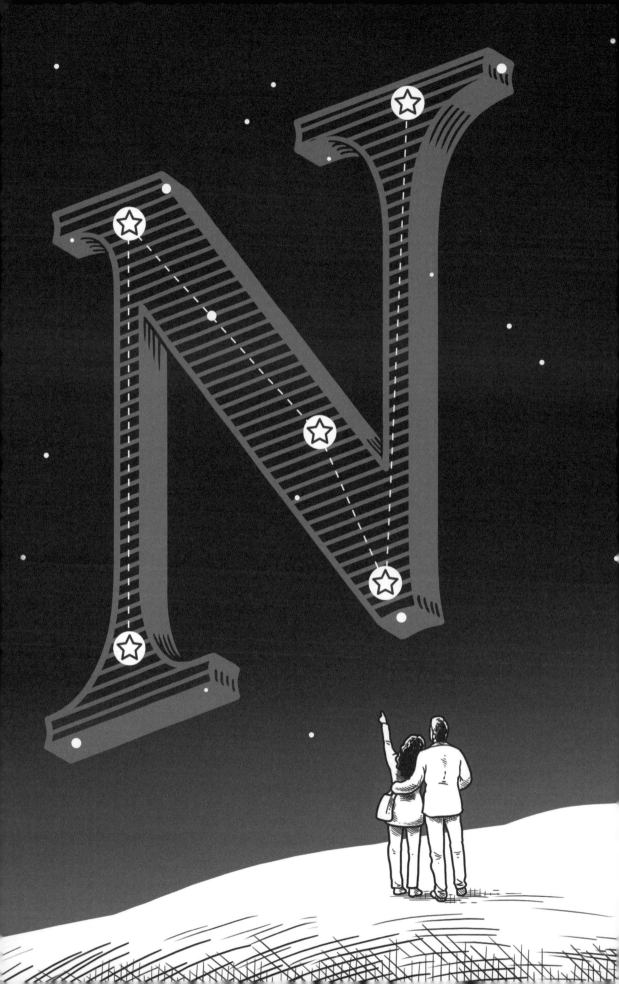

NOCTURNE

WHETHER YOU'RE JETLAGGED, insomniac or wired, London at night is a mysterious place. As the colours desaturate, the city changes: Pimlico slumbers and Vauxhall comes to life; Spaniards Road lies in thick shadow while neon paving stones flicker in Finsbury Avenue Square. With a significant proportion of London's population at home or asleep, there's more space for those who are up and about. By midnight, the city is a zone outside time: an obscure expanse to explore and enjoy without the personal or professional constraints of the day. London becomes a more extreme version of itself; wherever you go and whatever you do, you'll find that the night makes familiar places seem new, and new places seem familiar.

Of course, not everyone out at night is exploring or revelling. As London beds down, a nocturnal tribe sets to work, knitting up the city's ravelled sleeve, upgrading tube lines, sweeping streets, responding to emergencies, restocking shops, hoovering office floors and guarding warehouses. Bargers steer their freight boats from Northfleet to Fulham. Airborne police leave their base in Loughton and navigate the city using the shapes of unlit parks. In parallel, their shadier counterparts also get to work, the unlicensed employees of the night-time economy: dealers, prostitutes and thieves look for business; street artists decorate Hackney shopfronts; urban explorers eye up Battersea Power Station; and illegal cage fighters limber up in Leyton.

For many, simply surviving the night is a challenge. The Street Rescue team search for rough sleepers; and behind a door on Soho's Marshall Street, Samaritans listen to tales of suffering from across the city.

After 3am, when most late drinkers have stumbled on to night buses, even central London rolls over and tries to get some sleep. The dark hours before dawn work strongly on the imagination of those who are still awake. It's at this time that tales of the supernatural crawl out of the most caliginous corners. The pig-faced lady might be lurking nearby, or Queen Rat.

As dawn approaches and the sky lightens beyond Blackheath, sticky pavements, empty drug snap-bags and kebab-shop cabbage leaves emerge from the gloom. The high and low tidemarks of the previous evening are briefly visible on the early streets before they are swept away and the night and daytime populations trade places.

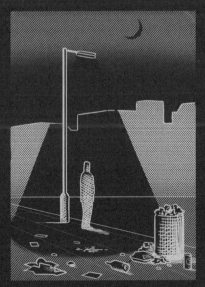

Now you can retire to sleep, and dream of your night. As H. V. Morton puts it, you have experienced in a London night 'a brief period of infinite possibility'.

TWILIGHT RITUALS

LAMP LIGHTING
There are still around 1,500 gas lamps burning each night on London's streets. At dusk, watch the filaments flicker into flame on Pall Mall, or outside Westminster Abbey, and look out for the team who maintain the lamps late at night.

DARK ART
To greet the weekend, the National Portrait Gallery holds free drawing classes every Friday at dusk (6.30pm). Sketch vampires congregating around Marc Quinn's blood head sculpture.[1]

BURIAL RITES
At 7pm on the 23rd of each month a crowd gathers by the gates of Crossbones Graveyard, the old paupers' and prostitutes' burial ground on Redcross Way, to commemorate the outcast dead through a ceremony of story and song. Bring a feather, flower or ribbon as a votive offering.

CEREMONY OF THE KEYS
This 700-year-old locking-up ceremony takes place daily at the Tower of London at 21.53. It's free and open to the public but you must apply in writing several months in advance.

NIGHT HOWLS
Dodie Smith's Twilight Bark in *The Hundred and One Dalmatians* took place on Primrose Hill.[2] To hear the modern equivalent, wander past Battersea Dogs & Cats Home.

RISING OF THE PISSOIR
In 2009, the council installed a pop-up urinal at the end of Electric Avenue, opposite Will Self's light-up *Brixton Speaks* artwork.[3] At night the Brixton pissoir rises phoenix-like from the tarmac. Be there to salute it.

[1] See p.35.
[2] The Dalmatians meet Martians on p.413.
[3] A wall covered with phrases Self earwigged in the area.

NIGHTS OF LONDON

'Beasts of prey and great cities alone in nature remain awake when darkness comes; the one in search of death, the other in search of an extra hour of life.' This was H. V. Morton's conclusion in *Nights of London*, his sublime and surreally humorous survey of the city's nocturnal habits.

LAST OF THE PROMS
Second Saturday in September
The Promenade Concerts were founded in 1895, and the concert on the Last Night has grown into a festival. Concertgoers bring balloons, dress up in patriotic fancy dress, and wave Union Jacks to nationalistic tunes. Huge crowds pack out the Royal Albert Hall and Hyde Park next door. If you're quick off the mark, you can get a standing ticket for £5.

BONFIRE
5 November
When Guy Fawkes was surprised on the night of 4 November 1605, he could not have known what he had ignited. By the mid-19th century, effigies of Fawkes were paraded through the streets accompanied by capering clowns, cross-dressers and drummers. Today the largest celebrations are on Battersea Park and Clapham Common, and the perfect vantage point for seeing fireworks across London is Primrose Hill.

TWELFTH
5 January
The wintry Twelfth Night[1] of Christmas is a time of revelry, governed by a Lord of Misrule who turns social norms upside down: kings become peasants and boys become bishops. Today Twelfth Night is celebrated with mummers, green men and Queen Peas in a free festival on Bankside, next to Shakespeare's Globe.

OWLS
London has wild populations of owls in Osterley Park and Abney Park Cemetery. Watch out for barn owls flying low over rough grass before dusk, tawny owls hooting after dark and little owls 'basking' in the trees on warm winter mornings. For a guaranteed sighting, visit Deen City Farm in Merton, where you can meet Edna the owl, who gives flying demonstrations in the early afternoons.[2]

SHAPES

Night-time's more of an economic entity than it used to be. Increasingly it's a packaged holiday. Lots of people travel to foreign cities purely to savour its nightlife. They do so because they think they can shapeshift, express their true selves, escape their civilian identity.
— *Sukhdev Sandhu*

LIGHTS

The very quality of the darkness in a great city like London is itself a study. The darkness of Pall Mall is different from the darkness of Bishopsgate; the lights of Piccadilly are different from the lights of Edgware Road.
— *H. V. Morton*

SOUNDS

London's soundfield transforms. Echoes, a hysterical cry, the threat of silence, a solitary bleep or thump or groan: all these are imbued with meaning.
— *Sukhdev Sandhu*

N —

---

[1] Eat Twelfth Night cake on p.90.

[2] Newham City Farm also has a number of birds of prey, including a majestic Indian eagle owl called Pegasus.

SLEEPEASY

A PRISON CELL

The cheapest overnight accommodation in London is a night in a police cell. This can be arranged quite simply by breaching the peace near your local nick. The beds are very firm, however, and room service is limited. If you like your creature comforts, try Clink 78, a converted Victorian magistrates' court near King's Cross. This hostel has transformed its 19th-century prison cells into bunk-bed accommodation, 'perfect for nostalgic ex-convicts and Dickens-loving punks'.[1]

SLEEPER BERTH

If you're not picky about where you wake up, we recommend kipping down in Euston Station, on the Caledonian Sleeper to Fort William. As darkness falls, every night of the week except Saturday, this bastion of the glamour days of rail travel trundles out of the city.[2] The rocking motion lulls you to sleep and you wake up on the bonnie banks of Loch Lomond.

THE HONKY TONK AFRO ROOM

Innocuous from the outside, the Pavilion Fashion Rock 'n' Roll Hotel on Sussex Gardens is an interior designer's horror show. Every themed room is crammed with stylistic clichés that will give you neon nightmares. The Honky Tonk Afro Room is a tribute to the 1970s with lime-green walls, leopard-print cushions, a pink feather boa frieze and a disco ball. It's supremely kitsch and totally groovy, baby. Apparently, Antonio Fargas ('Huggy Bear' from the original *Starsky & Hutch*) always asks for this room.

A ROOM FOR LONDON

There is a wooden boat on top of the Queen Elizabeth Hall with a bedroom inside it[3] and a panoramic view over the Thames. The boat is modelled on the *Roi des Belges*, the steamer that took Joseph Conrad through the Congo on the trip that inspired *Heart of Darkness*. Sign up to the Living Architecture mailing list for news of future booking ballots.

SUPERIOR SHARD ROOM

For a room with a view, fork out for a Superior Shard Room in the Shangri-La Hotel, which inhabits the 34th to the 52nd floors of the tallest building in the UK. Or track down Romeo, the fox discovered by construction workers at the top of the structure, and ask him what the view's like.

ROOM BY ANTONY GORMLEY

Immersive art carries a giant price tag at the Beaumont Hotel on Brown Hart Gardens, but you do get to sleep inside a crouching cubist self-portrait of Antony Gormley. *ROOM* squats above what used to be the reception of an AVIS garage. Inside the luxury suite, you climb narrow steps into a lofty wooden chamber, hung with wood-panelled cubes that draw your eye up into the statue's skull. Gormley suggests you think of *ROOM* as 'a cave, a tomb, a womb or a padded cell'. Sweet dreams!

---

[1] Visit more prison cells on p.280.
[2] Get into the spirit with a wee dram of Glenfiddich in the lounge car (£5) and some haggis, neeps and tatties (another £5).

[3] Inside the bedroom is a book in which guests are encouraged to write about their experience. You can read entries by 38 writers, musicians and artists in *A London Address*.

SPEAKEASY

Recently, London has been overrun with blind pigs and blind tigers. Speakeasies first emerged in Prohibition America, when moonshine was served in china cups, in bootleg joints fronted by respectable high-street businesses. The secret of London's speakeasies is their lack of secrecy. All of them are doing a roaring business and are highly visible online, yet the blatant charade still delivers an illicit thrill.

THE MAYOR OF SCAREDY CAT TOWN
The Breakfast Club, 12–16 Artillery Lane

Tell the waiter that you are here to see 'the mayor'.

You'll be led past unsuspecting all-day breakfasters and through a large Smeg fridge. From there you descend a staircase lit by a neon arrow advertising 'Thrills', past a flickering gas lamp and into a ranch-style underground bar, with an inflatable moose head and a portrait of the Queen as a rapper. The Bloody Marys are made with home-roasted cherry tomato juice.

EVANS & PEEL DETECTIVE AGENCY
310c Earls Court Road

Book an appointment and arrive with a mystery.

Enter the detective's office and present her with your unsolvable crime. She will usher you through her dusty bookshelves into a '20s-style dive bar with exposed brickwork, worn tiling and a wall of filing cabinets. Drinks are served in brown paper bags, or drawn from taps in the radiators. Try the tobacco-infused bourbon.

NIGHTJAR
129 City Road

Look for the door marked with a silhouette of a goatsucker.

Nightjar is the quintessential speakeasy: an elegant candlelit bar with live jazz, a burnished ceiling and mirrors etched with avian reliefs. Try a Beyond the Sea: a gin cocktail with oyster-leaf infusion, sherry, pink grapefruit, plankton air and yuzu salt. The menu is a pack of playing cards.

BARTS
Chelsea Cloisters, Sloane Avenue

Find a black door and press the doorbell in the Mickey Mouse room.

A little hatch flies open to reveal a pair of eyes. If accepted, you walk into a cluttered curiosity shop of antique oddities, dotted with teapot-strewn tables. There is a trunk of costumes if you want to blend in. Try Uncle Bart's Giant Teacup of Champions, which serves 8–10 people.[1] Once you become a regular at Barts, you'll get a key to let yourself in and out as you please.

EXPERIMENTAL COCKTAIL CLUB
13a Gerrard Street

The unmarked, battered door is manned by a bouncer with a children's book.

Behind the unpromising door, this secretive venue is arrayed over two floors of a Chinatown townhouse. Try the Opium Express: purple shiso-infused Ketel One, goji liqueur and syrup, dragon fruit, lemon juice and poppy seeds.

BYOC
Juice Club, 28 Bedfordbury

Hand over £20 at the Juice Bar.

This is a speakeasy with a difference: they don't have any alcohol. Bring your own cocktail spirit and the talented mixologist will use it to devise original masterpieces from their wide assortment of house ingredients. You are encouraged to swap booze with your neighbours to explore different combinations.

N —

---

[1] A whole bottle of Marquis vodka and a whole bottle of Prosecco are poured into an oversized teacup with apple, peach and berries.

THE LONDON ZODIAC

In the summer of 2011, artist Oscar Lhermitte created 12 new constellations above London: he strung stars in the sky between cranes and other high points in the city, each constellation representing a different London story.[1] Each constellation in this new London zodiac maps a different night-time itinerary. Prepare to hunt bats, play snooker, drink a Monkey Gland and jive till dawn.

STARS

When I was told by a teacher that the stars were other suns, I realised how far away they must be. I was fascinated by big numbers, and have been ever since. Humans throughout history have looked up in wonder at the dark starry sky. It's sad that young people in London never have this experience.

— *Lord Martin Rees, Astronomer Royal*

TELESCOPE [2]

The highest point in central London, the top of Hampstead Heath, is one of the best places for stargazing, even with the city's light pollution. For a closer look, visit the Hampstead Observatory: the Hampstead Scientific Society opens its telescopes for free from 8 till 10pm on Fridays and Saturdays, mid September to mid April. There is also free access to the UCL Observatory in Mill Hill.[3]

DREAM

For a blast of dream-like surrealism, walk along Camden High Street in the early hours. There are monsters crawling down the buildings: dragons, angels, silver scorpions and a giant white rocking chair. Sleepwalk along Regent's Canal towards the zoo. A Jolly Roger flaps over Pirate Castle and wild dogs prowl their canal-side enclosure. Bear north over Primrose Hill. Interpret your waking dream outside the house of Sigmund Freud, which has occasional late openings.

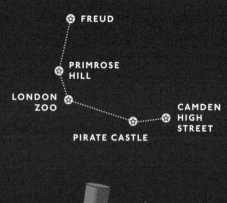

---

[1] For example, the 'Mosquito' above Mile End Park represented the unique species of mosquito breeding in the London Underground. See p.321.

[2] The telescope illustrated on the map is the Great Forty-Foot telescope designed by William Herschel in 1787. Today you can see a section of the original tube outside the Royal Observatory in Greenwich.

[3] One constellation you won't see in the sky is the Southern Cross, which is only ever visible south of the equator. Near Hyde Park Corner, however, six of the bronze 'standards' that form the New Zealand War Memorial are laid out in the pattern of the Southern Cross and are illuminated after dark.

COCKTAIL

You'll need to put on the ritz for this high-class bar crawl. Start with a Monkey Gland before midnight in the Ritz Rivoli Bar. Slide on to the Browns' naughty corner banquette for a Donovan Martini and live jazz.[1] The Westbury does excellent Mayfair Golds amid Swarovski Crystal fittings and the Connaught Bar offers a lesson in 'Bacchanology'. Finally hurry to Claridge's before 1am for a Regal. After that you can stay all night,[2] as long as you observe decorum.

BAT

The London Bat Group has an active events calendar. Go to Hyde Park to see pipistrelles, Europe's smallest bat, and noctules, Britain's largest, best seen flitting over the Serpentine. While you're there, consider the sinister aftermath of the lost film *London After Midnight*. This 1927 vampire flick was used as defence by Robert Williams, who murdered a girl in Hyde Park: he claimed the film had driven him temporarily insane.[3] Then walk from Hyde Park to Eon House at 138 Piccadilly, once the central London residence of Bram Stoker's Dracula.

SPECTRE

After spirits at the Black Lion Pub in Hammersmith, try this closing-time ghost tour. The pub itself is haunted[4] by Thomas Millwood, shot in 1803 by an excise officer who mistook him, ironically, for the 'Hammersmith Ghost'. During the ensuing murder trial, John Graham, a shoemaker, revealed that he was the Hammersmith Ghost and had been dressing up in costume to protest against ghost stories. Walk to Margravine Cemetery nearby, the site of one of Graham's attacks, and complete the tour by visiting Holland Park, where the Earl of Holland still carries his severed head; the Coronet Theatre, Notting Hill, where a spectral cashier haunts the stalls; and Cambridge Gardens to catch a phantom bus.

N ——————

MAP READING

The London Zodiac *is an astronomical chart of London at night. Each constellation is a short themed route to walk after dark. It references the 1680* Celestial Planisphere *by the Dutch cartographer Frederik De Wit; the six roundels contain adapted diagrams of the solar system. The two Pole Stars are the Royal Society of Astronomy and Gresham College, both of which run a regular programme of cosmological events.*

---

❶ The bar is named after the photographer Terence Donovan. His more risqué shots are confined to one corner.
❷ Or go to Grosvenor Square, toss defrosted chicken drumsticks over the railings and indulge in some urban foxhunting.

❸ Perhaps it's fortunate that the last known copy of the film was incinerated in 1967.
❹ Find another haunted pub on p.281.

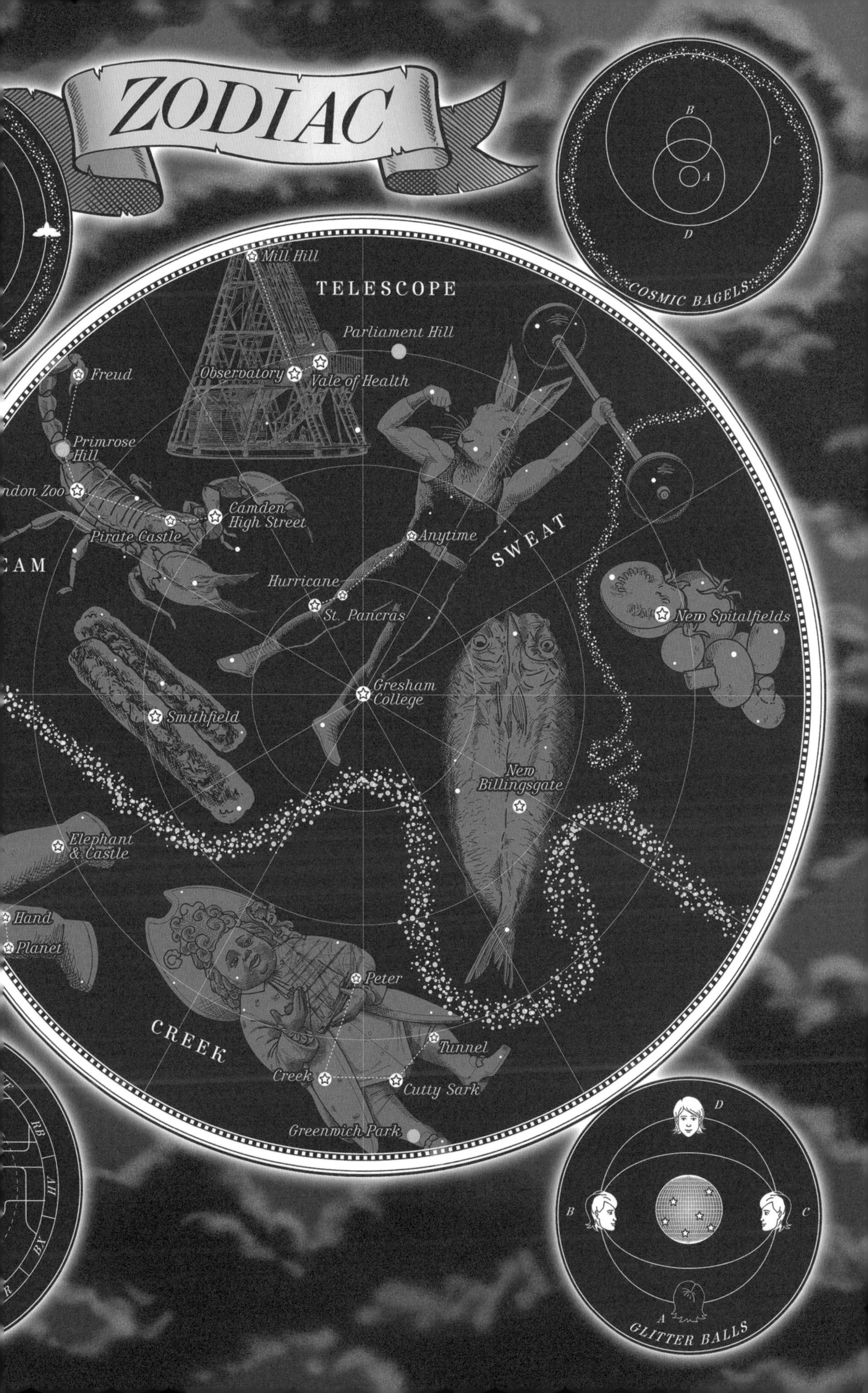

ZODIAC

COSMIC BAGELS

B

C

A

D

TELESCOPE

Mill Hill

Parliament Hill

Observatory

Vale of Health

Freud

Primrose Hill

London Zoo

Camden High Street

Pirate Castle

Anytime

SWEAT

Hurricane

New Spitalfields

St. Pancras

CAM

Smithfield

Gresham College

New Billingsgate

Elephant & Castle

Hand

Planet

Peter

CREEK

Creek

Tunnel

Cutty Sark

Greenwich Park

GLITTER BALLS

D

B

C

A

SWEAT

If you're counting the calories, remember that a night's sleep burns 500. If that's just not enough, head to King's Cross for alternative night-time exercise. Hit the treadmill at Anytime Fitness on Pentonville Road, then shoot some frames at the 24-hour Hurricane Pool and Snooker Club. Once you've warmed down, you can pile the calories back on at the all-night Costa in St Pancras Station.

- ⊛ ANYTIME
- HURRICANE ⊛
- ⊛ ST. PANCRAS

WEREWOLF

If it's raining, find a werewolf with a Chinese menu and follow him to Lee Ho Fook's for a big dish of beef chow mein. Listen to Warren Zevon's 'Werewolves of London' as you do so.[1] Fook's, on Gerrard Street, has since been renamed Dumpling's Legend and closes at 1am. If you miss it, try Mr Kong on Lisle Street, which closes at 2.45am. For more music, go to Ronnie Scott's Late Late Show on Frith Street or Ain't Nothin' But blues bar on Kingly Street. When the music stops, order a coffee at Bar Italia on Frith Street, which never shuts.[2] Lick on Greek Street serves gelato until half midnight on Fridays and Saturdays.

- BLUES ⊛ ········· ⊛ LICK
- SCOTT'S ⊛
- BAR ITALIA ⊛
- MR KONG ⊛
- DUMPLING'S ⊛
  LEGEND

ASTRONAUT

Take a space walk around London's most cosmic locations. Begin outside the mysterious British Interplanetary Society HQ on South Lambeth Road. There are often lights on late at night.[3] Not far away on Kennington Road, the west-side plane trees are labelled with the names of the Apollo astronauts. Visit them all and then camp outside the Virgin Galactic office, 50 Pall Mall, to be first in line for space tourist tickets in the morning.

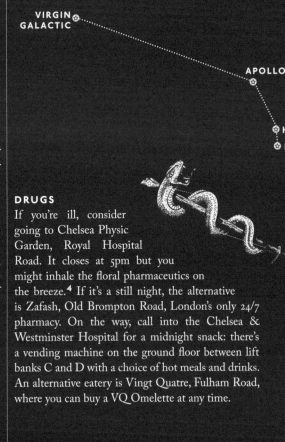

- VIRGIN ⊛
  GALACTIC
- APOLLO ⊛
- ⊛ H
- ⊛ P

DRUGS

If you're ill, consider going to Chelsea Physic Garden, Royal Hospital Road. It closes at 5pm but you might inhale the floral pharmaceutics on the breeze.[4] If it's a still night, the alternative is Zafash, Old Brompton Road, London's only 24/7 pharmacy. On the way, call into the Chelsea & Westminster Hospital for a midnight snack: there's a vending machine on the ground floor between lift banks C and D with a choice of hot meals and drinks. An alternative eatery is Vingt Quatre, Fulham Road, where you can buy a VQ Omelette at any time.

- ZAFASH ⊛
- ⊛ VINGT QUATRE
- HOSPITAL ⊛
- ⊛ PHYSIC
  GARDEN

---

[1] According to the song, you might also meet a well-groomed werewolf nursing a piña colada in Trader Vic's bar inside the Hilton on Park Lane.

[2] See p.181.

[3] This space advocacy organisation was founded in the 1930s by a group of enthusiasts. Anyone can become a member and attend events at their HQ (bis-space.com).

[4] Inhale herbal aphrodisiacs on p.77.

CREEK

The Greenwich Foot Tunnel[1] is open all night. Walk to the maritime borough under the Thames and emerge to admire the ghostly Cutty Sark, riding its cloud of illuminated glass. Then visit Up the Creek, South London's cult comedy venue, which hosts raucous after-parties until 2am on Fridays and Saturdays. If you fancy something quieter, walk to the mouth of Deptford Creek, where you'll find Peter the Great standing next to a dwarf.[2] Sit in his high-backed Russian throne, gaze along the river, and tune in to the shipping forecast at 00.48. Sail on the airwaves to Viking, Fair Isle, Biscay and Shannon.

PETER

TUNNEL

CREEK · · · · · · · · · · · CUTTY SARK

SHADES

Sometimes one night is too short, but in Brixton that doesn't have to be a problem. Begin Friday evening at Hootananny on Effra Road. Enjoy the ska in this characterful pub before migrating to one of many nearby clubs. Skank till dawn, then move on to Club 414 on Coldharbour Lane for their morning-after party. Come midday you'll be back on the street. Put on some shades and take a taxi to The Windmill, Brixton. It's always night-time in this windowless music cave.[3] Take shelter, catch a band or two, and hide out until night falls and you can begin again.

WINDMILL · · · · · · · · CLUB 414

HOOTANANNY

FRY-TINERARY

After a sleepless night there's nothing better than a fry-up, so why not spend the hours before dawn assembling the ingredients?

MUSHROOMS
Arrive at New Spitalfields Market (Leyton) for 1.30am to find the juiciest mushrooms and tomatoes. Then hop on the N26 and N242 to Smithfield (Farringdon, opens 3am).

BACON
Rifle the meat stalls for the perfect sausages and bacon, and drop into Tinseltown Diner for a snack (St John Street, closes 5am).

EGGS
Hop back on the N242 and catch the 344 via Elephant & Castle to New Covent Garden (Vauxhall). You can pick up freshly laid eggs among the flowers.

KIPPERS
Finally catch the 344 and 135 to New Billingsgate (Canary Wharf, opens 5am) for kippers.

N

❶ See p.325.
❷ Join the tsar in a wheelbarrow on p.381.
❸ There used to be a dog on their roof. See p.339.

HOUSELESSNESS

In the 1860s, Charles Dickens ran the magazine *All the Year Round* and lived above its offices at what is now the Charles Dickens Coffee House on Wellington Street. When he couldn't sleep he walked the streets:[1] the purpose of these walks was an 'education in a fair amateur experience of houselessness', bringing himself into 'sympathetic relations' with the homeless. He describes one of his routes in the essay 'Night Walks'.

WATERLOO BRIDGE
Set off at half past midnight and walk down to Waterloo Bridge. Dickens chatted to the toll-keeper here and recalled the 'chopped-up murdered man' who had recently been discovered below the bridge in a carpet bag.

THEATRE ROYAL, DRURY LANE
Dickens retraced his steps to the Theatre Royal, Drury Lane, and walked out on to the dark, empty stage, feeling like 'a diver might, at the bottom of the sea'.

NEWGATE PRISON
At Newgate Prison he paused at the 'wicked little Debtors' Door' (now the main entrance to the Old Bailey) with his back to the gallows where Oliver Twist witnessed Fagin's hanging.

BANK OF ENGLAND
He moved on and walked the perimeter of the Bank of England,[2] thinking of the treasure within and catching a glimpse of the 'guard of soldiers passing the night there, and nodding over the fire'.

LONDON BRIDGE
Then he walked south to London Bridge. As you cross the river, look up at the wild moon and clouds, 'as restless as an evil conscience in a tumbled bed', and drink in the 'shadow of the immensity of London [lying] oppressively upon the river'.

ANCHOR BREWERY
On the south bank, Dickens walked through the bustling Anchor Brewery with its 'smell of grains, and the rattling of the plump dray horses at their mangers'. The Anchor was once the largest brewery in the world; now all that remains is the old brewery tap, the Anchor Tavern on Park Street.

KING'S BENCH PRISON
Next he passed the King's Bench prison, which has also disappeared. The Scovell Estate is built on the site of this debtors' prison, where David Copperfield visits Mr Micawber.

BEDLAM
Outside Bedlam,[3] now the Imperial War Museum, Dickens has a protracted 'night fancy' about the equivalence of madness and sanity in the dreaming night-time. The gates are open for you to walk in between the huge naval guns.

WESTMINSTER ABBEY
Crossing Westminster Bridge, you can't get into the 'fine gloomy society' of Westminster Abbey at night as Dickens did, which is a shame, because he's buried in Poets' Corner.

---

[1] Dickens was a keen walker. Look for the illuminating plaque near Borough Station, which records the fact that 'Charles Dickens walked past here'.

[2] For more on this wall, see p.351.

[3] See p.291.

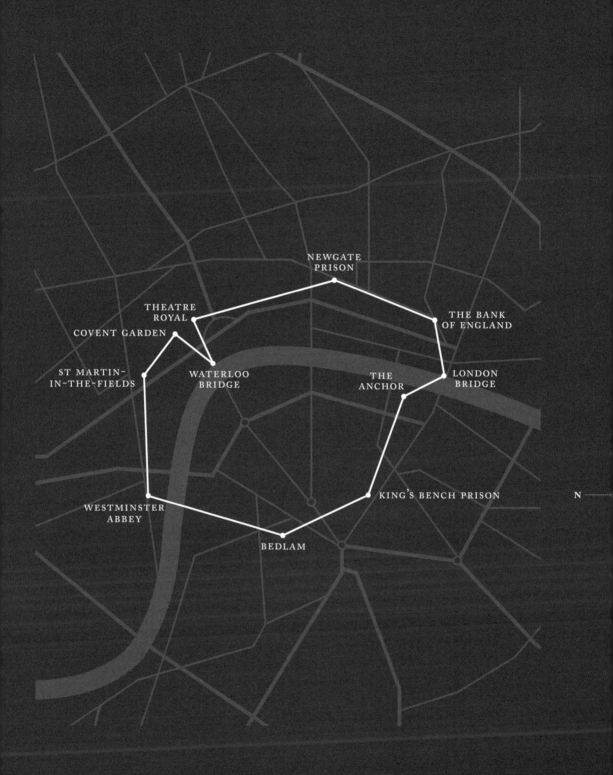

NEWGATE PRISON

THEATRE ROYAL

COVENT GARDEN

THE BANK OF ENGLAND

ST MARTIN-IN-THE-FIELDS

WATERLOO BRIDGE

THE ANCHOR

LONDON BRIDGE

WESTMINSTER ABBEY

KING'S BENCH PRISON

BEDLAM

N

ST MARTIN-IN-THE-FIELDS

Before you know it, it's 3am and you're in Trafalgar Square. Walk up the steps of St Martin-in-the-Fields. Dickens was on this spot as the clock struck three, and a figure rose up in front of him 'with a cry of loneliness and houselessness'.

COVENT GARDEN

Covent Garden was then a small-hours flower, fruit and vegetable jamboree with 'great waggons of cabbages' and dirty children making 'a blunt pattering of the pavement of the Piazza with the rain of their naked feet'. Today it's a deserted mall with a single street cleaner. A few steps more and you're back at Wellington Street.

ROUGH NIGHTS

London's homeless and runaways tend to cluster centrally, in the brightest, most moneyed and most anonymous parts of town: the backstreets between Charing Cross and Trafalgar Square, the covered walkways near Victoria Station, the arcade in front of the Ritz. Vauxhall is a hot spot as there are several hostels around the bus station and the *Big Issue* offices are nearby. In St James's Piccadilly and Notre Dame de France the local homeless sleep on pews.

Homelessness is so prevalent and visible in central London that it is hard to know how to react to it; and any individual's native generosity battles with an impossible level of demand. Saying that, many who've been homeless say that even a smile and a greeting goes a long way. And for those who want to get more involved in tackling this issue, there are many initiatives always looking for support and volunteers.

REPORTING

If you notice somebody sleeping rough, you can phone Street Link on their 24-hour hotline (0300 500 0914). They will notify the Street Rescue team who circulate around London, helping the homeless to access the right services. Their work is part of the 'No Second Night Out' initiative, started in 2011.

SUPPORTING

At Black Sheep Coffee on Goodge Street you can donate a discounted hot drink to a homeless person via their 'free coffee board'. Then pick up a coffee for yourself at the Old Spike Roastery on Peckham Rye. This coffee shop and social enterprise offers housing, training and employment to homeless people in the local area.

Shop for spruced-up furniture and electronics at the Emmaus boutiques in Lambeth and Greenwich. Emmaus communities offer room, board and a weekly allowance to anyone who is homeless, for as long as they need it (emmaus.org.uk). Residents work for 40 hours a week, learning to upcycle furniture and repair electronic appliances, which are then sold in shops. The proceeds fund the community.

SPITAL

In 1197, the Mayor of the City of London kicked out all the homeless people, the street sellers and the beggars, by creating a hostel a mile up the road from the City called the Hospital of St Mary Spital, and that is the origin of Spitalfields: the hospital fields.
— *The Gentle Author*

VOLUNTEERING

Help those who are sleeping rough by joining a Street Rescue team (thamesreach.org.uk). You'll explore the night-time city in a van, responding to sightings of rough sleepers and supporting them into emergency accommodation.

Get to know members of the homeless community better by volunteering at a St Mungo's Broadway hostel, running activities or acting as a mentor (mungosbroadway. org.uk).

If you have a spare room, become a Nightstop host and offer emergency accommodation to a vulnerable young person without a place to stay (depaulnights topuk.org).

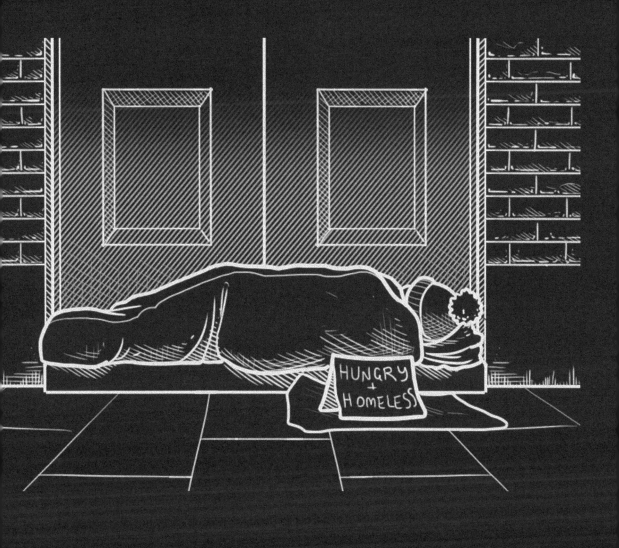

DOWN AND OUT

Take a copy of George Orwell's *Down and Out in Paris and London* and read it in Potters Fields, the open space behind City Hall. Orwell stayed in a dosshouse for the homeless on Tooley Street while researching the book and wrote parts of it in St Olave's Library, which used to stand on Potters Fields.

CHEESE & DREAMS

Spice up your night with a mind-altering substance: we recommend cheese. Take a stroll through London's pasteurised past, load up on Cheddar and Stilton, and prepare for some psychedelic shut-eye.

NEAL'S YARD DAIRY

The British Cheese Renaissance began in 1979 when Randolph Hodgson founded Neal's Yard Dairy. Their Park Street branch is next to the gourmand's paradise of Borough Market, which contains several other quality cheesemongers. It's an ideal place to start a cheese odyssey.

Eat some fine Cheddar and then head out of the market and across London Bridge.

PHILPOT LANE MICE

Wind past the Monument and find Caffè Nero on Eastcheap. If you look carefully, you'll spot a tiny sculpture of mice eating a ball of cheese on the side of the building. This piece of 19th-century street art commemorates two builders working on the Monument:[1] apparently they fought over missing cheese sandwiches and fell to their deaths; it was later discovered that their sandwiches were eaten by mice.

Walk along Eastcheap to Seething Lane Gardens.

PEPYS'S PARMESAN

In 1666, three nights after the Great Fire had started, Samuel Pepys climbed the spire of All Hallows Church and beheld the blaze, 'spread as far as I could see it'. He was concerned because he lived on Seething Lane nearby. To protect his most precious possessions, he dug a pit in his garden and buried his papers, his wine and his Parmesan cheese. His house survived the flames and there is usually a plaque in Seething Lane Gardens[2] marking the site, but it has been moved while the gardens are dug up to construct a three-storey basement car park. Now is the moment to bury your own Parmesan: just lob a piece into the enormous pit.[3]

Walk from Seething Lane along Pepys Street and turn left on to Savage Gardens.

CHEESE ROLLING

On the Late Spring Bank Holiday at the end of May, Coopers Hill in Gloucestershire is the site of a glorious fixture in the British sporting calendar: cheese rolling. Truckles of Double Gloucester are launched down the steep slope and competitors career after them. The gentle incline of Seething Lane is perfect for inner-city cheese rolling: Baby Boules.[4] Distribute Babybels, position the pig (a wax-coated Cheddar works best) and start rolling. Whoever's baby boule ends closest to the pig wins the cheese.

Turn left on to Crutched Friars, past the Cheshire Cheese, and then weave through French Ordinary Court towards Leadenhall Street.

THE CHEESEGRATER

The Cheesegrater is perfectly placed next to the Gherkin: soon we'll have all the architectural ingredients for a humungous Ploughman's lunch.

Continue left along Leadenhall Street.

THE SCIENCE

Cheese contains the amino acid tryptophan, which has been shown to reduce stress and induce sleep. Its precise effect on our dreams is harder to determine. In 2005, the aptly named British Cheese Board ran a survey, 'Cheese and Dreams', and discovered that …

IF YOU EAT	YOU'LL DREAM OF
Stilton	vivid and bizarre things, such as crying crocodiles;
Cheddar	celebrities;
Red Leicester	schooldays and childhood friends;
Brie	nice things if you're a woman, strange things if you're a man;
Cheshire	nothing – you'll have a dreamless sleep.

---

❶ See p.337.
❷ An ancient ceremony takes place here each year. See p.189.
❸ If the works have finished, grate some on to the rose beds instead.
❹ For traditional, cheese-free boules see p.232.

CHEESE AT LEADENHALL MARKET

Turn into Leadenhall Market, where cheese has been sold since at least 1397. This Victorian arcade, with its stunning gold-and-burgundy ironwork, occupies the site of the Roman forum. It was the Romans who first brought sheep's cheese-making techniques to Britain in 43 AD; go in to Cheese at Leadenhall Market and ask to taste a Roman-style ewe's milk cheese, such as Berkswell.

Across the street is Bell Inn Yard.

BELL INN YARD

Another Bell Inn is located in the village of Stilton on the Great North Road, where Stilton was first sold to travellers.[1]

Savour the mould as you weave through the labyrinthine alleyways to Cheapside.

MILK STREET

'Cheap' is the Old English word for market, and the two big market streets of medieval London were Cheapside and Eastcheap. Many of the side streets retain the identity of the products sold there: Bread Street, Wood Street and Poultry. Milk Street[2] was the centre of the medieval dairy trade.

Crumble some Wensleydale on your way to the west end of St Paul's.

WINGED COW

Look for the winged cow on the west front of St Paul's Cathedral, the god of cheese makers and eaters everywhere.[3] Eat some Stinking Bishop on this sacred site then walk down Ludgate Hill and up Fleet Street.

YE OLDE CHESHIRE CHEESE

Cheshire is the quintessential London cheese. In the 18th Century, Daniel Defoe described how it was shipped 'by river all over the country in enormous quantities, 14,000 tons a year going to London alone'. The cheese was sold in pubs, and lent its name to several in London. Ye Olde Cheshire Cheese is particularly atmospheric: Dickens was a regular and mentions it in *A Tale of Two Cities*. Finish your fromage foray by ordering the Welsh rarebit, which is traditionally made with Cheshire cheese.

LONDON DREAMS

WILLIAM ARCHER was at Watford Junction and wanted to get to London, but a sudden queue for tickets meant he missed his splendid *train de luxe*.

MARY ARNOLD-FOSTER was at a party at the Royal Society in Burlington House, attended by Lord Kelvin and other eminent scientists, and she demonstrated her method of flying by circling round the ceiling.[4]

LEWIS CARROLL took nine-year-old Marion 'Polly' Terry from her suburban home to see herself, the grown-up Polly, on stage at the Walter House theatre.

JOHN DEE was dead and disembowelled, but still mobile and able to speak to the Lord Treasurer who had come to burn his magic books in Mortlake.[5]

WALTER DE LA MARE had perpetrated a murder, the victim of which had lain a year in a house on a narrow deserted London street. He and the body were about to be discovered.

THOMAS DE QUINCEY was walking by lamplight in Oxford Street[6] with Ann the prostitute, as they had done 17 years earlier.

LORD MACAULEY's niece admitted that Pepys's *Diary* was all a forgery, and that she had forged it. 'What!' he expostulated. 'I have been quoting in reviews, and in my *History*, a forgery of yours as a book of the highest authority.'

SAMUEL PEPYS was making water on his doorstep and found it extremely painful. He discovered the cause by pulling a turd out of his 'yard'.[7]

N ———

---

❶ Stilton was never traditionally made in Stilton and it is now illegal to make it there. Stilton is one of very few legally protected British cheeses: it can only be made in Derbyshire, Leicestershire and Nottinghamshire.

❷ For a former resident of Milk Street, see p.6.

❸ This alate ungulate is actually the symbol of Luke the Evangelist and represents sacrifice, service and strength.

❹ Float to the ceiling on p.142.

❺ See p.361.

❻ For more on De Quincey's walking habits, see p.288.

❼ For a real-life encounter between Pepys and turds, see p.50.

NIGHT SHADES

The shadows of the night disguise lurking terrors.
Look out for these fearful figures when you're alone after dark.

THE PIG-FACED LADY OF MAIDA VALE

On a March night in 1912, Elliott O'Donnell witnessed a pig-faced lady haunting Maida Vale: 'It was the most sublimely horrible thing I ever saw. It was human and yet not human; the top part of the head covered with a tangled mass of long hair was that of a woman; the lower, with two obliquely set eyes and a thin, leering mouth, was that of a pig.' He saw her again a fortnight later.[1]

THE GOAT-MAN OF THE PARKLAND WALK

The Parkland Walk is a seemingly delightful strip of nature reserve that links Finsbury Park with Highgate Wood. Beware as you walk past Crouch Hill, however. This stretch of abandoned train line was haunted in the 1980s by a ghostly goat-man who terrified local children at night, and today the old railway arches near the abandoned station contain an enormous green spriggan, leaping out of the brickwork. Apparently, this unnerving sculpture inspired Stephen King to write his short story 'Crouch End', in which a man is swallowed into Crouch Hill by the horrific Goat with a Thousand Young. If you escape the Parkland Walk, recover by dropping down the hill to Kentish Town City Farm and petting Sharon, their resident nanny goat.

SPRING-HEELED JACK

In the 1830s, an agile gentleman terrorised the city. Reports of his physical appearance vary: sometimes he's described as a man in a black cloak, with a helmet and tight-fitting white oilskin; at other times he appeared as a devil, with clawed hands and fiery eyes. He would attack people viciously and was reputed to be able to leap over hedges and walls. The reports caused widespread panic, although only one victim's testimony seems to have involved a genuine attack.

THE FISH FIGURE AT CLEOPATRA'S NEEDLE

Cleopatra's Needle is almost 3,500 years old, carved more than a millennium before Cleopatra was born. When the 60-foot obelisk was given to the British government in 1819, there were rumours of a curse. Sure enough, the journey to London was disastrous: six seamen died in a storm that nearly sank the monument. In the 1950s, homeless people sleeping rough on the Embankment steered clear of the spot after sightings of a tall, nude figure with a pointed head and a body covered with scales. The figure would appear next to the Needle and then leap into the river, accompanied by hellish, mocking laughter.

THE QUEEN RAT OF BERMONDSEY

The 'toshers' of Bermondsey worked the London sewers, collecting scrap metal and valuable items to resell.[2] They told stories of a great Queen Rat who would listen to a handsome tosher talking, then appear to him at night in the form of his dream girl and sleep with him. The clue to Queen Rat's identity is that one of her eyes is blue and one is grey. If she's pleased with your performance, she gives you a love bite on the neck, which bestows great luck and warns other rats not to harm you. Go to St Saviour's Dock in Shad Thames. If you're lucky, you'll meet either Queen Rat or the modern troubadour Nigel of Bermondsey, who might regale you with 'One Eye Grey', his song inspired by the legend.

---

[1] A hundred years earlier, London had been agog with tales of the Pig-Faced Woman of Manchester Square. She is now overdue a 21st-century appearance.

[2] Henry Mayhew heard grizzly tales 'of sewer-hunters beset by myriads of enormous rats'. Meet the toshers' colleagues, the flushers, on p.55.

DAWN

ALL-NIGHTERS

WATCH FILMS
The Prince Charles Cinema on Leicester Place holds regular all-night film marathons. Pyjamas mandatory. Try their 'Frightfest' each Halloween.

EAT BREAKFAST
It's always breakfast time in Polo Bar on Bishopsgate. This greasy spoon is open 24-hours a day and has been serving fry-ups for nigh on 50 years.

READ A BOOK
LSE Library on Portugal Street is open 24/7 during term time for students and staff, and till midnight for visitors. Apply for a pass online.

OBSERVE A VIGIL
All-night adoration at the Tyburn Convent, near Marble Arch, is open to the public once a month. Contact the Vigilant Mistress for information.

CITY DAWNS

PEACEFUL
At sunrise every morning, a single Buddhist monk makes the short walk from his temple and home in Battersea Park to the riverside Peace Pagoda, beating a drum and chanting the Daimoku. Join the Reverend Gyoro Nagase for prayers at dawn.

WILD
Watch the early scullers from the Richmond riverbank opposite Eel Pie Island.[1] Take eggs and a camping stove, and enjoy having this wild slice of London to yourself.

POETIC
Relive Wordsworth's 'Upon Westminster Bridge': 'This City now doth, like a garment, wear / The beauty of the morning; [...] The river glideth at his own sweet will: / Dear God! the very houses seem asleep; / And all that mighty heart is lying still!'

TECHNICOLOUR
Every morning at 7.30am, there is a half-hour Morning Prayer service in Westminster Abbey. If you go in December or January, you'll see dawn breaking through the ancient stained-glass windows.

CETACEAN
Described by Will Self as a series of monumental whales' backs, 'as if a pod of these leviathans had been frozen in mid-motion', Stockwell Bus Depot is a surprisingly handsome structure. The best view is from Lansdowne Way. Linger nearby at 5.30am to witness shoals of buses dispersing on their daily migratory patterns.

N ———

[1] See p.125.

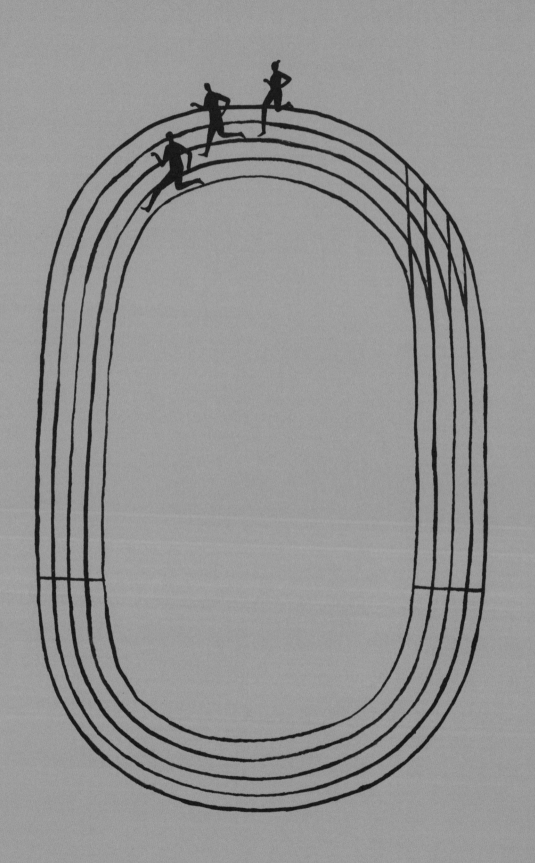

THE OTHER OLYMPIC GAMES

Olympic sports fall in and out of favour. The tug of war was retired in 1920 and perhaps now is the moment for others to follow suit and give way to a fresh intake. This is a blueprint for the capital's next Olympic Park, and a vision of the events we'll be glued to next time the interlocking rings hover over the city.

CHEESE BOWLING ①

The Hampstead Lawn Billiard and Skittle Club now concentrates solely on skittles. They play an old English variant of the sport, which involves lobbing a wooden 'cheese' at nine pins.[1] The cheese 'should swing like a pendulum' the club advises, with the power 'from the swing not from the elbow'. This mysterious society is situated in the basement of the Freemasons Arms on Hampstead's Downshire Hill. There is no mention of them on the pub's website, but all are welcome to the club's regular Tuesday evening games.

MOB FOOTBALL ②

Mob football, a medieval forerunner of the modern game, involves two crowds attempting to manoeuvre a stuffed bladder towards the opposing team's marker. It has few rules and no upper limit on players. Although mob football is still played outside the capital, it has all but died out in London itself. Londoners wishing for the full medieval football experience today will need to found their own club, or begin launching bladders into crowds of shoppers until someone joins in.[2]

ARM WRESTLING

Join the London Arm Wrestling Team at Peacock Gym in Canning Town and train up for the Arm Wars 'Capital Punishment' tournament at the O2 in September (londonarmwrestlingteam. com).

BEAR-BAITING

Elizabeth I was a particular fan of bear-baiting.[3] Variations included bull-baiting and rat baiting: the Artillery Arms on Old Street used to get through 700 rats a week.

CROQUET

The name 'Pall Mall' comes from *pallamaglio*, an Italian game like croquet. Set up your own croquet club in St James's, or head to Golders Hill Park to play with the Hampstead Heath Croquet Club (hampsteadheathcroquetclub.org. uk).

DODGEBALL

Form a team of six and enter the Dodgeball London League. Remember the five Ds of dodgeball: dodge, duck, dip, dive and dodge (dodgeball-london.com).

EGG & SPOON

In the V&A Museum of Childhood you can see a set of whittled wooden eggs and spoons designed especially for racing.[4]

FREERUNNING

Learn the techniques of freerunning in the Parkour Generations Chainstore Gym at Trinity Buoy Wharf, the UK's only indoor parkour training zone. They hold daily classes that will have you leaping between metal, concrete and wooden structures and prepare you for the playground of the city.

O

---

❶ The pins are made of hornbeam and the 4kg cheese is made out of lignum vitae, a dense wood that was used to make early police truncheons.

❷ Some early versions of football were played with the heads of enemies, something students of King's College London are rumoured to have done with the preserved head of Jeremy Bentham from their rival institution University College. UCL refute this. See p.349.

❸ Henry Mayhew recorded a 19th-century showman complaining of the difficulty of finding lodgings for his animal: 'Bears is well-behaved enough if they ain't aggravated'.

❹ In 1990, Dale Lyons completed the London Marathon in 3 hours 47 minutes while balancing an uncooked egg on a dessert spoon.

RUGBY NETBALL ③

Rugby netball, or netrugby, combines the robust physical contact of rugby with the nimble passing and shooting of netball. The aim is to throw a rugby ball into the opposing team's net. The sport has been played on Clapham Common for over a hundred years and is now played nowhere else in the world. Join the club and help maintain a dwindling pastime. Games are on weekday evenings and the season ends with a full-day World Cup (netrugby.org).

LUCHA LIBRE ④

Learn the art of masked Mexican Lucha wrestling at the Resistance Gallery, tucked away in a railway arch behind Cambridge Heath Road. Beginner classes are held on Monday nights. Once you've mastered the essentials of this high-flying martial art, you may be invited to intermediate classes, pro classes and, ultimately, offered a part in the Lucha Britannia show alongside wrestlers including Glamsexico, El Stupido and three-time champion Santeria (luchabritannia.com).

CHESSBOXING ⑤

Chessboxing began as a piece of Dutch conceptual art, inspired by a French post-apocalyptic graphic novel.[1] In 2003, artist Iepe Rubingh staged and won the first tournament of the hybrid sport, in which contenders face each other in alternate rounds of chess and boxing until someone achieves a checkmate or knockout. Rubingh's wry art project caught the imagination of other brainy brawlers and several clubs sprung up, including London Chessboxing in 2008. Join a Saturday morning class at Islington Boxing Club to begin honing your skills (londonchessboxing.com/classes).

ROAD SKATING ⑥

Roller skates have evolved considerably since their invention in 1760. John-Joseph Merlin, a Belgian inventor in London, is usually credited with creating the first pair and is said to have lost control and broken a mirror while demonstrating them at a Soho soirée.[2] To road skate in London now, join the weekly 10–15 mile London Friday Night Skate, a marshalled group outing that meets at Wellington Arch at 8pm. Less confident skaters and those wearing 18th-century prototypes should join the Sunday Roller Stroll instead, which meets on Serpentine Road at 2pm (lfns.co.uk).

GAELIC FOOTBALL

'Caid' was codified a quarter of a century after Association Football, to preserve some of the game's more ancient rules, such as carrying, bouncing, hand-passing and soloing the ball. There are Gaelic football clubs located across the city, including the Dulwich Harps in Peckham Rye (dulwichharps.com) and the Holloway Gaels in Haringey (hollowaygaels.org).

HAGGIS HURLING

In this traditional Scottish sport the contender stands on a whisky barrel and hurls a haggis as far as possible. The haggis must be edible after landing. On Burns Night, 25 January, set up your barrel and let the games commence.

IAIDO

Iaido is a Japanese martial art, which involves drawing a huge sword, striking your opponent, removing the blood and replacing the sword in its 'saya'. Learn with a *bokken*, or wooden sword, at the Central Hagakure Dojo in Marylebone, with sensei Len Bean (hagakure.co.uk).

JOUSTING

Each June, Eltham Palace hosts a 'Grand Medieval Joust'. Watch as knights in full armour clash on horseback. Expect colourful encampments and a cheeky jester.

KABADDI

Kabaddi is an ancient Indian contact sport, in which contestants hold their breath and make raids into the opponents' territory. If you can grapple without oxygen, consider joining the Singh Sabha team in Southall.

---

① *Froid Équateur* (1992).   ② Some reports suggest he was playing the violin at the same time.

SKINNY DIPPING ⑦

'There come moods when these clothes of ours are not only too irksome to wear,' wrote Walt Whitman, 'but are themselves indecent.' Those who agree and prefer to exercise unencumbered should attend Naturist London's Sunday Swim at the University of London Union pool, which takes place each week at midday (naturist.london/4SundaySwim.php).[1]

ICE CLIMBING ⑧

If London's landscape isn't rugged enough for your alpine appetites, go to Ellis Brigham Mountain Sports on Southampton Way. The back wall of the shop is made of ice and can be booked by those seeking to finesse their ice climbing without leaving the city. There are a number of routes up the frosty precipice, one of which includes a sharp overhang.

BAR BILLIARDS ⑨

Bar Billiards involves eight balls, nine holes and three wooden mushrooms. The objective is to pot the balls in the holes with the greatest value, while avoiding obstacles. Play in the games room of the Cheshire Cheese pub on Little Essex Street.

OCTOPUSH ⑩

To the spectator, octopush is little more than a wild watery skirmish. Besnorkeled players armed with 35cm batons pursue a lead 'squid' on the bottom of a swimming pool and try to propel it into their opponents' goal. The sport was created in 1954 as winter exercise for scuba divers.[2] There are London octopush teams in Islington and Lewisham who welcome newcomers.

BROOMBALL ⑪

Broomball is a Canadian sport rather like ice hockey, but with trainers instead of skates and rudimentary wooden paddles instead of hockey sticks. Broadgate Ice Rink holds tournaments on Tuesday nights in winter that anyone can enter. Write in advance to express your interest (broadgate.co.uk/Broomball). The world's first skating rink was called the Glaciarium and opened in Covent Garden in 1844. They couldn't use ice, because it melted, so people skated on a reeking mixture of pig fat and salts.

MAP READING

The Other Olympic Games draws on Soviet propaganda posters, with their block colours and healthy, active bodies, and turns the whole of London into an alternative Olympic Park.

LAWN BOWLS

The City of London Bowls Club occupies Finsbury Circus.[3] Matches take place on Tuesday evenings with the finals every September. Spectate from the Pavilion, the wooden clubhouse that has been converted into a wine bar.

MOUNTAINEERING

Chalk your hands and clamber around the Castle Climbing Centre near Finsbury Park, a converted Victorian pumping station that looks like a fairy-tale castle. Alternatively, climb trees in Trent Park (goape.co.uk/days-out/trent-park), or the granite boulder on Mabley Green in Hackney.[4] Or, like the cast of Monty Python, attempt to scale the north face of the Uxbridge Road between the junction of Willesden Road and the bus stop.

NETBALL

Go Mammoth is the largest social netball club in London, with nine venues across the city.

ORIENTEERING

Geocaching is an international treasure hunt craze for tracking down hidden 'caches' and signing your name. There is a geocache trail that crosses all the Thames bridges in London. Alternatively, turn up at a SLOW event organised by the South London Orienteers (slow.org.uk).

POLO

Ham Polo Club coaches polo in Petersham. Or head over to Newington Gardens in Elephant and Castle for a game of hardcourt bicycle polo (lhbpa.org.uk).

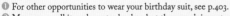

❶ For other opportunities to wear your birthday suit, see p.403.
❷ Many now call it underwater hockey, but the game's inventor, Alan Blake, decries the new name as 'unimaginative and non-descriptive' and insists that it is not 'an adapted land game'.
❸ The lawn is currently turfed up as part of the Crossrail development, but is due to be fully restored by the end of 2017. Meet the boring machines on p.323.
❹ The Mabley Green Boulder is one half of a giant artwork: the other rock is in Shoreditch Park.

URBAN GOLF ⑫

Disc golf adheres to the principles of golf but uses frisbees and elevated metal baskets instead of balls and holes. London's only 18-hole disc golf course is in Croydon's Lloyd Park. Old-fashioned golfers who cleave to their clubs may prefer urban golf, as pioneered by the Shoreditch Golf Club, who mapped out an 18-hole course around the streets of East London in 2004. A soft leather ball must be used to prevent injury or damage.

PÉTANQUE ⑬

Pétanque involves aiming light metal balls at a smaller wooden ball, known as a piglet. The French sport is thriving in London and the finest place to play is on the gravel of Cleaver Square in Kennington. The London Pétanque Club play there every Wednesday evening in summer and on the first Saturday morning of the month in winter (londonpetanqueclub.com). The tiny Prince of Wales pub on the corner of the square has a pétanque set for loan.

POWERPRAMMING ⑭

Although pushing a pram can be strenuous, it hasn't traditionally been considered a sport. Powerpramming has changed that, converting babe and buggy into fitness accessories. Groups jog through London parks pushing their prams and toning as they go. Free 'Buggy Exercise' sessions are run by Our Parks (ourparks.org.uk).

ULTIMATE FRISBEE ⑮

Chaucer and Shakespeare both reinterpreted the tale of the doomed lovers Pyramus and Thisbe. The story's latest incarnation is in the name of the Pyramus and Frisbee club, who meet on Clapham Common at 11am every Saturday (pafultimate.com). Ultimate frisbee is self-refereed and depends on good sportsmanship from all.

SHINTY ⑯

Some say that shinty was brought to Scotland by the mythic Irish hero Cúchulainn, after he had learned the arts of love and war on the Isle of Skye. Shinty players use an ash or hickory 'caman', which is slanted on both sides, to hit a worsted leather ball towards their opponents' goal. The London Camanachd play on Sunday afternoons on Wandsworth Common and hold occasional open days for prospective shinters (facebook.com/LondonCamanachd). On Remembrance Sunday they gather in Crown Court Church on Russell Street, next to the memorial to shinty players lost in the First World War.

QUIDDITCH

Grab a broom and join the London Unspeakables, the city's original quidditch team (facebook.com/UnspeakablesLDN). They hold regular training sessions on Hampstead Heath and play in matches and tournaments through the year.[1]

RUGBY

Visit the World Rugby Museum at Twickenham Stadium, the largest rugby stadium in the world. Attempt a virtual conversion in the 'Play Zone'.[2]

SNAIL RACING

The World Snail Racing Championships are based in Congham, Norfolk (scase.co.uk/snailracing), but there have been many gastropod gallops in London over the years. The London Snail Racing Championships used to be held at the O'Conor Don pub on Marylebone Lane, now the Coach Makers. Start a club of your own.

TEN-PIN BOWLING

For an authentically 50s-themed ten-pin bowling experience, go to Rowans at Finsbury Park. Look out for 'The Legend', a Rowans regular who deploys a special handshake every time he gets a strike.

UNICYCLE HOCKEY

Every Tuesday and Thursday evening, the LUNIs (London Unicycles) meet at Queensbridge Sports Centre to train for the UK Unicycle Hockey League (unicycle-hockey.co.uk/teams/about-the-team).

---

❶ The golden snitch dangles out of the snitchrunner's shorts.

❷ Rugby Union was an Olympic sport until 1924. As of 2016, Rugby Sevens has rejoined the pantheon.

ROLLER DERBY ⑰

Roller derby combines violence and high velocity. It involves two teams of four roller skaters travelling in the same direction around an oval track and tussling to overtake and lap one another. This all-female, full- contact sport was created in the USA and arrived in London in the mid 2000s. Try out for the London Rollergirls squad (londonrollergirls.com) or, if your scrimmage skills aren't up to snuff, sign up for the regular Friday evening Open Skate sessions in Bermondsey.

TUBE CHALLENGE ⑱

Elite runners in the London Marathon can finish a route in under two and a half hours. More stamina is required for the Tube Challenge, an endurance sport that began in 1959. The goal is to travel to all 270 stations on the network in a single uninterrupted burst. It requires meticulous planning to minimise distance and duplications, and anything under 17 hours is considered an impressive time. Buses may be used to travel between stations, but it's against the rules to use taxis, bikes or any other private means of propulsion. You can attempt the Tube Challenge any time you like, and as many times as you like: bring a logbook, a stopwatch and a camera and begin at the western end of the Metropolitan Line.[I]

OFFICE ABSEIL ⑲

If you have a head for high finance, make your way to Canary Wharf. Every May, hardy accountants take part in a 230-foot abseil down the face of the 50 Bank Street building at Canary Wharf.

VOLLEYBALL

During the 2012 Olympics, Boris Johnson described the beach volleyball players on Horseguards Parade as 'glistening like wet otters'. Glisten with the London Beach Volleyball Club at Shoreditch Park Court (londonbeachvolleyball.org).

WIFE CARRYING

The UK Wife Carrying Championships are held in Dorking, Surrey, a short trip outside London (trionium.com/wife). Holds include the piggyback, the fireman's carry and the adventurous 'Estonian-style', where the wife hangs upside-down with her legs around the husband's shoulders.

X-TREME IRONING

In this combined extreme sport and performance art, you take an ironing board to an austere location and iron. In 2011, a man filmed himself ironing on the M1 in London.

YUKIGASSEN

Yukigassen ('snow battle') is a Japanese snowball-fighting sport. There are seven players on each team. Why not set up a league on London's next snow day?

ZUI QUAN

The ancient Chinese martial art of 'drunken kung fu' is based on the Daoist tale of the sozzled Eight Immortals. You can observe unintentional masters of the art most Saturday nights, performing on the 262 bus from Stratford to Beckton.

❶ See p.407.

SWIM LONDON

Roger Deakin wrote *Waterlog* in 1999 about a great circumlocutory swim he made around Britain. He was inspired by 'The Swimmer', the short story by John Cheever in which the hero decides to swim home from a party through the long string of swimming pools in his neighbours' back gardens. Here is a similar swimming route across London.

HAM LAKE

Go to Ham Lake in the early morning and you'll feel like you're wild swimming in the depths of the countryside. The grit from this flooded gravel pit was used to build the Bank of England, Westminster Cathedral and Heathrow Airport.

THE SERPENTINE

Every Christmas Day at 9am, a shivering gaggle of swimmers lines up along a narrow jetty in Hyde Park and dives into the Serpentine.[1] To enter, join the Serpentine Swimming Club, the oldest of its kind in Britain (serpentineswimmingclub.com). Non-members can swim here in the summer months.

RAC CLUB

There was no pool at Buckingham Palace until 1938, and legend has it that Queen Elizabeth learned to swim in the this gentleman's club pool. Notice the elegant absence of odorous chlorine: the pool has been ozone-treated instead.

BROCKWELL LIDO

Brixton Beach, the paved terrace around the edge of Brockwell Lido, is a lively sunbathing spot in the summer. You can access the excellent Lido Cafe separately. Sit out by the pool at night, sipping a fine ale under palm trees.

THAMES BATHS

The architecture firm Studio Octopi believes it is 'every Londoner's right to liberate themselves from the intensity of the city by swimming in the Thames'. To this end, they are running a campaign to build a series of floating 'Thames Baths' in the river (thamesbaths.com).

MARSHALL STREET LEISURE CENTRE

A leisurely merchild bestride two dolphins observes your lengths under the white-and-blue barrel-vaulted ceiling of this remarkable Soho swimming pool. Roger Deakin was involved in the campaign to keep Marshall Street baths open to the public and thought it 'one of the most beautiful indoor pools in this country'.

OASIS SPORTS CENTRE

There is an oasis in the heart of the West End, tucked behind High Holborn. In 1954, a Pathé film called this pool 'a fashionable haven for typists and tycoons alike; resting actresses, bearded bohemians and not-so-busy housewives'.

IRONMONGER ROW BATHS

Before diving in to the pool on Ironmonger Row, read the oral histories pasted on the walls by the vibrant community who bathe here. After swimming, descend to the Turkish Baths and sample their hot and cold rooms before an icy plunge. Deakin compares the silent steam rooms to 'a Quaker meeting, but freely hedonistic'.

LONDON FIELDS LIDO

Saved by tenacious campaigners who stood in front of the bulldozers in 1990, London Fields Lido reopened in 2006. It's heated but barely. The on-site Hoxton Beach Café serves falafel.

---

[1] This chilly 100-yard race is known as the Peter Pan Cup because J. M. Barrie once presented the trophy. See p.141.

CANARY RIVERSIDE HEALTH CLUB

Buy a pair of sky-coloured trunks and go for swim at Canary Riverside. This is where James Bond swims in *Skyfall*. In the film the pool is in Shanghai; in reality it's not far from Limehouse. After a swim, book into room 712 for a rinse, the location of Bond and Severine's steamy shower scene.

AQUATICS CENTRE

Swim like an Olympian. Known as the Stingray, Zaha Hadid's 2012 Olympic Aquatics Centre is now open to the public. The price of entry is maintained at the average cost of local swimming pools.

THE GREAT LONDON SWIM

Each July, 3,000 swimmers take part in the one-mile Great London Swim between the towers of Canary Wharf. Enter the race, lather yourself in goose fat, twang your regulation swimming cap and jostle through the mosh of neoprene elbows.

CHARLTON LIDO

In Hornfair Park you can splash up and down a 1930s lido, heated and open all year, that has resurfaced in the current craze for outdoor aquatics. Gone are the days when algal blooms would phosphoresce around your fingers as you swam here.

WILD & WET

Ignore the rectangular lane-marked pool at Wild & Wet in Woolwich, and frolic instead amidst their waterfalls, wave machines, volcanoes, inflatables and giant snake flume.

POND LIFE

The most idyllic swimming locations in London are the three Hampstead Heath Ponds: the Mixed, the Men's and the Kenwood Ladies'. As Deakin puts it, the water here is 'green, smooth and cold'. These glorious, bucolic pools were 18th-century reservoirs, formed by damming the twin sources of the Fleet River. They have always been popular with swimmers and now they are the best way to step out of London into a parallel universe of bracing water and wildlife. Join the Winter Swimming Club to swim here throughout the year. You may need to break the ice.

Another pond has been added temporarily to the London swimmers' repertoire. The King's Cross Pond, to the north of the Granary Square development, is an immersive artwork planted with wild wetland flora which naturally filters the pond's canal water.

o —

VIRGIN ACTIVE REPTON PARK

A shower in place of the altar, a hydro pool in the apse, and 24 metres of water reflecting the stained glass: this is what you can expect when you swim in the former chapel of the Claybury Psychiatric Hospital, now a members-only Virgin Active pool.

PARALYMPIANS

London is swiftly becoming one of the most accessible cities in the world, and it is an excellent place to play sport if you are disabled.

DEAFLYMPICS

After the Olympic Games, the world's longest-running multisport event is the Deaflympics, an elite sporting contest for deaf athletes that began in 1924.[1] Recently Sport England reported that people who are deaf or hard of hearing are 'the least likely group to participate in sport'. As a result, the DEAFinitely Inclusive scheme was founded in 2014 and holds London events for deaf people of all ages, encouraging them to get into athletics, basketball, cricket, football, golf and tennis (ukdeafsport.org.uk).

BLIND TENNIS

Metro Blind Sport is London's leading sports charity for the blind (metroblindsport.org). Blind tennis, sometimes called 'Soundball Tennis', is played with an adapted sponge ball that makes a noise when it bounces. If you're totally blind, you're allowed three bounces; those with partial sight are allowed two. Metro also holds archery sessions in Wandsworth, with adapted equipment that includes a tactile aiming guide and foot locator.

WHEELCHAIR BASKETBALL

The most popular wheelchair sport is basketball. The London Titans are the capital's leading wheelchair basketball club. The rules are the same as regular basketball, although 'travelling' is redefined as an athlete touching his or her wheels more than twice while holding the ball. Everyone is welcome to the Titans' training sessions, which are held regularly at the Copper Box basketball arena in the Olympic Park.[2] Wheelchair basketball is mostly played by people with permanent lower-limb disability, but anyone is welcome to participate.

GOALBALL

Goalball was developed after the Second World War to help convalescing German veterans who had lost their sight. Teams of three aim to place a jangling ball in their opponents' goal. Sighted and partially sighted players wear eyeshades over eyepatches to ensure a completely level playing field. The game has a tactile court and extra-wide goals; the players use their whole bodies to block the ball. The London Goalball Club welcomes 'all visually impaired persons, their families and friends' to their training sessions in Barnet (londongoalball.org).

ACCESS

There are lots of small ways in which London helps those with disabilities to navigate:

- Feel below the control box next time you're waiting to use a puffin crossing: a little ridged bobbin swivels when it's safe to cross.
- All of London's 8,000 buses 'kneel' to the curb for wheelchairs.
- Public staircases have ridged 'corduroy' strips before the top and after the bottom step.
- TfL offers a free 'travel mentoring service' to help you gain confidence on your first few journeys around the city.

---

[1] The last and only time London hosted the Deaflympics was 1935.   [2] Competitive chairs are loaned to beginners.

o————

ARMCHAIR SPORTS

If you fancy a sedentary Sunday morning, go to Brick Lane and challenge the Brick Lane Chess Master. He wears a hat-umbrella, smokes a pipe and takes on several challengers simultaneously, swivelling between boards on his wheelie chair. Alternatively, visit Draughts board game cafe in Hackney or the Lamb in Surbiton, which specialises in super-sized versions of games, including giant Hungry Hippos and Buckaroo. Here is a selection of board games inspired by London itself.

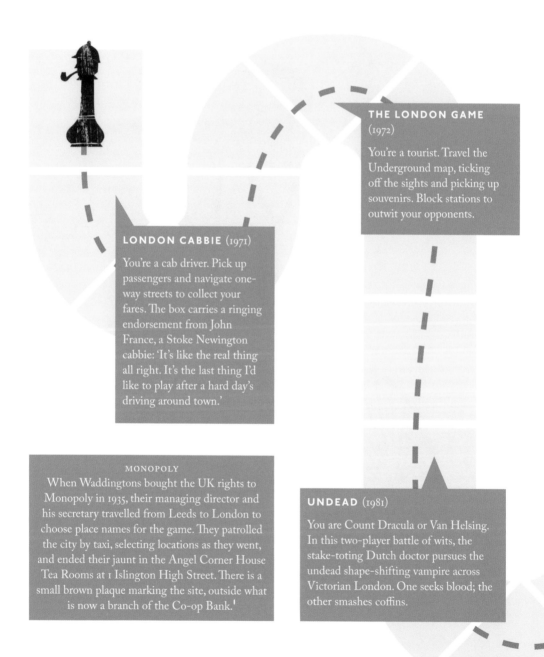

THE LONDON GAME (1972)

You're a tourist. Travel the Underground map, ticking off the sights and picking up souvenirs. Block stations to outwit your opponents.

LONDON CABBIE (1971)

You're a cab driver. Pick up passengers and navigate one-way streets to collect your fares. The box carries a ringing endorsement from John France, a Stoke Newington cabbie: 'It's like the real thing all right. It's the last thing I'd like to play after a hard day's driving around town.'

MONOPOLY

When Waddingtons bought the UK rights to Monopoly in 1935, their managing director and his secretary travelled from Leeds to London to choose place names for the game. They patrolled the city by taxi, selecting locations as they went, and ended their jaunt in the Angel Corner House Tea Rooms at 1 Islington High Street. There is a small brown plaque marking the site, outside what is now a branch of the Co-op Bank.[1]

UNDEAD (1981)

You are Count Dracula or Van Helsing. In this two-player battle of wits, the stake-toting Dutch doctor pursues the undead shape-shifting vampire across Victorian London. One seeks blood; the other smashes coffins.

---

[1] The most unlikely location they selected was Vine Street, a tiny cul-de-sac off Piccadilly containing nothing but service entrances to big buildings.

ON THE UNDERGROUND
(2006)

You're a railway company. Build Underground lines between popular destinations and collect passenger fares.

SHERLOCK

No one has inspired more London-based board games than Sherlock Holmes. Among the best are 221b Baker Street: the Master Detective Game (1975), in which everyone plays Holmes; Sherlock Holmes: The Card Game (1991), where the sequence of cards simulates the pursuit of villains through thick fog; and Sherlock Holmes Consulting Detective (1981), a one-player game that tests your mental powers of deduction. Among the worst are the plodding Sherlock Holmes: the Game of the Great Detective (1956), where each player takes it in turn to be Holmes; Sherlock Holmes (1967), a race to uncover six uninspiring clues; and Sherlock Holmes (1904), a card game published while Arthur Conan Doyle was still writing, in which players generate 'laughter and excitement' by capturing burglars, robbers and thieves.

SCOTLAND YARD (1983)

You're Mister X or a Scotland Yard detective. Mister X flees the law using the London transport system, while everyone else hunts him down.[1]

THE GREAT FIRE OF LONDON 1666 (2010)

You're a 17th-century property owner. As the Great Fire of London rages, you must fight to save your assets or fan the flames elsewhere. Use explosives to create firebreaks.

GAME OVER

If you're feeling exhausted after all that sport, have a rest on one of the colourful benches on the Southeastern High Speed platforms in St Pancras Station. These are the chopped-up fragments of the five huge Olympic rings that hung in the station for 18 months in 2011–2012.

LONDON (2010)

You're a city administrator. Over the course of 250 years[2] you must balance the pursuit of economic growth with public displays of largesse and the alleviation of poverty.

---

[1] If you are Mister X, you wear a black baseball cap with 'Mr. X' written on it.

[2] The game takes about 90 minutes.

CHAIN GANG

Certain names recur as you roam London's high streets. This is where some of the ubiquitous cafes, supermarkets and fast food outlets began.

BURGER KIN

A grey marble plaque inside 56 Powis Street in Woolwich explains that you are in McDonald's 3,000th branch and its first in the UK. Burgers have been flipped there since 1974 and another 200 stores have since taken root around the capital.

If you're thinking of setting up your own monolithic fast food empire, rent a shop on Coventry Street near Piccadilly Circus. Wimpy's first UK outlet opened there in 1954. 23 years later, Burger King opened their first London branch on the same site. It's now Crown Gifts, a souvenir shop.

Wimpy has suffered a long and undignified decline. There are now only 11 outlets in the city, and not one of them is in Zone 1. If you're craving their trademark 'Bender in a Bun', your most central options are now Streatham, Lewisham and Eltham. If you can't live without a West End Wimpy, why not open one yourself? Wimpy is a franchise so you can return it to its birthplace.

COPY CAFFS

Pret a Manger have given themselves a blue plaque in their Victoria Street branch. It tells you that 'the first Pret a Manger shop and kitchen was opened near here' in 1986. They've added 200 outlets in their first two decades.

Starbucks first landed on the King's Road in Chelsea in 1999. It's still trading at that location, but without a special plaque to mark the site. There are now about 250 branches across the city.

HIGH GROCERS

The very first Tesco grocery was opened by Jack Cohen at 9 Watling Avenue in 1929, after ten years running a market stall in Hackney. Today Tesco has moved to bigger premises on Burnt Oak Broadway and you'll find a branch of the chain Savers on their original site. Tesco now has about 500 stores across London.

Tesco's rival Sainsbury's began exactly 60 years earlier at 173 Drury Lane. Although Sainsbury's no longer have a shop there, they sell Drury Lane ham at their deli counters as an understated memorial to their first store.

P ———

COUNTER CULTURE

PEOPLE'S SUPERMARKET

Top up on groceries at the People's Supermarket on Lamb's Conduit Street, which was founded in 2010 as a reaction to the growing dominance of a few big chains. The staff are members who volunteer for four hours a month in return for 20% off[1] all of their shopping. They sell as much local produce as possible and minimise waste by cooking food approaching its best-before date and selling it in their People's Kitchen cafe.

FARESHARES

Fareshares, a volunteer-run wholefood shop at 56 Crampton Street in Walworth, began in 1988 as part of a squat. It now has a proper lease, but still aims to be 'an experiment in community', not a shop. There is almost no mark-up on any of the products and volunteers work regular two-hour shifts. You tot up your own bill with a calculator on the counter.

FOOD ASSEMBLY

Do a weekly shop through your local Food Assembly (thefoodassembly.com). You order what you want online and then pick it up directly from producers at a weekly gathering. The aim is to bypass supermarkets and make it easier for busy Londoners to buy direct from local food producers and farmers.

---

[1] The shop is near Great Ormond Street Hospital and all NHS staff receive a 10% discount.

A TIMELINE OF TRADE

Step in to the hushed, luxe confines of the Royal Exchange, next to Bank Station, and climb up to the mezzanine floor. John Stow described the Royal Exchange as the 'eye of London', and today, on the retina of its raised walkway, you can gaze back into the city's memory: 24 giant murals blaze a patriotic history of London's trade.[1] The capital's role as a global trading hub is the foundation of its wealth and influence. 'Unlike many European sites,' writes Roy Porter, 'London's *raison d'etre* was as a market, not a fortress.'

TIN (1)

Marvel at the Battersea Shield in room 50 of the British Museum. This elegant, 2,500-year-old object, decorated with swirling roundels and red enamel circles, was found in the Thames near Chelsea Bridge. It is made of bronze, the tin and copper alloy that underlaid European culture for three millennia. South-West England has rich seams of tin, and the valuable metal formed the basis of London's earliest international trade, attracting Phoenician merchants across the length of the known world. Tin is still a valuable commodity, traded at the London Metal Exchange on Leadenhall Street.[2]

GARUM (2)

When you next go for a coif at Nicholson & Griffin barbershop on Gracechurch Street, ask to see the remains in their basement. Downstairs is a brick arch, a remnant of the enormous forum-basilica that once stood at the centre of Roman Londinium. An important import was *garum*, fermented fish sauce, which gave Roman recipes their umami oomph. A 1st-century amphora discovered in Southwark, and now on display in the Museum of London, bears the strapline 'Lucius Tettius Africanus supplies the finest *garum* from Antibes'. Today's equivalent might be HP Sauce, the tangy brown condiment invented in 1895 by Frederick Garton and named after the Houses of Parliament,[3] where it is still served.

WOOL (3)

Legend has it that old London Bridge was 'built on woolpacks'. These spongy foundations are metaphorical: the bridge was paid for by taxes imposed on the wool trade. Wool was London's prime export in the Middle Ages.[4] When he wasn't writing about fartyng and thakkyng, Geoffrey Chaucer was the highly responsible comptroller of the wool customs.[5] Visit the House of Lords and examine the Speaker's chair: it's a red cushion known as 'The Woolsack', symbolising wool's erstwhile importance to the economy. In 1938 it was discovered that the Woolsack had been mistakenly stuffed with horsehair; it was hastily refilled with wool, gathered from across the Commonwealth countries.

---

[1] Commissioned in 1895, these images were used as standard illustrations in history textbooks until the 1950s.

[2] See p.196.

[3] Garton's sauce was in serious need of rebranding before it was dubbed 'HP': it had become known as 'The Handkerchief' after the unfortunate backwards reading of the name 'GARTON'S'.

[4] And the source of Dick Whittington's legendary fortune. See p.6.

[5] Hear one of his *Canterbury Tales* in a Tesco car park on p.408.

CLOTH ④

Raw wool is all very well, but its value trebles when it is spun into cloth. Cloth manufacture in London took off when Edward III imposed restrictions on imports of foreign fabric, encouraging skilled Flemish weavers to immigrate and set up their spinning wheels in the city. Soon the Company of Merchant Adventurers was selling British cloth across Europe. The domestic market was dominated by a 'Cloth Fair' at Smithfield, held every Bartholomew's Day.[1] John Betjeman lived in rooms at 43 Cloth Fair. Today his apartment is managed by the Landmark Trust; look out for a last-minute online deal and sleep in the fine Georgian house that still sports his William Morris wallpaper. Next door is the oldest residential house in London, an extraordinary survivor of the Great Fire.[2]

COFFEE ⑤

Attend a free public lecture by the Professor of Commerce at Gresham's College, Holborn. This philanthropic institution was founded in 1597 under the will of Sir Thomas Gresham, the man who built the Royal Exchange. Gresham's Exchange was an open trading courtyard where merchants from around the world gathered to haggle over sacks of sugar, spice, cotton, coca and coffee. In 1652, Pasqua Rosée, a Sicilian Greek trader in Turkish goods, cashed in on the exotic beans available at the Royal Exchange, and set up London's first coffee house in the warren of backstreets nearby.[3] The Exchange burned down twice; the current iteration was completed in 1844, a classical Temple of Mammon with the figure of Commerce at the centre of its pediment. Today it is a high-end shopping mall, but it still bears Gresham's personal emblem, the golden grasshopper.

TEA ⑥

After an aromatic pot of Assam in the V&A's lofty cafe, go to South Asia room 41 to see 'Tipu's Tiger', a life-size automaton of a tiger savaging a European. When you turn the crank handle, the tiger growls and the man screams in panic and waves his hand. This gruesome toy was made in the 1790s for the amusement of Tipu, Sultan of Mysore, who was holding out against the East India Company as it gradually tightened its grip over the whole Indian subcontinent. The East India Company was one of the world's first joint-stock corporations, with shares owned privately by wealthy merchants and aristocrats.[4] Its trade empire was governed from its City headquarters, known as the 'Monster of Leadenhall Street':[5] East India House contained a library of every book ever published on the subject of Asia, a collection that now fills nine miles of shelves at the British Library, and a three-storey museum of eastern souvenirs. The most popular exhibit was 'Tipu's Tiger'.

P ———

MAP READING

A Timeline of Trade *draws on Bruegel's crowded canvases and* November 5th, 1933 *by Eric Ravilious. The Thames forms a timeline running through the history of London trade. Father Time is sailing down the river.*

---

① The fair co-existed with the sideshows, acrobats and freaks of the riotous Bartholomew Fair nearby.

② Find another extraordinary survivor on p.328.

③ Samuel Pepys visited on 10 December 1660 and found 'much pleasure in it'. Jamaica Wine House now occupies the site in St Michael's Alley and still serves the bitter brew.

④ At its height, it oversaw half of the entire world's trade, particularly in raw commodities such as cotton, silk, indigo, salt and, increasingly, tea.

⑤ The site is now occupied by Richard Rogers's Lloyds Building. See p.26.

Everyone Everywhere'). Legend has it that Ronald Reagan called up to buy a baby elephant in 1967 and the operator enquired, 'Would that be African or Indian, sir?' And in 1921, when A. A. Milne dropped in to buy a present for his son Christopher Robin, he came out with a stuffed bear that is now more famous than the shop.[3]

SLAVES (7)

In 1698, in Jonathan's Coffee House on Change Alley, a broker named John Casting published the first list of company share prices, the progenitor of the FTSE 100.[1] Speculation spiralled out of control in the early 18th century, most spectacularly in the case of the South Sea Company, whose main commodity was African slaves. Encouraged by extravagant rumours and corrupt politicians, share prices shot from £100 to over £1,000 in August 1720. In reality the company's finances were disastrous and the 'South Sea Bubble' burst suddenly and violently, plummeting to the original flotation value. Investors were bankrupted and suicides became a daily occurrence.[2] Book an appointment to view Hogarth's *South Sea Scheme* print in the National Portrait Gallery archive on Orange Street. The centrepiece of this riotous image is a raised merry-go-round of investors, including a clergyman, a prostitute and a boot black, and a sign asking 'Who'l ride'. The South Sea Company continued to exist, mainly to manage the government's debt in the scheme, which was only fully paid off in February 2015.

OMNIA (8)

Take the Grade II listed escalator up six floors in the Egyptian Hall in Harrods. Above you in the zodiacal ceiling, three bright orbs mark Orion's Belt, the constellation that dictated the position of the Pyramids of Giza. Charles Henry Harrod, a grocer from Stepney, founded Harrods on its current site to cater for the crowds who flocked to the Great Exhibition of 1851. The motto of the world-famous department store is *'Omnia Omnibus Ubique'* ('Everything for

BEER (9)

Southwark Street is dominated by the blue-and-white hulk of the Hop Exchange, built in 1866. Today the Hop Exchange is mostly converted for office use, but rustic figures continue to pick hops above the iron gates. Behind the Exchange, in Borough Market, you can sit in the Market Hall indoor garden, amidst mobile orchards and screens of hops, intended one day for Borough Market Beer. If you can't wait, make for the Rake on Winchester Walk. This tiny speciality bar serves over a hundred beers.[4]

---

❶ For more on these early shares, see p.192.
❷ Eustace Budgell, Joseph Addison's cousin, rented a boat at London Bridge, rowed out into the Thames and jumped overboard with pockets full of stones.
❸ In Winnie's honour, Harrods now markets an 'Annual Bear'.
❹ To sample London's blossoming beer scene, see p.185.

RETAIL THERAPY

If all this rampant consumerism has worn you out, here are some places to unwind and declutter.

WORN OUT
Rummage through all 100 boutiques in Alfies Antique Market, housed in an old department store near Marylebone Station, then collapse with a scone in the rooftop cafe.

DISTRESSED
Brunswick House, a Georgian mansion opposite Vauxhall bus station, is jam packed with old radiators and distressed parquet. Stop for coffee beneath the second-hand chandeliers in its palatial cafe.

FLOORED
When you've scoured all seven floors of Peter Jones on Sloane Square, recover with a shortbread in their lofty glass-walled cafe, which has magnificent views over the museums of South Kensington.

FED UP
Rifle through the clothes in Ante on Brick Lane and then push through the black curtains at the back of the shop. Hidden inside is Back in 5 Minutes, a restaurant run by the Disappearing Dining Club.

ROUGH
Every record in Rough Trade East has a description stuck onto it to inform your browsing. Read as many as you can before being soothed by synthesisers at a free in-store gig.

DECLUTTERING

PAWNING
The three golden balls outside the Castle pub in Farringdon indicate that it holds a pawnbroker licence, supposedly granted by George IV after he left a royal heirloom as a security for a gambling loan. Find the painting of the king negotiating with the landlord, then trade away your possessions for pints and pork scratchings.

DONATING
'Nothing is useless but because it is in improper hands,' wrote Samuel Johnson. Gift your accoutrements to one of London's many charity shops. The charmingly cluttered Trinity Hospice shop on Streatham High Road is a fine place to start.

DISPLAYING
Robert Opie has spent his life as a 'supermarket archaeologist', collecting 'the packaging which would otherwise surely disappear forever'. His collection is now the spine of the Museum of Brands, Packaging and Advertising in Notting Hill.

CLOSING DOWN

Tobacco Dock in Wapping was meant to become the 'Covent Garden of the East End' when its warehouses were converted into a new shopping complex in 1990. It was awkward to get to, however, so the customers didn't come and it eventually went into administration. Tobacco Dock has stood vacant for 20 years and parts of it are now closed off.[1] Roam around the empty mall for London's ultimate anti-shopping experience.

GIVE AWAY

After the Good Friday service at St Bartholomew the Great, buttered hot cross buns are handed out by the choir in the churchyard. This is part of the annual Ceremony of the Widow's Sixpence, which has taken place since 1887.

You can't buy the baked goods in St Magnus-the-Martyr either. The church used to give bread to the poor every Sunday but its last batch was never distributed and is still mouldering on shelves next to the door.

---

❶ 2,500 soldiers were housed there during the 2012 Olympics.

ASHMOLEAN

NORTHWEST PASSAGE. 13 April 2015

SILENCE & WITNESS. UNITARIAN CHAPEL,
NEWINGTON GREEN. POWER OF VOICES
CONTAINED IN AN EMPTY BUILDING.
DISSENT BECOMES DELIRIUM.

    PATHS OPEN. SECRET WAYS
BEHIND THE CHAPEL. GLIMPSES OF
ARTHUR MACHEN'S TUNNEL THROUGH
TIME. DEPOSITING WALKER IN A
CORRIDOR OF MALIGNANT DOUBLES.
    THE FRINGE OF ABNEY PARK.
NEXT MOVE = RESOLUTION. OR
           ABDICATION.
  — NORTON

HENRY ELIOT,
MATT LLOYD-ROSE,
FLAT 2,
395 Hanley Road,
London N4

THE COLD COTTAGES
Chalk Farm[1] was an exposed, inhospitable spot for a dwelling. Cool down today at Marine Ices on Chalk Farm Road, a local ice-cream institution since 1931.

THE CHEESE FACTORY
Chiswick was a Saxon farm that specialised in cheese production. Today you can stock up at Mortimer & Bennett on Turnham Green Terrace and enjoy a cheese board in the formal gardens of Chiswick House.

THE NOOK OF LAND WITH FROGS
Keep an eye out for frogs' legs on the specials board at La Cage Imaginaire on Flask Walk, near Frognal.

THE HEATHEN TEMPLE
Harrow was a site of pagan worship before the early 7th century. According to the druid Chris Street, the centre of Harrow's Earthstar pentagram[2] is the church of St Mary, Harrow on the Hill.

THE MOSSY SPRING
When an unidentified king of Scots was 'strangely diseased', he was advised to take the water of a well in England called 'Muswell', and 'after long scrutation and inquisition' this was discovered at Muswell Hill. According to the Tudor historian John Norden, the cure was successful.

THE NOSE-SHAPED HILL
The Saxons thought that Neasden Hill looked like a nose.

THE VALLEY OF PEAR TREES
Visit the 'Maiden's Tomb' in the graveyard of the church of St Mary the Virgin in Perivale. Before she died in 1721, Elizabeth Colleton said that if there were a just God, trees would grow out of her tomb. They did.

THE RUSHES LEAP
Ruislip is the Old English name for a spot on the River Pinn, marked by rushes, where one could leap from one side to the other. Push through the undergrowth off the Celandine Walking Route and find out whether it's still possible.

NORTH-EAST

THE RIVER OF LIGHT
The River Lee comes from the Celtic root '*lug—*', meaning 'bright', so this major Thames tributary may have been dedicated to the Celtic god Lugus. In 2005 and again in 2011, Canada geese were seen disappearing below the surface of the Lee, leading to rumours of a dangerous predator.

THE OLD RED BRIDGE
A red bridge crossed the River Roding in the 18th century, where the A12 red route approaches the North Circular today.

THE WAYSIDE CROSS
Crouch End appeared around a road junction marked by a cross (*crouch*). Today the cross has been replaced by an ornate clock tower.

THE SUNKEN WAY
There is a tract of low ground between the heights of Highgate and Islington. The section of the Great North Road that runs along it is still known as the Holloway Road.

THE RED CLIFF
The Ratcliff Highway runs along a cliff of red soil, which gives the area its name. Martin Frobisher set out from Ratcliff in 1575, in search of the Northwest Passage. Today you can catch the Overground from Shadwell on a similar bearing.[3]

SOUTH-WEST

THE LOUD RIVER
The River Wandle's original moniker was Ludeburne.[4] The river was once famous for its brown trout, which disappeared for over a century until 2008, when trout were reintroduced by local schools participating in the 'Trout in the Classroom' project.

Q

---

[1] Despite the name, the soil here is London clay.
[2] See p.368.
[3] For another Northwest Passage, see p.288.

[4] The name 'Wandle' is a 16th-century back-formation from Wandsworth.

THE BEAUTIFUL PLACE

Beulah Hill comes from the Old French for 'beautiful place'. Beulah was John Bunyan's name for the Earthly Paradise and for William Blake it was the realm of the subconscious.

THE VALLEY OF WILD SAFFRON

Croydon lies in the valley of the River Wandle where *Crocus sativus* used to grow, a species of wild saffron introduced to Britain by wealthy Romans, who used it for dying cloth and daily 'saffron baths'. Today you need look no further than Savemore Spicy Foods on London Road.

THE HOUND'S MOUND

Hounslow was probably a settlement near the burial tumulus of a dog.

THE KEY

Kew is situated on a key-shaped spur of land.

THE STREAM OF YOUNG SALMON

Mortlake grew up around a stream (*lacu*) rich in young salmon (*mort*). Enjoy smoked salmon with your eggs royale at Annie's Restaurant on White Hart Lane.

THE LANDING PLACE OF HAWKS

Inspect the birds of prey at the Putney Common Open Day in September (wpcc.org.uk).

TREE STUMP SPRING

If an obstructive tree stump springs up in Stockwell today, call local firm Graftin Gardeners to remove it.

THE HILL OF WOAD

Woad, as popularised by Mel Gibson's face in *Braveheart*, was cultivated in the Middle Ages as a blue dye and farmed commercially in Britain until the 1930s. It used to grow wild at Waddon.

SOUTH-EAST

THE TURBULENT RIVER

The River Cray is a Celtic name from the British word *crei*, 'rough or turbulent'.

THE LONELY HOUSE

In the mid 19th century, Scottish silk merchant William Sanderson built the first house on a hilly part of Penge Common and called it Annerly, Scottish for 'only' or 'lonely'. Anerley is now a dense residential area.

THE GLADE OF BADGERS

Former Brockley resident Harold Hardiman has created a cartoon character called Badger, who lives in Brockley. Read *Badger's Day Out* on Brockley Common.

THE WILDCAT SHALLOWS

Although originally a river crossing known for its cats, Catford was famous in the 20th century for its dog-racing stadium. The stadium was demolished in 2003.[1]

THE DEEP FORD

Deptford is the fordable spot on the River Ravensbourne before it opens into Deptford Creek. Until the first Deptford Bridge was built, a resident hermit helped travellers across.

THE DILL MEADOW

The Saxons used dill medicinally for jaundice, headaches, boils and nausea. Residents on the Friern and Upland Roads in Dulwich find that dill still grows wild through the cracks in their patios.

THE MEADOW OF SWANS

The grounds of Eltham Palace are still lapped by the River Quaggy, but these pastures are no longer famous for their swans.

THE GREEN HARBOUR

Order fish and chips from the Green Village cafe in Greenwich and wander down to the old harbour.

THE WOOD'S END

The only Celtic name in London that isn't a river is Penge, which comes from *penn ced*, 'the wood's end'. It was originally a woodland swine pasture attached to the manor of Battersea.

THE VALLEY OF TRICKSTERS

Pratt's Bottom is an unfortunate address. A family called Pratt once lived at the bottom of this valley. The surname Pratt means 'tricky'.

THE WOOL PORT

Wool was London's most valuable export commodity in the Middle Ages.[2] Today the best trading post near Woolwich is Yarnia in Belvedere.

---

[1] You can still go to the dogs at Wimbledon Greyhound Stadium. See p.96.   [2] See p.246.

GENTEEL TAKEOVER

In 2008, twenty of the units in Brixton Village Market were unoccupied. Trade was brisk elsewhere in the market but here, on the wrong side of the railway line, footfall was dwindling and the beautiful old arcades were threatened with demolition. In an attempt to revive them, Lambeth Council worked with a company called Spacemakers, who offered the units rent-free for three months to anyone with a good idea (spacemakers.info). Artists, tailors, coffee grinders and chutney makers filled the gaps between the existing grocers, record shops and fishmongers. As these ventures attracted crowds, more cafes, shops and restaurants piled in after them.

Brixton Village is now buzzing, its old and new businesses cheek by jowl. But the unintended consequence of re-energising the market was to supercharge the area's gentrification. Brixton's edgy new bars have attracted near-constant crowds of moneyed young professionals. In parallel, the police have cracked down on drug dealing, schools have been improving and public spaces have been revamped. People who might not have considered living in Brixton before 2008 are now moving in. Shop rents and house prices have rocketed accordingly, edging out people who can no longer afford to be there. Some see the area as a shining example of creative urban renewal, others see a community being forced off its patch. Brixton has become London's premier pro- and anti-gentrification pin-up.

SKUNK

If you linger on the corner outside KFC you might still hear someone muttering, 'Skunk, weed, skunk, weed,' under their breath. But following a major police crackdown in 2011, and zero tolerance since, most of the dealers on the high street have moved elsewhere.

SOURDOUGH

Franco Manca pre-empted Brixton's new wave of restaurants[2] and its roaring success paved the way for others. This sourdough pizza specialist is now a rapidly expanding chain but has kept prices low and attracts a diverse crowd.

SQUARE

New public spaces, like leafy Windrush Square opposite KFC, have transformed the look and feel of Brixton town centre. The square was redeveloped to mark the 50th anniversary of the arrival of Caribbean immigrants on the *Empire Windrush*.[1] There is a charming pavement cafe outside the Ritzy Cinema.

WINDOW

The shop window of Foxton's Estate Agents has become an anti-gentrification rallying point. The agency replaced the much-loved low-cost eatery Speedy Noodle, and has been accused of deliberately pushing up house prices in the area. When Foxton's opened in 2013, the words 'YUPPIES OUT' were sprayed across the shopfront and in 2015 the window was smashed during a 'Reclaim Brixton' protest.

CASH

Stock up your store cupboard in Nour's Cash and Carry, a cavernous Middle Eastern shop with a deceptively small entrance. This iconic local business almost closed down after rent hikes, but was saved by a substantial protest.

CHAMPAGNE

No new arrival galvanised anti-gentrification sentiment as much as Champage + Fromage, a Covent Garden wine bar that opened its second branch in Brixton Village. The only alcoholic drink on the menu is champagne, and bottles start at £45.

Q

---

❶ See p.6.

❷ It replaced another pizzeria called Franco's. *'Franco manca'* simply means 'Franco is missing'. They use a sourdough starter that originated in Italy in 1730. See p.38.

STREETS IN THE SKY

Find the row of low concrete blocks at the back of Smithfield Market to see some of London's best knee-level street art. Each block is stencilled with a grid of windows, balconies and TV aerials so that it looks like a tiny tenement. Together they form a brutalist council estate in miniature. London's real social housing is varied and isn't, for the most part, contained in forbidding grey towers like these.

BOUNDARY

Stand in the bandstand on the mound at the centre of Arnold Circus. Beneath your feet are the crushed remains of the Old Nichol slum, 'the blackest pit in London', according to the novelist Arthur Morrison.[1] After the rookery was razed in the 1890s, London's first social housing sprung up in its place. The Boundary Estate consists of several handsome red-brick blocks radiating out from a central roundabout, where the ruins of the slum were heaped and landscaped. The estate is still largely council housing. Drop in to their community laundrette on Calvert Avenue for a chat with Marie, who's been managing this non-profit neighbourhood hub since it began in 1992.

EXCALIBUR

London's final pre-fab estate has been knocked down. The Excalibur Estate in Catford was assembled by German and Italian prisoners of war in 1945 to provide emergency housing in a bomb-scarred city. Although the simple units weren't meant to last, 187 of them survived until 2013, preserving the atmosphere of post-war London at the heart of Lewisham. Walk along Persant Road to see six surviving bungalows, which were listed by English Heritage along with the estate's church, which has a barrelled metal roof like an Anderson shelter.

BRANDON

Look for *Two Piece Reclining Figure No. 3*, the Henry Moore sculpture outside Kennington's Brandon Estate. It was commissioned by the council to inspire residents.

ROBIN HOOD

In the early days of social housing, Nye Bevan hoped that every estate would contain 'the living tapestry of a mixed community', with residents from all professions and walks of life. That hasn't always happened and certain estates, like Robin Hood Gardens in Poplar, with its streets in the sky, came to symbolise deprivation and social segregation. English Heritage declined to protect Robin Hood Gardens[2] when it was slated for demolition, stating that 'in the end it failed in its original brief to create a housing development which worked on human terms'.

ALEXANDRA & AINSWORTH

Walk through the avenue at the centre of the Alexandra & Ainsworth Estate in Camden. Its concrete flats are stacked up in distinctive typewriter-shaped terraces and the estate is frequently used as a film location.[3] Visit the recently restored park, where the tenants and residents association have beehives and are making their own honey.

---

[1] Morrison fictionalised Old Nichol in his novel *A Child of the Jago*. There is now a fashion boutique called A Child of the Jago nearby on Great Eastern Street, set up by Vivienne Westwood and Malcolm McLaren's son.

[2] The avant-garde novelist B. S. Johnson made an eerie film about the construction of Robin Hood Gardens for the BBC: *The Smithsons on Housing*. The corporation were deeply unhappy with it, but it was aired in 1970 and can still be found online.

[3] You can see clips of films shot on the estate on the tenants and residents association website (alexandraandainsworth.org/on-film).

RULES

WILLIAM WHITELEY founded London's first department store in the late 19th century. Whiteley's, which is still trading on Queensway, was famous for its draconian employee code of conduct: a catalogue of 176 rules and punishments. Standing on a chair carried a 6d fine, as did stopping for lunch at the wrong time. The final and most ominous penalty was for breaking 'Any rule not before mentioned'. Whiteley ran a tight ship, but his disciplinarian leadership came to an abrupt end when he was murdered in his own shop, shot by a man claiming to be his illegitimate son.

London itself is a rule-bound place, with an ambiguous attitude to rule-breakers. The atrocities of Jack the Ripper, Dr Crippen and the Krays have become the stuff of waxworks and walking tours. In 2015, a Ripper museum opened in the East End near the site of his killings.[1] Likewise, there was much excitement when the Metropolitan Police finally put part of the New Scotland Yard Crime Museum[2] on public display, including the nooses that hanged infamous offenders and implements from the Acid Bath Murders. In London, if you're sufficiently brutal, you can be sure of a lasting legacy.

Most of London's crime is not so grizzly and extreme: there are currently around 700,000 recorded offences in the city each year, as well as those that never come to light. More representative than the celebrity super-villains are long-forgotten criminals like the Forty Elephants, a gang of prolific female shoplifters from the 1920s who stashed stolen goods in specially adapted bloomers. Or Rodney Williams, a serial bag thief, who made headlines in 2014 when he became the first person to receive an Anti-Social Behaviour Order banning him from all of London's 35,000 bars.

'The more strictly we are watched, the better we behave', wrote Jeremy Bentham, and to put his theory into practice he designed the Panopticon prison for the site now occupied by Tate Britain. The prison's cylindrical design would enable a single guard to see into every cell from a central tower. Prisoners would act as though they were being observed even when they weren't, giving the guards unprecedented 'power of mind over mind'.[3]

The Panopticon was never built, but its principles live on in London's streetlights, CCTV networks and even its inhabitants. The city acts as a Panopticon because we expect conformity. As we cram on to the tube or pass in the street, we police one another.

> **PANOPTICON PIE**
> Bentham's plans for his prison were so far advanced that he'd even planned the menu. Prisoners would eat Devonshire Pie, filled with a scrumptious combination of potatoes, gooseberries, tripe, lung and spleen. The recipe was reprieved by the St John restaurant in Smithfield in 2013 and it's still occasionally served there – contact them beforehand to check the menu. Or, if you'd prefer to make one from scratch, you can find this and other recipes on UCL's 'Bake it like Bentham' web page (blogs.ucl.ac.uk/transcribe-bentham/2013/03/15/bake-it-like-bentham).

---

[1] To the outrage of the local community, who'd been informed that a women's history museum was being opened.

[2] Colloquially known as the Black Museum. In the 1950s, Orson Welles narrated a BBC series called *Tales from the Black Museum*, telling the stories behind the collection's most gruesome objects.

[3] To get a sense of how Bentham's omnipresent warden would have felt, climb up inside the dome of Tate Britain (now the members' room) and keep a watchful eye on the crowds from the circular balcony. For more on Bentham see p.349.

DIVISIONS

London is divided into places where we are and aren't supposed to go – and nothing says 'KEEP OUT' better than a set of spiked railings slathered with anti-climb paint.

SPIKES

The city's railings used to be brightly coloured and often featured elaborate spiky pineapple motifs. On the death of her husband, Albert, Queen Victoria had them all painted black[1] and most remain so to this day. Less sombre are the new railings on Triton Square near Warren Street. They're painted a lush, lurid yellow to evoke the inside of a pineapple.

STUBS

Only the sawn-off stubs of railings are left along Malet Street in Bloomsbury. The metal was removed and melted down for the war effort in 1940.[2] In fact it proved impractical to turn railings into tanks, so many of them were quietly dumped into the Thames.

STRETCHERS

Although the Second World War cost London its railings, it also provided replacements. Keep an eye out for the low mesh railings that sometimes surround blocks of council flats. They're made out of the stretchers used in the Blitz. You can see a set outside Mereton House, near Deptford Bridge.

SNAILINGS

On the railings outside L'Escargot restaurant on Greek Street, one of the spikes has been removed and replaced with a golden snail. There used to be a snail farm in the restaurant's basement and *escargots* are still on the menu. Order a bowlful, or take some garlic butter to Soho Square and grub around for your own.[3]

SURVIVORS

The railings outside the Firestone Tyre Factory have nothing left to protect. The factory was demolished by its owners the day before it was due to be declared a listed building. If you drive along Brentford's Golden Mile, you can still see the elaborate Egyptian-style railings,[4] which survived the demolition and were listed before further damage could be done.

STANDARDS

IMPERIAL

Look for the brass plaque at the north-east corner of Trafalgar Square showing the precise length of one foot, two feet and a yard. These Imperial Standards of Length were put here as a permanent, public reference point.

PLIMSOLL

Before setting off down the Thames in a merchant ship, draw a Plimsoll Line on the hull to check that you aren't dangerously overloaded. Copy the cryptic scale marked on to the base of Samuel Plimsoll's memorial on the Victoria Embankment.

MODULOR

The architect Le Corbusier thought that measures should correspond to the size of a human body, so he invented the Modulor scale. The basic Modulor unit is six feet, because, according to Le Corbusier, 'in English detective novels, the good-looking men, such as policemen, are always six feet tall'. Look for a policeman and ask if you can measure him.

---

❶ For more on Victoria's mourning, see p.122.
❷ In 2012, their ghost was resurrected: the stumps were fitted with sensors so that whenever someone walked past they would hear the sound of a stick being run along the phantom railings next to them.

❸ Find more snails on p.232.
❹ The Golden Mile is a stretch of art deco factories on the Great West Road. Find another Egyptian art deco mash-up on p.29.

RULE BREAKERS

Look for the childish painting of the Crucifixion in the Museum of London: in dark-red letters at the bottom left is the signature 'R. KRAY'. It was painted in 1972 by Ronnie Kray, three years after he and his brother Reggie had been jailed for the murders of fellow gangsters Jack 'the Hat' McVitie and George Cornell. The Kray twins have since achieved an almost mythic status for the criminal antics of their gang, the Firm. But while London's scurviest characters are amply celebrated, some of the city's more charming small-time rule breakers go overlooked.

FINE ARTISTS

When it comes to protecting library books, some boroughs adopt a tougher stance than others. Hillingdon charge 16p per day for an overdue book, Richmond 20p, the City of London 22p, and Lambeth a hefty 25p. The one borough you really don't want to upset is Islington, who took two young men to court for damaging their books. The young lovers Joe Orton and Kenneth Halliwell moved into 25 Noel Road, Islington, in 1959 and spent three years sneaking dozens of volumes out of the local library,

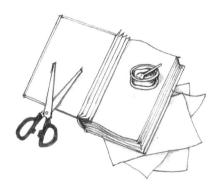

razoring out pictures and creating surreal photo collages on the covers[1] before covertly returning the books to the shelves. When the library discovered these guerrilla artworks, they went to great lengths to identify the culprits, who were given six months inside for 'malicious damage'. Orton went on to become a famous playwright and now 25 Noel Road is marked by a green plaque stating that he lived there from 1960 to 1967. It doesn't mention that he also died there, bludgeoned to death by Halliwell, who then killed himself. You can see some of the couple's doctored book covers in the Islington Museum.

BEAVER STEALERS

Under the 1777 Bugging Act, journeyman hatters could be given three months' hard labour for embezzlement. Rogue journeymen would switch expensive fabrics for the same weight of a cheaper material while moving it around the city. This was commonly known as 'stealing the beaver', as beaver felt made the finest, most sought-after headgear. Not only is it waterproof, some believed that wearing a beaver hat increased brainpower. If you fancy yourself in a beaver fedora, you can buy one at Bates on Jermyn Street. Or if you'd rather not wear a rodent on your head, pick up a baseball cap in Foot Locker at 105 Oxford Street: the store is inside Henry Heath's defunct hat factory and has four stone beavers perched on the roof.

NOUGHTY HOAXERS

On 7 February 1910, five years before publishing her first novel, Virginia Woolf put on a fake beard, a turban and a flowing robe and travelled to Paddington Station. Her brother Adrian had invited her to join a scheme to hoax the Royal Navy: a group of them would stage a fake visit by the Abyssinian royal family and go to inspect HMS *Dreadnought*. They sent bogus Foreign Office telegrams to senior officers, blagged a private train at Paddington and travelled in style from London to Weymouth. The visit was a great success and the prank didn't come to light until one of the hoaxers leaked the story to the press. Attempt to replicate the scam with a fancy-dress visit to HMS *Belfast*, which is moored next to London Bridge.

R

---

[1] On one edition of John Betjeman's work, a lithe, tattooed body has been pasted below the poet's head.

THE LONDON PANOPTICON

London is strung with an invisible mesh of conventions, standards and laws. When you cross one of those lines, you lose the guarantees of protection that we take for granted; instead, the city bites back and protects itself from you.

THE RIGHT SIDE OF THE LAW

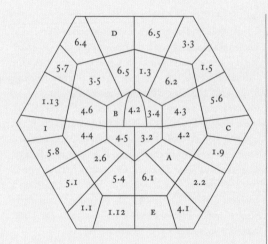

I. CODES OF CONDUCT

Commuters clash so frequently with tourists on Oxford Street that, in 2010, serious plans were mooted to create 'slow' and 'fast' Lanes on the pavements. Londoners have expectations of one another: not dawdling at rush hour, letting passengers off the train first, controlling umbrellas, not playing techno on a quiet bus. But this everyday etiquette is relatively transparent. Here are some less obvious edicts:

1.1 'Keep off the grass' on Elm Walk in Merton. The sign occupies most of this protected patch, which, at only 2 by 3 feet, is a strong contender for the smallest forbidden turf in the capital.

1.2 Gentlemen must wear a tie and jacket at all times in the Bar of the Ritz.

1.3 No suits or ties allowed at Big Red, a rock and metal dive bar on Holloway Road. Those in smart attire may not be admitted.

1.4 Do not attempt to transport venomous creatures on the tube: unthreatening dogs and any other 'inoffensive animal' are welcome.

1.5 Pens and post-it notes are strictly forbidden inside the reading rooms of the British Library.

1.6 'Hippies use side door' when shopping at Bookmongers on Brixton's Coldharbour Lane.

1.7 'No music, no machines, no television and no mobile phones' in the French House[1] on Dean Street.

1.8 Crowd surfers will be ejected from Brixton Academy. Look out for the prominent signs on either side of the stage.

1.9 No women were allowed at the bar of El Vino on Fleet Street until 1983. The bar is reputed to be the model for Pommeroy's, favoured haunt of Rumpole of the Bailey.

1.10 Don't sit down on the fine old chairs in Sir John Soane's house. A large thistle head is positioned on each seat to underline the point.

1.11 Don't go to the Cockpit on St Andrew's Place straight after a rugged hike. 'Persons with soiled clothing or dirty boots will not be served.'

1.12 'Please do not touch the walrus or sit on the iceberg' at the Horniman Museum.

1.13 No whistling, humming or singing in Burlington Arcade. Prostitutes used to whistle to warn pickpockets of approaching police officers. The beadles still enforce the rule today.

MAP READING

The London Panopticon imagines London as a prison. Its shape is inspired by Jeremy Bentham's plans for the Panopticon and the design of Millbank Prison. A–E on the map key are described on pp.282–3.

See p.377.

2. NUDGES

Increasingly, rule-makers attempt to gain non-forced compliance from citizens through positive reinforcement and subtle incentives. This behavioural science technique, known as nudging, is described by Richard Thaler and Professor Cass Sunstein as 'any aspect of the choice architecture that alters people's behaviour in a predictable way'. Look out for elements of your environment engineered to encourage certain decisions.

2.1 Enter the TfL Travel Etiquette Poetry competition and write a short stanza that gently chides your fellow commuters for poor choices and shows them a better way to travel.

2.2 After dark, go to the Woolwich crime hotspot Green's End in a fighting mood, and prepare to be pacified by the smiling faces of local babies. Infants were painted on to shop shutters following evidence that images of children's faces elicit warm, caring feelings.

2.3 Feel your tensions melt as you imbibe wisdom and perspective from Oval tube station's 'Thought for the Day' whiteboard.

2.4 If you look under 21, look out for signs reminding you not to feel offended if you're asked for ID when buying alcohol.

2.5 Don't forget that your bus journey is being recorded for your own safety. Screens on many routes allow you to watch your own commute in real time.

2.6 Relax to the soothing tones of Mozart and Mussorgsky in the ticket hall of Brixton tube. TfL now plays classical music in some stations to encourage civility.

3. DETERRENTS

Sometimes a nudge isn't enough and behaviours are actively discouraged. The severed heads of criminals used to leer down from spikes on London Bridge[1] as a gentle reminder of the consequences of crime; today their place has been taken by the sightless eyes of the capital's CCTV network. Around 7,000 council cameras capture over six million hours of footage a year, compiling a massive digital memory for the city: momentary lapses now have long lifespans.

3.1 If you're under 25, you may hear an irritating high-pitched buzz in certain locations. This is a mosquito alarm, set at a frequency only the very young can hear and designed to deter loitering.

3.2 Act in the knowledge that you are observed by hundreds of public and private cameras every day. Go to Newman Street and look for the cameras above the Post Office yard that failed to deter Banksy creating his work *One Nation Under CCTV* on the site. It was later painted over.

3.3 Do not park in an inappropriate place on Highbury Crescent in Islington. There's no scope for error; between two parking bays is one of the country's shortest yellow lines, at 18 inches.

3.4 Linger in the central garden of Walker House in Camden where, for a while, a robotic voice on a CCTV camera commanded loiterers to depart. It was silenced after residents' protests.

R

3.5 Don't drive a vehicle heavier than 7.5 tonnes from Carlton Hill into Maida Vale. To encourage larger road users to seek alternative routes, a camera with automatic number plate recognition technology has been installed there.

3.6 Be pleasant to police officers. Many are now sporting body-mounted cameras, recording their every interaction. This is also an incentive for them to be pleasant to you.

---

❶ The site is now marked by a 16-foot limestone spike.

THE LONDON PANOPTICON

4. TRIALS

The machinery of the law is surprisingly accessible to the general public. Trials, the moment when justice is meted out, are open to all.[1]

4.1 Start small. Go to Bexley Magistrates' Court, wait on a metal bench and watch an antisocial behaviour hearing.

4.2 Go to the opposite extreme and attend a trial in the magisterial Old Bailey building, which handles the most serious criminal offences.[2] Beneath you is Dead Man's Walk, the old path to the scaffold.

4.3 Sit in on a trial at the Royal Courts of Justice on the Strand, which houses the High Court and the Court of Appeal.[3] Then visit the Seven Stars pub, just behind the courts, and look at the 'Cabinet of Jurisprudence' in its window. The display contains animal skulls in judicial wigs and spectacles.

4.4 Pay £1 for a self-guided tour of Middlesex Guildhall, the Supreme Court, on Parliament Square. This court 'hears appeals on arguable points of law of the greatest public importance'.

4.5 Those found guilty of minor offences would be put in the stocks at the old Charing Cross pillory, now Trafalgar Square, and pelted with eggs, dead cats and, sometimes, rocks. Legend has it that when Daniel Defoe was pilloried for publishing a scandalous pamphlet the public threw flowers.

4.6 Order a cocktail in one of the former holding cells of the Great Marlborough Street Magistrates' Court, now a bar, and then go for dinner in the courtroom where Oscar Wilde was tried.

5. IMPRISONMENT

London is chock-full of dungeons, jails, nicks and clinks. Walking past a prison, it's sometimes hard to believe that only a few metres from you, filed away in a vast brick cabinet, are rows of Londoners who've been deprived of their liberty. Here are some ways to get behind bars if you haven't been formally sent down.

5.1 Start the day with breakfast cooked and served by inmates of HMP Brixton at the Clink Restaurant inside the prison. Book well in advance and don't fatigue the waiters with jokes about porridge.[4]

5.2 Toast your liberty at Vinopolis, next door to the Clink, Southwark's most infamous prison, now a museum.

5.3 Examine prisoners' graffiti in one of the cells from Wellclose Square Prison, which is now in the Museum of London.

5.4 Find all that remains of Marshalsea Prison on Angel Place, just off Borough High Street. Dickens spent Sundays here, visiting his incarcerated father, an experience he later fictionalised in *Little Dorrit*. The southern wall of the debtors' prison still stands and is marked with a plaque.

5.5 See inside the Fleet Prison in panel seven of Hogarth's *Rake's Progress* in Sir John Soane's house. Tom Rakewell and his fellow inmates are concocting schemes to repay their debts. Spot their alchemy equipment and homemade wings.[5]

5.6 The Execution Bell on display in St Sepulchre-without-Newgate used to be rung outside the cells of the condemned before their hanging at Newgate Prison.

5.7 Spot a portrait of the prison reformer Elizabeth Fry[6] on the gatehouse of HMP Wormwood Scrubs. While still governor, John McCarthy railed against overcrowding and described himself as 'the manager of a large penal dustbin' in a letter to *The Times*.

---

[1] Travel light as many courts don't allow bags and don't provide storage.
[2] For one of its most famous trials, see p.76.
[3] Civil servants use the majestic main hall for a weekly badminton club.
[4] Instead, order the eggs, laid by free-range chickens at HMP Send, a women's prison in Surrey.
[5] Find the last panel on p.291.
[6] Fry appears several million times on p.122.

STRAND

 'Let's all go down the Strand — Have a banana!' goes the old music-hall song. Buy a banana from the fruit stall on Twyford Place, and then go down the Strand, the ancient umbilical track connecting the cities of London and Westminster along what was once the wide, muddy foreshore of the Thames.[1]

When you reach the end of the Strand, continue east along the riverbank. Stop just before you get to Canary Wharf pier and take a seat on a talking bench: in *Speaking of the River*, people who live and work by the Thames describe the part it plays in their lives.[2] As you sit at the water's edge and listen to these intimate tales, consider the infinite strands that make up the story of London.

FAIRY TALES

The fairytale forest is a metaphorical place where you are lost and then find yourself. London is just such a place.

— *Marina Warner*

On walls we read plaques, panels, street names and graffiti: ghostly reminders of the lives, deaths, epiphanies and crimes that played out on those spots. These details lie in wait as we walk through the city and, whenever our paths intersect, their narratives intertwine with our own.

Every Londoner has their own thread through the labyrinth, but most of us tend not to stray too far from familiar territory: we follow signposts, obey directions and add our footsteps to well-worn routes. London has its physical and psychological outskirts, however: areas beyond the mainstream, which many of us rarely visit. Those who take up permanent residence there are the mavericks and the madmen.

London has spawned many eccentrics and visionaries, and none more spectacular than William Blake, the engraver, poet, painter, printer and prophet, who was born in the heart of Soho and only left London for three of his seventy years. 'There was no doubt that this poor man was mad,' wrote William Wordsworth about Blake, 'but there is something in the madness of this man which interests me more than the sanity of Lord Byron and Walter Scott.' Blake saw angels, ghosts and visions in the London streets and created a highly complex personal mythology. In his imagination, the city was a decrepit old man, led by a small child.

Blake ended his life in a garret off the Strand, but from his window he could see a small sliver of the Thames, shining 'like a bar of gold'. He was singing when he died.

SYMBOL

London itself is a symbolic place, its image shaped as much by fiction as fact. From the time I was young I wanted to make a character out of London.

— *Michael Moorcock*

---

❶ If you don't like bananas, buy a peach. In the poem 'Fulbright Scholars', Ted Hughes recalled buying a peach on the Strand after first seeing Sylvia Plath's face in a newspaper. He could 'hardly believe how delicious'.

❷ The artwork, an audio montage by Constance de Jong, connects London to New York and also includes interviews about the Hudson River.

PSYCHOGEOGRAPHY

Psychogeography was dreamed up in 1960s Paris by the French Situationist Guy Debord. He described it as the study of the 'effects of the geographical environment […] on the emotions and behaviour of individuals.' Debord believed it would one day be possible to create psychogeographical city maps – 'maps of influences' – to enable us to navigate 'new forms of labyrinths'. Psychogeography is now a label applied to a wide range of playful and political urban walking and writing.[1]

NAVIGATE THE NORTH-WEST PASSAGE
with THOMAS DE QUINCEY

Instead of waiting for a night bus, use nautical principles to navigate home. This was the essayist Thomas de Quincey's strategy: after taking opium on a Saturday night, he saw the city as a dreamscape, with alleys that tangled into knots and streets that became impassable. He would fix his eye on the Pole Star and seek 'ambitiously for a north-west passage'. Steer between the capes and headlands yourself.[2]

DRIFT AGAINST THE CURRENT
with GUY DEBORD

Observe the ways in which geography affects people's behaviour. Do you funnel along London's main thoroughfares? Are muzak and artificial aromas manipulating your emotions? Yes they are, according to Guy Debord, the French situationist and founding father of psychogeography. The antidote is the *dérive* or 'drift': an unplanned journey on which you ignore subliminal signs. Start in Leicester Square, the heart of London tourism, and drift wherever the mood doesn't take you.

SPELL OUT A SECRET MESSAGE
with IAIN SINCLAIR

Get out a map of London and scrawl a word on it in large letters, then walk the route of your word, one letter a day. Iain Sinclair performs an act of 'ambulant signmaking' in *Lights Out for the Territory*: he walks a 'V' from Hackney to Greenwich Hill and back along the River Lea to Chingford Mount. In Paul Auster's *City of Glass*, Quinn trails Stillman as he walks letter-shapes through the streets of New York.[3] Quinn wonders what the map would look like of all the steps he had taken in his life, and 'what word it would spell'.[4]

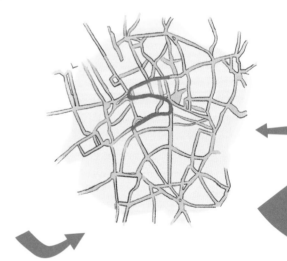

---

❶ Among London writers the term has become quite unfashionable. London artist Laura Oldfield Ford regards self-proclaimed psychogeographers as 'middle-class men acting like colonial explorers'.
❷ North Street Passage in Plaistow might prove a useful bearing.
❸ Stillman walks the letters OWEROFBAB. Quinn initially thinks it must be an anagram, but works out the phrase when he writes it as OWER OF BAB.
❹ The London-based artist Jeremy Wood is finding out: he's creating a GPS-plotted map of his entire life. Visit the V&A Museum and ask to see *My Ghost*, a snapshot of Wood's life in London so far.

DEEP TOPOGRAPHY

'Most of what passes for psychogeography is of no interest to me. Since the late 1980s I have wandered outwards from London by foot as far afield as Stonehenge, Southend and East Anglia, sleeping rough and writing retromodernist prose poems of interest to no one other than myself. I became aware that the magnitude of experience I had while doing so was off the beaten cultural track [...] and so I coined my own term for what I wrote as a consequence: Deep Topography.' — *Nick Papadimitriou*

FILM WHAT NO LONGER EXISTS with PATRICK KEILLER

Try to solve the 'problem of London' by filming a stroll around the city. 'The true identity of London is in its absence,' muses Patrick Keiller's unnamed narrator in his film *London*. The narrator and his companion, Robinson, attempt to embody the spirit of the Parisian flâneur as they confront the emptiness of the modern city.[1]

CROSS THE EMPTY QUARTER with WILL SELF

Next time you take an international flight, set out for the airport on foot, at least ten hours before your scheduled departure time. Will Self walked from Stockwell to Heathrow Airport, and then from JFK Airport to Manhattan, thereby traversing the 'true Empty Quarter' of the airport hinterlands. The first time Self attempted to walk to Heathrow, he reached the road tunnel below the runways and found a sign that read: 'No pedestrian access. Go back to the Renaissance.' The Renaissance is a hotel on the A4.

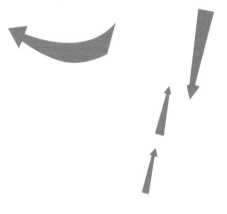

LONDON LABYRINTHS
Because of its irregular, twisting streets, London is sometimes compared to a labyrinth. A labyrinth is different from a maze, however: it's a single path without choices, sometimes used for meditation. The pavement labyrinth in Fen Court, for instance, is used by the London Centre for Spirituality (spiritualitycentre.org).

London's most striking labyrinth is the Mirror Labyrinth in Victory Park in Stratford: reflecting-steel sarsens create an increasingly claustrophobic shattered-mirror effect as you coil into the centre. The artist Mark Wallinger has installed a unique black-and-white labyrinth in all 270 stations on the Underground system, which invite tube travellers to compare the single meandering path to their own underground journey. Chigwell has a particularly good example: it has the same design as the medieval floor labyrinth at Chartres Cathedral.[2]

S

---

[1] For more on Robinson, see p.130.

[2] Labyrinth lovers should also visit the Chalk Labyrinth in Tower Hamlets Cemetery Park, the Flower Labyrinth in Ruskin Park and the Turf Labyrinth at Hall Place.

MAZES

There is a perverse delight to getting lost in a maze.[1] Enter this maze of London mazes and experience the thrill. Begin at Hampton Court Palace and make your way to the Minotaur.

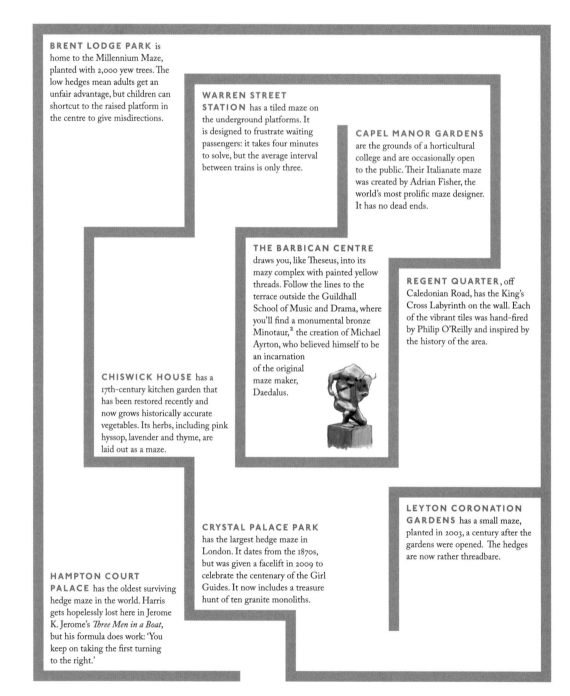

BRENT LODGE PARK is home to the Millennium Maze, planted with 2,000 yew trees. The low hedges mean adults get an unfair advantage, but children can shortcut to the raised platform in the centre to give misdirections.

WARREN STREET STATION has a tiled maze on the underground platforms. It is designed to frustrate waiting passengers: it takes four minutes to solve, but the average interval between trains is only three.

CAPEL MANOR GARDENS are the grounds of a horticultural college and are occasionally open to the public. Their Italianate maze was created by Adrian Fisher, the world's most prolific maze designer. It has no dead ends.

THE BARBICAN CENTRE draws you, like Theseus, into its mazy complex with painted yellow threads. Follow the lines to the terrace outside the Guildhall School of Music and Drama, where you'll find a monumental bronze Minotaur,[2] the creation of Michael Ayrton, who believed himself to be an incarnation of the original maze maker, Daedalus.

REGENT QUARTER, off Caledonian Road, has the King's Cross Labyrinth on the wall. Each of the vibrant tiles was hand-fired by Philip O'Reilly and inspired by the history of the area.

CHISWICK HOUSE has a 17th-century kitchen garden that has been restored recently and now grows historically accurate vegetables. Its herbs, including pink hyssop, lavender and thyme, are laid out as a maze.

LEYTON CORONATION GARDENS has a small maze, planted in 2003, a century after the gardens were opened. The hedges are now rather threadbare.

CRYSTAL PALACE PARK has the largest hedge maze in London. It dates from the 1870s, but was given a facelift in 2009 to celebrate the centenary of the Girl Guides. It now includes a treasure hunt of ten granite monoliths.

HAMPTON COURT PALACE has the oldest surviving hedge maze in the world. Harris gets hopelessly lost here in Jerome K. Jerome's *Three Men in a Boat*, but his formula does work: 'You keep on taking the first turning to the right.'

---

[1] Michel Foucault describes the experience as an 'act of Dionysian castration'.

[2] The minotaur is known locally as Colin.

BEDLAM

'They called me mad, and I called them mad, and damn them, they outvoted me.' – *Nathaniel Lee*

 Asylum doctors outvoted the 17th-century dramatist Nathaniel Lee and locked him away for five years. Bedlam, or the Royal Bethlehem Hospital, was the first institution in Europe to specialise in mental illness; it has become, in Roy Porter's words, a symbol for 'man's inhumanity to man', and 'bedlam' is now a byword for confusion and uproar. This hospital has haunted London for over six centuries and been through four incarnations.

THE HOSPITAL OF ST MARY OF BETHLEHEM

In March 2015, Crossrail excavations beneath the new Liverpool Street ticket hall unearthed 3,000 human skeletons. This was the burial ground of Old Bedlam, which began life as the 13th-century Priory of the Order of Bethlehem, built over a sewer that regularly overflowed. Conditions were appalling. In 1632, the clergyman Donald Lupton listened to the distressed inmates' 'cryings, screechings, roarings, brawlings, shaking of chaines, swearings, frettings [and] chaffings'. Stand in Liverpool Street and read from *The Honest Whore* by Thomas Dekker and Thomas Middleton. First performed in the nearby Fortune Playhouse, scene 15 features a number of Old Bedlam lunatics, including two who argue about flap-dragons and porridge.

BEDLAM HOSPITAL

When the number of inmates outgrew the building, Robert Hooke was commissioned to design a larger, grander Bethlehem Hospital nearby, which was completed in 1676. If you stand next to the obelisk on Circus Place, you are standing on the site of New Bedlam's main gates, which were once capped by large figures of 'Melancholy' and 'Raving Madness'. Alexander Pope called these sculptures the 'brainless brothers', and you can see them today in the Museum of the Mind in Beckenham. The final image in William Hogarth's series of paintings, *A Rake's Progress*,[1] is set in New Bedlam: Tom Rakewell, shaven and manacled, has been reduced to violent insanity. In the background, two well-dressed ladies giggle at the sight of a naked man with a large sceptre. Tourists could visit Bedlam for a penny to gawk at the inmates.

BETHLEHEM ROYAL HOSPITAL

When New Bedlam began to deteriorate, land was acquired in St George's Fields in Southwark, and a new hospital was completed in 1815. A Bedlam inmate, James Matthews, entered the competition to design the new building and some of his details were incorporated into the plans. The central block of the third hospital still exists and houses the Imperial War Museum today.

BETHLEM PSYCHIATRIC HOSPITAL

In 1930, the hospital moved to its current location near Beckenham in south-east London. It is still a specialist psychiatric hospital and includes the National Psychosis Unit and a residential anxiety unit.[2] The hospital's Museum of the Mind opened in 2015, displaying the shackles and padded straitjackets used in previous hospital buildings, and artwork by former patients. The most striking painting is *The Maze* (1953) by William Kurelek, which shows a skull-like labyrinth with a white rat trapped at its centre, which Kurelek identified as himself.

S

---

[1] The paintings are on display at the Sir John Soane Museum on Lincoln's Inn Fields. See p.21.

[2] A BAFTA-winning Channel 4 documentary called *Bedlam* was filmed there in 2013. You can watch clips online (channel4.com/programmes/bedlam).

GOLGONOOZA
WILLIAM BLAKE'S SPIRITUAL FOURFOLD LONDON

Here, on the banks of the Thames, Los builded Golgonooza

William Blake imagined a parallel London: an alternative city of 'Art & Manufacture', which he named Golgonooza. Constructing this city in his imagination, and in his epic, illuminated poems, was a symbolic and spiritual quest for Blake, an antidote to the dominance of Enlightenment rationalism.

This map follows 'Los', Blake's alter ego, as he walks through London in a sequence from the poem *Jerusalem*. Los's track is a thread through Golgonooza, connecting an array of fabulous figures from Blake's personal mythology. Walk the route yourself, building Golgonooza in your mind's eye.

THE FOUR ZOAS

'I must Create a System,' wrote Blake, 'or be enslav'd by another Man's.' Over the course of his life Blake created his own mythology, peopled with allegorical figures, giants, spectres and angels.

At the heart of Blake's system are the 'Four Zoas', which are the four fundamental aspects of the human psyche: man's body (Tharmas), his reason (Urizen), his emotions (Luvah) and his imagination (Urthona, or Los). All four aspects are present in everyone, and humanity's goal is to keep them in equilibrium. Each male zoa has a female counterpart, or 'emanation'. These are called Enion (the emanation from Tharmas), Ahania (from Urizen), Vala (from Luvah) and Enitharmon (from Los).

He came down from Highgate

LOS ①

Los symbolises poetry and the creative imagination, and is engaged in building the city of Golgonooza with his blacksmith's hammer. Blake had a fiercely powerful imagination. On the summit of Primrose Hill, he once conversed with the 'Spiritual Sun', not 'a golden disc the size of a guinea', he clarified, 'but like an innumerable company of the heavenly host crying "Holy, holy, holy"'.[1] Look online for a clip of Iain Sinclair's film *Ah! Sunflower*, in which Allen Ginsberg sits on Primrose Hill 'trying to raise the spirit of Blake over the city'.

Thro' Hackney & Holloway

ENITHARMON ③

Enitharmon represents spiritual beauty and provides Los with inspiration for his poetry. She is a version of Blake's own wife, soulmate and helpmeet, Catherine, whom he married in St Mary's Battersea ⑲ in 1782.[2] You can see a stained-glass window in the church celebrating the literary connection.

Towards London

ST PAUL'S CATHEDRAL ④

At the heart of the imaginary city of Golgonooza stands 'Cathedron'. This womb-like hall is a 'wondrous golden Building immense with ornaments sublime', which houses the looms of Enitharmon, where she weaves physical bodies for souls. There is a memorial to Blake in the crypt of St Paul's Cathedral.

Till he came to old Stratford

THE TYGER ⑤

In Blake's poetry, the tiger symbolises wrath, appearing as flames 'burning bright'.[3] Wrath can be beneficially harnessed as Revolution. There is a giant mural of the Tyger on Banner Street, not far from Bunhill Fields.

& thence to Stepney

---

① Today a stone circle commemorates the vision. The name Los is 'sol', or sun, backwards.

② Blake met Catherine Boucher in Battersea. At their first meeting he asked her, 'Do you pity me?' She replied, 'Yes, I do, most sincerely.' 'Then,' he said, 'I love you for that.' 'Well, and I love you,' she said.

③ Blake's 'Proverbs of Hell' remind us that 'the tygers of wrath are wiser than the horses of instruction'.

BUNHILL FIELDS ⑥

'I cannot think of death as more than the going out of one room into another,' said Blake. He was buried in an unmarked grave in Bunhill Fields, the dissenters' burial ground near Old Street. Today a large fig tree bends over a headstone placed 'near by' the remains of William and Catherine.[1] The monument always has an oblation of copper coins on the rim.

& the Isle
Of Leutha's Dogs

THE ISLE OF DOGS ⑦

'Leutha' is Blake's personification of sexual guilt, and Leutha's 'dogs' are base passions. The Isle of Dogs was notorious for prostitution, and Blake identifies it with Leutha's dogs, which accompany Los as he walks: 'at his feet they lap the water of the trembling Thames, then follow swift.'

Thence thro the narrows of the
River's side

LUVAH ⑧

Luvah, the 'Lover', symbolises all emotions, including love and hate, and he wears a crown of thorns. For Blake, the Tower of London ⑨ was a symbol of Luvah's hatred.

To where the Tower of London frown'd dreadful
over Jerusalem:
A building of Luvah builded in Jerusalem's eastern
gate to be
His secluded Court

VALA ⑩

Vala is the emanation of Luvah and represents the erotic aspects of war. In 1780, when Blake was an apprentice engraver, he was walking down Long Acre on his way to work when he became caught up in a crowd. He found himself carried to Newgate amidst the Gordon Riots and watched the prison burn to the ground.[2] Cross Blackfriars Bridge to Falcon Point.

Albion Mill, ⑪ the first steam-automated flourmill in London, once stood here. It burned down in 1791, possibly as a result of arson. Blake would have passed the charred walls of this dark satanic mill every time he walked into the City from his home in Lambeth.

Thence to Bethlehem,[3] where was builded
Dens of despair in the house of bread

PECKHAM RYE ⑫

Aged eight, Blake had a vision on Peckham Rye of a tree 'filled with angels, bright angelic wings bespangling every bough like stars'. There is a mural depicting the scene on nearby Goose Green. In 2011, the Blake Society planted a new Angel Tree on the Rye to commemorate the vision.[4]

Enquiring in vain
Of stones and rocks, he took his way, for human form
was none

URIZEN ⑬

Urizen, 'Your Reason', symbolises the rational mind. Blake saw the dominant rationalism of the Enlightenment as dangerously limiting. 'I turn my eyes to the Schools & Universities of Europe,' Blake wrote, 'And there behold the Loom of Locke, whose Woof rages dire, / Wash'd by the Water-wheels of Newton.' Look outside the British Library for Eduardo Paolozzi's sculpture *Newton (After Blake)*. ② Newton hunches over a set of dividers and his bronze body appears to be bolted together, as if he were himself a machine.

And thus he spoke, looking on Albion's City with
many tears:

S ——

MAP READING

Golgonooza: William Blake's Spiritual Fourfold London *uses Blake's descriptions of 'Golgonooza' from his prophetic poem* Jerusalem: The Emanation of the Giant Albion. *The strange geography of Golgonooza has south at its zenith, north at its nadir, west as the circumference and east at the centre, so in this map south is at the top and north is at the bottom.*

---

❶ Luis and Carol Garrido have located Blake's exact resting place, using the coordinates in the *Bunhill Fields Burial Order Book*: he was buried east-west 77 and north-south 32. When you know that Edward Scales's tomb is on north-south 32, and Matthew Wilks's fenced-off tomb is east-west 76, you can work out the precise location of Blake's physical remains: they lie close to a large London plane tree.
❷ The Old Bailey now stands on the site. See p.88.
❸ See p.291.
❹ It has since perished.

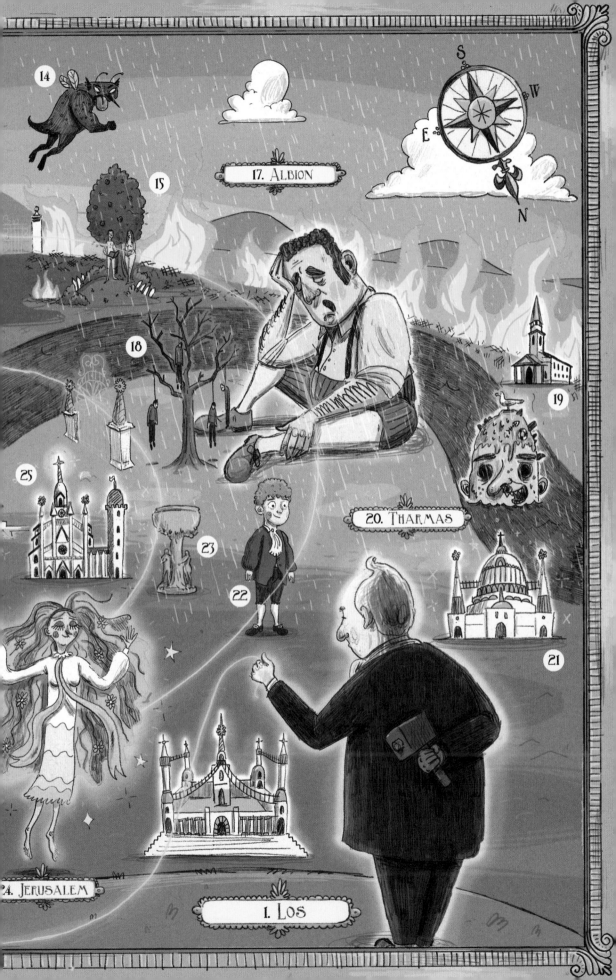

THE FLEA (14)

In 1819, Blake saw the ghost of a flea in the corner of his room. He kept his eye on it while his friend John Varley passed him drawing materials. Blake made a miniature tempura painting from his sketch, which you can visit in the Blake room at Tate Britain. (16) It shows a muscular, nude figure with a bull-like neck. Blake used gold leaf underneath the paint to give the flea an iridescent quality.[1]

'What shall I do? what could I do if I could find these Criminals?'

HERCULES ROAD (15)

From 1790 until 1800, the Blakes lived at 13 Hercules Buildings, in the small village of Lambeth. It was here that Blake's friend Thomas Butts stepped into their garden to find William and Catherine sitting naked, reading passages from *Paradise Lost*. 'Come in!' cried Blake; 'it's only Adam and Eve, you know!' Today the house has gone, but the site on Hercules Road is marked by a plaque. Underneath the railway arches opposite there are 70 mosaics inspired by Blake's images.

If I should dare to lay my finger on a grain of sand
In way of vengeance: I punish the already punish'd.

ALBION (17)

For Blake, Albion was both the giant who founded Britain and the progenitor of all humankind. At one point in *Jerusalem*, Albion sits down in Hyde Park, and a 'deadly Tree' springs up underneath his heel: the tree 'spread over him its cold shadows [...] They bent down, they felt

the earth, and again enrooting / Shot into many a Tree, an endless labyrinth of woe.' The deadly 'Tree of Mystery' is Blake's transmutation of Tyburn Tree, (18) the triangular gibbet at the end of Watling Street.[2] Visit the site today and arrange to visit the crypt shrine at the Tyburn Convent nearby.[3]

O whom
Should I pity if I pity not the sinner who is gone astray?

THARMAS (20)

Tharmas, the First Zoa, represents the physical body. Blake's 'vegetable' body was born on the corner of Marshall and Broadwick Streets in Soho, on Monday 28 November 1757. Aged four, the infant Blake was 'set ascreaming' by God putting his face to the window here. Today a brutalist tower block, William Blake House, marks the spot. If you ask, the receptionist will show you the Blake-inspired artworks in the foyer.[4]

O Albion, if thou takest vengeance: if thou revengest
thy wrongs,
Thou art for ever lost!

SOUTH MOLTON STREET (22)

17 South Molton Street, the only one of Blake's London houses to survive, now has a waxing salon on the ground floor.[5] The Blakes lived on the first floor from 1803 until 1821, and it was here that Blake, with help from Catherine, printed his two greatest prophetic works: *Milton* and *Jerusalem*. 'I write in South Molton Street what I both see and hear in regions of Humanity,' he wrote, 'in London's opening streets.'

What can I do to hinder the
Sons
Of Albion from taking
vengeance? or how shall
I them persuade?'

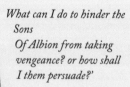

---

❶ When you visit the Tate, don't miss the octagonal gallery beyond the shop, which has a mosaic floor by Boris Anrep representing a selection of Blake's 'Proverbs of Hell'.

❷ See p.84 p.110 and p.281

❸ See p.110.

❹ Nearby, the 'Spirit of Soho' mural includes a portrait of Blake and a ceramic plaque commemorating local engravers.

❺ '2,000,000 bushes beautifully pruned'.

BALE
11

BALE
11

adidas

Producto
Oficial

Realmadrid

Henry Eliot x Matt Lloyd - Rose
Flat 2, 395 Hanley Road
London N4

18 MAY 2015 — Last night I went to Spain.
The English cemetery was disguised by a curtain
of the strangest, Humboldean handed. Dwellings
grown, not built. The former regime
freed any structure put up in a
single night, in the dark, for taxes.
When I opened my eyes, I was
held by the spite of
gravity, to London.

MADRID
Futbolín

HENRY ELIOT. MATT LLOYD - ROSE
FLAT 2, 395 HANLEY ROAD
LONDON   N4

②

→ Within the precinct of Queen Mary
College on Mile End Road, Jewish graves
were arranged like a garde of slate
postcards. A rassi told me the
history of expulsions: from the Promised Land
and   SPAIN. The ground where a Jew
is laid, he explained, belongs to that
person to the end of
time. NORTON

4PHOTOS
www.4photos.cat

TIMES

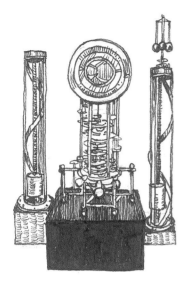

VISITORS TO LONDON often comment on the speed of the city, how everyone rushes, as if Londoners are living at a faster rate than the rest of the species. They're right that time operates strangely in the capital: it can disappear, as in 1752, when the switch to the Gregorian calendar meant that 11 days were lost forever;[1] and it can also be retrieved, as in 1995, when a flock of starlings landed on the minute hand of Big Ben and put the time back by five minutes. Nevertheless, London is a good place to get some perspective on time.

In the Royal Observatory at Greenwich you can touch the Gibeon meteorite, a 4.5-billion-year-old extra-terrestrial as old as the planet itself, older than any other rock on earth.

Across the river at Trinity Buoy Wharf you can hear the first performance of a piece of music called *Longplayer*. Kierkegaard observed that 'music exists only in the moment of its performance'; *Longplayer* is a computer-controlled composition for Tibetan singing bowls that lasts 1,000 years.[2] Listening to it enlarges one's sense of the present moment.

And in the Making of the Modern World gallery at the Science Museum, you can see the first prototype for the 'Clock of the Long Now'. The clock is powered by falling weights and designed to keep accurate time for the next 10,000 years. This model is the blueprint for a vast version, currently under construction in a cave below Nevada. If humanity becomes extinct, this hidden timepiece will continue to generate its own power far into the future using temperature changes in the Earth's crust.

SYNCHRONISE

SPEAK
Dial 123 on a BT line to talk to the speaking clock. This service began in London in 1936 with the voice of Ethel Cain, who won the 10-guinea prize after a search 'for the girl with the golden voice'. Today the golden voice belongs to Sara Mendes da Costa, from Brighton.

DROP
At 1pm every day, the large Time Ball drops on a pole at Flamsteed House in Greenwich Park, described in *Old and New London* (1878) as 'the most wonderful clock in the world'.

PIP
Tune into BBC Radio 4 and listen for the six pips that mark the start of each hour. They are generated by an atomic clock in the basement of Broadcasting House on Great Portland Street.

---

[1] Wednesday 2 September 1752 was followed by Thursday 14 September 1752. Go to Sir John Soane's Museum and look at Hogarth's 1754 painting *An Election Entertainment*. The campaign banner with the slogan 'Give us our Eleven Days!' is a reference to the ensuing Calendar Riots.

[2] Until 31 December 2999, when it will begin again. You can listen live online (longplayer.org/listen).

PAST TIMES

London has been the seedbed for many avant-garde movements, each rebelling against establishment ideologies until they become established themselves.

BLUE STOCKINGS

When the botanist Benjamin Stillingfleet wore blue worsted stockings to a literary breakfast organised by Elizabeth Montagu, the gatherings became forever associated with his informal hosiery. The Blue Stocking Society, which gathered on Hill Street, Mayfair, was revolutionary in encouraging and advocating women's intellectual independence. Today the celebrated sorority has been co-opted by a 'thinking women's cabaret' called The Bluestockings, who use burlesque to challenge 'social and cultural expectations about women' (facebook.com/The-Bluestockings-164155333599930).

P.R.B.

The Pre-Raphaelite Brotherhood had plans to take a house in Chelsea and install a cryptic plaque that would read 'P.R.B.'. Members would understand and outsiders would simply think it meant 'Please ring the bell'. The secretive P.R.B. was founded in 1848 at 7 Gower Street, where John Everett Millais lived with his parents.[1] They were reacting against the classical postures of Raphael and the 'sloshy' work of Sir Joshua Reynolds, and drew instead on the detailed, luminous aesthetic of late-medieval and early-Renaissance art. Visit Millais's *Christ in the House of his Parents* at Tate Britain, described by Dickens as displaying the 'lowest depths of what is mean, odious, repulsive, and revolting'.

BLOOMSBERRIES

'Bloomsbury paints in circles, lives in squares, and loves in triangles,' quipped the American poet Dorothy Parker. The Bloomsbury Set writers and artists were highly influenced by the philosopher G. E. Moore, who taught that the prime objects in life are 'love, the creation and enjoyment of aesthetic experience and the pursuit of knowledge'. The group is also remembered for their complicated love geometries: for example, Vita Sackville-West – Virginia Woolf – Leonard Woolf; Dora Carrington – Lytton Strachey – Ralph Partridge – Frances Marshall; and Duncan Grant – Vanessa Bell – Clive Bell. Channel the spirit of the Bloomsberries by visiting 46 Gordon Square with several lovers of both sexes. This building was home to Virginia Woolf and subsequently the economist John Maynard Keynes. It's now home to the Peltz Gallery, exhibiting today's Bloomsbury set: the staff and postgraduates in the School of Arts at Birkbeck.

FLAPPERS

When you refer to the cat's pyjamas, the bee's knees or you go to see a man about a dog, you're flapping.[2] A flapper was a radical young woman in the Roaring Twenties with a short skirt, bob haircut, full make-up and a cloche hat.[3] She listened to jazz and smoked profusely. If you want to get flapping yourself, book online for the next Prohibition Party, held regularly at secret locations (prohibition1920s.com). Brush up your Charleston in the refresher class beforehand.

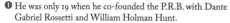

ANGRIES

On 8 May 1956, audiences at the Royal Court Theatre gasped at the shockingly domestic sight of an ironing board on stage. The press release for *Look Back in Anger* described the playwright, John Osborne, as an 'angry young man', and the name came to represent a generation of passionate middle- and working-class writers in the 1950s.[4] The Royal Court on Sloane Square continues to stage 'restless, alert, provocative theatre' and always sells playtexts instead of programmes.

---

❶ He was only 19 when he co-founded the P.R.B. with Dante Gabriel Rossetti and William Holman Hunt.

❷ Flapper vocabulary included 'big cheese', 'floorflusher' (insatiable dancer), 'giggle water' (booze), 'junk' (opium) and 'whoopee'.

❸ The US actress Colleen Moore (illustrated here) was the flapper to whom the term was first applied.

❹ The 'Angries' included Osborne, Kingsley Amis, Colin Wilson, Harold Pinter and Alan Sillitoe.

CURRENT AFFAIRS

'What the British public wants first, last and all the time is News,' says Lord Copper in Evelyn Waugh's great Fleet Street novel *Scoop*. Lord Copper, proprietor of the *Daily Beast*, knew better than most that all newspapers have an angle. Those printed in London today are no exception; each has views to impart and is loosely positioned at a different point on the political spectrum. This is a working guide to reading your way across a London newsstand.

Time Out (founded 1968, free since 2012) started in London as an edgy, counter-cultural pamphlet.[1] It is now the city's leading things-to-do magazine and an international media group with a readership of 40 million across 39 countries.

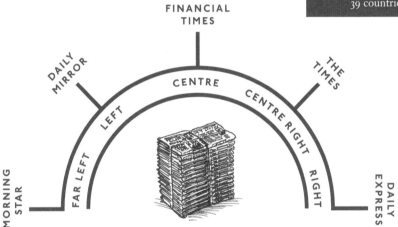

THE MORNING STAR
True to its communist ideals, the *Morning Star* is wholly owned by its readers. Anyone can join the co-operative: shares in the People's Press Printing Society cost £1 and you can buy them directly through the *Morning Star* website (morningstaronline. co.uk). Britain's only socialist daily newspaper was founded in 1930 by the Communist Party of Great Britain and was originally distributed on Tabernacle Street.

THE DAILY MIRROR
The *Daily Mirror* began life on Carmelite Street in 1903 before moving to Holborn Circus and eventually Canary Wharf. Originally it was a newspaper for women, run by women, but over the years it's lost this feminine emphasis, and has frequently courted political controversy. An early editor was Lord Rothermere, a friend of Mussolini and Hitler.

THE FINANCIAL TIMES
The *FT* was co-founded by the grand swindler Horatio Bottomley, as the friend of 'The Honest Financier and the Respectable Broker'. It was originally printed on undyed pink paper as a cost-saving device; now the distinctive salmon pages have to be specially coloured.

THE TIMES
The Times is the oldest London newspaper still published today. The London Library has a '*Times* Room' that contains original copies spanning more than 200 years. A dystopian version of *The Times* features in George Orwell's *Nineteen Eighty-Four*, where it appears as the one-sided organ of a totalitarian ruling party.

THE DAILY EXPRESS
On 2 November 1924, the first crossword was published in a British newspaper. The *Sunday Express* ran a puzzle by Arthur Wynne, the inventor of the 'Word-Cross'.[2] Look out for the art deco Daily Express Building on Fleet Street, made from vitrolite, glass and chromium. It was nicknamed the 'Black Lubyanka' by *Private Eye*, after the KGB headquarters in Moscow.

---

[1] In 1976, it printed a list of 60 supposed CIA agents operating in the city.

[2] The first crossword included the clues 'Cosy little room' and 'Home of a certain animal'.

FUTURE TRENDS

Medieval 'sumptuary laws' prescribed precisely what the different echelons of London society were permitted to wear. Only aristocrats were allowed to wear pointy boots, and yeoman's wives were strictly banned from wearing silk veils. Clothing still expresses identity today, although the ever-changing laws of London's sartorial tribes are now written by fashion labels. Influence the future of couture by becoming a designer yourself.

1. DEVELOP YOUR STYLE

Start by working out what you like to wear. Browse Dover Street Market, an achingly hip multi-brand concept store, which displays clothes alongside art installations in an 'atmosphere of beautiful chaos', in the words of its founder Rei Kawakubo. Although the store is called Dover Street Market, it migrated from Dover Street in 2016 and now occupies Burberry's former HQ on Haymarket. Once you've shopped, stop to admire your customised dazzle pants and spandex dungarees in the Rose Bakery on the top floor.

2. LEARN THE ROPES

Once you've defined your personal style, go to the Fashion and Textile Museum, whose bombastic pink-and-orange façade dominates Bermondsey Street. In keeping with its subject, the Fashion and Textile Museum has no permanent collection and changes its entire contents from one season to the next. The museum is also a college and has a busy programme of workshops: sign up for a course in crochet or avant-garde tapestry weaving. Alternatively, you could enroll on a degree course at the London College of Fashion in Shoreditch and bag a BA in Fashion Bags and Accessories. Check out the competition at their annual summer degree show.

3. GET INSPIRED

Now you know your godet from your gusset, take inspiration from past fashion masters. On the first floor of the Horse Hospital, an underground art venue behind Russell Square, you'll find Contemporary Wardrobe, a collection of 'rare and exotic street fashion', pieces from which have been hired by stars from David Bowie to PJ Harvey. Looking further back, the V&A Museum's fashion collection is the most comprehensive in the world.[1] Examine 18th-century side-hoop underskirts, which tripled a woman's width, then admire Jean-Paul Gaultier's corsets, described as 'armour for a late 20th-century cyber-woman'. The V&A also hosts regular 'Fashion in Motion' live catwalk events.

4. HIT THE CATWALK

In both February and September, London Fashion Week[2] grips the fashion world. To apply for your own catwalk, you need to have been in business for at least three years, with a minimum of six stockists. It pays to be superstitious: 'I always go to Holland Park before my fashion shows,' says Paul Smith, 'so I can see a rabbit, because rabbits are good luck for me. If you see a tall person in fashion week holding 84 carrots, you know it's Paul Smith.' Your catwalk will be streamed live on the LFW website.

THE DANDY

A Dandy[3] is a Clothes-wearing Man, a Man whose trade, office and existence consists in the wearing of Clothes. Every faculty of his soul, spirit, purse and person is heroically consecrated to this one object, the wearing of Clothes wisely and well: so that as others dress to live, he lives to dress.

— *Thomas Carlyle*

---

❶ You can find the world's oldest dress on p.166.
❷ In 2015, LFW moved to an unexpected new venue. See p.97.
❸ Find a dandy on p.111.

FREEZE FRAMES

Here are some ways to catch time as it rushes past.

SLOW LIFE DOWN

Look at Eadweard Muybridge's Animal Locomotion photographs at the Kingston Museum. Muybridge, who was born and died in Kingston, spent years photographing animal movements that are too quick for the human eye to process. Look at his sequence of prints showing a horse running; as your eye moves along the frames, you can make out exactly when and how the horse lifts each leg – and you can see the moment when the horse flies, with all four legs off the ground. Muybridge used these photographs to slow life down and break actions into their constituent parts. Take your own rapid bursts of photos of pigeons taking off and commuters dashing for tubes.

DOCUMENT THE EVERYDAY

'DO NOT PASS ME BY' reads a hand-painted sign outside a house on Brixton's Railton Road. 'TRY SAM THE GREATEST CYCLE REPAIRER.' This is the home and workshop of Clovis Salmon, now in his 80s, who arrived from Jamaica in the 1950s. As well as his legendary talent for rebuilding bike wheels, Clovis became well known for documenting everyday life in Brixton with a Super 8 camera. His film *The Great Conflict of Somerlyton Road* begins in the 1960s with the plight of Jesus Saves, a Pentecostal Church demolished to make way for the Barrier Block,[1] and ends with footage of burnt-out cars after the 1981 riots. Watch it online (samthewheels.co.uk),[2] then head out with a Super 8 to film your London.

STOP TIME

Life stands perfectly still in Dennis Severs's House at 18 Folgate Street in Spitalfields. Severs bought the property in 1979 and spent 20 years changing it back to the way it might have looked when it was home to Huguenot weavers in the 18th century. The house now exists in an eternal present; half-eaten meals, still-burning candles and discarded clothes give the impression that each room has only just been vacated by its occupant. Severs lived in the house while he worked on it. 'With a candle, a chamber pot and a bedroll, I began sleeping in each of the house's 10 rooms', he wrote, 'so that I might arouse my intuition in the quest for each room's soul.' Whenever you need respite from the churning city, book onto one of the evening visits, which take place in complete silence.

T ——

---

[1] Find out why the Barrier Block looks the way it does on p.93.

[2] You can also see a 2008 interview with Clovis, in which he states that nobody but him 'can build a wheel that three men can stand on that wheel and never break'. Next time you have cycle trouble, pay him a visit.

THE TIMES OF LONDON

THE SEASONS

Let the seasons be your calendar in London: in April the swallows start to arrive; in August they depart; in September the stags rut in Richmond Park; ① in late autumn the tawny owls re-establish their territories in Rainham Marshes; ② and, for a few short weeks each summer, adult stag beetles emerge after six years as grubs and the males lock horn-like mandibles.[1]

You can also use the ornamental cherry trees that line London's suburban streets: follow the cherry cycle through buds (February), blossom (March), green leaves (April–July), fruit (August), red leaves (September), abscission (October) and bare branches (November–January). Supermarkets are another way to divine the time of year: dowse the shelves for chocolate eggs, sun cream, back-to-school kits and festive merchandise.

THE NIGHT SKY

It's technically possible to use the Pole Star and the Plough to create a celestial clock face and tell the time to the nearest hour. This works perfectly each year on 7 March.[2] The sky's most sophisticated timepiece, however, is the moon. Both clock and calendar, its phases shape our months and its tides give a rhythm to our days. If you've ever mistaken a waxing gibbous for a waning crescent, visit the Astronomical Clock

built for Henry VIII at Hampton Court. ③ As well as time, date and zodiac signs, this 16th-century marvel shows the moon's phases and the time of high tide at London Bridge.

The same concept has been radically updated downstream at Trinity Buoy Wharf. Look for the tide-powered lunar clock at the wharf's south-east corner. ④ It uses three concentric rings of light to visualise the moon's monthly wax and wane, its position in the sky and the cycle of the tides. This lunar clock is a prototype for an immense model, intended to sit

alongside the Millennium Dome. Visit at high tide, when the Thames tolls the *Time and Tide Bell*, a sonorous sculpture attached to the river wall nearby. ⑤

THE SUN

The sun turns through the sky like a giant hour hand, marking morning, noon and night, and this predictable diurnal arc has long been harnessed to tell the time. The oldest surviving sundial in London is on the wall of the Charterhouse Great Hall, funded by Thomas Sutton in 1628; more recently, three precision-steel sundials were installed to celebrate the millennium at Greenwich, Blackfriars and Chatham.

The pointer of a sundial is called a 'gnomon', meaning 'the one who knows'. The earliest known gnomons are Egyptian obelisks. Cleopatra's Needle on the Embankment, for instance, was once the gnomon of a giant sundial in Heliopolis, the 'City of the Sun'. ⑥

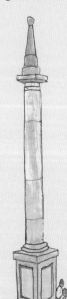

Visit and chalk Cleopatra's hours on to the southbound carriageway of the A3211. The central column of Seven Dials is another architectural gnomon: the six sundials on the dialstone are accurate to within ten seconds[3] and the column itself turns the circular shopping district into the seventh dial. ⑦ [4] For a tour of 12 variations in sundial design, follow the sundial trail at the Horniman Museum, which boasts a stained-glass dial, a ceiling dial, a 'tea-time' dial and an armillary octahedron. ⑧

---

① Stag beetles are Britain's largest beetle and their UK stronghold is the 'urban heat island' of London.

② Unfortunately, with each successive day the technique becomes four minutes less accurate and demands increasingly complex arithmetic.

③ A plaque at the base of the column explains how to convert readings to GMT.

④ The column is a modern replica, but you can see the 1693 original at Monument Green in Weybridge, on the Thames. The original dialstone is next to Weybridge Library.

WATER

In ancient Egypt there were 12 hours between dawn and dusk every day without fail. The length of an hour expanded and contracted with the seasons, and the Egyptians used adaptable water clocks to measure out the shifting segments of their days. Look in the British Museum for the remains of a black basalt water clock: a trough with a small hole at its base which would gradually empty over the course of a day. ⑨ Sets of lines incised on the inside indicate the time, differently spaced for each month of the year.

The water clock was a much-used technology until the advent of clockwork, but, unlike the sundial, it hasn't endured. Today the most elaborate water clock in London is above the Holland and Barrett health food shop on Shorts Gardens. At the centre of this bizarre 1980s contraption is a transparent pipe, marked with quarter hours, which slowly fills with water. When the level reaches a full hour, water cascades from the roof through a series of buckets, ringing bells and filling the watering cans of a team of mechanical gardeners. The gardeners empty their cans into a trough behind the shop sign, causing a floating flower garden to appear.

SANDS OF TIME

Sandglasses follow a similar principle to water clocks. You can see proto-egg-timers, used by priests to time their sermons, in the Measuring Time gallery of the Science Museum. ⑩

MAP READING

The Times of London *imagines London as a clockwork mechanism, inspired by Heath Robinson's contraptions and London's many public clocks. William Heath Robinson was born in Stroud Green and lived in London all his life.*

FLOWERS

In 1678, Andrew Marvell observed that 'sweet and wholesome hours' spent gardening should be measured by 'herbs and flowers'. Eighty years after Marvell wrote 'The Garden', Carl Linnaeus proposed the *Horologium Florae* or 'Flower Clock'. A flower clock works by planting 'circadian' flowers that open and close at precise times each day, independent of sunlight. There is no record of anyone planting one successfully, but why let that deter you? Find a plot and lay out some bristly ox-tongue (opens 4am), mouse-ear hawkweed (opens 8am), blue sow-thistle (closes 12pm) and proliferous pink (closes 1pm).[1]

Alternatively, use the scent of flowers to tell the time. ⑪ The wild thyme on Foots Cray Meadows in Bexley releases its aromas in the heat of the day; evening primroses in Spitalfields City Farm release their sweet, lemony fragrance at dusk. Since the time of the Song dynasty, Chinese temples have coiled winding trails of slow-burning incense and lit them in the morning: the trail burns throughout the day, and distinctive scents mixed into portions of the incense indicate the time.[2] Other horological odours include Borough Market in the morning (freshly baked bread); the Thames beach at low tide ('damp basement', according to master perfumer Roja Dove) and clubs before nightfall (disinfectant and urinal cakes).

T ———

---

[1] Linnaeus's clock was synchronised for Uppsala's latitude of 60°N in Sweden. London is at 51.5°N, so you may need to make some adjustments.

[2] You can see a maze-like Chinese incense clock in the Science Museum.

BELLS

Big Ben may be a radio star, but the largest bell in London is Great Paul at St Paul's Cathedral. [1] ⑫ The sound of bells has beaten the rhythm of London's days for several hundred years, and none more famously than the bells of St Mary-le-Bow Church. ⑬ It is said that true cockneys are born within earshot of the Bow bells, but despite their nursery-rhyme prominence [2] they have had a troubled past: they were destroyed in both the Great Fire and the Blitz, and silenced for two years in the mid 19th century at the request of a local woman who believed that the sound of the bells would kill her. Listen out for them on Cheapside, and, once they've tolled for you, tour some of the city's other chimes.

St Mary Woolnoth no longer strikes nine in the unusual way immortalised by T. S. Eliot, but inside the church you can see the bell's former mechanism behind glass, inscribed with lines from *The Waste Land*. At St Dunstan's-in-the-West on Fleet Street, two pocket-sized giants [3] strike the bells above its clock, which was the first in the city to sport a minute hand.

As well as the city's church bells, there is a Swiss glockenspiel clock in the north-west corner of Leicester Square, which marks the hour with a 27-bell extravaganza and a procession of cows, goats and alpine folk; ⑭ and in a Gothic spirelet above 24 Old Bond Street the 23-bell Atkinson carillon is played on Friday evenings and Saturday afternoons.

PENDULUMS

In 1670, William Clement invented the grandfather clock in London. Clement's stroke of genius was to invent an 'anchor' escapement, which reduces the pendulum's swing to 6° and means it can be enclosed in a case. By contrast, you can see a dramatic exposed pendulum in the V&A Museum entrance hall: the 'turret clock' was installed in 1857, soon after the museum first opened. The dials show Day in a chariot, Night in a cloak and Time with an hourglass and scythe. Between the numerals, the letters spell 'IRREVOCABLE'. [4] Today the huge bob pendulum hangs motionless and the clock is powered by electricity.

Tim Hunkin's automaton clock at London Zoo has a more active pendulum, with two toucans apparently acting as a gravity escapement. ⑮ On the hour it goes through a magical transformation, releasing mechanical birds into the sky above your head.

If you want to buy someone a grandfather clock on the morn of the day that they are born (one that will always be their treasure and pride), go to Pendulum of Mayfair, Maddox Street, a ticking treasure trove of antique clockwork.

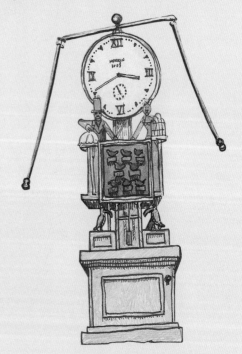

---

[1] Although it has a faulty mechanism and hasn't been heard above the city for several years. Its smaller counterpart, Great Tom, sounds the hours and another, 'the banger', is rung before 8am services.

[2] 'I do not know,' says the great bell of Bow. St Clement's on the Strand plays the 'Oranges and Lemons' tune every day at 9am, noon, 3pm and 6pm.

[3] Gog and Magog. See p.396.

[4] See p.316.

SPRINGS

Look for an over-sized pocket watch in the Royal Observatory, Greenwich. ⑯ Although its size and weight would stretch even the roomiest waistcoat, this impractical timepiece, known as H4, solved one of the great scientific problems of its age.

In 1714, the British government offered £20,000 to anyone who could create a device that would work accurately at sea. The joiner John Harrison ⑰ spent much of his life trying to crack the problem of longitude, creating a series of ingenious chronometers with spring-loaded balance wheels and a brass and steel strip that adjusted for fluctuating temperatures (his beautiful but bulky first attempt, H1, is also on display in the Royal Observatory). ⑱ H4 was his winning model, losing only 39.2 seconds on a sea journey of 47 days. Once you've admired it, look for a memorial plaque to Harrison on the floor of Westminster Abbey.[1] In the 1996 Christmas special of *Only Fools and Horses*, Del Boy and Rodney find and sell H6, a mythic missing Harrison chronometer, and finally become millionaires. ⑲

ELECTRICITY

Before the Apple Watch we had the Potato Clock. Go to Borough Market and buy two cutting-edge potatoes. Push a galvanised nail into each and a length of copper wire into the opposite sides. Connect the potatoes to a small LED clock: zinc ions react with copper ions, the potato acts as a buffer and the rest, as they say, is electrochemistry.

Electric clocks all rely on something that can generate a regular frequency. This frequency is then packaged up as seconds and minutes and communicated as the time. Your potato-powered LED clock uses the consistent resonance of a quartz crystal; some clocks use the vibration of a tuning fork; others use the mains alternating current itself. The Ham Yard Hotel has combined analogue and digital formats in their lobby: on the wall, the electric hands of 135 analogue clockfaces rotate to form hypnotic changing patterns, revealing the time every minute in a giant digital format.

ATOMS

You may think that a second is one eighty-six-thousand-four-hundredth of a day, but think again. The earth's wonky rotation, and the inconsistent days it produces, have long been considered far too imprecise to use as the foundation for international time. Instead, it's now more accurate to describe a second as nine-billion-one-hundred-and-ninety-two-million-six-hundred-and-thirty-one-thousand-seven-hundred-and-seventy vibrations of a caesium-133 atom. Today we live by atomic clocks, which beat time to the frequency of an agitated atom.

The first successful atomic clock, Caesium 1, was made in 1955 at the National Physics Laboratory in Teddington.[2] ⑳ Caesium 1 would slip a second every 300 years, shockingly inaccurate in comparison to recent models, which lose a second every hundred quadrillion years. If you're a stickler for punctuality, Frost of London, on New Bond Street, is one of the only places in the city where you can buy an atomic wristwatch: yours for just over £30,000. Nowadays, Coordinated Universal Time, the successor to GMT, is based on the average time from 400 atomic clocks around the world.

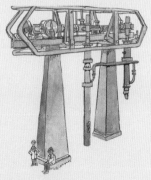

T ———

---

❶ His surname is bisected by a brass and steel meridian line, inscribed with its longitude: 000° 7' 35" W.

❷ This chunky contraption is now on display in the Making the Modern World gallery of the Science Museum.

THE HOURS

James Joyce's novel *Ulysses* takes place over the course of a single day known as 'Bloomsday', 16 June 1904. Every year on that date, Dubliners dress up as characters from the book and trace the narrative around Dublin, with readings and events along the way.

Virginia and Leonard Woolf were offered the opportunity to publish *Ulysses* in 1919. The scale of the novel was too great for the Hogarth Press, however, which they ran out of their Richmond townhouse, but Virginia read Joyce's epic, and, in 1925, published a novel of her own that also takes place over a single day, and is similarly composed of its characters' streams of consciousness.

Woolf's working title was *The Hours*. Set in London, the novel is punctuated by the chimes of Big Ben, whose 'leaden circles' dissolve in the air and mark the passage of time across the book. The novel became *Mrs. Dalloway*, one of the greatest achievements of modernist literature.

We hereby propose the introduction of an annual DALLOWDAY in London, to be held on the middle Wednesday of June each year.[1] You should begin Dallowday on Barton Street in Westminster, at the Dalloways' house.

6AM	7AM	8AM	9AM	10AM

10AM, THE FLOWERS

Decide to buy the flowers yourself. Make your way to Victoria Street for 10am. Listen out for Big Ben. There! 'First a warning, musical; then the hour, irrevocable.'

Enter St James's Park from Queen Anne's Gate, and walk past the 'slow-swimming happy ducks'. Turn right along Piccadilly to Hatchard's bookshop.[2]

Retrace your steps and walk up Bond Street with 'its flags flying'. Look out for a salmon on an iceblock.

When you get to 42 New Bond Street, walk in through the swing doors. In 1925, this was the location of G. Adam & Co., florists and fruiterers to the king, and the model for Mulberry's in the novel.[3]

While inside, imagine the 'pistol shot in the street' that Mrs. Dalloway hears, and picture the crowds gathering to inspect the intriguing motor car that backfired.

Some people should now follow Mrs. Dalloway back to Barton Street with the flowers; anyone who feels like the world has 'wavered and quivered and threatened to burst into flames' should follow Septimus and Rezia Smith to Regent's Park.

---

[1] Dallowday dates for 2017–2021:

2017	14 June
2018	13 June
2019	12 June
2020	17 June
2021	16 June

[2] Look in the window for copies of *Jorrocks' Jaunts and Jollities*, *Soapy Sponge*, *Mrs. Asquith's Memoirs* and *Big Game Shooting in Nigeria*.

[3] Today it is an outlet of Coach, a luxury handbag brand.

11AM, THE VISIT

Head upstairs to mend your dress.

At 11 o'clock, receive a surprise visit from an old flame. Have an emotional conversation and leave the house in a flurry like Peter Walsh.

Stride up Whitehall, glaring at the statue of the Duke of Cambridge.

Notice an extraordinarily attractive young woman in Trafalgar Square and follow her up Cockspur Street. Stalk her up the Haymarket, across Piccadilly and up Regent Street until she disappears into a flat red house off Great Portland Street.

No matter. Continue to Regent's Park. Find a bench in the Broad Walk and sit down, smoke a 'rich benignant' cigar and start snoring.

When you wake up, watch a little girl run into a lady's legs. Then walk to Regent's Park tube station.

As you exit the park, arrange for a battered old woman to be singing. Picture the 'old bubbling burbling song, soaking through the knotted roots of infinite ages', then give her a coin, and leave Peter Walsh to catch his cab to Lincoln's Inn while you walk along to Harley Street.

1PM, THE LUNCH

Walk to Oxford Street, as Hugh Whitbread does, pause outside Clarks and gaze 'critically, magisterially, at socks and shoes'. Then go for lunch on Brook Street.

You are dining with Lady Bruton, so bring red carnations. Head to the Silver Room at Hush, 8 Lancashire Court. Order a chicken casserole, coffee and soufflé.

2PM, THE ROSES

Leave Lady Bruton as she begins to snooze. Contemplate a silver two-handled Jacobean mug in the window of Peter Edwards on Conduit Street, and then, like Richard Dalloway, buy red and white roses and walk back towards Westminster.

As you walk through Green Park, notice families sprawling in the shade and 'children kicking up their legs'. Walk past the memorial to Queen Victoria 'billowing motherliness'.

As you pass through Dean's Yard, Big Ben begins to strike.

11AM	12PM	1PM	2PM	3PM

11AM, THE PARK

Find a bench in the Broad Walk and sit down.

Look up at the sky and imagine an aeroplane far above you, spelling out letters in the sky. Bring toffees in case you get peckish.

Watch the gulls flying overhead and listen to the bells strike 11.

When you feel drained by your husband's post-traumatic stress disorder, walk to the Ready Money Drinking Fountain.[1] Cry, 'I am alone; I am alone!'

Maisie Johnson asks you the way to Regent's Park tube station – wave her away with a jerk of the hand.

Feed your saved crusts to the squirrels and look at Maisie. You can't help smiling at a girl like that.

A child should now run into you, fall flat and burst out crying. Stand her upright and dust down her frock.

Go back to your husband, who is watching the ghost of his dead comrade walk past. It's time to leave.

As you exit the park, listen to an old woman singing. Walk along Marylebone Road to Harley Street.

12PM, THE APPOINTMENT

As you walk down Harley Street, listen for the strokes of Big Ben. Walk into Harley Therapy (1, Harley Street), a private psychotherapy practice that specialises in post-traumatic stress disorder. Try to wangle a visit that lasts three-quarters of an hour, the length of Septimus's appointment with Sir William Bradshaw.

As you step back into Harley Street, listen for the sound of 'shredding and slicing': the clocks of Harley Street nibbling away at the day.

3PM, THE NAP

As the sound of Big Ben floods the drawing room, give Clarissa the roses. Bring a pillow and a quilt so that she can have a nap. Why not have a post-prandial snooze yourself?

Your daughter, Elizabeth, disturbs you, entering very quietly. She and Miss Kilman leave to visit the stores. As Big Ben strikes the half-hour, the old lady in the house opposite moves away as if she is connected to the chimes.

The delayed chimes of St Margaret's break, 'like the spray of an exhausted wave', upon your body as you walk with Elizabeth down Victoria Street. Enter the cool, fragrant perfume department of House of Fraser.[2]

Browse the petticoats in the lingerie department and then nip down to Caffè Nero in the basement for tea and a chocolate éclair. When Elizabeth finds you repulsive and leaves, imagine Miss Kilman blundering towards the Abbey to raise her hands in prayer.

T

---

[1] This fountain was donated in 1869 by Sir Cowasjee 'Ready Money' Jehangir, a wealthy Parsee industrialist.

[2] Until 2005, this branch of House of Fraser was known as the Army and Navy Stores.

9PM, THE PARTY

Oh dear, it is going to be a failure, a complete failure.

Let the yellow curtain with the birds of paradise blow as if there were 'a flight of wings into the room'.

When the prime minister arrives, escort him down the room, sparkling on the waves. You still have that gift; to be; to exist. You are the party!

The noise! The sign of success. When Lady Bradshaw confides that one of her husband's patients, a young man, has killed himself, you picture it, the ground flashing up.

4PM, THE OMNIBUS

Wait for a bus in Victoria Street, outside Westminster City Hall (stop SA). Step forward and board the No. 11, competently, and take a front seat on the top deck.

The bus is an impetuous creature – a pirate – starting forward, springing away; you have to hold the rail to steady yourself as it rushes 'all sails spread' up Whitehall.

Ride on along the Strand, past Somerset House and the Strand churches. Alight at the Royal Courts of Justice (stop M). Head down Middle Temple Lane, catch a glimpse of the Thames and walk along Pump Court to the Temple Church. Lose track of time. Enjoy the 'sisterhood, motherhood, brotherhood' of the crowd.

When you get cold feet, let Elizabeth Dalloway mount the bus back to Westminster, but you should catch a cab to Guilford Street, and the Grenville Hotel.

7PM, THE DINNER

Enter the Jacques Wine Bar and find a table for one. Firmly order the 'Bartlett pears' to command the respect of other diners.

After dinner, enjoy a cigar on the hotel steps, then fetch your coat and walk out into the evening.

4PM	5PM	6PM	7PM	8PM	9PM	3AM

6PM, THE HOTEL

Leave and turn left along the street. You hear an ambulance, as Peter Walsh does, turning a corner and disappearing beyond Tottenham Court Road.

Walk to the Tavistock Hotel.[1] When you reach the hotel, cross the art deco hall and collect the key to your room and a letter in a blue envelope.

Read the note from Clarissa. Pull off your boots and empty your pockets. Wash, shave and get dressed for dinner.

8PM, THE EVENING

Stroll down Bedford Way and observe the loitering couples in Russell Square, 'dallying, embracing, shrunk up under the shower of a tree'.

As you walk down Whitehall this summery evening, does it appear 'skated over by spiders'? Move past 'looming houses, high houses, domed houses, churches, parliament' until you come to Barton Street, with cabs 'rushing round the corner like water round the piers of a bridge'.

5PM, THE WINDOW

Ask for a front-facing room at this Bloomsbury guest house. Lie on a sofa while your wife makes a hat. Watch the 'watery gold' light glow and fade on the wallpaper.

There are bars on the window, so when your doctor comes to remove you forcibly, you will not be able to sit on the sill. 'I'll give it you!' Septimus Smith cries as he flings himself vigorously, violently down on to the area railings.

Instead, drink some brandy shakily and listen to a clock striking somewhere.

3AM, THE END

Watch the old woman opposite, quite quietly, going to bed alone. She pulls down her blind and Big Ben begins to strike the hour.

Fear no more the heat of the sun. You must go back to the party.

---

❶ The Tavistock Hotel was built on the site of 52 Tavistock Square, where Virginia Woolf wrote *Mrs. Dalloway*.

TIME OUT

BUY THYME

Fortnum & Mason sell thyme in Tin No. 20. Keep track of the time you spend in the shop by clocking the 18-bell chimes emanating from the large timepiece above the main entrance: on the hour, automaton versions of Mr Fortnum (carrying a teapot) and Mr Mason (carrying a candelabra) emerge from alcoves and bow to each other.

MAKE TIME

The Clockmakers' Collection of historical horological devices has its own gallery at the Science Museum. This is the oldest collection of clocks and watches in the world.

MARK TIME

The Millennium Dome was constructed with time in mind: it has 12 metal struts, it is 52 metres high and has a diameter of 365 metres.

DRINK TIME

At Ziferblat[1] on Shoreditch High Street, 'everything is free inside except the time you spend there'. When you arrive, you are given a clock. Make yourself a coffee that costs 3p per minute.

FATHER TIME

High above Lord's Cricket Ground, the cowled figure of Old Father Time can be seen hunched over a wicket, removing the bails, a reference to Law 16(3) of Cricket: 'After the call of Time, the bails shall be removed from both wickets.'

TAKE TIME

St George the Martyr in Borough has four clock faces. Three of them are white and illuminated at night, but the clock facing east is black and unlit. When the church was being refurbished in the 1730s, local parishioners were asked to stump up cash. The people of Bermondsey, to the east of the church, refused and so, as they had no time for St George, St George had no time for them. That side of the clock tower was left blank, and the black odd-clock-out was added at a later date.

STOP TIME

The clock in the Dolphin Tavern on Red Lion Street stopped when a Zeppelin dropped a bomb on the pub on 9 September 1915. It was never started again, and still shows the fateful hour of 10.40.

MERIDIANS

The 'World Time Today' clock in Piccadilly Circus Station ticket hall is a map of the world with an illuminated band of times tracking across its centre: the band keeps pace with the earth's rotation, so that the clock always shows, simultaneously, the correct time for everywhere in the world.

G.M.T.

Greenwich is the prime meridian of the world, the line of longitude from which all others are measured. At the Royal Observatory you can stand with one foot in the world's eastern hemisphere and one in the west. At night, a powerful green laser beam cuts through the sky above Greenwich Park, marking the meridian line. It passes directly over Pole Hill in Epping Forest and shoots past the obelisk erected on the Bradley Meridian.[2]

O.K.

King George III attempted to establish a rival meridian in Kew, 18 minutes and 53 seconds west of Greenwich, running through his King's Observatory. His 'Arcadian Meridian' is still marked by a line of four obelisks, three of which you can visit in Richmond Old Deer Park, and there are plaques marking the two spots where the line crosses the Thames path. This ground zero never ousted the Greenwich meridian, but observatory papers were stamped 'O.K.' (Observatory of the King), which is said to be the origin of the popular exclamation.

T ———

---

❶ The name Ziferblat translates as 'clock face' in Russian and German.

❷ The earlier Bradley Meridian is 6 metres west of today's official meridian longitude.

UNDERGROUND

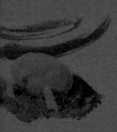

THERE'S AN URBAN LEGEND that the first London Underground baby, born on the Bakerloo Line in 1924, was named Thelma Ursula Beatrice Eleanor, so that her initials would remind her of her birthplace.[1] The Underground itself began life in 1863 and has inspired fascination and frustration in equal measure ever since. It's a masterpiece of engineering that yokes the city together, adored for its timeless design - its roundel, art deco stations, seat fabrics and fonts - and despised for its heaving crowds.[2]

The tube makes it easy to spend a lot of time deep below the streets. It can become so routine that you forget you're separated from the surface by thousands of tons of soil. But don't be taken in by the neat tiles and strip lights: you're in a completely alien environment, surrounded by plague pits, ruins, secret military installations and underground rivers. There's even an underground farm growing sorrel and rocket 100 feet below Clapham High Street (growing-underground.com). The climate below London is so different that there's a strain of mosquito unique to the Underground, incapable of breeding with its terrestrial counterparts. *Culex pipiens molestus* feeds on mice, rats and humans and is markedly more aggressive than the common house mosquito.

Underground sites are often abandoned when they're no longer needed and London is riddled with tantalising buried places. Some are easy to access, but many lie undisturbed and open very rarely to the public. Nevertheless, with persistence, good luck or an appetite for trespass you can lift the lid on more of these hidden recesses than you might imagine.

A city's underground isn't purely physical. It's also a byword for the radical creative activity taking place below the radar, movements like punk, hatched on the Kings Road in the '70s, or grime, which recently burst out of East London.

The allure of the underground – literal and metaphorical – is irresistible. So put away your oyster card, top up your thermos, and wrench off the nearest manhole cover: London's underworld is waiting for you.

URBAN LABYRINTHS

The stories in the *Arabian Nights* are set in urban labyrinths with underground spaces opening up to reveal stashes of treasure or ghastly hell holes; they take place behind mysterious walls in gorgeous private houses; their heroes are castaways, wanderers, fortune-seekers, lovers. According to the rules of fairytale hope and justice, the poor sometimes take possession of such palaces and come to rule in such cities ...

— *Marina Warner*

[1] This isn't true: the baby's name was Marie Cordery. The final letter of her first name and first letter of her surname do offer a clue to the station where she was born, however: see p.330.

[2] Find its most congested spots on p.39.

UNDERGROUND OVERGROUND

Before descending, here are some places where you can look down on the underground from above.

WELLS

WELL ENDOWED
Sadler's Wells Theatre houses an ancient well with healing waters. Up the stairs at the right of the foyer you can look down the well through a glass porthole on the floor.

WELL PRESERVED
Walk from the theatre to 16 Farringdon Lane and peer through the window at the handsome old Clerks' Well, from which Clerkenwell draws its name. If you'd like a closer encounter, call Islington Local History Centre to arrange a free visit (020 7527 7988).

WELL RESEARCHED
Camber Well was unearthed in 2009, following research by an enthusiastic local historian. It's in the back garden of Mrs Noreen Morrin of Grove Park and is not currently open to the public.

CRYPTS

FRIARFIELDS
The logo of the law firm Freshfields is the Archangel St Michael holding a spear. Perhaps this religious leaning explains why the firm has the crypt of a medieval monastery in the basement of its Fleet Street headquarters. You can see it from Magpie Alley, a pedestrian passage behind their offices. Before being absorbed by a multinational company, the crypt was part of the Whitefriars Carmelite priory.

UNDER & OVERY
Not wishing to be outdone, Freshfields' competitor, Allen & Overy, unearthed a medieval charnel house in the basement of their new building on Bishop's Square in Spitalfields in 1999. The charnel house belonged to the St Mary Spital priory and was used to store the bones displaced when new graves were dug in the cemetery. The remains of over 10,000 people, including 100 Romans,[1] were excavated before Allen & Overy could move into their London base. You can see the 14th-century crypt through the glass pavement outside the office.

> #### STATION IN THE SKY
> The highest subterranean site in London is West Ashfield Underground station, several storeys above street level in Ashfield House, a TfL building in West Kensington. To prepare their staff to work on the network, TfL have created a detailed replica of a District Line tube station[2] inside an office block. The platform can be made to vibrate and a fan simulates the gust from an approaching train.

---

[1] There are more Romans on p.397.

[2] Look out for another fake District Line station, Walford East, in the soap Eastenders.

GOING DOWN

DIG

Every generation cracks London open in different places. Crossrail is the latest great excavation, opening up vast craters, like the one at the top of Charing Cross Road, and burrowing beneath the city with eight boring machines: Ada (Lovelace), Phyllis (Pearsall), Elizabeth (the First), (Queen) Victoria, Mary (Brunel), Sophia (Brunel), Jessica (Ennis-Hill) and Ellie (Simmonds). Before long, Crossrail will clean up after itself and there'll be no trace of this immense Soho canyon and its eight tunnelling ladies.[1]

FIND A SECRET PORTAL

Neil Gaiman's novel *Neverwhere* takes place in 'London Below', a fantastical realm occupied by 'people who fell through the cracks in the world'. To get there, visit Hanway Place, just off Tottenham Court Road. It's normally a dead end, but if you go on a good day, you'll be able to take a left at the end on to Orme Passage, the entrance to London Below. If this portal doesn't work, look for the secret door in Kilburn that leads to UnLondon, a perilous subterranean world dreamed up by China Miéville in his novel *Un Lun Dun*. Watch out for binjas.[2]

LIFT A GRATE

Little Compton Street only exists under London. You can see its street sign by looking through a grate on the traffic island in the middle of Charing Cross Road at the junction with Old Compton Street. Wait until you're unobserved before lifting the grill and climbing down.

TAKE AN ESCALATOR

Go underground in Earls Court tube station, the site of the network's very first escalator. Bumper Harris, a one-legged engineer, was hired to ride it non-stop on the first day to reassure nervous travellers.[3] You can see a model celebrating his maiden voyage at the London Transport Museum's depot at Acton.

URBAN EXPLORATION

Exploring the city has completely ruined my ability to get anywhere on time. Everywhere I look now I see manholes, ventilation shafts into the tube, drainpipes I can shimmy up and open windows I can crawl through. I am constantly taking notes, photos and logging GPS points to return to in the middle of the night. — *Bradley Garrett*

U

---

❶ Boring machines are often named after women. The 1999 Jubilee Line extension was created by Sharon and Tracy, the names of the lead characters in the TV series *Birds of a Feather*.

❷ Dustbins trained in martial arts.
❸ The threat was real: nine dresses were torn during the escalator's first week.

LONDON UNDERFOOT
BURROWS & CAVES

CHALK MINES ①

Budding troglodytes should take the train from London Bridge to Chislehurst and spend time in the ancient chalk mines. Chislehurst Caves achieved notoriety in 1903 when a leading archaeologist claimed they had been dug by druids. The caves went on to have an intriguing century: they housed the Kent Mushroom Company between the wars; sheltered 15,000 Londoners during the Blitz, and then became an underground music venue[1] from the 1960s. Join an illuminated guided tour or sign up for one of the live roleplay games that take place in darkness.

CADE'S CAVERNS ②

Look for carvings of a horned god in Blackheath. If you see them, you may be at the entrance to Jack Cade's Caverns, a mysterious cave system of uncertain origins. The caverns enjoyed a brief period as a risqué night spot in the 19th century, and rose to prominence once more in 2002 when a road above them collapsed, leaving a crater at the junction of Blackheath and Maidenstone Hills. The original entrance, now sealed, is said to be in the garden of 77 Maidenstone Hill.

MERLIN'S CAVE ③

The Pen Ton Mound contains a druidic monument to the mother goddess in a cave accessed by a tunnel. The tunnel used to be in the cellars of Merlin's Cave Tavern at 16 Merlin's Place, but was bricked up in the early 20th century. The cellars are now somewhere below Charles Rowan House on Merlin Street.

MOLE MAN'S BURROW ④

Already riddled with tunnels, subterranean London is not an easy place to be a mole. This didn't deter William Lyttle, the Hackney mole man, who spent four decades burrowing under his home[2] before being evicted by the council for jeopardising the structural integrity of the street. He was relocated to a flat and died soon afterwards. When the house was put up for auction in 2012, with planning permission to redevelop the site, it was bought by two artists intent on preserving it and honouring Lyttle's handiwork. There's now an unofficial blue plaque outside the house at 121 Mortimer Road stating that William 'Mole Man' Lyttle 'lived and dug here'.

> **LABOURERS**
> The collective noun for moles – a labour – reflects the constant effort of these creatures' hidden lives. You can see a labour of 18 preserved in a single jar in case 12 of UCL's Grant Museum.

---

[1] Hosting the Rolling Stones in its heyday and the Strolling Bones tribute band in its 1980s decline.

[2] 'I thought I'd try for a bit of a wine cellar, and found a taste for the thing,' said Lyttle.

TUNNELS

FOOT Ⓥ

The Brunels' foot tunnel beneath the Thames was the first underwater tunnel ever constructed. It was a painful process: there were several high-profile floods while they were digging the tunnel, leading the Brunels to host an underground dinner party to assuage public anxiety. When it opened in 1843, it was hailed by many as the eighth wonder of the world, and in its first four months a million visitors paid a penny to experience the novelty of walking underwater. To enjoy a similar thrill today, go to Greenwich and take a free stroll through its foot tunnel, then walk back south through the tunnel at Woolwich.[1] You can travel through the Brunels' original tunnel on a London Overground train. Or, if you'd like to walk it, the Brunel Museum leads excursions along the tracks during planned engineering works.

ROAD Ⓥ

Aspiring skateboarders and street artists should visit Leake Street in Waterloo. Banksy ran a graffiti festival in this old road tunnel in 2008, and ever since, painting has been authorised here.[2] If you want some quiet practice, arrive early in the day with your favourite cans and nozzles. Once you've done your worst, grab your board and go into the former Old Vic Tunnels, where an American shoe manufacturer has set up a free indoor skate park. Hone your ollies, slides and grinds, then graduate to the graffiti-covered Southbank undercroft, which narrowly escaped redevelopment in 2014 after years of protests and petitions. If your board snaps, throw it off the southern end of the Hungerford Bridge on to the long-established Skateboard Graveyard.[3]

MAP READING

London Underfoot *depicts the territories below the city, peeling off the surface to reveal an abandoned underground kingdom.*

TRAMWAY Ⓥ

In 1954, the BBC's *Goon Show* revealed that a No. 33 tram had spent two and a half years hiding in the Kingsway Tramway Subway after the network had been decommissioned. The driver was determined that his would be the final tram in London and refused to leave the tunnel until he was presented with a marble clock at a 'last tram ceremony'. When he was finally discovered, his only passenger, Eccles, was patiently waiting for the tram to arrive at its Kingsway destination. Take the 521 bus from Waterloo, which passes through part of the subway, now the Strand Underpass.

CABLE Ⓥ

In 1980, the journalist Duncan Campbell found a way in to the deep cable tunnels beneath the city and located Q-Whitehall: a government communications facility 100 metres beneath Trafalgar Square.[4] In an exposé for the *New Statesman*, highlighting the facility's vulnerability, Campbell recommended that members of the public visit and jog along 'the only pollution-free running track to be found in (or under) central London'. The tunnels have since been secured, but underground fitness fanatics can console themselves with the fact that plans are afoot to convert disused tube routes into cycle tracks.

SUBWAY Ⓥ

Subway Gallery opened on 06/06/06 in the infernal regions beneath the Edgware Road. This tiny art gallery in a 1960s glass and steel kiosk is best known for its life-size waxwork of the art magnate Charles Saatchi. The venue also successfully petitioned for the name of its lair to be changed to the 'Joe Strummer Subway' and installed signs in honour of the Clash frontman who used to busk there.[5]

U

---

[1] If you enjoy your time below the riverbed, you may wish to join FOGWOFT (Friends of Greenwich and Woolwich Foot Tunnels; fogwoft.com).

[2] For some unauthorised Banksy, see p.188 and p.277.

[3] Obituaries for broken boards are posted online (hungerfordbridge.pbworks.com).

[4] An easier way to get under Trafalgar Square is to visit the crypt cafe of St Martin-in-the-Fields. Go early for a hearty fry or late on Wednesdays for tomb-top jazz.

[5] There is a mural of Strummer on the side of a bead shop on Portobello Road.

CELLARS & VAULTS

WINE CELLARS (x)

When the Ministry of Defence building was constructed on Whitehall after the Second World War, Henry VIII's wine cellar had to be dug up and relocated so that it wouldn't be damaged. A steel and concrete casket was built around the 1,000-tonne room before it was shunted 9 feet west and 19 feet down. It's now entombed below the MoD and only opens by request to interested parties. While your application is being considered, go to the candlelit cellar of Gordon's Wine Bar on Villiers Street and order a bottle of their finest Chablis. Then visit the cellars of Berry Bros. & Rudd at 3 St James's Street, a wine merchant founded in 1698, the same year the Palace of Whitehall burned down, marooning Henry's cellar.

STACKS (xi)

The British Library has one of London's roomiest basements:[1] five floors deep, it extends south to Euston Road and north until it meets the Northern and Victoria Lines. Go to the library and order a copy of *Selected Caves of Britain and Ireland*. While you wait for the mechanical book retrieval system to send your tome skywards, take the escalator to the lower ground floor and look for *Paradoxymoron*, Patrick Hughes's trompe l'oeil painting of an infinite library.

STRONGROOMS (xii)

If you're looking for secure document storage, what better place than a bomb shelter? The Goodge Street shelter is now a privately owned storage company on Chenies Street, named the 'Eisenhower Centre' after its Second World War associations with General Dwight D. Once you've archived your confidential files, go to the former vaults of Coutts Bank, now the basement of the Hard Rock Cafe at 150 Old Park Lane. It contains valuable holdings including a harpsichord played by the Beatles and one of Madonna's bustiers.

GIN CELLARS (xiii)

Gin is extracted from giant copper aquifers under London. Prospectors sink wells through the subsoil and siphon it off. You can watch the process at the City of London Distillery on 22 Bride Lane. Through a glass wall in their basement bar, gin-swillers have a clear view of the bulbous stills. Once you've savoured their botanicals, visit 214 Bermondsey Street. This gin cellar stocks Jensen gin, bottled in a railway arch nearby, and manufactures its own tonic.[2]

PINDAR (xiv)

When Alexander the Great destroyed the city of Thebes in 335 BC, he spared a single house, which had belonged to the Greek poet Pindar. In 1984, inspired by this image of resilience, the British government gave his name to a secret bunker beneath Whitehall. 'Pindar' is a crisis-management centre, sturdy enough to survive surface shocks of any kind. It's London's final refuge if disaster strikes and it never opens to the public.[3] When naming Pindar, MPs could have looked closer to home. Sir Paul Pindar, a 17th-century merchant, lived in a timber-framed mansion on Bishopsgate that narrowly survived the Great Fire, standing firm amidst the embers. Many years later, when Liverpool Street Station was expanded and the area was razed, the fragile structure escaped destruction a second time. Go to the Medieval and Renaissance galleries of the V&A and look for the preserved façade of Pindar's house.

---

[1] Consult one of their strangest books on p.353.
[2] Find more gin makers on p.175. Alternatively, install a thumper, doubler and slobber box in your basement and bottle your own.

[3] The photographer David Moore was admitted and documented its scuffed, spartan interior in his book *The Last Things* (davidmoore.uk.com/projects/the-last-things).

BUNKERS

BLAST DOOR (xv)

There's a steel blast door at the base of Pear Tree House, a block of council flats on Lunham Road in Gipsy Hill. The flats were constructed during the Cold War with an 18-room nuclear bunker in the basement. In the 1980s, Lambeth declared the borough 'nuclear free' and decommissioned the facility.

RAT TRAP (xvi)

The nuclear blast that obliterates London in James Herbert's novel *Domain* irradiates the city's rat population, massively increasing their size, strength and taste for human flesh. Human survivors battle the rats from a network of tunnels below Chancery Lane. You can see the unassuming entrance to the complex, which was occupied by MI6 in the Second World War and later housed the Cold War hotline between the US and USSR, at 39 Furnival Street. Once you've found it and overcome any mutant rodents with your ultrasonic cell disruptor, walk up Gray's Inn Road and steady your nerves with a brandy at the Water Rats pub. Reassure yourself with the fact that elsewhere in London the evolutionary power of rats is being harnessed for human good: researchers at Queen Mary's University are mapping the genome of naked mole rats[1] to investigate their longevity and resistance to cancer.

DEEP SHELTER (xvii)

Look for the memorial mural covering Stockwell's Second World War deep bomb shelter[2] at the junction of Clapham and South Lambeth Roads. At the centre of the painting is the story of Violette Szabo, resident of Burnley Road, who trained as a Special Operations Executive agent and conducted several undercover missions in France before being captured and killed.

IGNORED ROOMS (xviii)

There was an alarming moment during the Blitz when the Cabinet War Rooms below Whitehall began filling up with smoke. They hadn't been hit; the cause was a blocked chimney, obstructed by the prime minister who was sitting on it to keep warm while he watched the air raid from the roof. Although this site is now a popular tourist attraction, the alternative War Rooms remain little known. Churchill disliked the back-up bunker in Neasden, code-named 'Paddock', and only held meetings there twice. Council flats were subsequently built on the site and the War Rooms were forgotten. Paddock is still there, completely bare and unrestored. You can visit on one of Network Stadium Housing Association's two annual open days (networkstadium.org.uk).

U

---

❶ Naked mole rats look, according to one of the research scientists, like 'sabre-toothed sausages'.

❷ 'The danger here is not bombs, or even burial or typhus,' wrote G. W. Stonier in *Shaving through the Blitz*, 'but of going native and not coming up again till after the war, when you will emerge with a large family and speaking another language'.

THE TUBE

The protagonists of *A London Life* by Henry James venture across the city 'in a romantic, Bohemian manner [...] taking the mysterious underground railway'. Nowadays we tend to rush through, rather than romanticise, the tube. Here are some places to pause as you navigate the network.

The tube's last wooden escalator was removed from **GREENFORD** in 2014. Today, the next best thing are the stairs of In Cahoots, which are styled to look exactly like a wooden escalator. The setting for this tube-themed bar in Soho is **KINGLY COURT**, an invented station.

Look at the tiled reproductions of vintage TfL posters along the passageways in **HANGER LANE**.

Don't be alarmed if you hear a tube driver annou over the intercom that 'hell is other people'. **PICCADILLY LINE** drive were all given a book of quotes to inject some spi into their announcemen

There's always an art installation in the alcoves of the disused platform at **GLOUCESTER ROAD**.

MARK LANE

One of my favourite tricks for sharing the wonders of subterranean London with visitors is to show them an abandoned tube station. If you board a Circle or District Line train west from Tower Hill, for instance, and then cup your eyes against the glass so you can see into the tunnel as you head toward Monument, you will get a glimpse of Mark Lane, a station that was open from 1884 to 1967. — *Bradley Garrett*

In his poem 'The Underground', Seamus Heaney recalls rushing to the Proms with his wife Marie along the pedestrian tunnel at **SOUTH KENSINGTON** station. The buttons pop off her white coat as she runs.

In 2001, **ST JAM** trialled coating f with a pleasing f that would be re by passengers' foo Following passe complaints the s not introduced t network.

BALHAM was used as an air-raid shelter dur the Blitz. Look for the subdued grey plaque commemorating thos who died in October when a 140kg armou piercing bomb penetr 32 metres below groun and exploded in the s

Take a mackerel[3] to Spooky, the station cat at **ARNOS GROVE**. The elegant cylindrical entrance hall was inspired by Stockholm City Library.

A spiral escalator was trialled at **HOLLOWAY ROAD** in 1906. It was deemed unsafe and decommissioned.

Look for Cary Grant being pursued by a light aircraft in **LEYTONSTONE**. The station commissioned a series of 14 mosaics depicting scenes from Alfred Hitchcock[4] films to celebrate the centenary of his birth in the borough in 1899.

Look for a mysterious sign on the platform at **FARRINGDON**. It reads: 'DRIVERS Do not forget to drop the Pantograph!'

Look for the brass plaque at **BARBICAN**, which commemorates their much-loved station cat, Pebbles, who died in 1997.

High on the wall of the westbound platform at **EAST HAM** is an old painted sign advertising 'TEA 2D per cup'.

As you wait on the platform at **ALDGATE**, you're standing on a plague pit where a thousand bodies are still interred.[5]

ALDWYCH, the best known 'ghost station', was closed in 1994. You can still see the entrance on the Strand and TfL occasionally open it for visits.[2]

A TfL notice board outside **TEMPLE** warns travellers that the curvy 1932 tube map on display there is for interest only. Beck's geometric design was adopted the following year.

U

Marie Cordery was born below ground in 1924 at **ELEPHANT & CASTLE**.

The geometric tiling on the platforms at **BRIXTON** is a visual pun and shows a ton of bricks.

❶ The fragrance was meant to have 'a fresh, watery floral bouquet of rose and jasmine, combined with citrus top notes, tiny touches of fruit and herbs, giving way to woody accents and a hint of sweetness in the base'.

❷ Or explore it yourself in the guise of gun-toting archaeologist Lara Croft. London level 2 of the *Tomb Raider 3* computer game is set in the station. Make sure you pick up the Uzi and Masonic Mallet.

❸ There is only one tube station that shares no letters with the word 'mackerel'. It's mentioned on p.297.

❹ See a giant, pouting bust of Hitchcock in the courtyard of Gainsborough Studios in Shoreditch.

❺ Look into the pit on p.42.

PUNK

PINK

One of London's most conspicuous punks is a TfL employee at Oxford Circus Underground station. Look out for his tall Mohican, dyed the same red and black as the train doors. Punk style was born in 1974 at Malcolm McLaren and Vivienne Westwood's shop SEX at 430 King's Road.[1] Behind the striking façade, with its pink foam sign, they were dreaming up the ratty, ruined style that would become the hallmark of punk. McLaren was also beginning to assemble the Sex Pistols,[2] bringing together three of his customers and one of his shop assistants to form the band. In 1976, SEX was rebranded Seditionaires and began selling clothes with the rips, straps and zips for which punk is famous. By 1980, Westwood's interests had evolved and she renamed the shop Worlds End, which is still trading today. Instead of a sign, there's a large clock outside with a 13 where the 12 should be.

PISTOLS

Flick through John Lydon's autobiography *Rotten* in the bookshop hush of Foyles on Charing Cross Road. You're in the old St Martin's art school building where the Sex Pistols played their first gig in November 1975 with Johnny Rotten screaming at the helm. Joy Division's Bernard Sumner recalls seeing them live before he became a musician: 'They were terrible. I thought they were great. I wanted to get up and be terrible too.'

POGO

Sid Vicious, the Sex Pistols' second bassist, claimed to have invented the pogo in 1976. This simple dance involves stiffening the body and bouncing up and down on the spot like a pogo stick. Vicious invented it at the Punk Special in the 100 Club and it caught on rapidly. This two-day festival brought London's emerging punk acts together and propelled the movement forward.[3]

The venue is still in the basement of 100 Oxford Street; go and pogo at their next punk gig.

POST-PUNK

'History is for pissing on,' said Malcolm McLaren. Despite the insult, history has been kind to punk, which is already a treasured part of London's heritage. Perfectly styled punks in leather and red tartan bounced to the Sex Pistols' 'Pretty Vacant' at the 2012 Olympic Opening Ceremony and you can find crowds of young enthusiasts around the punk outfitters of Camden Market, an old stomping ground of many of punk's greatest acts. As you browse the racks at Punkyfish, decide whether you agree with Laura Oldfield Ford that the anarcho-punk look has been 'totally emptied of its radical critique'.[4] Deck yourself out in anti-authoritarian clobber and recreate the cover of the Clash's first album. The photo was taken on a narrow slope, now a staircase, just to the left of the main High Street entrance to the Camden Stables.

CYBER-PUNK

Look for two tall robotic sentinels in the corner of the Camden Stables market. They guard the entrance to the underground lair of Cyberdog. Even if you don't tend to dress in fluorescent dungarees or self-define as a cyberpunk, you should visit. Walk past the in-store dancers into a domain permanently bathed in trance music and ultraviolet light.

PROLONGED PUNK

Some of punk's pioneers still grace London stages. Look out for the Mekons,[5] one of the few first-wave groups who still play together. The Camden Rocks festival is always a good place to catch old punks (camdenrocksfestival.com). Glen Matlock, the Sex Pistols' first bassist, headlined in 2015. He was ejected from the band for being too musical.

---

[1] The shop sold fetish gear under the slogan 'rubberwear for the office'. Buy your rubberwear on p.67.
[2] Originally known as the Swankers.
[3] It ended badly when Sid, drumming for *Siouxsie and the Banshees*, threw a pint glass which smashed and blinded a woman in one eye.
[4] If you disagree, get a green mohican at Pepi's hairdressers and have a safety pin put in your ear at Cold Steel.
[5] They often play the Brixton Windmill.

GRIME

RINSE

'When I'm in London I listen to the pirates as much as I can,' said the DJ John Peel in 2004. 'There's a station I like called Rinse FM, which is somewhere in the area banded by Kiss FM and Classic FM.' In 2005, after 20 years of illegal bedroom broadcasts, Rinse was shut down by Ofcom, and one of its leading figures, DJ Slimzee, received an ASBO banning him from rooftops in Tower Hamlets to prevent him installing transmitters. Rinse FM was the first home of grime and the place where Wiley, the MC and producer now considered the Godfather of Grime, built his audience. Today Rinse has a licence and you can hear it on 106.8FM.

RIDDIM

'After punk rock, this is the truest music Britain has produced,' says Ghetts, a Newham grime MC. Like punk, grime is an underground music scene that's grown up organically, expressing the frustrations of young people in the inner city. Grime began in East London with Wiley's Roll Deep collective (E3). They were followed by others including the Newham Generals (E7), Boy Better Know (N17) and N Double A Est (SW9). To get a sense of how locally rooted grime collectives are, watch the Southside Allstars' video 'Southside Riddim'. The video cuts rapidly between squares, skate parks and street corners across South London as local MCs state their name and postcode.

RASCAL

Listen to *Boy in da Corner*, released by Dizzee Rascal in 2003 when he was 18, living on the Crossways estate in Bow. The album is full of barbed reflections on East London life, the things 'going on under people's noses whether they like it or not', as he said to one journalist.[1] The backing tracks are harsh – juddering rhythms made of sirens, ringtones and computer game bleeps – and Rascal raps about everything from creps, skengs and shotters,[2] to ninja turtles, Tropicana and his low-slung trousers. Asked about the title, he said, 'I'd been that kid in the corner of the classroom, the street corner. I had my back against the wall in general.'

RAVES

When Dizzee Rascal performed his song *Bonkers* at the 2012 Olympic Opening Ceremony,[3] not far from the streets where grime began, it became difficult to argue that it was still an underground scene. But although certain artists have broken into the mainstream, grime remains half-hidden and is hard to hear in the city's clubs. Many venues refuse to host grime nights following police warnings that they attract violent crowds.[4] If you're searching for grime in the capital, Wiley hosts Eskimo Dance at Indigo in the Millennium Dome, Peckham Palais hold a grime night called Boxed, and Love Music Hate Racism often include grime MCs in their line-ups (lovemusichateracism.com). 'I'm happy that grime remains underground', says Skepta, a Tottenham MC. 'A lot of people talk like it's some underrated or ignored genre, but to me that's the beauty of it. You've got our voices recording the heart and the aggressiveness of London.'

U

---

[1] 'You can try and ignore it,' he continues, 'but if you ignore something that's under your nose, sooner or later, it'll punch you in the face.'

[2] Trainers, knives and drug dealers.

[3] In a red-and-white 'E3' jacket and a red cap stamped with the letters LDN.

[4] 'Pow (Forward)' by Lethal Bizzle was banned in many clubs despite reaching No. 11 in the charts. The 2004 track features a groups of MCs making violent threats and gained a reputation for provoking fights.

BURIED RIVERS

Dowse for the subterranean waterways that still babble below London.

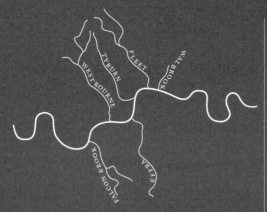

THE FALCON BROOK

The Falcon Brook flows below the Falcon pub in Clapham Junction. This pub was once popular with undertakers, especially after the lease was taken by a landlord called Robert Death. An 1801 engraving shows a gathering outside the pub, with the caption 'Undertakers regaling themselves at Death's Door'. In 2007, the river flooded and Falcon Road became a stream again.

THE WESTBOURNE

Constable's painting of the source of the Westbourne is on display in room 87 at the V&A Museum.[1] The river's meander through Hyde Park was dammed in 1730 to form the Serpentine,[2] and you can stand below the stream at Sloane Square tube station, where it is carried above the platforms in an enormous riveted iron pipe. If you stand by the Thames in Battersea Park, you can see the large mouth of the Westbourne in the embankment opposite, below the Royal Hospital Chelsea.

THE TYBURN

At the mouth of the River Tyburn, on the embankment west of Vauxhall Bridge, a plaque details its course.[3] Visit an exposed tributary in the basement of Grays Antiques on Davies Street, netted off and full of

goldfish, and then join the Tyburn Angling Society, who are campaigning to reopen the entire river for salmon fishing.

THE EFFRA

There is an urban myth that a coffin once collapsed into the Effra below West Norwood Cemetery and floated all the way to the Thames. Visit the mouth of the river: a storm outlet below the MI6 building.

THE FLEET

On 10 October 1859, the *Daily Telegraph* revealed that the River Fleet's upper reaches in Hampstead 'shelter a monstrous breed of black swine, which have propagated and run wild among the slimy feculence'[4]. Previously, in 1844, a Smithfield butcher had lost a young boar in the Fleet Ditch. When he recovered it five months later, it had fattened up and 'improved in price from 10/- to 2 gns'. Before the river's lower reaches were covered, they had become an acrid sewer: Jonathan Swift described the 'Sweepings from Butchers Stalls, Dung, Guts and Blood, / Drown'd Puppies, stinking sprats, all drench'd in Mud'. Listen for feral oinks through the grating outside the Coach and Horses pub on Ray Street, where you can still hear the Fleet flowing; then dive into the river's dammed tributaries on Hampstead Heath.[5]

THE WALBROOK

The River Walbrook is named for its course below the Roman city wall[6] west of All Hallows-on-the-Wall. Step down to the Thames beach at the end of Cousin Lane and find the 'Dowgate', now a storm drain where the Walbrook flows into the Thames. On 18 June 1999, the activist collective Reclaim the Streets[7] opened hydrants along the course of the Walbrook to 'release the river'.

---

❶ *Hampstead Heath, Branch Hill Pond.* Today the pond has disappeared, but the boggy site is still accessible below Whitestone Pond in Hampstead.

❷ Swim in the Westbourne on p.234.

❸ The source of the Tyburn, the Shepherd's Well on Fitzjohn's Avenue in Hampstead, is marked by another plaque.

❹ In Neil Gaiman's *Neverwhere*, the Great Beast of London is a feral boar grown obese on Fleet sewage, see p.323.

❺ See p.235.

❻ Trace the line of London Wall on p.15.

❼ See p.83.

OVERGROUND UNDERGROUND

To readjust to life at sea level, here are some underground hang-outs that feel as though they're above the surface.

MURALS

The lush, rolling landscape of Rex Whistler's mural in Tate Britain's basement restaurant transports diners to the Duchy of Epicurania. Whistler spent several months below ground painting *The Expedition in Pursuit of Rare Meats*,[1] which tells the story of seven travellers who set out from a land where cream crackers are the only available foodstuff in order to expand their national cuisine. Eat a packet of dry Bath Olivers as you explore the Tate, then plunge down to the restaurant for a slap-up feed.

WINDOWS

It's always Sunday morning in Communion, a basement cocktail bar on Camberwell Church Street styled to feel like a sunlit chapel. Order yourself a Corpse Reviver[2] and bask in the celestial glow from the backlit stained-glass windows.

MIRRORS

The most direct route from London to Paris is hidden below the neons of Piccadilly Circus. Walk down the stairs at the back of the French cafe at 20 Sherwood Street and you'll find Zédel, an immense brasserie with high ceilings, mirrored walls and marble columns. Zédel is far cheaper than its appearance suggests: enjoy tripe sausages and breaded frogs legs in immaculate *belle-époque* surroundings.

GLASS CEILINGS

Look for a portrait of arch-tunneller Isambard Kingdom Brunel in room 27 of the National Portrait Gallery, then head underground to the cafe. The glass ceiling allows you to look up at Charing Cross Road from below and is best enjoyed in the rain.

OUTDOORS

Walk through the unmarked blue door at 57 Greek Street and you'll find the New Evaristo Club, a basement bar known to most as Trisha's after its owner. Gangsters, boxers and popes grin down at you, and the Dead Wall near the door commemorates deceased regulars.[3] Although the bar itself is a dark, candlelit space, there is a subterranean smokers' courtyard out the back beneath a narrow patch of sky.

SURFACING

You have plenty of time to prepare for life above ground at Angel tube station, which contains two banks of escalators, the second of which is the longest on the tube network.

Depending on which measure you use, Hampstead or Westminster is the deepest tube station. Hampstead is 58 metres below street level and offers the longest lift ride to the surface. But Hampstead is on a hill and Westminster, at 32 metres below sea level, is technically deeper. Fortunately Westminster is also a spectacular place to come up for air. Navigate its futuristic nexus of concrete columns and criss-crossing escalators and leave through Exit 3, which brings you out at the base of Big Ben.

U ——

---

[1] Six weeks after its completion, the mural was completely submerged by the 1928 Thames flood. See p.340.
[2] Gin, Cointreau, Lillet Blanc & lemon juice in an absinthe-washed glass.

[3] Look out for the mysterious bottles of wine behind the bar with photos of Hitler and Mussolini on their labels.

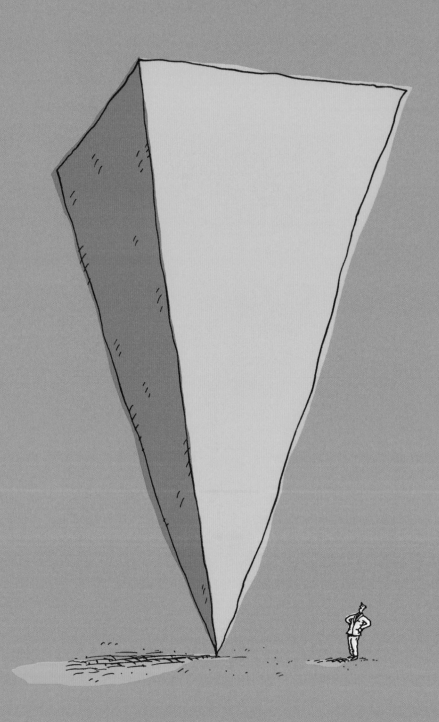

COLLISION

Nobody knows for certain why the driver didn't slow down as his train approached the dead end on Platform 9 of Moorgate Station. After the crash in 1975, TfL implemented a series of measures known as 'Moorgate Protection' to prevent the same thing happening again. There's now a plaque outside the station and the names of the 43 people who died are listed on a memorial in Finsbury Square.

ARSON

Police investigating the fire that consumed two clubs at 18 Denmark Place in August 1980 initially wondered whether it was due to a dispute between competing fast food vendors, after they found charred hot dog stands on the premises. They later discovered that the blaze had been started by an angry punter who'd been ejected, returned with a can of petrol, poured it through the letterbox and thrown in a match. Thirty-seven people died, but there's no memorial and the fire is relatively little known, despite being one of the most serious mass murders London has ever seen.

TERROR

Four backpacks full of homemade bombs were detonated in London on 7 July 2005, killing 52 people. The memorial in Hyde Park consists of 52 plain steel columns, clustered to show the number lost in each of the four blasts. The names of the victims are also inscribed on plaques at the bomb sites in Tavistock Square, King's Cross, Edgware Road and Aldgate East.[1] 'Even after your cowardly attack,' said the Mayor Ken Livingstone, 'you will see that people from the rest of Britain, people from around the world will arrive in London to become Londoners and to fulfil their dreams'.

ASSASSINATION

Two weeks after the 7/7 bombings, a surveillance officer code-named Frank was filming a house in Tulse Hill, waiting for a suspected terrorist to appear.[2] If he hadn't put down his camera to go the toilet, it's likely that police would have realised that the person leaving the building was not their man. From that moment, a disastrous chain of mishaps and mistakes unfolded, leading to Jean Charles de Menezes, an innocent Brazilian electrician, being gunned down in Stockwell tube station. There's now a memorial mosaic outside the entrance.

DESPERATION

Since 1996, at least twelve people have died trying to enter London by hiding in the undercarriage of aeroplanes.[3] Some have frozen, others have fallen out of the sky. On a quiet Sunday morning in September 2012, Jose Matada, a young man from Mozambique, landed on the pavement of Portman Avenue, a residential street in Mortlake. He was buried in an unmarked grave in Twickenham and it took three months for him to be identified. In 2014 he was flown home to his family.

v ——

---

❶ You can find out more about the people who died that day in a book of tributes created to celebrate their lives. It's on display at the Museum of London.

❷ One of the perpetrators of the failed terrorist attack on 21 July 2005. Only the detonators of the devices exploded.

❸ Only three recorded attempts have been successful.

UNREALISED CITY

For every grand scheme of London that has come to fruition, there have been dozens that died on the drawing board. This map is a memorial to the unrealised plans that could have changed the face of the capital, but didn't.

UNFRUITFUL ①

When the spire of Old St Paul's was struck by lightning in 1561,[1] the surveyor John Revell was tasked with the renovation. He only got as far as constructing a marzipan model, which he presented to Elizabeth I on New Year's Day 1562. A hundred years later, and six days before the Great Fire broke out, Christopher Wren proposed a new design to the Royal Commissioners, featuring a dome topped with a colossal pineapple. It wasn't approved and Wren worked through four iterations before construction finally began in June 1675. Look for the gold pineapples he did manage to smuggle on to the western towers.

UNBENDING ②

In 1796, the architect Willey Reveley proposed a simple but radical solution to the growing demand for docks: unbend the Thames by carving a straight river channel directly from Wapping to Woolwich Reach across the Isle of Dogs. Not only would this create three enormous ox-bow docks and three new islands (Ratcliff, Greenwich and Blackwall), it would remove the inconvenient loop past Greenwich, greatly reducing the sailing time up the river. This 'novel, grand and captivating' scheme was kyboshed and London has been lumbered with the distinctive Thames meander ever since.[2]

UNLADYLIKE ③

In 1799, artists were invited to submit plans for a 'naval pillar or monument' in London. John Flaxman suggested a whopping 230-foot sculpture of Britannia. She would have stood on the summit of Greenwich Hill with a British Lion peeping around her leg and tiny visitors awestruck at her base. He had an engraving made by his friend, William Blake, which you can request in the British Museum Prints and Drawings room (1894,0612.35.1). Despite royal support the plan was controversial; indeed a musical satire entitled 'The Naval Pillar, or Britannia Triumphant' was staged at Covent Garden. The scheme was eventually dropped and in Britannia's place today stands the comparatively diminutive effigy of General Wolfe. You can see a five-foot maquette of Flaxman's Britannia in the crypt of Sir John Soane's house.

UNDEAD ④

There have been many schemes for Primrose Hill. Over the years a pagoda, a casino, a botanical conservatory and an Olympian statue of Shakespeare have been proposed for its summit. The most spectacular suggestion came from Thomas Willson in 1829: to plant a great pyramid of death on the charming knoll. This 94-storey mausoleum, taller than St Paul's with a 15-acre base, would have had ample accommodation for 5,167,104 dead Londoners. Helical ramps were to spiral up a central access shaft, allowing porters ingress to 215,296 catacombs with berths for 24 coffins each. As each crypt filled up, it would be sealed for eternity, until the entire granite-faced polyhedron was completely blocked up. Willson hoped his Grand Mausoleum would 'impress feelings of solemn awe and admiration upon every beholder'. He announced an application to Parliament in May 1829, but the plans fell through and the mighty necropolis of Kensal Green Cemetery[3] was built instead.

---

① See p.98.
② The unfortunate Reveley's other project in the 1790s was drawing up plans for Jeremy Bentham's Panopticon, which was also never built. See p.273.

③ Visit all of the Magnificent Seven cemeteries on p.60.

UNREFORMED (5)

As the Reform Bill gathered momentum in the early 1830s, Richard Trevithick dreamed of an appropriate monument to symbolise the 'beauty, strength and unaffected grandeur' of the new British Constitution. He drew up plans for a 1000-foot tower, covered in gold and fitted with a steam-powered airlift to propel visitors to the pinnacle.[1] After the Reform Bill was passed in June 1832, Trevithick submitted his plans to William IV but he died two months later, taking the plans for the Reform Column to his unmarked pauper's grave in Dartford. Celebrate his memory by visiting the Trevithick steam engine in the Energy Hall of the Science Museum.

MAP READING

Unrealised City *maps projected construction projects that were never built.*

UNHOUSED (6)

Westminster Reference Library on St Martin's Street is the site of the house where Sir Isaac Newton lived from 1710 until his death in 1727. In 1834, Thomas Steele commissioned drawings of a stepped pyramid, topped by a giant stone globe, which would encase and preserve the great scientist's dwelling. The scheme never materialised: in 1849 Newton's house was stuccoed, later the square observatory tower was removed and in 1913 the building was demolished.

UNMANNED (7)

Instead of Nelson's Column, designed by William Railton, we might have had any of 120 different designs, submitted in 1837 for a 'Nelson Testimonial' in the newly christened Trafalgar Square. The designs included Nelson on a globe, on a dome, on an anchor and even lolling against the base of his column. Some designs abandoned Nelson altogether, such as the plan for an 80-foot trident – 'nothing more than a large toasting fork', according to *Art-Union*.

UNTRAINED (8)

Ten years before the first underground line opened in 1863, railway engineers James Samuel and John Heppel teamed up to work on the 'Thames Viaduct Railway': a raised line that would run above the centre of the Thames from London Bridge to Westminster with stops at each bridge along the way. The express journey would have taken just five minutes. Today Thameslink trains pause on Blackfriars Bridge, where you get a sense of what the Viaduct Railway might have felt like.

UNGEOGRAPHICAL (9)

In 1862, Dion Boucicault, an Irish actor-manager, took over the lease on Astley's Amphitheatre in Lambeth. Eschewing geography, he rechristened it the 'New Theatre Royal, Westminster', and then announced his plan to pull down eight adjacent houses and expand the playhouse into a leisure complex of epic proportions, with a replica Alpine village on the rooftop, complete with waterfalls, pine trees and snow-peaked mountains. Frustratingly for Boucicault, the project coincided with a scandalous law suit involving him and a young American actress, which caused his backers to withdraw and his creditors to sue. That summer he was declared bankrupt.

UNCROSSED (10)

The chief difficulty for planners submitting designs for what is now Tower Bridge was how to retain access for tall ships. The strangest suggestion came from Sidengham Duer in 1872. He proposed an iron gangway, 80 feet above the river, to which horses, carts and foot passengers would be raised on hydraulic platforms. He estimated that the bridge could accommodate up to 500 carriages an hour. You can get a flavour of Duer's Dream by crossing the pedestrian bridge over Royal Victoria Docks.[2]

V ———

---

[1] Having admired the view, thrill-seekers would descend by releasing air valves and returning to earth with 'the same shock [...] as jumping off a 9-inch door-step'.

[2] See p.182.

WYRD

DEEP IN THE TEMPERATURE-CONTROLLED VAULTS below the British Library, there is a 1,000-year-old manuscript known as the *Lacnunga*, or 'Remedies'. It is an Anglo-Saxon leech-book, a compendium of medical, magical charms. If you have an infected wound, for instance, it prescribes singing the 'Nine Herbs Charm' three times, while preparing a concoction of mugwort, cockspur grass, lamb's cress, plantain, mayweed, nettle, crab apple, thyme and fennel. Applying this salve, and praying to the god Woden, will sort you out in no time.

Professor Brian Bates, former director of the Shaman Research Project at the University of Sussex, is the world's leading authority on Anglo-Saxon magic.[1] For Bates, the concept of 'Wyrd' is at the root of ancient English magic. It corresponds roughly to 'fate' or 'destiny': literally it means 'that which has turned' or 'that which has become', implying that one's fortunes are always in flux.[2]

There are many magical books resting on London shelves, waiting quietly to spill their secrets: the Wellcome Library has a late-15th-century magical codex; University College London holds the 'Harry Price Library of Magical Literature'; and the Warburg Institute has a copy of the *Picatrix*, the largest and most comprehensive of all magical grimoires, containing the collected secrets of 11th-century Arabian sorcerers. The British Library's own extensive Sloane Collection contains the magical writings of London's great magicians, including the famous Elizabethan astrologer Dr John Dee.

This is an unusual concentration of arcane literature, but then London is a weird city. Charles Davies wrote in *Mystic London* (1875) that there is 'in its midst an element of the mysterious and occult utterly undreamed of by the practical people'. This is still true today. In London you can join a witches' coven, worship with druids, scry into the future, cast spells and channel earth mysteries.

Charles Fort, the American writer who popularised 'anomalous phenomena', lived on Marchmont Street for seven years while researching at the British Library. Fort's writings inspired 'Fortean' societies around the world, and today the London Fortean Society runs a packed series of event in the vaults below Dirty Dicks on Bishopsgate, with lectures on mummies, UFOs and zombies (forteanlondon.blogspot.co.uk). The South East London Folklore Society also runs regular events (selfs.org.uk). Both societies open the door to the occult side of London; this chapter invites you to step through that portal and embrace the Way of Wyrd.

---

[1] Bates spent years studying the *Lacnunga* and in 1983 published his own magical leech-book in the form of a novel, entitled *The Way of Wyrd*.

[2] Bates's revelation was to comprehend the 'Web of Wyrd', the way in which everything is both connected and in a state of constant change. A magician is someone who knows how to read the web and how to manipulate one part of it to produce effects in another.

THE WHEEL OF THE YEAR

Pagans celebrate eight high festivals each year, and most occult activity in London is concentrated around these solstices, equinoxes and cross-quarter days.

SAMHAIN
Halloween

When the harvest has been reaped, the Goddess descends into the underworld. Spirits roam abroad in this liminal time. Costumed mummers pass from door to door, reciting verses in exchange for food, lighting their way with turnip lanterns carved into grotesque faces. Bring your toothsome pumpkin to the shrine of the Black Madonna of Willesden.¹ Leave it as an offering to the dark Lady of the Oak.

MABON
Harvest

As the sun's strength wanes, the king is sacrificed and descends into the earth. The fruits of the earth are blessed and the earth's benison is shared in festivals of the harvest. At the autumnal equinox, step over the railings into the enclosure of Boudicca's Mound on Parliament Hill. Channel the spirit of the alpha female, the Warrior Queen Initiatrix, and leave a cryptic arrangement of pinecones.

LUGHNASADH
Lammas

When the land is at its most fertile, the Mother gives birth to the harvest. Bilberries are eaten, mountains are climbed and athletic contests held. This is an auspicious season for handfasting. Human-shaped loaves are baked from the first corn and eaten. Bake your own gingerbread figure and take it along to Queen's Woods near Highgate to join the annual 'Pan's Picnic', a masked afternoon of drums, dreams, food and frolics, held within the ring of 13 oaks known as the 'Witch's Coven'.

LITHA
Midsummer

At midsummer, the sun becomes the Solar King, at the height of his power. Bon-fires of bones and wake-fires of wood protect against evil spirits. The wheel turns. Walk down to Old Billingsgate Market for sunset, and invoke the druidic King Belinus, who was cremated and preserved in a golden urn on this spot.

YULE
Christmas

The sun, the solar child, emerges out of midwinter darkness. At this season, the Great Horned God, with his long white beard, leads the Wild Hunt across the winter sky, and gifts are exchanged. On the winter solstice, pay your respects to the Holly King by sipping hot wine in the Holly Bush pub in Hampstead. Then celebrate with pagan carols, divination and festivities at the Treadwell's Yule party, noisy merrymaking that should guard against the dark spirits of midwinter.

IMBOLC
Spring

When spring arrives, the Maiden rises refreshed from the dark winter earth. This is the season of hearth and home, a time of spring-cleaning, new lambs and initiations. Holy wells are visited and blessed with milk. Sprinkle some semi-skimmed around the Roman altar in the crypt of St Bride's Church.[2]

OSTARA
Easter

The sun grows in strength. The fecund Maiden, keeper of the apples of youth, is honoured with painted eggs, and the frisky badinage of March hares is sacred. At the vernal equinox, join the London Pagan and Heathen Circle at Cleopatra's Needle on Victoria Embankment for an Egyptian rite of Isis.

BELTANE
May Day

The Maiden blossoms into the Flower Bride. Garlands of yellow mayflowers decorate doorways, windows and cattle, and poles are erected to commemorate the primordial world tree. Bathe your face in the dawn's liquor to ensure beauty and prolonged youthfulness, then spend the afternoon in Trent Park, Enfield, where you'll crown your lover with flowers, dance around the maypole and leap over a flaming cauldron. In the evening, the Pagan Federation of London hosts an Open Ritual at Conway Hall facilitated by aphrodisiacs; photography is banned.

W

❶ Willesden has had a black image of Mary since the 10th century. Some say Black Madonnas descend from Kali, the Hindu goddess who wears a necklace of skulls and dances on the corpse of her husband.

❷ Built beside a holy well, this ancient site is sacred to Brighde, the druidic goddess of poetry and the spring. See p.396.

OCCULT SHOPS

TREADWELL'S
33 Store Street

If you're looking for a magic wand, you'll find one at Treadwell's. Perhaps a slender gnarl of hawthorn, carefully selected from English woodland, trimmed, polished and prepared for consecration, or a length of striated oakwood presented in a satin case. This is the boutique of choice for all your magical supplies: ceremonial daggers, cauldrons, wooden pentagrams and velvet witches' *haute couture*. The ground floor is lined from floor to ceiling with out-of-print books on spiritualism and the paranormal; the basement hosts events and workshops, including initiations into the arts of incense-making, tarot-reading and Haitian voodoo.

ATLANTIS
49a Museum Street

The Atlantis Bookshop was founded in 1922. There's a blazing fire inside and a cosy armchair. Snuggle down with the latest issue of *Pagan Dawn* and invoke the spirits of Aleister Crowley, Dion Fortune and W. B. Yeats, all of whom were customers here. It was in the basement of Atlantis that Gerald Gardner initiated the modern revival of witchcraft in the 1950s, and it was here that he met Ross Nichols, founder of OBOD.[1] Atlantis hosts regular events, including the Psychic Café every month.

> Witchcraft is the only religion Britain has given to the world and The Atlantis Bookshop is where the modern revival started. We are a necessary touchstone for people from all over the world – princes and pop stars included. Our Mysteries are western in flavour, suited to the magical land of Albion.
> — *Geraldine Beskin*

MYSTERIES
9-11 Monmouth Street

A New Age shop with an enviable array of crystals, smudge sticks, dreamcatchers and ear candles. Walk in for same-day psychic readings. You can consult their psychedelic website to see who will be scrying that day.

WATKINS'
19-21 Cecil Court

Watkins' Bookshop is one of the world's oldest esoteric suppliers. Founded in 1893, its shelves overflow with tomes on mysticism and the occult, as well as tarot cards, magazines and mystic videos. Despite recent financial problems, during which the shop closed temporarily, Watkins' is once again thriving. Consult their GeoSpiritual Map for an up-to-date compendium of occult happenings in London (watkinsbooks.com/ushahidi).

DENLEY'S
24 Brydges Place

Zanoni, Edward Bulwer-Lytton's occult novel of 1842, opens with a description of 'an old-book shop, existing some years since in the neighbourhood of Covent Garden', containing 'the most notable collection, ever amassed by an enthusiast, of the works of alchemist, cabalist, and astrologer'. The shop was based on a real emporium run by the eccentric antiquarian John Denley. Sadly it now appears to have disappeared, at least to the uninitiated, but when you squeeze down Brydges Place, the narrowest alleyway in London, there's still a chance you'll receive a mysterious encoded manuscript from an elderly stranger, as happens to the narrator in *Zanoni*.

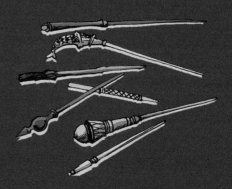

❶ See p.365.

TREADWELL'S

ATLANTIS

MYSTERIES

WATKINS'

DENLEY'S

W

WITCHES

In London most witches' covens are private and unlisted. If you feel drawn towards the modern witchcraft religion of Wicca, start attending public pagan events and in time you may be approached to join a coven.

NEW MOON

The Nova Stellar Wicca Meeting Group gathers on the second Tuesday of every month at 6.30pm in the Castle pub, Farringdon. It's a safe environment for newcomers to meet initiates from covens across London. You can ask questions about Wiccan practices before starting down the path of the Moon Goddess yourself.[1] For a more formal introduction, Alison Spiritweaver holds regular introductory courses in New Addington, Croydon, during which you will experiment with spell-craft and ritual magic, including an open-air sojourn with the Horned God.

WAXING CRESCENT)

You can explore the world of Wicca from your own home by setting up an account with life-simulator Second Life. Go to Witches Island, a sacred isle with standing stones, open-air temples and a maypole, created and administered by the British witchcraft organisation Children of Artemis (witchcraft.org). Your personalised avatar can attend classes and rituals on the island and even bust mystic grooves at a disco in the Artemis Tavern. If you'd prefer a more real-world experience, the Witches Inn Moot[2] gathers in the Feathers, Merstham, on the first Wednesday of every month. This friendly open gathering, run by traditional witch Rebecca Bird, is a good way to make new pagan friends.

FIRST QUARTER)

Once you are a witch, you will want to conduct rituals, but this can be difficult on your own. For solitary pagans, Treadwell's Bookshop hosts communal 'Open Circles' on the first Monday of every month, with discussions, chanting and ritual activity. Alternatively,

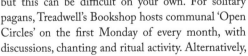

you could attend an event organised by Rain, a witch in Romford. Her shop, Cobwebs and Cauldrons, hosts workshops in scrying, numerology and palmistry.[3]

WAXING GIBBOUS

Full initiation into London's Wiccan scene must include tickets to Witchfest International in the Fairfield Halls, Croydon. This is the largest witchcraft festival in the world: it includes workshops in wand-making and moving magic, lectures on shamanism and psychic self-defence, and music from the likes of Rumpledrumskin and Spriggan Mist. An opening blessing launches a schedule packed with events: you might find yourself reciting spells, watching the Hunter's Moon morris dancers or linking hands and dancing a ritual spiral late into the night.

FULL MOON

Wiccans celebrate the phases of the moon with 'Esbats', as opposed to solar 'Sabbat' rituals. At the full moon, Esbat rituals take place across London. In the north-east, the Global Wicca Earth Healing Temple holds a Full Moon Esbat in Walthamstow at a 'private location' (meetup.com/Global-Wicca-Earth-Healing-Temple-London).[4] Alternatively, in the south-west, Wiccan High Priest Mani Navasothy leads a Full Moon Esbat on Wimbledon Common for the London Woodland Witches, Wiccans, Eco-Magicians and Outdoor Pagans (meetup.com/London-Woodland-Witches-Outdoor-Pagans). Navasothy is a Sri Lankan High Priest with 20 years' experience of witchcraft. He integrates 'creativity, magic, eclectic shamanism and the primal side of Witchcraft' into his events. He also leads night-time candle-lit rituals on the Terrace Gardens, Richmond.

---

❶ Events occasionally feature guest speakers, such as the shaman Gordon the Toad, author of *Sacred Animals*.
❷ Other monthly moots around London are listed on p.370.
❸ Rain also organises an annual coach trip to the 'Wytches Market' in Glastonbury, an occult bazaar of artisan crafts.
❹ Reserve a place online and meet at the St James Street station with your ritual tools.

DRUIDS

In 50 BC, Julius Caesar described Britain as the home of druidic wisdom, which concerns 'the stars and their movements, the size of the cosmos and the earth, the world of nature, and the powers of deities'. There are still many ways to follow the druidic path in London.

FIRST CONTACT

As well as courses on animal communication, past-life exploration and finding your astral wings, the College of Psychic Studies on Queensberry Place holds public introductory classes on the mysteries of druidry. Arthur Conan Doyle was a former president of the College of Psychic Studies; a week after he died, thousands of admirers summoned his spirit during a seance in the Royal Albert Hall. Become a member yourself to access their library of over 6,000 esoteric titles.

PARTIAL ECLIPSE

As you explore the potential of druidism, you could consider attending an event organised by the London Pagan & Heathen Circle. These include meetings on Maidenstone Hill in Greenwich, celebrating the art of the bard through storytelling, poetry and music, as well as recreations of robed rituals practised by the Priestesses of Atlantis (meetup.com/London-Pagan-Circle). You could also attend one of the happenings organised by Hern's Tribe, London's woodland shamanic group, which specialises in reworking fairy tales as tribal ritual dramas: they tend to gather in London's urban woodlands, usually near Croydon (hern-tribe.org).

FULL ECLIPSE

When you feel the time is right, take the plunge and join the Order of Bards, Ovates and Druids (druidry. org). Membership of the Order is not cheap, but you will receive a self-directed course of *gwersi* (lessons), with step-by-step instructions on becoming a druid.[1] Between *gwersi*, relax by tuning in to either of the two leading druidic radio stations (both currently internet-based): Pagan Radio (paganradio.co.uk) and

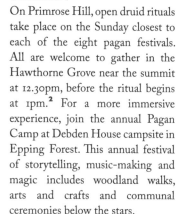

Wyldwood (wyldwoodradio.co.uk), which have eclectic music programming, from medieval plainsong to heathen heavy metal. There is also a druids' podcast, Druidcast, hosted by Damh the Bard (druidcast. libsyn.com). If you need a longer break from your studies, book yourself into Caer Corhrain, a shamanic retreat on the Isle of Sheppey, which has a stone circle and a sacred sweat lodge.

CORONA

On Primrose Hill, open druid rituals take place on the Sunday closest to each of the eight pagan festivals. All are welcome to gather in the Hawthorne Grove near the summit at 12.30pm, before the ritual begins at 1pm.[2] For a more immersive experience, join the annual Pagan Camp at Debden House campsite in Epping Forest. This annual festival of storytelling, music-making and magic includes woodland walks, arts and crafts and communal ceremonies below the stars.

TOTALITY

Once you are a fully initiated and practising druid, there are two key dates for your London diary. The first is the Pagan Federation of London Annual Conference, held in Leystonstone at the end of June. This all-day event includes talks on pagan history and sacred places, workshops on scrying and rewilding, opening and closing rituals and a pagan market, as well as live performances from pagan rock bands and a chance to connect with other druids across the country. Then the next day, you can attend London's Pagan Pride Parade. Bring your broomstick, floral crown and heathen hammer to Russell Square Gardens and walk with giants, fairies, floats and banners on a circular march through the streets of London, affirming your right to your beliefs while also celebrating pagan diversity.

W ——

---

❶ The course opens with an initiation ritual and introduces you to sacred circles, directions and elements.
❷ Look for the memorial stone on top of Primrose Hill, which commemorates the first 'Gorsedd' or sacred druid gathering

organised there by the Welsh stonemason Iolo Morganwg, on midsummer's evening 1792. He surrounded a small group with a sacred circle of scattered pebbles.

THE TAROT OF LONDON

'It's said that the shuffling of the cards is the earth, and the pattering of the cards is the rain, and the beating of the cards is the wind, and the pointing of the cards is the fire,' wrote the novelist and occultist Charles Williams. 'But the Greater Trumps, it's said, are the meaning of all process and the measure of the everlasting dance.'

Tarot cards have four suits: swords, wands, coins and cups. Each suit has cards numbered ace to ten, and four court cards, but there is also a 21-card suit of Great Trumps, known as the 'Major Arcana', with names including Death, Strength and the Hanged Man.

Although some claim its roots lie in ancient Egypt, Tarot is first recorded in Italy in the 15th century. It soon became a popular tool for divination: the cards reveal present situations and shed light on future consequences. If you would like to explore Tarot, book ahead at Treadwell's Bookshop, which offers readings seven days a week. Or if you want to experiment with the cards yourself, buy a copy of the iconic Rider-Waite deck.[1]

In this map we deal out London's Tarot, turning up key figures from the city's long association with the occult.

THE WITCH ①

Witchcraft has a long history in London. Stand on London Bridge and remember the witch drowned here in 963 for possessing a nail-studded effigy; or stroll through Pimlico, over the fields where a severed head and grimoire were incinerated in 1371; or stand at the junction of Edgware Road and Bayswater and picture Margaret Hacket, hanged at Tyburn in 1585 for killing a young man with witchcraft.[2]

THE WITCH.

London's most notorious medieval witch, however, was Eleanor Cobham, Duchess of Gloucester. Eleanor was born and brought up in the Palace of Placentia[3] in Greenwich. She married the Duke of Gloucester, Henry VI's uncle, who was regent during the young king's minority. Seduced by power, she conspired with a witch and a necromancer to murder the 20-year-old king by magical means. She planned to melt a wax effigy of Henry in the Bishop of London's hunting lodge in Hornsey (now the site of Highgate Golf Club), while a priest said a mass for the dead. When this treasonous plot was discovered in 1441, she was charged with necromancy, sorcery, witchcraft, heresy and treason, and did penance in the London streets before being banished to Peel Castle on the Isle of Man, where she founded a Manx coven that still meets today.

More recently, the retired civil servant Gerald Gardner founded the witchcraft religion of Wicca in 1954, which now has 800,000 adherents worldwide. He held regular naked covens in an Elizabethan cottage in the grounds of his Five Acres Country Club in Bricket Wood in north-west London, including one wild, orgiastic night with members of the band Pink Floyd. Gardner's cottage still stands in the grounds with his ritual circle and pentagram inscribed in the floor. Five Acres was, and still is, a naturist club, so to see the cottage you'll need to strip off.

---

❶ The Rider-Waite Tarot was created in London: commissioned by the mystic A. E. Waite, designed by artist Pamela Coleman Smith and published by the Rider Company in 1910. Coleman Smith was a member of the Hermetic Order of the Golden Dawn, and her evocative images are the result of magical visions induced by music.

❷ She had 'rotted his bowells and back bone asunder'.

❸ Later Oliver Cromwell's cracker factory, see p252.

THE MAGICIAN ⓘ

Look deep into Dr John Dee's black mirror in the Enlightenment Gallery at the British Museum.[1] Dr Dee was Elizabeth I's astrologer and advisor in magical matters. When Elizabeth heard that a spiked portrait of herself had been buried in Lincoln's Inn Fields, for instance, she consulted Dee, who promptly found and disposed of the voodoo object.

He lived on the Thames at Mortlake, where he had an observatory, a laboratory and an extensive library of occult books. His house was a pilgrimage destination for esoteric scholars from all over Europe, and Elizabeth herself visited him there. Make a journey to the site, on the north side of Mortlake High Street, opposite the church of St Mary the Virgin. The apartments to the west of the church, John Dee House, stand in what used to be Dee's orchard and you can find the last remnant of Dr Dee's house outside the church's west end: a stretch of old bricks embedded in the wall.[2]

THE MAGICIAN.

THE ALCHEMIST ⓘ

Elias Ashmole was a Renaissance man: a mason, a lawyer, an astrologer and an alchemist. He described himself as 'Mercuriophilus Anglicus', the 'English Mercury-Lover', and he was drawn to a variety of fringe beliefs.[3] Alchemists are concerned with transformation, both physical and spiritual, and their ultimate goal is the creation of pure gold from base metal. In 1653, a philosopher revealed to Ashmole the secret of the *materia prima*, the essential material from which the Philosopher's Stone is created. In 1679, Ashmole's library in Middle Temple was

MAP READING
The Tarot of London is a vision of a sorcerer's table, strewn with esoteric items. A dark map of occult London is overlaid with a set of new tarot cards, inspired by the Rider-Waite deck. The key locations in the texts are identified with stars on the map.

destroyed by fire and all his carefully accumulated books on alchemy, hermetic magic and astrology went up in flames. Raise its memory by walking along the 275-metre walkway on the east side of Liverpool Street station. At each end of the passageway, the roof beams are painted a leaden grey, but as you walk the colour changes subtly, like a finely gradated paint chart, until you reach a central golden joist. This is *Alchemy*, one of London's least noticeable public artworks.

THE ALCHEMIST.

Afterwards visit the luxuriant Alchemist on Bevis Marks, where expert mixologists juggle flasks above Bunsen burners, dispensing Fools Gold cocktails as they quest for the Philosopher's Stone.

HOW TO MAKE A PHILOSOPHER'S STONE
Get some dried lemon balm (*Melissa officinalis*) and some good brandy. Grind the herb into a powder and mix with the brandy; seal and leave in a warm place for a day. Then strain the mixture and seal the liquid. Meanwhile, spoon the infused herbal matter on to a baking tray and burn off the alcohol, then place in a very hot oven until the herb reduces to a white ash. Let the ash cool and grind it into a powder, then add the alcohol drop by drop, mixing thoroughly, until it combines into a grey waxy substance: this is the vegetable form of the Stone. Alchemists believe that a small amount, mixed with water and drunk, will improve your physical and spiritual strength.

W

---

❶ This smooth, obsidian disc was crafted by Aztec priests to communicate with the god of sorcerers, Tezcatlipoca.

❷ Dee's surviving manuscripts are held at the British Library, but you can browse them online (esotericarchives.com/dee). Look for his descriptions of Enochian script, revealed to him by angels and written from right to left.

❸ Once he had a cold, for instance, and hung three live spiders around his neck, following Robert Burton's advice in *The Anatomy of Melancholy*. See p.34.

THE WITCH.

THE EMPRESS.

THE MAGICIAN.

THE HIGH PRIESTESS.

THE EMPRESS ⒁

'There is no religion higher than Truth' is the motto of the Theosophical Society. Attend a public event at the Society's London headquarters, 50 Gloucester Place, and browse their library of arcane books: non-members can visit the library on Sundays by appointment. 'Theosophy' means 'wisdom of the gods': it is the ageless wisdom, the 'Light which shines through the many coloured lamps of religion'. Members of the Theosophical Society have included Oscar Wilde, W. B. Yeats, George Bernard Shaw, Thomas Edison and Annie Besant.

It was founded in 1857 by Madame Helena Blavatsky, who had conducted seances in Cairo, studied occult sciences in Tibet and become a Buddhist in Sri Lanka. She arrived in London in May 1887. 'What's the use of asking me to go to London?' she asked, 'What shall I, what *can* I do amidst your eternal fogs and the emanations of the highest civilisation?' She set up a journal called *Lucifer* and a personal 'Blavatsky Lodge' in her home at 17 Lansdowne Road. The Theosophical Society became London's predominant occult movement, and since Blavatsky died on 8 May 1891, the date has been celebrated by theosophists around the world as 'White Lotus Day'. Her last words were: 'Keep the link unbroken! Do not let my last incarnation be a failure!'

THE DEVIL ⒱

The successor to the Theosophical Society was the Hermetic Order of the Golden Dawn, founded in 1888. Members included writers Arthur Machen, E. Nesbit and Algernon Blackwood, as well as the most notorious of all London's occultists, the 'wickedest man in the world',[1] Aleister Crowley. Crowley was born into a repressive and religious family in 1875. His mother soon began to suspect he was the Anti-Christ, and referred to him as the 'Great Beast'. He moved to London in 1898 and took rooms at 67 Chancery Lane under the name Count Vladimir Svareff. There he created two temples: the white with six huge mirrors to contain magical forces, and the black with an altar and a human skeleton, which He fed with blood and dead birds. Both had magic circles and pentagrams drawn on the floor.[2] He used powerful drugs in many of his rituals and incorporated inventive sexual activity, with both men and women, learning his craft from the Ordo Templi Orientis, the top grades of which include magical masturbation and intercourse.[3] Crowley later founded his own magical order, the Argentinum Astrum (or A. A.), which follows the religion of Thelema, named after the abbey in Rabelais's *Gargantua and Pantagruel*, which has the motto 'do what you will'. You can apply to join the A. A. here: thelema.org.

---

❶ Crowley was described thus in 1923 by the tabloid newspaper *John Bull*, which also described him as 'a man we'd like to hang'.
❷ When the site was renovated in 2006, builders found a human skull in the basement and a pentagram made of sticks.

❸ The O.T.O. AMeTh Lodge is still active and recruiting in London (ameth.oto-uk.org).

THE HIGH PRIESTESS ⓘⅤ

If you had stood on Peter's Hill, between St Paul's and the Millennium Bridge, one and a half millennia ago, you would have been standing within the precincts of a Roman temple to Isis, the Egyptian goddess of nature.[1] In the 1930s, the cult of Isis was revived by Dion Fortune. Occultist, author and psychologist, Fortune operated out of the Belfry on West Halkin Street, which is now Mosimann's, a private dining club.[2] The owner of the building, Sir Vincent Henry Penalver Caillard, installed a lift so that Fortune could appear dramatically at the climax of each ritual, dressed as the Egyptian goddess.

Fortune founded an esoteric community, the Fraternity of the Inner Light, which still exists as the Society of the Inner Light (innerlight.org.uk). To become a member, you must apply in writing and undertake an extensive 'supervised study course'.

THE ARTIST ⓥⅡ

'His inventive faculty is stupendous,' wrote a critic, when the artist Austin Osman Spare held his first West End exhibition, 'and terrifying in its creative flow of impossible horrors'. As a child, Spare moved with his family close to the ancient Kenning Ton, at 15 Kennington Park Gardens. Here, it's claimed, he was seduced by a witch and initiated into black arts. He was involved briefly with Crowley's A. A., but soon developed a personal occult system, writing three grimoires: *Earth Inferno, The Book of Pleasure* and *The Focus of Life*.

He experimented with magical artistic techniques, including automatic drawing and sigilisation (the use of hermetic symbols). Contorted, surreal and sexual, Spare's artworks depict voluptuous nudes, winged heads, thorny satyrs, flaming hands and goatish skulls. Spare claimed that Hitler had once asked for a portrait, but he refused the commission. Very little of his work is on public display in London, although you can see some of his wartime portraits at the Imperial War Museum. 'Spare's medicine,' commented George Bernard Shaw, 'is too strong for the average man.'

THE DRUID ⓥⅢ

On William Blake's birthday in 1781, Henry Hurle revived the 'Ancient Order of Druids' in the Kings Arms Tavern, 23 Poland Street, five doors from where Blake would later live. The Ancient Order of Druids was a philanthropic organisation, which by 1933 had over 1.5 million members, including Sir Winston Churchill. In 1918, the alternative 'Ancient Druid Order' was founded in Clapham by committed socialist and vegetarian George Watson Macgregor Reid. This order still exists and they hold public ceremonies on Primrose Hill at the autumnal equinox, and at Tower Hill at the vernal equinox. Members are distinguished at public ceremonies by their white robes and cowls. A West London headmaster called Ross Nichols joined the Ancient Druid Order in 1954, and a decade later founded the Order of Bards, Ovates and Druids (OBOD), now one of the world's largest magical groups.

THE DRUID.

W ——

---

❶ You can see the remains of her altar in the Museum of London.

❷ The vaulted garret where Fortune performed the Rites of Isis is now called the Garrard Room.

LONDON'S LEYS

Ley lines were revealed to Alfred Watkins on 30 June 1921. The 66-year-old photographer realised, in a flash of inspiration, that ancient sacred sites are aligned across the British landscape in a network of perfectly straight lines, each one 'a fairy chain stretched from mountain peak to mountain peak.' He called these chains 'leys' after the Saxon word for a clear strip of land. The first of Alfred Watkins' London leys was The Strand Ley. Start by walking along the southern pavement of Pall Mall, which runs directly along the ley line.

ST MARTIN-IN-THE-FIELDS
The bones of an eight-foot human were disinterred below St Martin's.[4] The ley passes through the north–west corner of the building.

ST MARY LE STRAND
Built in the middle of the road, St Mary le Strand was once the site of a 134-foot maypole, last erected to celebrate the restoration of Charles II.[5]

ST CLEMENT DANES
Between 1189 and 1222 St Clement Danes was under the care of the Knights Templar. Though it's built in the middle of the Strand, it's orientated at an angle along the ley.

ST DUNSTAN'S IN THE WEST
The figures of Gog and Magog strike the hours outside St Dunstan's in the West.[6]

ST BRIDE'S, FLEET STREET
Sacred to the goddess Brighde.

THE TEMPLE
The Temple Church was consecrated by the patriarch Heraclius. Inside, a 13th-century effigy of Heraclius rests on a dragon.

Physicians' was buried here. No one knows why.

CORONATION STONE, KINGSTON-UPON-THAMES
An ancient sarsen stone, where seven Anglo Saxon kings were crowned .[2]

WESTMINSTER ABBEY
Built on the sacred Thorn Eyot, an ancient island in the Thames, Westminster Abbey is the traditional place of coronation and burial for British monarchs.[3]

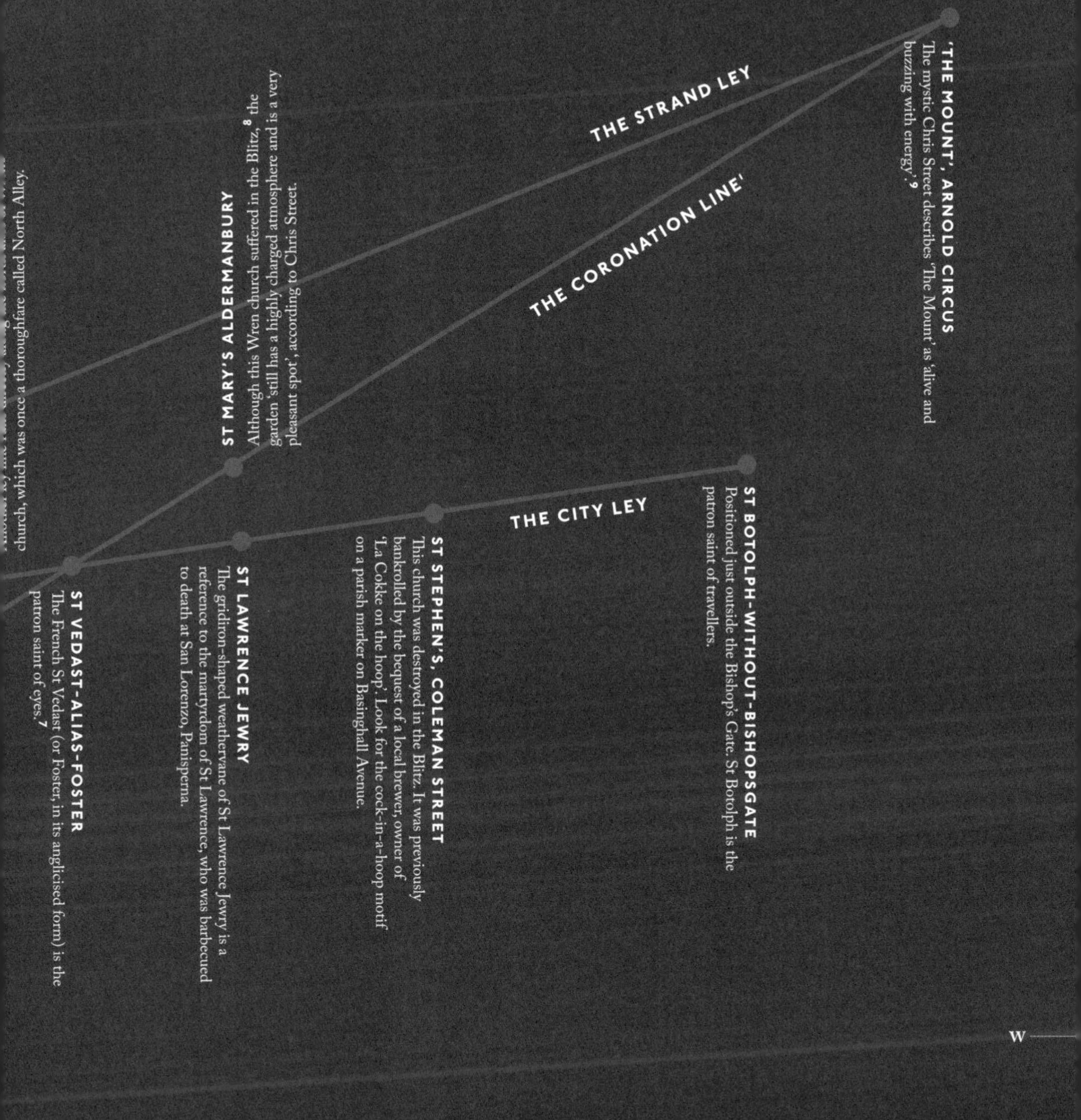

THE STRAND LEY

THE CORONATION LINE¹

THE CITY LEY

'THE MOUNT', ARNOLD CIRCUS
The mystic Chris Street describes 'The Mount' as 'alive and buzzing with energy'.⁹

ST MARY'S ALDERMANBURY
Although this Wren church suffered in the Blitz,⁸ the garden 'still has a highly charged atmosphere and is a very pleasant spot', according to Chris Street.

Another 1,/ the Fish Street/ burg church, which was once a thoroughfare called North Alley.

ST VEDAST-ALIAS-FOSTER
The French St Vedast (or Foster, in its anglicised form) is the patron saint of eyes.⁷

ST LAWRENCE JEWRY
The gridiron-shaped weathervane of St Lawrence Jewry is a reference to the martyrdom of St Lawrence, who was barbecued to death at San Lorenzo, Panisperna.

ST STEPHEN'S, COLEMAN STREET
This church was destroyed in the Blitz. It was previously bankrolled by the bequest of a local brewer, owner of 'La Cokke on the hoop'. Look for the cock-in-a-hoop motif on a parish marker on Basinghall Avenue.

ST BOTOLPH-WITHOUT-BISHOPSGATE
Positioned just outside the Bishop's Gate. St Botolph is the patron saint of travellers.

W

❶ The line connecting coronation sites was discovered by Chris Street (see EARTHSTARS on the next page). He noticed that Westminster Abbey and St Paul's Cathedral are aligned along the solstice azimuth. In other words, standing at Westminster the midsummer sun appears to rise directly behind St Paul's; conversely, standing at St Paul's, the midwinter sun appears to set behind the Abbey.
❷ See p.402.
❸ See p.134.
❹ Find another eight-foot human on p.123.

❺ James Bramston mourned its loss in 1729: 'What's not destroyed by Time's devouring hand? / Where's Troy and where's the May-Pole in the Strand?'
❻ See p.396.
❼ The current Wren-Hawksmoor church on the medieval site is regarded as having the finest-sounding bells in London.
❽ Its remains were subsequently dismantled and transported to Westminster College in Fulton, Missouri.
❾ See p.268.

LEY HUNTING

Watkins provided instructions for finding new ley lines. First you need to get hold of a good map: the *London A–Z Premier Map* is suitable. Start by pinning it to a board and circling as many ancient stones, mounds, wells and churches as you can find.

Then: 'Stick a pin into an undoubted mark-point (as a mound or traditional stone), place a straight edge against this and move to see if three other ringed points (or two and a piece of existing straight road or track) can be found to align. If so, rule a pencil line (provisionally) through the points. You may then find on that line fragments here and there of ancient roads and footpaths; also bits of modern roads conforming to it. [...] When you get a good ley on the map, go over it in the field.'

If you want company, join the Society of Ley Hunters (leyhunters.co.uk), the current incarnation of the Old Straight Track Club, of which Watkins was a founding member. The society publishes a quarterly newsletter and hosts two ley hunts each year.

EARTHSTARS

Chris Street, a mystic and 'reluctant visionary', has taken London's ley lines to a cosmic level. According to his Earthstars theory, ley lines in London are not isolated alignments: they interconnect 'to create a vast and beautiful design resembling an immense mandala covering the whole of Greater London'.

Starting with a central ley line running from Camlet Moat to Pollard's Hill in Norbury, Street has extrapolated a geometrical series of increasingly complex star patterns that form 'a vast landscape temple', manifesting the 'soul of the city'. Find out more on the Earthstars website (earthstars.co.uk).

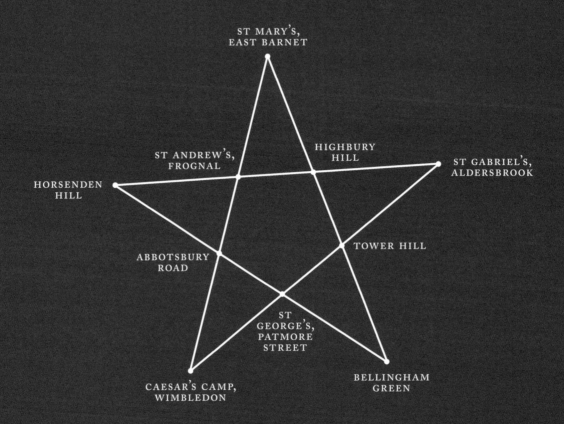

SQUARE & COMPASS

If you walk east of Covent Garden in the late afternoon, you are likely to see small groups of men in black suits, each carrying a briefcase. These men are Freemasons, and their cases each contain a small apron, a pair of white gloves and a magic wand. The Grand United Lodge of England on Great Queen Street was founded in 1717 and is the oldest Masonic Grand Lodge in the world.[1]

Today Freemasonry advertises its transparency, but the motto of the Grand United Lodge is still '*Audi Vide Taci*': 'Hear, See and Be Silent'. To become a mason at the Grand United Lodge, there is an online form to complete (ugle.org.uk/contact-us/interested-in-joining). You will then be invited to an interview and the lodge will hold a ballot on your application. All men of good character are welcome to apply; women should apply to the Order of Women Freemasons, the oldest Masonic organisation for women in the UK.[2]

Once accepted into a lodge, you declare a belief in a Supreme Being, swear to protect the secrets of your initiation and promise to support fellow Freemasons in distress, within the limits of the law. Then you will commence your journey into the 'craft', gradually being initiated, passed and raised through the three degrees of Apprentice, Fellow and Master Mason, learning secret grips, signs and passwords along the way. Masonic rituals are based on sacred knowledge handed down from Hiram Abiff, the chief stonemason and architect of the Temple of Solomon in the 10th century BC.

Have a drink at the Freemasons Arms on Long Acre, or browse the regalia in the various Masonic shops on Great Queen Street, and consider the order's illustrious membership list, which has included King George VI, William Hogarth, Josephine Baker, Rudyard Kipling and Nat King Cole.

W ——

---

❶ The monumental temple is open to the public, with several free tours on weekdays and free access to the Library and Museum of Freemasonry.

❷ Founded in 1908. It is based in the masonic temple behind 27 Pembridge Gardens, Notting Hill (owf.org.uk).

MOOT POINTS

A moot is a social gathering of pagans. There are public moots held every month in London.

First Monday of every month:

SACRED HART
The Edge Bar, Romford, 7pm

A well-established public moot with guest speakers and merchandise.

First Tuesday of every month:

COBWEBS & CAULDRONS
The White Horse, Chadwell Heath, 7.30pm

Friendly speaker events with time for socialising.

First Saturday:

HENDON HEATHENS
The Greyhound, Hendon, 6pm

Discussion over a pint and a pizza, followed by dancing at the Jammy Dodgers Variety Club.

Second Monday:

EAST MOLESEY MOOT
The Bell, East Molesey, 8pm

A social gathering for people on all pagan paths.

Second Wednesday:

ICKENHAM MOOT
The Coach and Horses, High Road, 7.30pm

Real ale in a cosy atmosphere.

Second Thursday:

ENFIELD TOWN CIRCLE
The Crown and Horseshoes, Horseshoe Lane, 7pm

Sofa-based discussion around a large fireplace.

Third Thursday:

CHILDREN OF ARTEMIS CROYDON
1 Matthews Yard, Surrey Street, 8pm

A friendly evening with talks, discussions and celebrations. The first Children of Artemis gathering established in the UK.

Third Sunday:

DAWN OF THE OAK
The Castle, Farringdon, 3pm

A casual, safe environment for pagans to meet over a pint.

Last Tuesday:

CHERTSEY MOOT
The Golden Grove, Ruxbury Road, 8pm

A sociable and open moot for all forms of pagan.

UXBRIDGE MOOT
The Swan & Bottle, Oxford Road, 8.30pm

A friendly and informal gathering.

PRAY TO THE BLACK SUN

Visit the Chapel of Our Lady in Notre Dame de France on Leicester Place. The chapel's mural was painted in 1959 by French poet, writer and occultist Jean Cocteau. Look for the Black Sun, an occult symbol associated with the mystic aspects of socialism.

CAST RUNES

Make your own set of runes, or purchase some from Oswald the Runemaker (runemaker.com). Choose a quiet location for casting, perhaps a corner of the British Museum where the runic Kingsmoor finger-ring inspired Tolkien to write *The Lord of the Rings*.[1] Clear your mind and focus on a simple question. Swirl the runes and select one. Hope for ᚠ, Fehu (reward, wealth, nourishment), rather than ᛁ, Isa (ice, stagnation, lack of emotion).

WORSHIP THE THAMES

The Tamesa London Circle works 'magically and spiritually with the River Thames', celebrating its guardian deity, Tamesa. Their lunar rituals are suitable for beginners and take place at various locations along the riverbank at key points in the lunar cycle (tamesa.info).

MEET A MUMMY

In the Ancient Egyptian galleries of the British Museum, exhibit 22542 is the 'Unlucky Mummy', a wooden sarcophagus of an unknown priestess who died in 950 BC. The story goes that the four Victorian explorers who first acquired the artefact died in mysterious circumstances and the man who delivered it to the museum died within a week. The photographer who took its picture committed suicide and it was even said to be aboard the *Titanic* when she sank.[2]

SPOT A YETI

If you're seeking the elusive yeti, drop into the Hunterian Museum on Lincoln's Inn Fields before you set off for Nepal. The museum has a papier-mâché cast of a yeti foot in its collection, as well as yeti teeth, hair and faeces, collected by the primatologist Professor Osman Hill.[3]

STARDUST

If things get a bit hectic, lean against a tree or a sun-warmed old stone wall to earth you. Breathe, have a drink and a snack or look at the river and then your spirit will be restored too. We are all made of earth, air, fire, water and spirit, as everyone has a teeny-weeny speck of stardust in them. — *Geraldine Beskin*

AUTOHAGIOGRAPHY

I am afraid that my adventures have lost me the citizenship of the world. Alastor is my name, the Spirit of Solitude, the Wanderer in the Waste. I am only at home in the Elysian Fields, conversing with the mighty men of old. I dislike London, not because it is busy and noisy and dirty and dark and sordid, and so on, but because it is so pettily provincial. I live in a city beyond time and space; how much beyond the ticking centuries and the itching inches of London!
— *Aleister Crowley*

W

---

[1] The Museum is also the setting of a key episode in M. R. James's terrifying story 'Casting the Runes'.
[2] The abandoned British Museum tube station, which closed in 1933, is said to be haunted by the ghost of a mysterious Egyptian princess. She screams so loudly you can hear her on the Piccadilly Line platforms at Holborn.
[3] They also have a yeti finger, but a BBC investigation in 2011 revealed that it's actually human.

JAMAICA (87,467)

Large numbers of Jamaicans began to arrive in London in the late 1940s, to meet the post-war labour shortage. Many of them settled in Brixton, which soon became London's largest and liveliest West Indian community. The UK's first black heritage centre, the Black Cultural Archives, opened on Windrush Square in July 2014. Browse the ephemera, letters and photographs telling the stories of black Britons, and then enjoy shark fillets and jerk chicken in Fish, Wings and Tings in Brixton Village Market.[1]

FRANCE (66,654)

In 2012, London was declared France's sixth biggest city with a French population bigger than that of Bordeaux. The French Parliament created a new constituency and 37-year-old Axelle Lemaire became the first French 'MP for London'. Traditionally South Kensington has been the French heart of London, with the Institut Français[2] offering a programme of cultural events. Elsewhere, you can sip a half-pint – full pints are banned – in the French House on Dean Street, where Charles de Gaulle wrote his famous speech '*A tous les Francais*', and don't miss the almond croissants along the road at Maison Bertaux, London's oldest patisserie.

KENYA (64,212)

When Kenya gained independence in 1968, the government expelled British passport-holding South Asians, as did Uganda in 1972. 13,000 Kenyan Asians arrived in London in 1967 and 10,000 Ugandan Asians followed in 1971. A remarkable Kenyan contribution to the city is on display at 575 Wandsworth Road. Once home to Khadambi Asalache, a Kenyan-born poet, novelist and British civil servant, the whole house is now a work of art, with every wall and surface covered in ornate pine fretwork. Asalache began this 20-year labour of love in order to cover damp stains in his dining room but it became an obsession and he ended up handcrafting every square inch. His house is now owned and operated by the National Trust.

UNITED STATES (63,920)

The *Mayflower* left Rotherhithe in July 1620 to pick up the Pilgrim Fathers at Plymouth.[3] They established the colony of Virginia, and 156 years later the United States declared themselves independent of Britain. Before the states were quite united, however, Texas had its own embassy in London; you can see the commemorative plaque in Pickering Place, off St James's Street. For a slice of Americana today, order an 'Original Fat Boy' with extra patty in Fatboy's Diner on Trinity Buoy Wharf, a New Jersey diner built in 1941 and later transported to London. Alternatively rack up the pins at Bloomsbury Lanes off Tavistock Square and head for celebratory cocktails in the Stafford American Bar, which is decorated with hundreds of gifts from hotel guests.[4]

ITALY (62,050)

Until the 1960s, Clerkenwell was known as 'Little Italy' and was home to a lively population of street entertainers, knife grinders, ice-cream sellers and musicians. The Italian Church of St Peter's on Clerkenwell Road still hosts a procession of Our Lady of Mount Carmel on the third Sunday in July, an annual tradition since 1883. Finsbury Park also has a lively Italian community, centred on Pizzeria Pappagone, which describes itself as 'a nice'a place to stuffa your face', and the Italian Farmers delicatessen. Other Italian hotspots include the Estorick Collection of modern Italian art in Canonbury Square and the eccentric Bunga Bunga bar in Battersea, with gondolieri barmen, yard-long pizzas and a Berlusconi Bellini cocktail, served in a replica of the former prime minister's head.

x ——

---

[1] See how the market has been changing on p.267.
[2] Try a French art-house film in the institute's Ciné Lumière, or browse its Médiathèque library, the largest collection of French books, magazines and films in the UK.
[3] The atmospheric *Mayflower* pub in Rotherhithe was once the only place in the UK licensed to sell American stamps. Find a model of the *Mayflower* on p.137.
[4] Supposedly the Stafford's congested collection began when an American guest donated a wooden eagle to alleviate the bareness of the walls.

WO

HARROW

BARNET

BRENT

HILLINGDON

EALING

CA

HOUNSLOW

HERMITH
FULHAM

KENSIN
&CHE

RICHMOND

KINGSTON

MERTON

TURKEY (59,596)

In 1627 there were only 40 Turkish Muslims living in London, but the community has grown hugely following the influx of Kurdish refugees and Turkish Cypriots.[1] The community has several Turkish-language newspapers and its own radio station. Relax with the *Turkish Times* over a peeling-foam-aroma package at the Hamam Turkish Bath in Dalston. Then, if it's May, you can sample the best of Turkish film-making at the Rio Cinema as part of the annual Turkish Film Festival, before heading to Clissold Park for the Anatolian Cultural Fete, where you'll be gripped by shadow puppetry, Ottoman marching bands and the Turkish National Oil Wrestling Team.

GERMANY (55,476)

Just outside the entrance to the Imperial War Museum in Lambeth you can touch a panel of the Berlin Wall, taken from the Brandenburg Gate in 1989. It still blazes an image of a gaping mouth by graffiti artist Indiano and the words 'CHANGE YOUR LIFE'. After this slice of German history, go to Katzenjammers Bierkeller in the basement of the old Hop Exchange on Southwark Street, for lederhosen, *weissbier* and live oompah brass on Friday nights.

PORTUGAL (41,041)

Vauxhall is 'Little Portugal', a bustling *barrio* of Portugese bars, cafes and shops, strung along South Lambeth Road. Not to be missed is the *bacalhau* salt cod from Tony's Delicatessen, and the *pastel de nata* custard tarts from Casa Madeira on Albert Embankment. For a surprising Portuguese encounter, try Madeira Só Peixe, a fishmonger with a secret barbecue cafe at the back. After a brochette of beef, watch the world go by outside Estrela Bar with a shot of *ginjinha*.

CHINA (39,452)

Limehouse was London's original Chinatown, an enclave of Cantonese sailors marooned without return tickets. Tower Hamlets is still the London borough with the largest number of Chinese residents, and there are fleeting glimpses of the old community – a dragon sculpture on Mandarin Street, the Chun Yee Society old people's drop-in centre on Birchfield Street – but the maze of opium dens and Chinese laundries, the fictional haunts of Fu Manchu, have evaporated. After the Second World War, Chinatown moved to Soho, and has been actively promoted by Westminster Council since 1986, when the Chinese pagoda was erected in Gerrard Street. Every spring, Chinese New Year celebrations take over the streets. Escape the crowds in Westminster Chinese Library on Charing Cross Road, and browse their selection of 50,000 Chinese-language books.

JAPAN (20,637)

London's first Japanese arrivals were Christopher and Cosmas, who returned with Sir Thomas Cavendish in 1588 after his marauding westbound circumnavigation of the globe. The Land of the Rising Sun can be found today on Shaftesbury Avenue in the Japan Centre. What began life as a bookshop and martial arts store in 1980 is now a vast emporium with a Japanese supermarket, bakery, Yoshino deli counter and homeware department. If you need some peace and quiet, try the Kyoto Garden in Holland Park, the Japanese Garden in Peckham Rye, or the Roof Garden at SOAS, accessible through the Brunei Gallery on Thornhaugh Street.[2] Then cling on at the Natural History Museum Earthquake Room, where you can stand inside a lifelike simulation of the 1996 Great Hanshin earthquake.

---

[1] Visit the Western Kurdistan Association museum and library on King Street W6 to learn about Kurdish heritage and browse their collection of Kurdish nappies.

[2] The most apologetic building in London. See p.29.

RUSSIA (16,757)

London has been connected with Russia since the 12th century, when the Hanseatic League harnessed trade routes across the Baltic. One early Russian visitor was Tsar Peter the Great, who rented John Evelyn's house in Deptford in 1698.[1] For Russian culture today, Pushkin House hosts a sparkling calendar of events in Bloomsbury Square, and the Russian Bookshop at the top of Waterstones Piccadilly has 1,200 square feet of Russian literature. For a more sensuous experience, try the Russian *banya* on Micawber Street, where you can steam, plunge and be thwacked with dry leaves. For something more covert, sidle along to the Brompton Oratory. Inside the entrance is a small altar: check the space behind the column on the left-hand side. KGB agents used this recess as a dead letter drop as recently as 1985.

SWEDEN (14,747)

The first Swedes in London were Vikings, some of whom were involved in a grisly encounter at Greenwich.[2] Today London's Swedish residents are less bloodthirsty. Drop into Ulrika Eleonora Church on Harcourt Street for Swedish newspapers, coffee and cinnamon rolls, stock up on herring and Abba fishballs in Totally Sweden on Crawford Street, and then kick back in the Harcourt Arms, London's Swedish pub, with a pint of Kopparberg and a plate of *köttbullar e pyttipanna*.

LEBANON (11,258)

Edgware Road is known to some as 'Little Beirut'. Middle Easterners have been settling here since the late 19th century, and the trickle became a stream during the Lebanese Civil War of the 1970s. Stock up on self-serve tabbouleh, *shrinam* and *jeliab* from Beirut Express, or visit one of its sister restaurants nearby, Maroush, Ranoush and Maarouf. Then relax outside Al Dar and choose which shisha to puff through their giant hookahs. Shisha cafes were hit hard by the England-wide smoking ban in 2007, but on a warm evening you can sit outside with a mint-flavoured smokepipe and feel like the Sheikh of Watling Street.[3]

THAILAND (10,250)

In the heart of residential Wimbledon, off Calonne Road, there is a tranquil retreat. Wat Buddhapadipa was built in 1965, the first Thai Buddhist temple in Europe, and has been at its current location since 1976. The interior walls of the bright-white temple depict florid episodes from the life of the Buddha; look out for portraits of Queen Elizabeth II and Charlie Chaplin hidden in the murals. There is a path that winds through the garden with words of wisdom at regular intervals, and glimpses of al fresco shrines through the trees. For a more lively experience, attend Songkran, the Thai New Year water festival on 13 April, when you can sample Thai food and crafts, watch traditional dances and bathe Buddha's image.

SOUTH KOREA (8,850)

New Malden is London's 'Little Seoul', with the densest concentration of Koreans outside South Korea. Since the 1970s the community has been growing around the former residence of the South Korean ambassador in Lord Chancellor's Walk. Show off your knowledge of the Korean pop scene in Han, on the High Street, an upmarket karaoke venue.

BELARUS (1,707)

For all your Belarusian literary cravings, look no further than the Francis Skaryna Belarusian Library, 37 Holden Road, North Finchley. This unprepossessing suburban house contains more than 30,000 volumes in Belarusian, as well as Belarusian LPs, archive documents and maps, and there is also a small museum with historic Belarusian stamps and *slutskiia paiasy* girdles, woven with gold.

X

---

[1] The tsar spoiled Evelyn's prize holly hedges by romping through them in a wheelbarrow.

[2] According to the *Anglo-Saxon Chronicle*, Viking raiders kidnapped Alphege, Archbishop of Canterbury, and pelted him to death 'with bones and the heads of cattle'. Nicholas Hawksmoor's church of St Alphege marks the spot.

[3] Explore the rest of Watling Street on p.2.

AROUND THE WORLD IN EIGHT ENTRÉES

Set off from the Reform Club in a balloon and try and sample all eight of these eateries in a single weekend.

HIDEG ÍZELÍTŐ

Order a plate of *hideg ízelítő*[2] and a glass of Frittman Kunsági Kékfrankos at the Gay Hussar on Greek Street. The wood-panelled walls of this 60-year-old Hungarian institution are hung with 60 caricatures of some of the establishment political figures[3] who have eaten there in recent years: the cartoonist Martin Rowson had an arrangement with the restaurant's owner to pay for each meal he ate there with a pen portrait of a notable figure dining that day.

POUTINE

Pick up a hot pot of poutine from the Poutinerie stall at Brick Lane Market one Sunday. This French Canadian speciality consists of chips and thick salty cheese curd doused in gravy. It's not the lightest snack, but it's a welcome pick-me-up on a cold day or when recovering from a night of excess.

ROPA VIEJA

The walls of Cubana on Lower Marsh are covered with revolutionary photos and old rifles. A fine place for a mojito and a bowl of *ropa vieja*,[1] this bar was founded in 1998 by former Tory politician Phillip Oppenheim, who buys the rum and sugar directly from Cuban producers.

PALM NUT SOUP

The Gold Coast is a Ghanaian gastro-pub in Norwood. Go on a Saturday night, when a DJ plays West African dance music, and fuel up on *kelewele*[4] and yam balls. Then return on Sunday lunchtime, the only time in the week when their special peanut and palm nut soups are served.

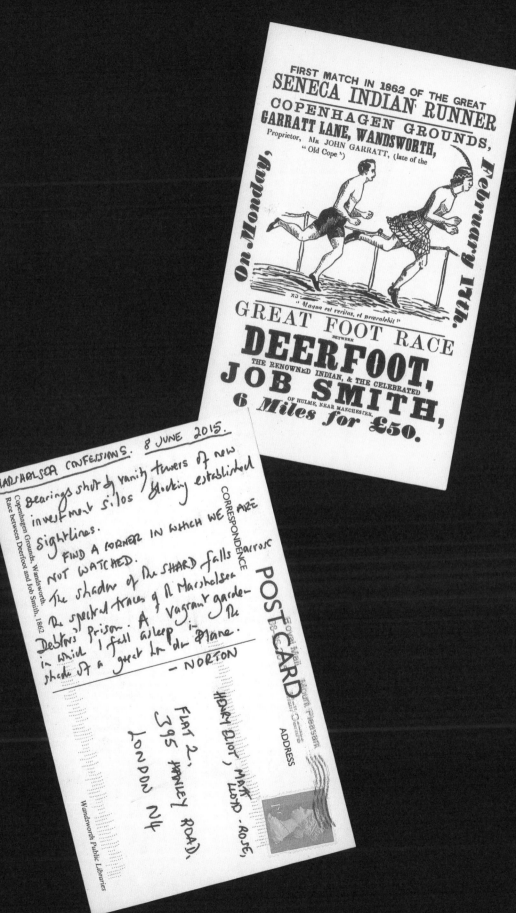

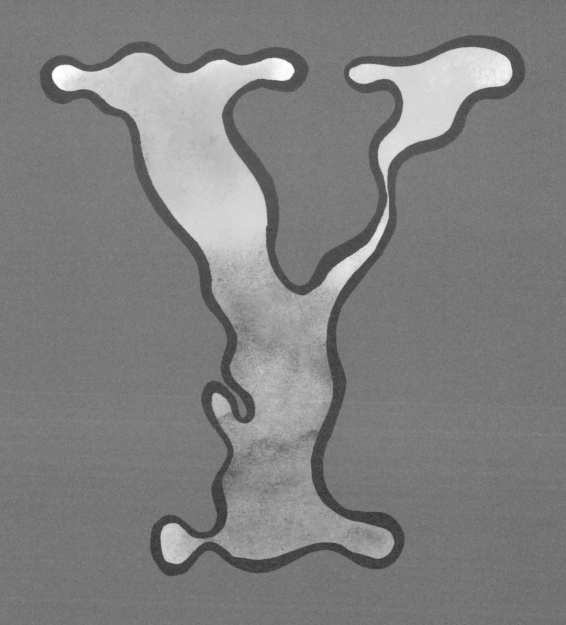

H 1

HYDROGEN

Hydrogen[6] was first identified in Soho in 1766. Henry Cavendish produced 'inflammable air' in his laboratory on Great Marlborough Street, and realised it was an elemental constituent of water. Visit Costa Coffee, which stands on the site of Cavendish's laboratory, and savour a glass of tap water in his honour.

Ar 18

ARGON

At UCL in 1894, William Ramsay identified argon for the first time, and in 1895 he isolated helium. In 1898, he discovered three more 'inert' gases, xenon, krypton and neon, and bagged the last, radon, in 1910. Today UCL's hall of residence on Maple Street is called Ramsay Hall; its communal areas are lit by neon strip lights.

K 18

POTASSIUM

Sir Humphrey Davy discovered several new elements in the basement of the Royal Institution on Albemarle Street, starting with potassium in 1807. 'When he first saw the minute globules of potassium burst through the crust of potash, and take fire as they entered the atmosphere,' recalled his assistant, 'he could not contain his joy — he actually danced about the room in ecstatic delight.' Over the next year Davy discovered six more elements: barium, boron, calcium, sodium, strontium and magnesium. He also identified chlorine in 1810 and iodine in 1812.

Pd 46

PALLADIUM

There are four precious metals that require a hallmark: gold, silver, platinum and palladium. Palladium was discovered in 1803 by William Hyde Wollaston in his house near Fitzroy Square. Wollaston marketed the metal as 'new silver' in a jewellery shop at 26 Gerrard Street, which is now the London Chinatown restaurant. After crab dim sum, buy a pair of palladium earrings from Garrard's, London's oldest jewellers, and wear them to a show at the London Palladium.

1. For more on air pollution, see p.58.
2. The London Fire Brigade museum is scheduled to reopen in the late 2010s, in their former headquarters building on Albert Embankment.
3. It gets less rain than Paris, Berlin or Lisbon, and is arid compared to Brussels, where it rains most days of the year.
4. On a Thursday, call by Andrew Coram's stall at the weekly Spitalfields Antiques Market and ask him to show you a boar's tooth mounted in silver from the Frost Fair of 1715.
5. Most Christmases are white according to this definition, but only four Christmases in over 50 years have seen widespread snow on the ground.
6. Hydrogen accounts for three-quarters of the mass of the universe.

Y ——

PREHISTORY

Wind back the years and imagine London's prehistory in these numinous locations.

STANWELL CURSUS

If you are waiting in Heathrow Terminal 5 departure lounge, you are sitting at one end of the enormous Stanwell Cursus. This prehistoric earthwork consists of two ditches 20 metres apart with a ridge of soil running between them. The cursus is aligned with the setting sun at the midwinter solstice and acted as a prehistoric runway for ritual processions.

AMBRESBURY BANKS

William Morris loved to visit Ambresbury Banks in Epping Forest. This Iron Age hill fort is now a gently rippled earthwork circle in the woods, but once it had steep banked sides and a deep defensive ditch. Legend has it that Queen Boudicca took her last stand against the Romans here.

RIDDLESDOWN DITCH

Riddlesdown Common near Croydon is crossed by a prehistoric trackway known as the Newe Ditch, and several Neolithic[1] stone axes have been found nearby. Animals still graze this common ground and the local residents' association hosts an annual fun day.

FARTHING DOWNS

Farthing Downs is an extensive area of chalk downland, next to Happy Valley in Coulsdon, where Neolithic pottery has been discovered. Today it is a strip of unspoilt grassland with pockets of ancient woods. It's an important habitat for the yellow-rattle plant.

LIVING HISTORY

TREE

The oldest living thing in London is the 2,000-year-old Totteridge Yew in St Andrew's churchyard, which stands on the 'Tott Ridge'[2] promontory of Barnet. In its youth, this tree witnessed the Romans establishing their camp at nearby Brockley Hill in 45 AD. Creeping inside its hollow trunk is the closest thing in London to genuine time travel.

VINE

London's gnarliest grapevine is the 250-year-old Black Hamburg vine at Hampton Court. This 118-foot creeper was planted in 1769, and is now housed in its own bespoke 'Vine House', constructed in 1969. It still produces between 500 and 700 bunches of black dessert grapes every year, which you can buy from the palace shops in September.

SHRUB

The 200-year-old wisteria at Fuller's Griffin Brewery[3] in Chiswick is England's oldest. This purple-flowering climber was planted in 1816, from a Chinese sapling. Its twin at Kew Gardens withered and died; water your wisteria with Fuller's London Pride[4] to keep it perky.

---

[1] 'Neolithic' means 'of the new stones' and refers to the last phase of the Stone Age, from c.4000 until c.2500 BC in Britain.

[2] A tot was an artificial Celtic beacon hill, arranged along a solstice line. The most famous tot hill in London was in Westminster and lent its name Tothill Fields and Street.

[3] For more beer, see p.185.

[4] London Pride takes its name from a small white-and-pink flower, which sprung up on bombsites during the Blitz. The flower also goes by the names 'None-so-pretty', 'Look up and kiss me' and 'St Patrick's Cabbage'.

FOUNDATIONS

As you walk through London, imagine the geological strata stretching down below your feet and then look at those same foundations all around you. 'The Earth around London,' wrote Christopher Wren, '[...] will yield as good brick as were the Roman bricks'. Even London's stones hold traces of the primordial. 'There are ancient oyster shells within the texture of Mansion House and the British Museum,' observes Peter Ackroyd. 'Seaweed can still be seen in the greyish marble of Waterloo Station.'[1]

But a city is built on more than physical foundations. London's identity is also constructed through stories, such as the legend that Julius Caesar established a camp at St Pancras in the 1st century BC, or that St Paul visited London and preached from Parliament Hill. Origin myths combine with archaeological narratives to form a single Rorschach image, in which everyone reads their own version of London's distant past.

MYTH	HISTORY

KYMRY

The first Britons were Armenian. Go to Jakob's, the Armenian cafe on Gloucester Road, and read *The British Kymry*, in which the Reverend Richard Morgan describes how two ancestral Britons escaped the primordial flood in a ship called *Nevydd Nav Neivon* and settled in Armenia, the 'Summer Land'.

Their descendants called themselves the Kymry, and later returned to the island of Britain.[2] As you enjoy your Jakob's cream tea, bear in mind the linguistic links between the 'Crimea' and the Welsh 'Cymru', and that Cornwall and Armenia are the only places in the world that make clotted cream.

AUROCHS

Stand in front of a huge horned auroch skull in the Museum of London. Half a million years ago, our Neanderthal forebears faced a menagerie of ferocious animals in the Thames valley.

Walk with the spirits of wolves along Cheapside, lions in Chelsea and crocodiles in Islington. Mammoths have been excavated at King's Cross, straight-tusked elephants in Hackney, bison in Putney, brown bears in Woolwich and hippopotamuses in Trafalgar Square. Watch out for reappearances of the *HippopoThames*, a 21-metre-long wooden hippo who nosed along the river in 2014.

BRAN

Visit the Tower of London and examine the ravens closely: the one with the grey ankle band is called Bran. In Welsh legend, the raven-god Bran the Blessed was beheaded, but his head continued to speak and was buried at Bryn Gwyn, the White Hill of the Tower of London, to protect the country against the threat of invasion.

The country remained impregnable until King Arthur removed Bran's head, but the ravens at the Tower preserve the god's memory. It is said that if ever they leave, the kingdom will fail.

PLOWONIDA

10,000 years ago, a band of *Homo sapiens* established a camp in Uxbridge, exploiting the annual migratory patterns of reindeer and trapping local beavers, swans and wild pigs. The camp is known as the Three Ways Wharf and is now a traffic island on the Oxford Road roundabout.

Look for the 6,000-year-old timber piles sticking out of the Thames foreshore in front of the MI6 building at low tide. These stumpy staves are the remnants of a Mesolithic structure built by the earliest Londoners[3] at the confluence of the River Effra and the Thames.

Y

---

[1] Outside Green Park tube station, John Maine has created an artwork out of Portland stone, which is naturally rich in spiral gastropod fossils. In some places you can see the sharp conical gaps left by these 150-million-year-old marine creatures; in others, Maine has incised their shapes at a much larger scale.

[2] When they arrived, they found 'no living creature on it but bisons, elks, bears, beavers and water monsters'.

[3] Visit the London Before London gallery at the Museum of London and gaze into the eyes of the Shepperton Woman, a facial reconstruction of a female Londoner from 5,500 years ago.

TROIA NOVA

MYTH

BRUTUS ⊕

At the Lord Mayor's Parade, every second Saturday of November, two enormous wicker figures are wheeled through the streets, representing the giants Gog and Magog. London was once populated by giants, and the largest and fiercest was called Goemagot.

According to Nennius, a 9th-century Welsh monk, Brutus, the grandson of Aeneas,[1] teamed up with a band of exiled Trojans, discovered Britain and named it after himself. He slaughtered all the native giants, except for Goemagot, who died in a dramatic cliff-edge wrestling match with Brutus' general Corineus. Brutus then founded a city on the Thames and called it Troia Nova, 'New Troy', after his home town.

A 3,000-year-old two-handled cup from Asia Minor was discovered in the Thames in 1913; its presence in London is unexplained.

CAER LLUDD

The Celtic descendants of Brutus were an eccentric dynasty. Brutus' son, King Locrinus, dug a dungeon below Troia Nova and locked up his mistress for seven years; King Bladud was a necromancer who built wings for himself and flew above the city. The flight was a success until he struck the Temple of Apollo and fell to his death λ. Bladud's son was King Leir, notorious madman and father of three daughters.

The most significant Celtic monarch, however, was King Lludd, who began his reign in 72 BC. He renamed the city Caer Lludd and built a huge limestone wall ⊗. He is buried beneath Ludgate, the western gate of the city. If you stand outside 12 Ludgate Circus today and look up, you can see his face high above you.

HISTORY

BRONZE

The prehistoric Thames was much wider and shallower than the river today; it was bordered by mudflats fringed with sedge and willow. You can get an idea of prehistoric London today by travelling up or downstream. Go to Maidenhead to see a surviving stretch of interconnecting waterways and swampy river islands; alternatively, the Kentish marshes give a sense of the treacherous quicksands that also once characterised central London.

During the Bronze Age, hunting and herding were gradually replaced by farming, and a land once dominated by sacred monuments was drained and divided into fields. Walk into Greenwich Park through Croom Hill Gate and you'll find yourself amidst the tumuli of a Bronze Age cemetery.

CAER LLANDAIN

Admire the horned helmet at the British Museum, which was discovered in the river at Waterloo, probably thrown in ritually as an offering to the horned Celtic god Cernnunos. Remnants of the Horned God persist today. Visit the Wrestlers in Highgate and take part in their twice annual 'Swearing on the Horns' ceremony for new drinkers. Afterwards, stand on Waterloo Bridge and drop your wallet and keys into the river as an offering to the gods.

Two Celtic tribes lived in the London area: the Trinovantes[2] and the Catuvellauni. They prayed to their fertility goddess, Brighde. Visit the crypt of St Bride's Church, just off Ludgate Circus. This is an ancient site that has passed through many denominations. It is thought to have begun as a Celtic temple to Brighde.

MAP READING

Foundations is an image of the city's myths and history mingling in the primordial soup. Next to each image is a rune, which links to the text that describes it.

---

[1] Virgil immortalised Aeneas' story in the *Aeneid*, and told how his descendants, Romulus and Remus, founded Rome. Less familiar is Nennius's *Historia Brittonum*, a fan-fiction sequel that focuses on Brutus.

[2] Some etymologists connect the Trinovantes with Troia Nova, 'New Troy'.

AUGUSTA

Conrad's *Heart of Darkness* opens on a cruising yawl in the Thames estuary. The narrator imagines a Roman commander leading the first expedition up the Thames, to 'the very end of the world, a sea the colour of lead, a sky the colour of smoke [...] sand-banks, marshes, forests, savages, – precious little to eat fit for a civilized man, nothing but Thames water to drink'.

CAESAR

Track down Caesar's Well, a circular brick basin in the woods on Keston Common. Legend has it that it was discovered by thirsty Roman troops following a raven.[1] Julius Caesar led the first Roman invasion of Britain in 55 BC and you can visit two 'Caesar's Camps' in London: an earthwork in the grounds of Holwood House in Keston and a hill fort at the southern end of Wimbledon Common.

BOUDICCA 🕦

The Romans founded Londinium in 43 AD, but 17 years later the city was utterly destroyed. In the archaeological record there is a layer of cremated clay, wood ash and oxidised iron that marks 60 AD with a thick red line. The devastation was wrought by Boudicca, queen of the powerful Iceni tribe. Incensed by her ill treatment at the hands of the Romans, she marched on Londinium. The Roman forces were away battling Welsh druids, so she razed the fledgling city to the ground. Today her statue rears above a chariot on Westminster Bridge, and legend has it she's buried between Platforms 9 and 10 at King's Cross Station.

LONDINIUM

Despite this early setback, Britain was a Roman colony for 350 years, with Londinium as its capital. You can see a model of Londinium in the crypt of All Hallows by the Tower, as well as the traces of an original Roman pavement. The Romans grew wine in London, a practice that has been reintroduced by Forty Hall Vineyard in Enfield,[2] London's first vineyard since the Middle Ages.

MITHRAS

Southwark Cathedral was once a Roman temple and St Paul's may have been a temple to Diana. In 1954, a Temple to Mithras was discovered beside the River Walbrook. The mysterious cult of Mithras was popular among Roman soldiers: underground temples hosted initiation feasts and role-play rituals. London's Mithraeum will soon be open to visitors, as part of the Bloomberg Building at Walbrook Square.

GLADIATRIX

Beneath the Guildhall Art Gallery you can stand in the centre of a Roman amphitheatre, where gladiators once fought in the sand with wild animals. When they weren't revelling in gore, the Romans went swimming. A leather pair of bikini bottoms was found in a Roman well on Queen Street in 1953; they're now on display at the Museum of London. Take yours to the bogus Roman Baths on Strand Lane, an underground site you can visit on Wednesday afternoons by appointment.

CUCUMIS

There's a body at the base of the Gherkin.[3] When the skyscraper was built, the skeleton of a Roman girl was uncovered. On its completion she was reinterred outside, below a flagstone engraved with a laurel wreath. Nearby you can read an inscription, translated into Latin: 'To the spirits of the dead the unknown young girl from Roman London lies buried here'.

AUGUSTA

The Roman city began to decline in the 3rd century, and it was renamed 'Augusta' in a failed rebranding exercise. As public services deteriorated and buildings became unsafe, the city and the Roman lifestyle were abandoned within a single generation. By 410 BC Augusta was a ghost town.

Y

---

1 Caesar's Well is the source of the River Ravensbourne. Find more of London's rivers on p.334.

2 This 10-acre social enterprise blends winemaking with therapy for vulnerable adults in its local community (fortyhallvineyard.com).
3 Or *Cucumis anguria*, as the Romans would have called it.

LUNDENBURGH

MYTH

ARTHUR ⓟ

Chris Street, the mystic, believes he has located the site of King Arthur's Camelot in Cockfosters. Go to Trent Country Park and look for the ancient earthwork known as Camlet Moat. It shows traces of having had a drawbridge, thick walls and a dungeon. It's now haunted by a spectral Grail Maiden.[1]

It was at Camelot that Arthur's illegitimate son, Sir Mordred, assumed the throne and insisted on marrying his stepmother, Queen Guinevere. She persuaded him to let her go to the markets of London to buy the necessaries for their nuptials. When she got to the capital, she barricaded herself within the Tower on Bryn Gwyn.

BLUETOOTH

According to Marvel Comics' version of the Norse myths, Greenwich is destroyed in the final battle of the Second Dark Elf Conflict.[2] To access your Nordic roots, go to the Danish Church in Regent's Park and touch a modern replica of the Jelling Stone. It's brightly painted, covered in runes, and combines religious traditions, showing Christ crucified on Yggdrasil, the Nordic World Tree ⓕ.

The ancient original was erected by Harald Bluetooth in the Danish town of Jelling in the 10th century. His grandson King Cnut was the first monarch of England to build a palace on Thorney Island[3] – and legend has it that it was on the river shore that he famously attempted to hold back the tidal Thames ✳. Try attending one of the moots, blots or althings organised by the Kith of Yggdrasil, a heathen organisation recreating Norse traditions (kithofyggdrasil.org.uk). Their annual Althing is held at the Moat Mount campsite in Barnet in June.

HISTORY

ALFRED

The Saxon settlement of Lundenwic developed in the area that is now the Strand; 'Wic' signifies a market town and the site of Lundenwic today is Aldwych: the 'old wic'. Two hundred and fifty years later, Britain's first and worst celebrity chef, Alfred the Great, moved the Saxon settlement back within London's walls. A plaque on the Riverside Walk near Southwark Bridge commemorates his restoration of the Roman fortifications.

Take a burnt Victoria sponge to Trinity Church Square in Southwark and share it with the statue of King Alfred, the oldest open-air effigy in the capital.

FORKBEARD

In the 10th century, Vikings controlled all England. Except for one small town of indomitable Saxons, which held out against the invaders: Lundenburgh. In 994, however, Swein Forkbeard came to London with 94 ships, and besieged the city for two decades. By the end of 1016, the English King Aethelred was dead without an heir, and Forkbeard's son Cnut was accepted as king of all England.

In the Viking London gallery at the Museum of London you can see a decorative slab discovered in St Paul's Churchyard, commemorating a member of Cnut's court. When Cnut acceded to the Danish throne in 1018 and assumed control of Norway, London became the headquarters of a powerful Scandinavian empire.

---

① You can consult Merlin on p.324.
② Consult *Thor: The Dark World* (2013) for details.

③ Westminster. See p.134.

ARCHAEOLOGY

Archaeology in London is overseen by the Museum of London. If you want to get your hands dirty, consider volunteering with MOLA (Museum of London Archaeology): you could be sifting and cataloguing archaeological finds or combing the Thames foreshore as a FROG volunteer (Foreshore Recording and Observation Group).

If that doesn't appeal, take inspiration from Indiana Jones and replicate some of his archaeological adventures.

HOARDERS OF THE LOST ARK

The Ark of the Covenant lies in a secret vault below the British Museum: it takes the form of 11 wooden tablets wrapped in purple velvet. Museum staff are forbidden to enter its vault. These sacred *tabots* were looted from Ethiopia by the British in 1868, and it is sacrilegious for anyone other than senior clergymen of the Ethiopian Church to look on them. As you infiltrate the museum's basement, watch out for booby traps and big stone balls.

THE LOST CADAVER

There is a mummy in the tower of St James Garlickhythe, Garlick Hill. In 1855, an embalmed 18th-century man was discovered in the church vaults; he was dubbed 'Jimmy Garlick' and put on display in a glass cabinet. Today he stands out of sight in the church tower, but the verger may be persuaded to give you a peek. Try to leave the church without getting tangled up with a fanatical Nazi crusade.

> ## THE TEMPLE CHURCH OF DOOM ❶
> The Knights Templar, the 'Poor Fellow-Soldiers of Christ', were one of the wealthiest international organisations in Europe. In 1185, they built a round church in London, mirroring the circular Church of the Holy Sepulchre in Jerusalem. Visit the Temple and admire the recumbent knights on the floor. Then try to solve the riddle from *The Da Vinci Code*.[1] Be prepared to meet a bloodthirsty cult with a taste for human sacrifice.

THE HOLY GRAIL

Finding the Grail is less of a slog than you might imagine. Quest along Haymarket and turn on to Norris Street, an overlooked passageway where you'll find nine alcoves embedded into the wall. They contain breathtakingly precious treasures, including the original Grail from the 1989 film *Indiana Jones and the Last Crusade*. This plain wooden cup conveys eternal life on whoever drinks from it. Go into Planet Hollywood and persuade the Grail keepers to serve you a coke in the chalice.

Y ——

---

❶ 'In London lies a knight a Pope interred.
His labour's fruit a Holy wrath incurred.
You seek the orb that ought to be on his tomb.
It speaks of Rosy flesh and seeded womb.'
*Clue: knights in the Temple Church are effigies not tombs;
the riddle's answer lies in Westminster Abbey.*

MYTHICAL SAFARI

In *Mother London*, Michael Moorcock saw 'monsters, by mud and giant ferns' lurking beside Hungerford Bridge; a 'Megalosaurus, forty feet long or so' waddles up Holborn Hill in *Bleak House*;[1] and in *London Bridge*, Louis-Ferdinand Celine pictured the buses of Piccadilly Circus as a 'raging herd of mastodons'. Mythical beasts abound in the capital. Start at Westminster Underground station and bring a fire blanket, because here be dragons …

WINGED HORSE

Continue down the Strand, until you pass the flying horse at the entrance to the Inner Temple on your right. Pegasus is the divine, winged horse-child of Poseidon, who bore Perseus to rescue Andromeda. He has been the emblem of the Inner Temple since the 16th century.

TEMPLE DRAGON

Go up to the Strand and walk east until you reach Temple Bar. Perched on an imposing plinth is one of the City's largest and most frightful sentinel dragons, brought to life by the BBC in 2008.[5]

WINGED SPRINGBOK

Springboks are known for their long jump but they don't usually fly. On the east side of the square you can see the former logo of South African Airways: a golden gazelle taking flight from the South African Embassy.

CLEOPATRA'S SPHINXES

Turn east along Victoria Embankment until you reach Cleopatra's Needle.[3] Sphinxes are famous for flanking pyramids and eating those who answer riddles incorrectly. These two are guarding an 1878 time capsule containing a box of cigars, a baby's bottle, a rupee, 12 photographs of the best-looking English women of the day, a map of London and a portrait of Queen Victoria.[4]

FOUNTAIN MERFOLK

Walk back along Whitehall to Trafalgar Square, where mermaids and mermen spew water in a fishy fantasia. Merfolk lure victims with their siren calls before drowning them. These muscular examples commemorate John Jellicoe, Admiral at the Battle of Jutland in the First World War.

START

HOTEL MERLIONS

Walk down Northumberland Avenue, past the Citadines Hotel. Fishtailed lions[2] adorn this building, which used to be the headquarters of the Royal Commonwealth Society. When Singapore gained its independence in 1965, the merlion was chosen as the symbol of the new country.

SPANISH DRAGON

Turn left down Horseguards Avenue and cross Whitehall into Horseguards Parade. Supporting a 200-year-old French cannon is a cast-iron dragon, a gift from Spain to thank the British for their help in lifting the siege of Cadiz in 1812.

BURMESE CHINDIT

Walk east along Victoria Embankment until you meet the Chindit. This leonine Burmese beast usually guards Buddhist temples. Symbol of the dysentery-ridden British India 'Special Force' operating behind Japanese lines in the Second World War, this memorial now guards the Ministry of Defence.

---

[1] The Crystal Palace megalosaurus was unveiled the year after the last instalment of *Bleak House* was published; see p.163.

[2] For a fishtailed squirrel, see p.162.

[3] Look out for the winged sphinxes on the benches, and beware of tall, scaly figures; see p.220.

[4] For more time capsules, see p.420.

[5] Look up the 'BBC 2 City Season' trailer online and, for more on sentinel dragon, see p.15.

MEAT DRAGONS
Turn right along Charter House Street to Smithfield Market. Vicious silver-blue dragons inspect fresh deliveries at Smithfield Market.

WAX UNICORNS
Walk along Gresham Street. Above the entrance to the Wax Chandler's Hall sit two unicorns, representing the Virgin Mary. The ferocious unicorn can only be captured by a virgin maiden: he forgets his temper and falls asleep in her lap.

RED HERRING
Cross Cheapside and walk along Gresham Street. Stop for a drink in the Red Herring.[1]

LIBRARY WYVERNS
Make a detour down Basinghall Street, and spot the wyverns outside the Library Chambers: they are scrawny two-legged cousins of the dragon.

MITSUBISHI CHIMERA
Emerge and walk to 24 Lombard Street. A chimera is a portmanteau animal: usually a lioness with a snake's-head tail and the head of a goat on her back. This one is more feminine and sphinx-like and protects the Mitsubishi Trust and Banking Corporation.

GOLD DRAGONS
Walk east along Cheapside until you reach the Bank interchange. Dragons traditionally stand over subterranean treasure hoards. Creep through the Bank subway, past the dragons that guard the nation's gold reserves nearby.[2]

FINISH

LEADENHALL DRAGONS
Turn left at Gracechurch Street and right into Leadenhall Market. Silver dragons preside over cheese, meat and flowers, gathered like a flock of pigeons in the centre of the market.

ST MARY-LE-BOW DRAGON
Walk south to Cheapside, and look up to the weathervane of St Mary-le-Bow's slender spire. At its pinnacle, a golden dragon is in flight, streaming into the wind.

FIRE DRAGONS
Walk south to the Monument. Clutching its base, flame-breathing dragons support the column that commemorates the Great Fire of London.[3]

VIADUCT DRAGONS
Continue to Ludgate Circus and walk left along Farringdon Street. Pass below Holborn Viaduct, where rampant red-and-gold dragons roost.

Y

BRIDGE DRAGONS
Walk over London Bridge. Guarding the south end is a final pair of barb-tongued silver brutes.

[1] A red herring is a particularly strong kipper used to disorientate hounds.
[2] For more on this dwindling asset, see p.197.
[3] See p.337.

STONES

Sarsen stones litter the chalk downs of southern England and were used to build Stonehenge. Britain's best-loved henge visited London twice in 2012: Jeremy Deller brought an inflatable Stonehenge to Greenwich Park so that people could bounce between the trilithons, and Škoda commissioned a replica made out of cars, which appeared on Potter's Fields. London is bristling with sarsens of its own, however.

LONDON STONE

Through the grille in the wall of WHSmith's opposite Cannon Street Station you can see a single block of oolithic lime known as the London Stone.[1] Some think it's a druidic index stone and an ancient site of human sacrifice; others that it's a Roman milliarium. Some say it is a Brutus Stone installed by ancient Trojans; others that King Lludd set it in place. The first mayor of London was named Henry Fitz-Ailwin de Londonestone, and when Jack Cade led his rebellion in 1450 he struck the stone with his sword to stake his claim as the Lord of the City. Ultimately, admitted John Stow in 1598, 'the cause why this stone was set there, the time when, or other memory hereof is none'.

THE STONE OF DESTINY

Examine the empty space in the base of King Edward's Chair in Westminster Abbey. The Stone of Scone, a red oblong sarsen, was the Scottish coronation stone, but in 1296 it was seized by Edward I of England and brought to London, where it remained for 650 years inside the coronation throne. On Christmas Day 1950, however, four Scottish students stole the stone and returned it to Scotland,[2] and in 1996 it was officially transferred to Edinburgh Castle, where it now rests among the crown jewels of Scotland. It returns to Westminster for coronation ceremonies.

THE CORONATION STONE

The sarsen that stands outside the Guildhall in Kingston is known as the 'Coronation Stone'. According to legend, seven Saxon kings were crowned there.

BOUNDARY STONES

The 'Yantlet Line' runs across the mouth of the Thames between the Crow Stone in Southend-on-Sea and the 'London Stone' obelisk at the mouth of Yantlet Creek. It has been marked since 1285 and signifies the eastern limit of the City's river rights. Upstream, at Staines-upon-Thames,[3] a London Stone marks the westernmost limit. In the 19th century, the Lord Mayor of London would travel to Staines by water to touch the stone ceremonially with his sword.

THE LEYTON STONE

Leytonstone lies on an ancient track to Stratford. The sarsen is at the junction of Hollybush Hill and New Wanstead and is now topped by an 18th-century obelisk.

THE ELTHORNE STONE

There is a sarsen in Elthorne Park in Hanwell, discovered in 1899 on the site of an ancient riverbed. It is the same age, origin and composition as the sarsens that form Stonehenge.

---

❶ You can get a better view by stepping behind the magazine stand inside the shop.

❷ They were abetted by John Josslyn, 21st great-grandson of Edward I.

❸ The name Staines means 'stones'.

402

SKINS

When Shakespeare's King Lear contends with the fretful elements, he meets Edgar, naked and reduced to the 'most dejected thing of fortune'. Lear marvels at the 'bare, forked animal', stripped of social position, sanity and clothes, and in the clarity of his revelation he tears off his own garments. To get back to elemental humanity yourself, try exposing your own skin to the elements.

BASK
On Hampstead Heath, the Highgate Men's Pond changing yard has a slab of concrete dedicated to nude sunbathing; women sunbathe topless at the Ladies' Pond.

SWEAT
At the Ironmonger Row Baths[1] spa, Tuesdays are men-only and Fridays are just for women. Strip off and sweat it out in the tepidarium or laconium. Then jump into the icy plunge pool.

STREAK
Raise money for Sumatran tigers by running naked through London Zoo in August. Most people paint their bodies orange with black streaks (zsl.org/zsl-london-zoo/whats-on/streak-for-tigers).

MODEL
Learn to life-model with Spirited Bodies at Millman Street Community Centre (spiritedbodies.com). Professional models will help you pose to best advantage. Once you feel confident, sign up to the RAM (the Register of Artists' Models, modelreg.co.uk). Then consider the monthly pop-up restaurant Supper in a Pear Tree, which pairs life drawing with a three-course meal in Battersea's Lavender Hill Studios.

MINGLE
If you're after something more public, wait for artist Spencer Tunnick to return to town and participate in one of his mass naked photographs. You can see a large print of his Greenwich photo shoot on the wall of the Admiral Hardy Pub on College Approach.

POSE
Enrol on a four-week course of Naked Yoga in South London, exploring various nude postures (nakedyogalondon.co.uk).

CLIMB
Take inspiration from the trio of naked blue musicians scaling the façade of Maya House, dangling their instruments above Borough High Street.

READ
Twice a month, at the Ace Hotel in Shoreditch, you can attend a Naked Boys Reading event. These are aimed at 'lovers of naturism with a well-endowed library'.

RELAX
Elixir is a naturist massage centre in Alexandra Palace. Book your deep-tissue massage and cast away your cares between the Nordic sauna, steam room and hot tub.

Y ————

---

❶ For more on these baths, see p.234.

ZONES

STAND OUTSIDE CHARING CROSS STATION, at the centre of the city.[1] Thousands of strangers push past, open-top bus operators thrust leaflets at you, and queues of black cabs muscle around the one-way system. The commotion is relentless and overwhelming. But if you feel tired of London, it doesn't necessarily mean you're tired of life: maybe you just need a change of scene. The traditional remedy is to leave Zone 1 behind and head for the leafy suburbs of Zones 5 to 9. Board the Northern Line at Charing Cross and travel ten miles to its terminus, the dreamy edgelands of Edgware.

'We moderns ask much more before we are content than the ancients,' declared a 1920s marketing brochure, 'and Edgware is designed to give us that much more.' The city's new suburbs embodied the possibility of 'a healthy country life within easy reach of London'. As the tube network broke new territory, Londoners were encouraged to follow and settle in the homes springing up along the lines. One particularly striking poster from 1924 depicts a bleak townscape of identical grey boxes. Below it are the words 'LEAVE THIS AND MOVE TO EDGWARE'.

When you step off the tube at Edgware today, a fishing rod and picnic hamper at your side, you may not feel you've entirely escaped the metropolis. The idyllic fields and lanes are long gone, and the station is now on a busy road facing a Nando's and a branch of Snappy Snaps. H. G. Wells predicted that 'the London citizen of the year 2000 AD may have a choice of nearly all England and Wales south of Nottingham and east of Exeter as his suburb'. And, indeed, for a while it seemed as though London might just sprawl endlessly across southern England. To prevent this, the Green Belt was established in the 1940s: a ring of protected land that stopped the city in its tracks. It remains in place today, but London is straining against it, bulging outwards, upwards and downwards. The city is currently being transformed at an extraordinary pace and – although visions and predictions abound – there's little consensus about what will come next.

According to Iain Sinclair, we're in a 'limbo between cities'. This is 'the last of a certain kind of London and the new has not emerged or defined itself exactly yet.' This chapter trespasses beyond the outer limits of London, going from Zone 1 to Zone 9, from centre to suburb, interior to exterior, real to imagined, fact to fiction, and from the present into the future.

> **TWILIGHT COUNTRY**
> The suburbs have been much maligned. The novelist Beryl Gilroy[2] described them as 'a sort of twilight country, indeterminate between sleeping and waking, muted and barely alive.' For Walter Besant, suburban existence was 'as dull a life as mankind ever tolerated'. And Karim in Hanif Kureishi's *The Buddha of Suburbia* satirises the small worlds of suburbanites by suggesting that when they 'drowned they saw not their lives but their double-glazing flashing before them'.

Z ——

---

[1] Find the centre of London on pp.200–201.　　　　[2] Gilroy was London's first black headteacher.

ZONING OUT

ZONE 9
The end of the line is
CHESHAM, the furthest tube
station from the centre of
London. It's still much as it was
when it opened in 1889. Admire
its water tower and handsome
signal box.

ZONE 6
When you hit MOOR PARK,
you're over the Greater London
boundary. Hop off the tube and
leave from the rear exit, which
brings you straight out into
woodland. In the film, Betjeman
fluffs a putt on a nearby golf
course.

ZONE 5
As he passes through PINNER,
Betjeman remarks on the
'medieval fair in Metro-Land'.
You can still attend Pinner Fair,
which has been held every May
since 1336.

ZONE 8
At just under four miles, the
journey from CHALFONT &
LATIMER to Chesham is the
longest uninterrupted stretch
between any two stops on the
network. Why not get out and
walk? The Chess Valley walking
route connects the two stations.

ZONE 4
Betjeman describes Wembley as
'an unimportant hamlet where
for years the Metropolitan didn't
bother to stop'. Imagine the long
departed 'slushy fields and grass
farms' as the train pulls into
WEMBLEY PARK.[1]

BEYOND
Travel on to VERNEY
JUNCTION under your own
steam. This tiny hamlet is a
chunk of London that got away.
Until 1936, it was the end of the
Metropolitan Line and primed
to become another booming
suburb. As it is, the connection
was severed and it's barely
changed for a century. 'The
houses of Metro-Land never
got as far as Verney Junction,'
says Betjeman at the end of his
documentary. 'Grass triumphs
and, I must say, I'm rather glad.'
Ignore the signs still warning
pedestrians of oncoming
trains, step off the edge of the
crumbling platform and amble
along the weed-covered tracks.

ZONE 7
Until 1961, passengers had
to change from an electric
locomotive to a steam train
at RICKMANSWORTH. The
next stop is CHORLEYWOOD,
described by Betjeman as
'essential Metro-Land'. It seems
to have retained its idyllic
character: a 2004 study declared
it the English neighbourhood
with the highest quality of life.

❶ Find Betjeman in Wembley on p.346.

Every time London threatens to slip beyond its reach, TfL adds another fare zone to bind the city back together again. Transport for London's zones are a series of concentric circles, rippling out from the centre like the energy waves of an expanding universe. Zones 1 to 5 were introduced in the early 1980s. Zone 6 followed in 1991, and then Zones 7 to 9, which spill over the boundary of Greater London. In 2013, still more were added: the mysterious and rarely mentioned Zones B, C, G and W.

Leave the city on the oldest tube line, the Metropolitan, which rolls all the way from Zone 1 to 9. This is the journey John Betjeman took for his documentary *Metro-Land*, which explored the territories at the edge of the city, and the calmer, semi-rural existence they promised. Follow in Betjeman's footsteps as you zone out of London.

ZONE 3
The Metropolitan Line doesn't stop at all in Zone 3, but it goes right past NEASDEN. Betjeman describes Neasden[1] as the 'home of the gnome and the average citizen'.

ZONE 2
When the tunnels were being dug at FINCHLEY ROAD, soil analysis showed that an enormous glacier, which had covered Britain in the last ice age, came to a halt at the station.[2] Finchley Road is the only Metropolitan Line station in Zone 2.

ZONE 1
Take the escalator up to the platforms in ST PANCRAS STATION and look at the vast ceiling with its sky-blue ironwork and 18,000 panes of self-cleaning glass. Not far from you, and just as dazzled, is a statue of John Betjeman,[3] holding on to his trilby as he tilts his head back to admire the building he fought to save in the 1960s. Go down to the Underground and take the westbound Metropolitan Line.

Betjeman begins his journey to the suburbs at BAKER STREET, in the grand Chiltern Court Restaurant above the station. It's now the Metropolitan Bar, a branch of Wetherspoon's. Stop in for an All Day Brunch, then return to the tube.

Z ——

---

❶ The background music at this point in *Metro-Land* is 'Neasden' by Willie Rushton. 'Neasden! You won't be sorry that you breezed in', he sings.

❷ Follow its progress on p.389.

❸ 'And in the shadowless unclouded glare', reads the inscription at his feet, 'deep blue above us fades to whiteness where a misty sea-line meets the wash of air.' It's his description of the Cornish coast, which applies equally to the extraordinary light in the station.

DEPARTURES

EXPLORE THE WORLD

Stock up on walking socks and mint cake at Ellis Brigham in Covent Garden before leaving on a voyage of discovery. Set off from 'Hot and Cold Corner' at the back of the Royal Geographical Society,[1] beneath the statues of two of Britain's most celebrated explorers: on one side is Dr Livingstone in light jungle gear, on the other, Shackleton is kitted out in full oilskins and winter woollies.

GO ON A PILGRIMAGE

Talbot Yard is an unremarkable alley that runs along the back of Guy's Hospital in London Bridge. But it was here, at the Tabard Inn, that the pilgrims in Chaucer's *Canterbury Tales* rallied before setting off for Canterbury. There's now a blue plaque marking the spot. Tramp the 65-mile route in their footsteps, pausing to tell their tales in the same locations. 'The Knight's Tale' is first up, just along the Old Kent Road at the holy stream of St Thomas-a-Watering.[2]

CATCH A TRAIN

There's an air of romance around train stations. E. M. Forster described the way that they evoke their destinations: 'In Paddington all Cornwall is latent and the remoter west; down the inclines of Liverpool Street lie fenlands and the illimitable Broads; Scotland is through the pylons of Euston; Wessex behind the poised chaos of Waterloo.' The sprawling old parcel office in King's Cross is a fine place to linger before a journey. It was turned into a surprisingly charming nook-filled pub when the new station concourse was built.

DISAPPEAR

David Rodinsky vanished at the end of the 1960s, but it wasn't until 1980 that anybody opened his room in the attic of 19 Princelet Street.[3] When they did, it looked as though he'd just nipped out for a moment, his newspapers and breakfast lying where he'd left them. The story of Rodinsky's life and disappearance was unravelled by the East London writer Rachel Lichtenstein in the book *Rodinsky's Room*. She finally tracked him down in Waltham Abbey Cemetery. You can pay your respects to one of London's most elusive characters at plot WA25, row T, No. 708.

TRAVEL MENTALLY

Sail on the wings of your imagination in front of the charmingly incoherent mural on Mauleverer Road in Brixton. Residents were allowed to choose what would be painted on the section visible from their front windows, and so the scene shifts abruptly from a puppet show to a forest to a bandstand, according to the fantasies of each household. The hot white beach was chosen by a Caribbean man who wanted to see the sea from his living room.

END UP WHERE YOU STARTED

'Here 24,859' states an official-looking signpost on the Thames Path near the Millennium Dome. Set off on foot in the direction it indicates and, after a bracing 24,859-mile circumnavigation of the globe, you'll find yourself back in exactly the same place.

---

[1] You could get ideas for your trip at one of their regular talks and exhibitions.

[2] There is now a branch of Tesco on the site. Stand in a trolley and regale shoppers in your finest Middle English.

[3] For more on 19 Princelet Street, see p.373.

z ———

SHERLOCK'S HOMES

Some fictions become fixtures in the real city. Their stories are so powerful that they leap off the page on to the streets, irreversibly altering the place where they were set.[1] No London character is as pervasive as Sherlock Holmes, a figure who has colonised significant chunks of the capital since his first appearance in 1887. 'Perhaps the greatest of the Sherlock Holmes mysteries is this:' wrote T. S. Eliot, 'that when we talk of him we invariably fall into the fantasy of his existence.'

The recent BBC TV series created another version of Sherlock's flat in central London, transplanting 221b Baker Street to 187 North Gower Street. Speedy's, the cafe featured in the show, is not fictional. Admire the fan art on the walls as you devour a Sherlock and Watson wrap.

Baker Street stopped at No. 85 when Arthur Conan Doyle wrote his stories, but in the 1930s, London obligingly morphed to fit the fiction; Baker Street was extended and Sherlock was able to go home at last to 221b. Unfortunately Abbey National moved in before he could, but they were good enough to employ a full-time secretary to handle his correspondence.

When Sherlock decided to set up a museum, Abbey National was still banking in his bedsit, so he had to suffer the indignity of moving in to 239 Baker Street instead. Fortunately, Westminster Council agreed to bend geography for him. In 1990, the Sherlock Holmes Museum went from 239 to 221b without moving an inch. Look out for the eccentric numbering, which jumps from 237 to 221 to 241.

This didn't go down well with Abbey National, who insisted on continuing to handle Sherlock's fan mail until the branch shut in 2005. Now all letters addressed to 221b are delivered to the museum instead of being answered by a high-street bank, and the original 221 Baker Street is a large block of flats. Sniff around for signs of the super sleuth in Francesca's Cucina Familiale on the ground floor.

There are plaques around London that describe Sherlock as though he were a genuine historical figure. A plaque in the Criterion Bar on Piccadilly explains that here 'Stamford, dresser at Barts met Dr. John H. Watson and led him to immortality and Sherlock Holmes'.

There's a third contender for Holmes's official London residence on Northumberland Street. Go to the Sherlock Holmes pub and look at their immaculate reconstruction of his study. It was made for the Festival of Britain in 1951 and toured the world before settling here. Steer clear of the stuffed head of the Hound of the Baskervilles in the bar.[2]

Finish your exploration of Sherlock's homes by meeting Holmes and Watson, a pair of bristly pigs at Spitalfields City Farm.

Find the plaque in Barts Hospital, which states that Holmes and Watson first encountered one another there in 1881. Leave a memento in the unofficial phonebox shrine next to the spot where Holmes appeared to leap to his death in the second series of *Sherlock*.

Z

① King's Cross Station has been compelled to glue the back half of a trolley on to a brick wall to deter gung-ho Harry Potter fans from careering into the pillars dividing Platforms 9 and 10.

② Elsewhere in the world, there is a meticulous recreation of the interior of 221b in Meiringen in Switzerland (near the Reichenbach Falls), another in Lucens in Switzerland, and another in the University of Minnesota.

FRANKEN-FICTIONS

London is almost as crowded with fictional characters as it is with real people. What happens when they collide? We've taken some stories that share a setting and overlapped them, stitching together Franken-quotes with half a line from each book.

MRS TRIFFID-DAY

'Mrs Dalloway decided to buy a couple of the triffid guns and went out into the garden of Russell Square.'

London's last sighted survivors grouped behind the gates of UCL's Senate House before fleeing the triffid-infested city. If you dare, look for the bust of Virginia Woolf among the plant life in nearby Tavistock Square.

Mrs Dalloway, Virginia Woolf (1925)
The Day of the Triffids, John Wyndham (1951)

TINKER TAILOR MUGGLE SPY

'Smiley had closed the passport and was examining a very thin scar on his forehead which was shaped like a bolt of lightning.'

Charing Cross Road is full of secrets. If you're a spy, call in on George Smiley at the Circus (MI6), now HSBC on Cambridge Circus. And then, unless you're a muggle, you'll be able to slip through the Leaky Cauldron to Diagon Alley, the Oxford Street of the wizarding world. If you can't find it, walk to Store Street and pick up a wand in Treadwell's instead.[1]

Tinker Tailor Soldier Spy,
John Le Carré (1974)
Harry Potter and the Philosopher's Stone, J. K. Rowling (1997)

JEEVES AND DORIAN

'They found hanging upon the wall a splendid portrait of their master and could see that, if not actually disgruntled, he was far from being gruntled.'

Bertie Wooster and Dorian Gray are both Mayfair bachelors trying to avoid marriage by any means. Unfortunately Jeeves isn't around to keep Dorian on the straight and narrow. Have a bracing plate of eggs and b. at the Wolseley before admiring the portraits in the Dover Street galleries.

The Picture of Dorian Gray, Oscar Wilde (1890)
The Code of the Woosters, P. G. Wodehouse (1938)

❶ See p.356.

KEEP THE ASPIDISTRA, PADDINGTON

"I'm not a criminal," said Paddington, hotly. "I'm colourless, spectacled, and intensely disagreeable."'

The misanthropic anti-consumerist Gordon Comstock attempts to live without money just off the Edgware Road. He would have admired Paddington's frugality but not his addiction to marmalade and easy acceptance of middle-class life. Buy an aspidistra, Comstock's symbol of bourgeois conformity, and leave it on the bear's plinth in Paddington Station.

A Bear Called Paddington, Michael Bond (1958)
Keep the Aspidistra Flying, George Orwell (1936)

THE DEMON PAPER OF FLEET STREET

'Lord Copper, however, who normally lunched at one, was waiting to cut them up for Mrs Lovett's pies.'

Not far from the offices of the *Daily Beast*, the demon barber Sweeney Todd pepped up Mrs Lovett's pastries with fresh human meat. If you survive a hot towel shave at Fetter Barbers, just off Fleet Street, pop along to Bell Yard, the site of Mrs Lovett's shop, where the Old Bank of England still specialises in savoury pies.

Scoop, Evelyn Waugh (1938)
Sweeney Todd, The Demon Barber of Fleet Street, Christopher Bond (1973)

MR MOLE AND MR HYDE

'And to think that I, Adrian Mole, alone in the ranks of mankind, was pure evil.'

Now 30, Adrian is cooking offal in a highbrow Soho eatery, while Edward Hyde commits dreadful crimes in the surrounding streets. Write your diary in the schizophrenic Star Cafe on Great Chapel Street: gourmet greasy spoon by day, comprehensive gin cellar by night.

Adrian Mole: The Cappuccino Years, Sue Townsend (1999)
The Strange Case of Dr Jekyll and Mr Hyde, Robert Louis Stevenson (1886)

THE HUNDRED AND ONE MARTIANS

'What did surprise the Dearlys was the way Pongo and Missis paused, rigid, to hear if the Martian had thrust its tentacles through the opening.'

Primrose Hill is the location of the Twilight Bark[1] and where the last of the invading Martians are torn apart by dogs. If the wind is right, you can hear the wild dogs in London Zoo.

The Hundred and One Dalmatians, Dodie Smith (1956)
The War of the Worlds, H. G. Wells (1897)

---

❶ Listen out for the bark on p.204.

DYSTOPIAN LONDON

Perhaps there will be no apocalypse. In 1828, William Heath drew an exciting vision of future London where pineapples are easily available, mechanical horses leave 'No Slopage on the Road', a flying pig transports convicts to New South Wales and a Grand Vacuum Tube shuttles travellers directly from Greenwich Hill to Bengal. More recently, the artist Nils Norman's *Above Ground* poster on the Piccadilly Line foresees a cheerful 2050 with residential algae factories in Mayfair, a Buckingham Palace adventure playground, citywide biosphere accommodation and a magic mushroom facility in Hammersmith.

Don't get your hopes up however. The end is more likely to be nigh. A selection of postcards from the future arrived in 2010:[1] these disconcerting images show Tower Bridge surrounded by pack ice, paddy fields in Parliament Square, a caravan of camels approaching the desert oasis of Horseguards Parade and an aerial shot of London, flooded after the sea breaches the Thames Barrier.

As we know from H. G. Wells's *The Time Machine*, Richmond in 802,701 AD will be a tropical ruin, home to two divergent classes of human: the peaceable, apathetic Eloi and the cannibalistic cave-dwelling Morlocks. And in 30 million years' time it will be the shore of an oily sea, covered in poisonous-looking lichen and inhabited by giant white butterflies and monstrous crabs.

This map is an emergency manual for the future, designed to equip you with useful protocols.

WHAT TO DO WHEN YOU ...

...GET FROZEN

If you decide to wait out the revolution and freeze yourself cryogenically, be sure to cancel your bank account. Otherwise you may wake up in the year 2100 to discover that your money has accumulated while you slept and been used to found a worldwide plutocratic order.[1] In this circumstance, unless you want to become a pawn in a succession of political coups, run away and become a kamikaze pilot with a gang of Croydon insurgents.

...GET SCORCHED

If you find yourself walking down a deserted Fleet Street and there's a sickly orange glow, it may be that rogue nuclear testing has altered the planet's orbit, sending us hurtling too close to the sun.[2] You'll need to release nuclear warheads in Siberia to correct the planet's trajectory. To sound the alarm, run to the Imperial War Museum and ask to crank up their Cold War air raid siren.

...GET TORTURED

If your job's getting you down, if the news is always about war, if you find yourself eating synthetic meals in front of another repeat of *Big Brother*, you are probably under surveillance from the thought police.[3] Do not antagonise your colleagues in Senate House, aka the Ministry of Truth, and steer well clear of Conference Room 101[4] at BBC Broadcasting House, a torture chamber containing 'the worst thing in the world'.

AFTER LONDON

It became green everywhere in the first spring, after London ended. — *Richard Jefferies*

...GET WIPED

The world's information infrastructure may be destroyed overnight by a giant magnetic storm. In this eventuality, a nature-worshipping pagan elite may come to power. Go underground with a renegade band of 'memorialists' and help recreate the myth of the 'inter-net'.[5]

---

[1] This is what happens to Graham in H. G. Wells's *The Sleeper Awakes* (1910).
[2] This would be a good moment to watch the instructional video *The Day the Earth Caught Fire* (1961).
[3] As Winston Smith is in George Orwell's *Nineteen Eighty-Four* (1949).
[4] This room, where Orwell sat through tedious meetings, was demolished in 2003, but not before artist Rachel Whiteread had taken an enormous interior plaster cast. *Untitled (Room 101)* was displayed in the V&A cast courts for a year and is now in the Centre Pompidou in Paris.
[5] This was the plot of Hari Kunzru's novel *Memory Palace*, an experimental 'walk-in book' exhibition at the V&A in 2013.

...GET BRAINWASHED

If you're caught after a surfeit of moloko plus, in-out in-out and ultraviolence, you may be brainwashed with Ludovico aversion therapy. Stay in your apartment at the top of Canterbury House in Borehamwood,[1] which is marked today by a commemorative mosaic. Do not venture along School Lane, Bricket Wood: you might meet your old droogs-turned-policemen, who would giggle as they introduced you to a cattle trough.

...GET MAROONED

When the ice caps melt in 2145, sea levels will rise, temperatures will soar and London will become a flooded, tropical lagoon. Install yourself in a penthouse apartment at the Ritz,[2] amid the iguanas, giant mosquitos and screaming bats. You'll soon come to love the Triassic urban landscape. Get comfy by booking into the Ritz's Berkeley Suite before the deluge arrives.

...GET TURNED INTO A PARROT

If things get surreal after nuclear fallout, hold tight and you may become the Queen of England through lack of competition.[3] Alternatively you may be eaten after turning into a parrot.

MAP READING

Dystopian London *shows a flooded, disaster-ridden city, with the apocalyptic scenarios from various London fictions striking simultaneously. It references the Penguin cover of J. G. Ballard's* The Drowned World *(1962) and Walter Nessler's painting* Premonition *(1937), an image of a blitzed London from before the Blitz, which you can see in the RAF Museum in Hendon.*

...GET NUKED

If London is rebuilt as a steam-punk 'traction city' after a 60-minute nuclear war,[4] escape to the 'Out Country' for some perspective. The mechanical moving city, shaped like a wedding cake with St Paul's on top, will be roaming around the blighted country, subsuming smaller towns. You'll need to infiltrate and bring down the sinister authorities.

...GET INFECTED

If you wake up from a coma in St Thomas's Hospital and stumble across a deserted Westminster Bridge, you may be in the middle of a nationwide bioengineered plague. The last 28 days have probably witnessed the spread of a 'Rage' virus that has turned the population into ferocious infected killers.[5] Beware the maniacal priest of St Anne's Church, Commercial Road. Instead, try banding together with survivors in the River Heights tower block in Plumstead.

...GET STUNG

If a rampant species of mobile carnivorous plants turns nasty,[6] avoid looking at any dazzling meteor showers that could damage your eyesight. Otherwise, the triffids will take advantage of your blindness and eat you.

...GET THE GOSPEL

When London is underwater in 523 AD (After Dave), dig around for the irate rantings of an ancient black-cab driver and use them to found a new religion. Move in with the 'Hamsters'[7] and enjoy a diet of wheat and gulls' eggs. Your community must obey the misogynistic rule of law handed down by the cab driver Dave Rudman.

Z

---

[1] Stanley Kubrick was living in Barnet when he directed the 1971 film adaptation of Antony Burgess's *A Clockwork Orange* (1962). Most of the film's locations are nearby in North London.

[2] As Robert Kerans does in J. G. Ballard's *The Drowned World* (1962).

[3] This is what happens to Mrs Ethel Shroake of 393a High Street, Leytonstone in Richard Lester's film *The Bed Sitting Room* (1969).

[4] This is what happens in Philip Reeve's *Mortal Engines* (2001).

[5] Danny Boyle explores the consequences in *28 Days Later* (2002).

[6] As in John Wyndham's *The Day of the Triffids* (1951).

[7] The residents of Ham, an isolated island formed by the top of Hampstead Heath in Will Self's *The Book of Dave* (2006).

...GET ENHANCED

If you're a TfL engineer extending the Underground system to Hobbs End, look out for ancient human remains and mysterious metal objects. If you find anything, it's likely to be a Martian spacecraft: proof that the Martians arrived on earth five million years ago and artificially enhanced our species' intelligence.[1]

...GET FEUDAL

When life becomes so tranquilly bureaucratic that monarchs are appointed randomly as benign administrators, be prepared for a prankster king who upends society's rules just for fun.[2] He might turn London's boroughs into independent nation states as a joke, only to find that the patriots of Notting Hill take his edict over-seriously, rip up their spearhead railings and defend their territory until the blood runs 'in great red serpents' along Notting Hill High Road.

...GET INVADED

If the Daleks dominate London, they'll drive human survivors into underground hideouts. Follow the Doctor's example[3] and use magnets to pull the robots into a deep shaft, plunging them to the centre of the earth.

...GET DRAINED

When Space Vampires arrive, they'll drain our 'life-force' and flit from body to body. Send urgent missives to the Nioth-Korghai, their native race, who will hopefully come and retrieve the miscreant energy-beings.[4]

...GET THROUGH IT

If you survive the apocalypse, things may still be difficult. You could become embroiled in territorial skirmishes between rival tyrants.[5] Go for a reflective paddle across the poisonous marsh covering 'the deserted and utterly extinct city of London'.

...GET TO PARADISE

Let's hope, however, you find yourself in a new Golden Age.[6] Go for a swim in the Thames at Hammersmith and when you surface, the 'smoke-vomiting chimneys' of the soap and lead factories will have disappeared, and Hammersmith Bridge will have been replaced by 'a wonder of a bridge' with graceful arches, booths, shops, painted vanes and gilded spirelets. You will have leapt forward in time to a post-apocalyptic, socialist, agrarian utopia, with common ownership of property, no courts, no prisons and no class system. Row up the Thames to join a rustic Oxfordshire community, labouring happily in the fields.

---

[1] This is the theory put forward in the film *Quatermass and the Pit* (1967): the Martians weren't able to survive in earth's climate, so they imbued our species with dormant Martian memories.

[2] In G. K. Chesterton's *The Napoleon of Notting Hill* (1904), Auberon Quin is selected by chance, with disastrous consequences.

[3] In *Daleks – Invasion Earth: 2150 A.D.* (1966).

[4] These are the guidelines laid out by Colin Wilson in his novel *The Space Vampires* (1976).

[5] As in *After London* (1885) by Richard Jefferies.

[6] While reading Jefferies's *After London*, William Morris described how 'absurd hopes curled around [his] heart'. Five years later he published *News from Nowhere* (1890).

TWILIGHT ZONES

There are cracks through which the fantastic and unreal seep into the city. These are London's twilight zones: the in-between places where reality warps and the laws of science no longer apply.

MAGIC LANTERN

Dickens called London the 'magic lantern', and I often have that phrase in mind when thinking about the city. What's projected and what's behind the screen? How do image and reality blend? — *Monica Ali*

FAKE FRIENDS

Dickens and Dostoevsky had a fictional encounter in London in 1862. The writer A. D. Harvey published accounts of their made-up rendezvous under fake names in a range of scholarly journals. His fabrication was accepted as fact in academic circles for a decade, and was only exposed in 2013.

BEND GEOGRAPHY

Chelsea is north of the Thames, so how did a chunk of it end up opposite Brixton tube station? South Chelsea College, above the Body Shop, is either misleadingly named or a geographical irregularity worthy of proper investigation. Visit to experience being both south and north of the river simultaneously.

WARP TIME

There's a time warp in the Lloyd's building on Lime Street. Go up[1] to the 11th floor of this hypermodern inside-out skyscraper and step into an 18th-century dining room, complete with marble fireplaces, sash windows, panelled walls and spectacular chandeliers. This remnant of a Wiltshire mansion travels with the company and is meticulously reconstructed whenever they change headquarters.

PASS THROUGH A PORTAL

On a patch of scrubby ground on Mandela Way, just off the Old Kent Road, there is a rusting Soviet T-34 tank which seems to have rolled straight out of the Prague Spring of 1968. There's no explanation next to the vehicle: it's just there, neglected and overgrown.[2] Wade through the weeds until you find the portal to 1960s Czechoslovakia.

TELEPORT A SQUID

Book a tour around the Natural History Museum's Spirit Collection. Among their 22 million pickles is Archie the giant squid, who was fished, frozen and shipped to London in 2004. Giant squid specimens are incredibly rare because they're delicate and decay rapidly.[3] Archie was painstakingly defrosted and now lies in a 9-metre tank. But he's not only of interest to the scientific community: China Miéville's 2010 book *Kraken* revealed that Archie is an embryonic god with the power to end the world. Join the Church of Kraken Almighty, an underground squid-worshipping cult attempting to liberate their leader using teleportation.

Z ——

---

[1] Unless you have mystical powers or a career in insurance, you'll need to visit on Open House weekend. See p.29.
[2] It had been a prop in the 1995 film *Richard III* and was subsequently bought and installed by a local resident.
[3] For an alternative solution to the decay of marine invertebrates, see p.163.

TIME CAPSULES

Time capsules are the most effective way to leave a message for those who come after you.
Add to one of London's existing troves or bury your own.

Look for the old signalling box in the ticket hall of Tottenham Court Road tube station. It was sealed in 2013 and will be opened in 2063 on the bicentenary of the London Underground. It contains, among other things, a special edition Oyster Card and a 'Baby on Board' badge.

Blue Peter buried a capsule beneath the Millennium Dome in 1998. It will be cracked open by the futuristic youth of 2050.

When the Senate House was built in 1933, a capsule was buried in its foundations. It will only be opened on the building's demolition.

The time capsule in Kew Gardens is more useful than most. Their Botanical Ark, buried in 1985, contains the seeds of a range of basic crops and endangered plants in case they're all wiped out. [1]

INTO THE FUTURE

HITCHHIKE WITH THE DOCTOR

Cadge a lift with everyone's favourite time-travelling doctor. Dr Who is currently parked up outside Earls Court tube station. Wait by the blue police box until he gets back, or try and jemmy open his tardis with a non-sonic screwdriver. [2]

VANISH THROUGH A WORMHOLE

In *A Subway Named Moebius*, [3] obsessive improvements to Boston's tube system render it infinitely complex. [4] This tears the space-time continuum, causing a No. 86 train that set off in March to vanish until May. Go on your own Möbius trip around an infinite loop on the London Underground. Take the Victoria Line north from Euston to King's Cross. At King's Cross travel north on the Northern Line to Euston. Continue north on the Victoria Line from Euston to King's Cross. Then go north on the Northern Line from King's Cross to Euston. Exploit this inadvertent glitch in the tube network until you're transported through a temporal wormhole.

COMMANDEER A TIME MACHINE

In Brompton Cemetery [5] look for an Egyptian-style mausoleum containing a trio of mysterious spinsters. It has no key and no architectural plans can be found. It is thought to be a time machine created by the disgraced maverick inventor Samuel Warner, who is buried nearby. Read the conspiracy theories online, then crack open the door and step into the future.

BUILD YOUR OWN

'Jacob von Hogflume 1864–1909 Inventor of time travel lived here in 2189' read a blue plaque at 23 Golden Square. The plaque has since disapparated, just as its predecessor did. [6] Von Hogflume dips in and out of London past and future, and plaques come and go, marking his visits. Ask after him in Soho and see if he'll show you how to construct your own time machine. Look out for your own name on plaques commemorating your future self.

---

[1] Find another time capsule on p.400.
[2] Real Gallifreyan Sonic Screwdrivers are on sale at the Dr Who shop and museum on Barking Road. 'THIS IS NOT A TOY', the website warns.
[3] A 1950 novel by A. J. Deutsch. A Möbius strip is a twisted single-sided surface often used as an image for infinity.
[4] Every single station connects directly to every other station.
[5] Explore the cemetery on p.60.
[6] The previous plaque recorded Von Hogflume's residency on the square in 2063. Photos of both exist online.

Clapham Junction   2 July 2015

Finally, after all these months, I had it.
London on a system of caves, one leading
into the next, beneath an elevated
railway, the colour of an old Penguin
book by Graham Greene or Aldous
Huxley.

THE ONLY WAY <u>OUT</u> IS ROUND.
Every day I walked I met the same
mop-headed madman. He was always
pursued by minders, who filmed his
every move. Today, his fat
gloves pointed out the answer to
my quest. Keep circling, it's
endless. Time becomes space. No past,
no future. Railway is warped spine.
                    — NORTON

POSTSCRIPT

A yellowing article framed on the wall of Mr G's Cafe in Stepney Green informs the reader that his establishment once came second in a National Fry Up Competition run by *The Daily Mirror*. Mr G's award-winning breakfast comprises 'a perfect egg', 'a couple of slabs of pink, porky bacon', and 'tons of chips, a delicious blend of soft and crunchy', all bobbing in 'a welcoming sea of beans'. The overall effect, the piece continues, is 'a visual feast as well as being very tasty.'

London is blessed with an abundance of fine greasy spoons, serving competition-grade fry ups. The grandest is perhaps the art deco Regency Cafe in Pimlico, its commanding black-tiled exterior softened by red-and-white gingham curtains. Less imposing are Brixton's Phoenix Cafe, with its spartan décor and gregarious staff, and Marie's Cafe, a cosy refuge on Lower Marsh, which is greasy spoon by day and Thai restaurant by night. Those seeking bustle should try Bar Bruno, where you can watch Soho wake up from a green leather booth, or Gino's opposite Marylebone railway station, which serves high-speed eggs and b. to passengers rushing for trains to the Chilterns. If you're fresh from a wintry swim in the Hampstead ponds, head for the Royal Cafe on Fleet Road, which has an extensive menu, listing and re-listing the components of a fry-up in every conceivable combination; Veggie Breakfast #3 is a particular highlight. In all of these places prices are low and portions are mountainous.

Happy breakfasting, and remember Samuel Johnson's philosophy: 'I mind my belly very studiously, and very carefully; for I look upon it, that he who does not mind his belly, will hardly mind anything else.'

TIMELINE

PEOPLE

SELECTED COLLECTIVES

ARTISTIC
Angry Young Men, 306; Blake Society,
293; Bloomsbury Group 197, 198, 306;
Blue Stocking Society, 306; City Pickwick
Society, 184; Pre-Raphaelite Brotherhood,
271, 306; William Morris Society, 159

DIETARY
Acclimatisation Society of Great Britain,
375; National Temperance League, 44;
Sublime Society of Beef Steaks, 90;
Vegetarian Society, 10, 44, 346

LOCAL INTEREST
Camden Society, 173; Friends of Foots Cray
Meadows, 299; Friends of Greenwich and
Woolwich Foot Tunnels, 325; Friends of
Nunhead Cemetery, 60; Friends of West
Norwood Cemetery, 60; Pearly Kings and
Queens, 241; Thames and Field Mudlarking
and Metal Detecting Society, 149; Tyburn
Angling Society, 334

MUSICAL
Beatles, 91, 179, 328, 442; Blues and Ballads
Club, 82; Blur, 97, 269; Clash, 97, 325, 332;
English Folk Dance and Song Society,
82, 163; Friends of Dorothy Society (bell
ringing), 34; London Cabaret Society, 67;
Mekons, 332; Morris dancing troupes, 82;
the Nest Collective, 82; Pink Floyd, 102, 141,
360; Queen, 96; Roll Deep Collective, 333;
Seekers, 112; Sex Pistols, 332; Spice Girls, 6;
T-Rex Action Group, 111

PARANORMAL
Fortean Society, 353; Society of the Inner
Light, 365; Society of Ley Hunters, 368;
South East London Folklore Society, 353;
Theosophical Society, 364

POLITICAL
Chartists, 83, 385; King Mob, 84, 143;
Labour Party, 80; People's Press Printing
Society, 307; Reclaim the Streets, 83, 334;
the Southall Black Sisters, 79 Special
interests: British Interplanetary Society,
212; John Snow Society, 54; Last Tuesday
Society, 158; London Psychogeographical
Association, 201; Nightingale Society,
116; Roundabout Appreciation Society,
126; Royal Geographical Society, 412;
Royal Photographic Society, 13; Society
of Aurelians (lepidopterists), 167; Society
for the Reformation of Manners, 285;
Spitalfields Mathematical Society, 158; the
Wynkyn de Worde Society, 159

SPECIAL INTERESTS
British Interplanetary Society, 212;
John Snow Society, 54; Last Tuesday
Society, 158; London Psychogeographical
Association, 201; Nightingale Society,
116; Roundabout Appreciation Society,
126; Royal Geographical Society, 412;
Royal Photographic Society, 13; Society
of Aurelians (lepidopterists), 167; Society
for the Reformation of Manners, 285;
Spitalfields Mathematical Society, 158;
Wynkyn de Worde Society, 159

LANDMARKS

EATING & DRINKING

PUBS & BARS

PUBS WITH CHARACTER & FINE ALE

Albert Tavern, Westminster, 77
French House, Soho, 226, 276, **377**
George Inn, Borough, 2, **184**
Gun, Canary Wharf, 302
Holly Bush, Hampstead, 58, 355
John Snow, Soho, 54, **75**
Mayflower, Rotherhithe, 377
Morpeth Arms, Millbank, 281
Prince of Wales, Kennington, 232
Princess Louise, Holborn, 82, 260
Prospect of Whitby, Wapping 95
Rake, Borough, 250
Red Lion, Mayfair, **25**
Seven Stars, Holborn, **280**
Viaduct Tavern, Newgate, **285**
Ye Olde Cheshire Cheese, City, 184, 219
Ye Olde Mitre, Farringdon, 283

For London beer and breweries see p.185

THEMED BARS WITH A MEMORABLE AMBIENCE

Bar Kick (table football), 225
Bounce (table tennis), 224
Bunga Bunga (Silvio Berlusconi), 377
Cubana (revolutionary Cuba), **382**
Drink, Shop & Do (handicrafts), 144
Katzenjammers Bierkeller (German oompah), 380
Kingly Court (London transport), 330
Maggie's Club (Margaret Thatcher), 51
Reserve Stock Exchange Bar (high finance), 192
Sherlock Holmes (pipe-smoking detectives), 389, **410**
Stafford American Bar (gifts from guests), 377

BARS IN UNEXPECTED PLACES

CellarDoor (former public toilet), 51, **67**
Frank's (multi-storey car park), 64
Madeira Só Peixe (fishmongers), 380
Courthouse Hotel Bar (former magistrates' court), 280
Tamesis Dock (1930s Dutch barge), **49**, 134

GLOOMY BASEMENTS, GOOD FOR CONVERSATION

Gordon's Wine Bar, 328
New Evaristo Club, **335**
Phoenix Artist Club, **90**
The Star at Night, 413

WATERING HOLES FOR MUSIC LOVERS

Ain't Nothin' But (blues), 212
Hootananny (roots, reggae, world), 213
Big Red (heavy rock, metal), 276
Ronnie Scott's (jazz), 212
Royal Vauxhall Tavern (cabaret), **75**
Windmill (indie, punk, alternative), 213, 332, **339**

For folk clubs see p.82

CAFES & RESTAURANTS

CAFES IN UNEXPECTED PLACES

Brunswick House (architectural salvage company), 255
Ernst & Young foyer (professional services firm), 197
Host (church of St Mary Aldermary), 20
Jamyang (Buddhist centre), **128**
Lido Cafe (outdoor swimming pool), 234
Look Mum No Hands! (bike shop), **96**
RIBA cafe (industry association), **18**
Rolling Scones (industrial estate), 244
Waterside Cafe (narrow boat), **137**
V&A Museum (tiled hall), 247

CAFES WITH A SOCIAL PURPOSE

Black Sheep Coffee, 216
Cafe of Good Hope, 151
Hackney Pirates' Ship of Adventures Cafe, 144
inSpiral Lounge, **35**
Old Spike Roastery, 216
People's Kitchen, 245

OLD HAUNTS

Bar Italia, **181**, 212
E. Pellicci's, **181**
Maison Bertaux, 377
M. Manze, **5**
Syd's Coffee Stall, **242**

For London's oldest eateries see p.184
For new chain cafes and restaurants see p.245

SOPHISTICATED DINING OPTIONS

Andrew Edmunds, 64
Bibendum, **21**
Bob Bob Ricard, 64
Mildred's, 44
Quo Vadis, x, 7
Rex Whistler Restaurant, **335**
Roast, 38
Simpson's-in-the-Strand, 58, 297
St John, 273, 349, 375
Wolseley, **5**, 412

RESTAURANTS WITH DISTINCTIVE STAFFING ARRANGEMENTS

Bonnington Cafe (community run, rotating chefs), 13, **136**
Clink Restaurant (prisoners from HMP Brixton), 280
Dans Le Noir (blind and visually impaired waiting staff), 64
Mazi Mas (women from refugee and migrant communities), **385**
Pale Blue Door (transvestite front of house staff), **77**
Sarastro (operatic waiting staff), 90

SUPERLATIVE INTERNATIONAL CUISINE

Balthazar, 120
Bar Estrela, 380
Beirut Express, 381
Brasserie Zédel, **335**
Dumpling's Legend, 212
Fatboy's Diner 301, 377
Fish, Wings and Tings, 377
Franco Manca, 38, **267**
Indian YMCA, 10
Kennington Tandoori, 80
Pizzeria Pappagone, 377

For more international options see pp.382–3

MUSEUMS

CALENDAR

ANNUAL

JANUARY

Burns Night (25th), p.228
Ice Sculpting Festival, p.196
No Trousers Tube Ride, p.285
Twelfth Night (5th/6th), p.90, 205

FEBRUARY

Blessing of Sore Throats (3rd), p.110
Big Count, Thames River Watch, p.374
Chinese New Year 380, p.384
Clowns Service (first Sunday), p.148
Fashion Week, p.308
Imbolc (2nd), p.355
Pancake Racing (Shrove Tuesday), p.226
Trial of the Pyx, p.187

MARCH

Cherry trees blossom, p.310
Inter-Livery Bridge Tournament
    (first Monday), p.178
Night sky forms a celestial clock face (7th), p.310
Ostara (21st-22nd), p.355
Squirrels in season, p.375
Swearing on the Horns, p.396
World Water Day (22nd), p.390

APRIL

Ceremony of the Widow's Sixpence
    (Good Friday), p.256
Chair Lifting (Easter Monday), p.82
Oxford & Cambridge Goat Race, p.226
Royal Maundy Service (Maundy Thursday), p.190
Songkran (13th), p.381
Swallows arrive, p.310
Vaisakhi (13th), p.376

MAY

Anatolian Cultural Fete, p.380
Beating of the Bounds (Ascension Day), p.14
Beltane (1st), p.355
Boishakhi Mela (second weekend), p.376
Burlesque Festival, p.67
Coffee Festival (early bank holiday), p.180
International Workers Day rally (1st), p.85
Jack in the Green (1st), p.82
Mild Month in May campaign, p.185
Pinner Fair, p.406
Wild garlic picking, p.149

JUNE

Camden Rocks Festival, p.332
Dallowday (middle Wednesday), p.316
Gherkin Challenge, p.26
Kith of Yggdrasil Althing, p.398
Knollys Rose Ceremony (second Monday), p.189
Medieval Joust, Eltham Palace, p.228
Naked Bike Ride, p.96
Pooh Sticks Championships, p.155
Pride in London, p.34, 74
Streatham Common Kite Day, p.98
Summer Solstice (21st–22nd), p.354, 359

JULY

Chap Olympiad, p.226
Doggett's Coat & Badge Race, p.226
Great London Swim, p.235
Human Race Swim, p.302
Museum of Childhood Summer Festival, p.154
Our Lady of Mount Carmel procession
    (third Sunday), p.377
Soapbox Race, p.226
Sewage Week, p.56
Swan Upping (third week), p.179
Waiters Race, p.226

AUGUST

Brixton Splash (first Sunday), p.34
Lughnasadh (1st), p.354
Notting Hill Carnival, p.34, 89
Streak for Tigers, p.403
Swearing on the Horns, p.396

SEPTEMBER

Arm Wrestling tournament, p.227
Blackberrying, p.149
Brixton Bolt, p.226
Fashion Week, p.308
Great Gorilla Run, p.226
Great River Race, p.226
Hampton Court grapes in season, p.392
Horseman's Sunday (penultimate Sunday), p.153
Last Night of the Proms (second Saturday), p.205
Mabon (21st-23rd), p.354
Open House Weekend, p.29, 157, 419
Pumphandle Lecture, p.54
Putney Common Open Day, p.266
Stags rutting, p.310
Straw Jack, p.82
Totally Thames Festival, p.384

MONTHLY

* More monthly moots listed on p. 370.

WEEKLY

MONDAY

Alligator's Mouth storytime (also Tuesdays), p.143
Lucha Wrestling beginner classes, p.228
St Martin-in-the-Fields lunchtime
   concert (also Tuesdays and Fridays), p.5
Wigmore Hall lunchtime concert, p.128

TUESDAY

Broadgate Ice Rink tournaments (in winter), p.229
Cinema Club, Rotherhithe Picture
   Research Library, p.169
City of London Bowls Club matches, p.229
City of London Police Museum opens
   (also Wednesdays), p.283
Hampstead Lawn Billiard and Skittle
   Club games, p.227

WEDNESDAY

London Pétanque Club matches (in summer), p.232
Prime Minister's Questions, p.80
Roman Baths, Strand Lane, visitable
   by appointment, p.397
Shami Kebabs served at Tayyabs, p.383
St Martin-in-the-Fields jazz in the crypt, p.325

THURSDAY

Grow Heathrow community workday, p.136
Kick Babyfoot Association tournaments, p.225
Somerset House free tour, p.19
Trad Academy Sea Shanty Choir rehearsals, p.138
UCL politics lectures (during term time), p.80

FRIDAY

Belly Dancing, Pasha, p.383
Friday Night Skate, Wellington Arch, p.228
Hampstead Observatory opens
   (September to April, also Saturdays), p.208
National Portrait Gallery drawing classes, p.204
Old Bond Street 23-bell carillon
   (also Saturdays), p.314
Old Police Station Art Centre cell parties, p.283
Oompah Brass, Katzenjammers Bierkeller, p.380
Open Skate sessions, Bermondsey, p.233
Terry and Julie cross over the river, p.302
Up the Creek after-party (also Saturday), p.213

SATURDAY

Burlesque Cream Tea, Volupté, p.67
Charing Cross Collectors' Fair, p.190
Chessboxing, Islington Boxing Club, p.228
Maltby Street Market, p.243
Somerset House free tour, p.19
Speed Surgery, Old Operating Theatre, p.43
Tin Tabernacle opens, Kilburn, p.137
Ultimate Frisbee, Clapham Common, p.232

SUNDAY

Barbican Conservatory opens, p.24
Battersea Car Boot Sale, p.134
Brick Lane Market, p.382
Carrom, Brick Lane, p.225
Chatsworth Road Market, p.173
Columbia Road Market, p.243
Garrick's Temple to Shakespeare opens
   (in summer), p.120
Hackney Marshes football, p.224
London Camanachd matches,
   Wandsworth Common, p.232
National Gallery magic carpet storytime, p.143
Marylebone Farmers' Market, p.107
Naturist London Swim, p.229
Peanut and palm nut soup served
   at Gold Coast, p.382
Petticoat Lane Market, p.243
Roller Stroll, Serpentine Road, p.228
Swedenborgian Service, West Wickham, p.113
Theosophical Society library visitable
   by appointment, p.364

DAILY

5.30	Buses disperse from Stockwell Bus Garage, p.221
Dawn	Peace Pagoda prayers, Battersea Park, p.221
7.30	Morning Prayer, Westminster Abbey, p.221
11.30	Changing of the Guard, Buckingham Palace, p.5
1pm	Time Ball drops, Royal Observatory, p.305
2.30pm	Pelican feeding, St James's Park, p.145
3.30pm	Tyburn Tree pilgrimage (also at 10.30 and 5.30pm), p.110
6pm	'Oranges and Lemons', St Clement's (also at 9am and 3pm), p.314
Dusk	Lamp lighting, Pall Mall, p.204
9.53pm	Ceremony of the Keys, Tower of London, p.204
11.50pm	Caledonian Sleeper leaves Euston, p.206

FURTHER READING

The following inspired or informed *Curiocity*.

LONDON HISTORIES & GUIDES

London Labour & the London Poor by Henry Mayhew (1851)

Nairn's London by Ian Nairn (1966)

London As it Might Have Been by Felix Barker & Ralph Hyde (1982)

London: A Social History by Roy Porter (1994)

London: The Biography by Peter Ackroyd (2000)

A Dictionary of London Place Names by A. D. Mills (2001)

London in the Twentieth Century by Jerry White (2001)

London Calling: How Black and Asian Writers Imagined a City by Sukhdev Sandhu (2003)

London: From Punk to Blair edited by Joe Kerr & Andrew Gibson (2003)

The London Compendium by Ed Glinert (2003)

Medical London by Richard Barnett and Mike Jay (2008)

London Lore by Steve Roud (2008)

London: The Illustrated History by Cathy Ross & John Clark (2008)

Secret London: An Unusual Guide by Rachel Howard and Bill Nash (2009)

City of Sin: London and its Vices by Catharine Arnold (2010)

Discovering London's Docklands by Chris Fautley (2011)

London's Lost Rivers by Tom Bolton (2011)

London: A History in Maps by Peter Barber (2012)

Spitalfields Life by The Gentle Author (2012)

London: The Information Capital by James Cheshire & Oliver Uberti (2014)

The Temples of London by Roger Williams (2014)

LONDON TRAVELS

The Uncommercial Traveller by Charles Dickens (1875)

The Nights of London by H. V. Morton (1926)

Down and Out in Paris and London by George Orwell (1933)

The Unofficial Countryside by Richard Mabey (1973)

Lights Out for the Territory by Iain Sinclair (1997)

Rodinsky's Room by Rachel Lichtenstein and Iain Sinclair (1999)

London Orbital by Iain Sinclair (2002)

Night Haunts by Sukhdev Sandhu (2010)

Savage Messiah by Laura Oldfield Ford (2011)

Walk the Lines by Mark Mason (2011)

Londoners by Craig Taylor (2011)

Scarp by Nick Papadimitriou (2012)

This Other London by John Rogers (2013)

FICTION

A Journal of the Plague Year by Daniel Defoe (1722)

Bleak House by Charles Dickens (1853)

The Complete Sherlock Holmes by Arthur Conan Doyle (1887–1927)

Mrs Dalloway by Virginia Woolf (1925)

Mary Poppins by P. L. Travers (1934)

The Lonely Londoners by Sam Selvon (1956)

The Dwarfs by Harold Pinter (1965)

Concrete Island by J. G. Ballard (1974)

The Borribles by Michael de Larrabeiti (1976)

Mother London by Michael Moorcock (1988)

The Buddha of Suburbia by Hanif Kureishi (1990)

White Teeth by Zadie Smith (2000)

Brick Lane by Monica Ali (2003)

Pattern Recognition by William Gibson (2003)

POETRY

Songs of Experience by William Blake (1794)
Selected Poems by T. S. Eliot (1954)
Wordsounds and Sightlines by Michael Horovitz (1994)
Selected Poems by Linton Kwesi Johnson (2006)

DIARIES

The Diary of Samuel Pepys (1660–69)
The Diary of Virginia Woolf (1918–41)
The Journal of a Disappointed Man
    by W. N. P. Barbellion (1919)
Adrian Mole: The Cappuccino Years
    by Sue Townsend (1999)

BOOKS ON CITIES

The City in History by Lewis Mumford (1961)
The Death and Life of Great American Cities
    by Jane Jacobs (1961)
Invisible Cities by Italo Calvino (1972)
Soft City by Jonathan Raban (1974)
Non-Places by Marc Augé (1995)
The City and the City by China Miéville (2009)
Infinite City: A San Francisco Atlas by Rebecca Solnit
    (2010)
Explore Everything by Bradley Garrett (2013)

BOOKS ON MAPS

Maps of the Imagination by Peter Turchi (2004)
You Are Here by Katherine Harman (2004)
Atlas of Remote Islands by Judith Schalansky (2010)
Cartographies of Time by Daniel Rosenberg
    & Anthony Grafton (2010)
Great Maps by Jerry Brotton (2014)

MISCELLANEOUS

A Dictionary of the English Language
    by Samuel Johnson (1755)
The Old Straight Track by Alfred Watkins (1974)
Waterlog by Roger Deakin (1999)
Lipstick Traces by Greil Marcus (1989)
The Book of English Magic by Philip Carr-Gomm
    & Richard Heygate (2009)

FILMS

The Heart of the Angel by Molly Dineen (1989)
London by Patrick Keiller (1994)
Lift; All White in Barking; and Men of the City
    by Marc Isaacs (2001–09)
The London Perambulator by John Rogers (2009)
London – the Modern Babylon by Julien Temple (2012)
1000 Londoners by Chocolate Films (ongoing)

WEBSITES

The following websites are a trove of London-related
information and ideas:

bollardsoflondon.blogspot.co.uk
diamondgeezer.blogspot.co.uk
greatwen.com
ianvisits.co.uk
londonist.com
londonremembers.com
london-underground.blogspot.co.uk
peterberthoud.co.uk/blog
secret-cities.com
subbrit.org.uk
timeout.com/london/blog
tiredoflondontiredoflife.com

ILLUSTRATORS

TAKAYO AKIYAMA

Congestion & Xenophilia

Takayo Akiyama is a Hackney-based Japanese illustrator and cartoonist. Her intricate narrative-based work has been exhibited at solo exhibitions in London, Tokyo and France. Takayo loves to explore different techniques, such as animation, textile design, printmaking and pottery. She is the illustrator of *Where's Ringo?* Look out for the errant Beatle on her maps.

takayon.com
@takayo_aki

STEVEN APPLEBY

Eros & Vanitas

Steven Appleby is a creator of absurdist comic strips, radio, theatre and the animated television series *Captain Star*. He has published over 25 books and his paintings and drawings have appeared in numerous gallery exhibitions. He lives, works and daydreams among his unusual family in South London.

stevenappleby.com
@stevenappleby

DANIEL DUNCAN

Hagiolatry & Strand

Daniel is a freelance illustrator who creates most of his work in an old stable just outside London. He likes to illustrate narratives and create vibrant characters and environments. Daniel graduated from Middlesex University in 2013 and was shortlisted for the New talent in Children's Books category at the 2014 Association of Illustrators Awards.

dunksillustration.co.uk
@DanielDuncan

ISABEL GREENBERG

Atlas & Zones

Isabel Greenberg is a London-based comic artist and illustrator. Her first graphic novel, *The Encyclopedia of Early Earth*, was published in 2013 and has been translated into several languages. She is currently working on her second book, as well as a series of history books for children that will be published in 2016.

isabelnecessary.com
@isabelgreenberg

MIKE HALL

Nocturne

Mike is an illustrator from London specialising in decorative illustrated maps and architectural drawings inspired by antique prints. He has produced work for many publications, including the maps for issues C and E of *Curiocity* magazine. He now lives and works in Valencia, Spain.

www.thisismikehall.com
@thisismikehall

NICK HAYES

Knowledge & Pearls

Nick Hayes is an illustrator and graphic novelist living in London. He has written two grpahic novels, *The Rime of the Modern Mariner* and *Woody Guthrie and the Dust Bowl Ballads*, both focusing on man's relationship with the environment. For his next book, he is working on an adaptation of the poet Arthur Rimbaud's life story.

NICOLE MOLLETT

Isle & Rules

Nicole Mollett's drawings focus on forgotten wonders and the underbelly of human existence. Recent projects have included creating an artistic *Atlas of Kent*, driving a mobile art space to obscure places, and performances with Magic Lanterns. She lives in South London, but regularly escapes the smog to the Isle of Sheppey. Nicole drew a map of London as a dissected body for issue D of *Curiocity*.

nicolemollett.co.uk
@KENTBaton

FAYE MOORHOUSE

Mint

Faye Moorhouse is a freelance illustrator based in Brighton. Her work is inspired by strange stories, and she enjoys making her own self-published books and zines. In 2014 and 2015, Faye was shortlisted for the Association of Illustrators and London Transport Museum's Prize for Illustration.

fayemoorhouse.co.uk
@fayemoorhouse

ALICE PATTULLO
Livery & Olympia

Alice Pattullo is an illustrator based in East London. Research is at the heart of Alice's personal practice and much of her work has a focus on British traditions, superstitions and folklore. Alice works predominantly with screen print, producing limited editions to sell and exhibit across the UK.

alicepattullo.com
@alicepattullo

LEVI PINFOLD
Folkmoot & Underground

Levi Pinfold has enjoyed working as an illustrator for the best part of nine years and has created children's books including *Black Dog* and *Greenling*. When not at the drawing board, he likes reading, painting and going exploring. He currently lives in
New South Wales, Australia.

levipinfold.com

CHRIS RIDDELL
Juvenalia & Quarters

Chris Riddell is the 2015–17 UK Children's Laureate and the political cartoonist for the *Observer*. He has written and illustrated a huge number of books for children, including the *Ottoline* and *Goth Girl* series. *Goth Girl and the Ghost of a Mouse* won
the Costa Children's Book Award in 2013. Chris lives in Brighton with his family.

chrisriddell.co.uk
@chrisriddell50

JOHN RIORDAN
Blocks & Ylem

John is an illustrator and comic artist who lives in London. He won an Association of Illustrators award for his project *Capital City*. He co-creates the psychedelic, musical comic book *Hitsville UK* and he wrote and drew *William Blake, Taxi Driver* for *Time Out* magazine.

johnriordan.co.uk
@johnnyriordan

STEPH VON REISWITZ
Dust & Wyrd

Steph is an artist and illustrator drawn to mysterious, darkly humorous subjects. Her work includes large-scale drawings, graphic stories, murals and installations. She is a core member of London art collective LE GUN and has exhibited in the UK, Europe, the US, Japan, and China. She lives and works in London.

stephvonreiswitz.com

EDWARD WARD
Grid & Times

Edward qualified with an MA in Illustration from Camberwell Art College in 2012. He is fascinated by the mechanical world, particularly aviation, and specialises in elaborate cut-away drawings of imaginary machines and vehicles. Edward lives with his wife and daughter in East Sussex.

tedwarddraws.wordpress.com
@mr_smashing

CONTRIBUTORS

Monica Ali is the author of *Brick Lane*, *Alentejo Blue*, *In the Kitchen* and *Untold Story*.

Catharine Arnold has written four books about London: *Necropolis*, *Bedlam*, *City of Sin* and *Globe*.

Peter Barber is the former Head of Map Collections at the British Library.

Geraldine Beskin is an occult bookseller. She runs the Atlantis Bookshop on Museum Street.

Bidisha is a writer and broadcaster. Her fifth book, *Asylum and Exile: Hidden Voices of London*, is based on her work with asylum seekers and refugees in the capital.

Shami Chakrabarti is a human rights campaigner and the former director of Liberty, the National Council for Civil Liberties. She is the author of *On Liberty*.

Dr Irving Finkel is the curator in charge of the cuneiform tablet collection at the British Museum. He is the founder of the Great Diary Project.

Mick Floyd is a former Special Constable with the Met Police.

Dr Bradley Garrett is a social geographer and the author of *Explore Everything*, *Subterranean London* and *London Rising*.

The anonymous **Gentle Author** has been writing daily about the culture and characters of the East End at spitalfieldslife.com since 2009.

The poet **Michael Horovitz** was characterised by Allen Ginsberg as a 'Popular, Experienced, Experimental, New Jerusalem, Jazz Generation, Sensitive Bard'.

Richard Mabey is the author of *The Unofficial Countryside*, *Weeds: The Story of Outlaw Plants* and *Nature Cure*.

Robert Macfarlane is the author of *The Old Ways* and *Landmarks*.

Michael Moorcock is the author of *Mother London*. He was born in London at the start of the Second World War.

Nick Papadimitriou is a deep topographer and the author of *Scarp*.

Philip Pullman is the author of the *His Dark Materials* trilogy and is the President of the Blake Society.

Lord Martin Rees is Astronomer Royal. He was President of the Royal Society from 2005 until 2010.

Sukhdev Sandhu directs the Colloquium for Unpopular Culture at New York University and is the author of *London Calling* and *Night Haunts*.

Brett Scott is an economic anthropologist who worked as a derivatives broker in Mayfair before writing *The Heretic's Guide to Global Finance*.

Kelly Smith lives in Islington and plays for Arsenal Ladies Football Club.

Marina Warner is a writer of fiction and non-fiction who was born in London and has worked there since 1969. Her most recent book is *Once Upon a Time: A Short History of the Fairy Tale*.

Dame Fiona Woolf is an energy lawyer. She was Lord Mayor of London in 2013/14.

CREDITS

Every effort has been made to contact copyright holders. The authors and publisher would be glad to amend in future editions any errors or omissions brought to their attention.

Grateful acknowledgement is given to the following for permission to reproduce copyrighted material.

p.6 for lines from *London is the place for me* by Aldwyn Roberts (Lord Kitchener), courtesy of Kernal Roberts.

p.72 for lines from 'Annus Mirabilis' by Philip Larkin, courtesy of Faber & Faber.

p.75 for lyrics from 'Mad About the Boy' by Noël Coward, courtesy of Alan Brodie Representation.

p.151 and p.284 for lines from Selected Poems by Linton Kwesi Johnson, courtesy of Penguin Books.

p.259 for lines from 'The Whitsun Weddings' by Philip Larkin, courtesy of Faber & Faber.

With thanks to Faber & Faber for their blessing in relation to material inspired by T. S. Eliot's *The Waste Land* on pp.300-1.

We are very grateful for all the Twitter contributions we have received.

@AbneyParkN16
@ActionAidUK
@activeNewham
@Alex_Jerman
@amanda_autopsy
@andrewpclark
@artistsmakers
@BadBoysBakery
@barnthespoon
@BartleyS
@BartsPathology
@_BCT_
@BeaBTCharles
@BiblioDeviant
@Bit_Burgers
@BlairCowl
@BluePlaquesGuy
@BoardGameHour
@brixtonwindmill
@cabbiescapital
@caitlinuk
@calverts
@ChickAndTheDead
@cityandlivery

@DanielleWaller_
@dave_skin
@davidpiran
@doctorbarnett
@elmabrenner
@EssexAtheist
@ForageLondon
@ForteanLondon
@FourRedShoes
@GardenMuseumLDN
@Geograph_Bob
@GrantMuseum
@GreatOrmondSt
@GreenManPutney
@Grzeg
@HandelHouse
@Harrods
@HeritageASK
@holbornwhippet
@holland_barrett
@IFB_uk
@ImogenStaveley
@IslingtonMuseum
@I_W_M
@jemchallender
@jwoodx
@jykang
@KingstonMuseum

@LDNchessboxing
@LNWH_NHS
@londiner
@londonquakers
@mafunyane
@malcolmeggs
@MarysiaT
@metoffice
@MrTimDunn
@7iggerbird
@MuseumChildhood
@MuseumofBritish
@MuseumofLondon
@Nickuae
@NovAutomation
@OccultLondon
@ParasolUnit_
@Pastpreservers
@peter_watts
@Psythor
@Quirkative
@RaeGoddard281
@sciencemuseum
@ShanesTravels
@simon3862
@suitpossum
@teabolton
@TheDanishChurch

@TheFanMuseum
@theoldnunshead
@tootingfolk
@ToynbeeHall
@treadwells
@typecooke
@ukpubbitch
@urban75
@vertchill
@visitparliament
@WeAreSpacelab
@WelhamSteve
@WellcomeLibrary
@wellcometrust
@whatcan1choose
@Whatfroth
@WildLondon
@willagebbie
@WindmillBrixton
@wllmkstr
@wordonthewater
@writtleboy190
@YasminSelena
@zsllondonzoo
@7iggerbird

445

ACKNOWLEDGEMENTS

Our heartfelt thanks go first to three great friends and collaborators, Tom Kingsley, Andy Wimbush and Ed Posnett.

Tom helped devise the original folded format of *Curiocity* magazine, designed all six printed issues, and encouraged us throughout the creation of this book. He has been a touchstone for creative decisions and provided invaluable feedback. Above all he's been a great friend to us both, and we are immensely grateful for his limitless energy and good humour.

Andy has also been involved with *Curiocity* from the outset. He helped us glue the first covers, wrote pieces for the magazine, drew illustrations, created our second map, designed and maintained our website and gave feedback on chapters as we were writing. He is a tremendously insightful and supportive friend.

We gave the Best Man speech together at Ed's wedding a week before we got the deal to write this book. Ed is one of our dearest friends and he has been a great companion as we've worked on *Curiocity*, discussing it over many a lunch or long walk and looking at succesive drafts.

Several other people have been instrumental in supporting and shaping *Curiocity*, in particular Sonya Barber, Ed Blain, Matt Brown, Jen Feroze, Jess Heal, Bill Higgins, Mark Mason, Julia Minnear, Huw Moore, Luke Roberts, Belinda Sherlock and Brett Scott. Sincere thanks to them all.

We wouldn't have thought of making a book of *Curiocity* without the encouragement of Patrick Kingsley, and we wouldn't have known where to begin without the advice, sharp eyes and enthusiasm of our extraordinary agent Patrick Walsh. Thanks also to Carrie Plitt and the rest of the team at Conville & Walsh. We are also very grateful for the superb instincts of Louis Mikolay, who designed the sample chapter that accompanied our book proposal.

It's been a pleasure working with such a creative team at Penguin. Thanks in particular to Cecilia Stein, who has been a consummate editor and a great support throughout, and to Emma Bal, Alice Burkle, Helen Conford, Emma Horton, Rebecca Lee, Ingrid Matts and Jim Stoddart. Thanks also to Caz Hildebrand, Tom Key, Josh Shires and Venetia Thorneycroft at Here Design. Venetia designed the book and we're hugely grateful for her brilliant imagination and tireless commitment to this project.

It has been a privilege collaborating with so many exceptionally talented artists. Enormous thanks and credit to Takayo Akiyama, Steven Appleby, Daniel Duncan, Isabel Greenberg, Mike Hall, Nick Hayes, Nicole Mollett, Faye Moorhouse, Alice Pattullo, Levi Pinfold, Chris Riddell, John Riordan, Steph von Reiswitz and Edward Ward, all of whom managed to translate our sometimes eccentric conversations into spectacular maps and illustrations. Many thanks also to Stanley Donwood for creating such strange, stunning endpapers, Paul Bommer for designing the riddle tiles, and Iain Sinclair, who sent us a postcard each month charting his forays around the capital.

We are extremely grateful for written contributions from Monica Ali, Catharine Arnold, Peter Barber, Geraldine Beskin, Bidisha, Shami Chakrabarti, Dr Irving Finkel, Mick Floyd, Dr Bradley Garrett, The Gentle Author, Michael Horovitz, Richard Mabey, Robert Macfarlane, Michael Moorcock, Nick Papadimitriou, Philip Pullman, Lord Martin Rees, Sukhdev Sandhu, Kelly Smith, Marina Warner and Dame Fiona Woolf. Thanks also to Monica Parle, Emily Webb and the young people at First Story.

We have received valuable advice and feedback from Ned Beauman, Imogen Corke, Matt Evans, Christina Hardyment, Molly Hawn, Luke Ingram, Fiona Maddocks, Rebecca Nicolson, Justine Raja, Xa Shaw Stewart and Tom Williams. We were sent helpful recommendations from our friends Helen Babbs, Mark Boldin, Imogen Eyre-Maunsell, Sammy Jay, Richard Loncraine, Ralegh Long, Maz Kemple, Chris Kennedy, Tess Riley and Edward Stanners; and we have also had useful suggestions from Helen Anderson (City of London Open Spaces), Jack Ashby (Grant Museum), Nick Bodger (City of London Corporation), Joanna Bolitho (V&A Museum of Childhood), Anjali Christopher (Museum of London), Simon Clarke (Thames Explorer Trust), Joe Coggins (Canal and River Trust), Bryony Davies (Freud Museum), Adam Dennett (Centre for Advanced Spatial Analysis), Scott Edwards (Royal Geographical Society), Colin Gale & Heather Reed (Museum of the Mind), Phil Harper (English Heritage), Stephanie Hay (Horniman Museum), Evie Jeffreys (British Library), Frankie Kubicki (Keats House), Murray MacKay (Natural History Museum), Lucy Mathews (Royal Opera House), Alison McClary (Society for the Protection of Ancient Buildings), Lucinda Morrison (National Theatre), Josie Murdoch (London Transport Museum), Rupert Nichol (Garrick's Temple to Shakespeare), Esther Saunders-Deutsch (National Gallery), Nicola Stacey (Heritage of London Trust), Catherine Starling (London Wetlands Trust), Stephanie Taylor (Florence Nightingale Museum), Alec Ward (Medical Museums), Tim Webb (RSPB) and Emma Weeks (Down House).

Curiocity began life in 2009, when we started making a folded map-magazine with that title. We made two hand-made issues (1 & 2) and printed six more, lettered A to F. We are indebted to everyone who contributed: Chiara Allsup, Georgia Ashworth, Richard Barnett, Nigel of Bermondsey, Pete Berthoud, Tom Bolton, Tom Chivers, Lucie Conoley, Merlin Coverley, Alice Ford-Smith, Matt Gilbert, Philip Ginsberg, Alex Holmes, Chris Kennedy, Kathryn Mason, Rose McLaren, Alex Morris, Fiona Roberts, John Rogers, Oli Rose, Moya Sarner, Kelley Swain and Peter Watts; and to Annie Gould, who came up with the original strapline, 'London Unfolded'.

And we are extremely grateful to everyone who helped with its production and distribution: printers Arthur Stitt and Cherry Haynes, and the whole team at Calverts; the hand finishers at Busy Fingers; Bill Norris, Mark Chilver and Mike Drabble at Central Books distribution; and all our London stockists, Marion Akehurst (Blackwells, Wellcome Collection), Jason Burley (Camden Lock Books), Gideon Cleary (East London Design Store), Joana Espirito Santo, Gavin Read & Heather Baker (Foyles), Inma Ferrer, Andrew Bright & Giedrius Jastremskis (City of London Information), Georgina Gutcher (British Library), John Harrington (ICA), Malcolm Hopkins (Housmans), David Mantero (Stanfords), Josh Palmano (Gosh Comics), Laura Soar (London Review Bookshop), Sarah Tilley (Blackwells), Brett Wolstoncroft (Daunt Books) and Marc Smith (Rough Trade East).

We would also like to thank Boris Allen, Claire Armitstead, Mark Banting, Laura Bates, Nicola Beauman, Bali Beskin, Bethan Bide, Miriam Cantwell, Jay Carver, James Cheshire, Isabel Choat, Ivo Dawnay, Constanza Dessain, Margaret Dickinson, Danny Dorling, Rachel Douglas, Geoff Dyer, Seb Emina, Gabriella Ferrari, Richard Fortey, Alasno Goosequill, Katy Guest, Alice Hamlett, Tim Heath, Marc Hutchinson, Marc Isaacs, Catrin Jones, Tom Jones, Patrick Keiller, Stephen Lawlor, Jenny Lord, Brooke Magnanti, Henry Marsh, Paul Maskell, Spud Nut, Ollie O'Brien, Fran O'Hanlon, Brother Philip Thomas, Victoria Pinnington, Eric Reynolds, Alex Sheppard, David Shrigley, Stephen Walter, Rachel Woolley and N. Quentin Woolf.

FROM HENRY: I was particularly looking forward to showing this book to two people who didn't live to see it completed: Simon Whitworth, whose quiet intelligence and generous wit made him an inspirational godfather, and Adam Crick, poet, pilgrim and friend, who had an explosive laugh and was the best of walking and swimming companions. I am hugely grateful to them both and miss them very much.

I am indebted to everyone who has indulged my interest in London's eccentricities, especially Sue Cloke and the team at Cheese, everyone at Cardboard Citizens, Stephen Coates, Suzette Field, Daniella Huszár, David Rorke, Shikha Sharma and Joe Watson. Many thanks to my parents, Olivia and Simon, who first introduced me to London, and to my wonderful sister Georgina. My family's love and support is a constant bedrock — they are my benchmark for how to live with integrity, good humour and curiosity. Lastly, thank you Georgie, for sharing the highs and lows, for administering encouragement and perspective when necessary, and for exploring this extraordinary city with me; I couldn't have done it without you.

FROM MATT: Certain people have supported and encouraged me for longer than I can remember. Thanks above all to my amazing parents, Julie and Stephen, and to my sister Jennifer, who I'm incredibly proud of. Huge love and thanks also to Sheila Lloyd, Pauline and Tony Roberts, Bryan and Ann Whittaker, Barbara and Alan Trevitt, Helen Gayton, Brenda and Kevin Williams, and Sarah and Wilf Pomarin. I'd also like to thank Simon Barker and Lindsey Boucaud, two teachers whose influence was formative. Thinking of more recent years, my hearty thanks go to Hugo Azérad, one of the most inspiring people I've encountered, and to Reggie and Peeb, great men I trust completely.

I began writing this book immediately after moving to Buenos Aires in January 2015, trading the depths of winter for heat and mosquitos. While it's been surreal writing about London from 7,000 miles away, it's also been a hugely enjoyable and invigorating time, in large part due to new friends, including Manu and Anita, Pablo and Cande, and Filipe and MariCris. Thanks in particular to Denise Neuman, who taught me Spanish and became a great friend in the process.

Most of all, though, my thanks go to my wife, Lydia: my closest friend and the finest person I know. I cannot begin to express the love and gratitude I feel for her, and this last year, living above Buenos Aires zoo together, has been one of my happiest. Lyd came up with the name *Curiocity*.

A NOTE ON THE TYPE

TITLES

THE TITLES IN THE BOOK, AND THE TITLE ON THE COVER, ARE SET IN JOHNSTON, WHICH WAS CREATED SPECIFICALLY FOR LONDON'S PUBLIC TRANSPORT AUTHORITIES IN 1916, AND HAS BEEN IN USE EVER SINCE. THE DESIGNER EDWARD JOHNSTON'S BRIEF WAS TO CREATE A TYPEFACE WITH 'THE BOLD SIMPLICITY OF THE AUTHENTIC LETTERING OF THE FINEST PERIODS'. HE TOOK INSPIRATION FROM 15TH-CENTURY ITALIAN HANDWRITING, AND DEVELOPED THE FONT WITH THE HELP OF HIS STUDENT ERIC GILL. JOHNSTON'S BLUE PLAQUE AT 3 HAMMERSMITH TERRACE IS ONE OF ONLY FOUR BLUE PLAQUES IN LONDON THAT USE HIS JOHNSTON TYPEFACE.[1]

BODY TEXT

The rest of the text in the book is set in Caslon, which was used to print the United States Declaration of Independence in 1776. It was invented in London in the 1720s by William Caslon, a gunsmith and typefounder. You can find his foundry on p.159, and you can view many of his original punches and matrices at the St Bride Type Foundry (p.168). After William's death, the business stayed in the Caslon family. Visit their family tomb in the churchyard of St Luke Old Street.

THIS PARAGRAPH

The elegant Venetian-style Doves Type was designed in 1899 by Thomas Cobden-Sanderson, with input from his business partner Emery Walker. They used it at The Doves Press, which they established at 1 Hammersmith Terrace.[2] Cobden-Sanderson and Walker fell out disastrously, and Cobden-Sanderson began to destroy every one of the Doves Type typeface matrices, by sneaking them out in his pockets and dropping them into the Thames under cover of darkness. It took him five months of clandestine trips to dump the entire 2,600lb of stock and ensure that Emery Walker was never able to lay claim to them. The font was thought to be lost forever, but in January 2015 the designer Robert Green organised a speculative dive in the water below Hammersmith Bridge and Port of London Authority frogmen recovered bucketfuls of the original matrices. Green has now been able to recreate the entire typeface, which we have used for this paragraph only.

---

[1] The others commemorate three more pioneers of transport design: Harry Beck, designer of the topological tube map (p.13), Frank Pick, chief executive of London Transport, and Lord Ashfield, its first Chairman.

[2] The Doves Press was named after the nearby riverside pub The Dove, which is still serving.

A RIDDLE

We have stuck six ceramic tiles in unusual places around London.

Pictures of these tiles are hidden throughout this book, on pages that reveal their locations in the city.

To solve the riddle, you will need to visit each of these tiles. You may have to hunt around to find them, but they are all easy to access and you never need to move anything to see them.

When you find each tile, make a note of the letters and numbers in the corners.

Once you have found all six, combine the letters and numbers to reveal a seventh and final location, and a codeword.

Go there and say the codeword to add your name to the roll of honour of those who have successfully cracked the *Curiocity* riddle.

We will list the names of all those who solve the riddle in future reprints of *Curiocity*.

The tiles were designed and fired by the artist Paul Bommer, who also created the Huguenot Plaque on Hanbury Street, site of London's first Huguenot Chapel (paulbommer.com).

FOR YOUR OWN MAPS & NOTES

Henry Eliot and Matt Lloyd-Rose are old friends and *Curiocity* is their first book. Henry likes mazes, maps and literature. He leads cheese walks through the City and has lectured on Geoffrey Chaucer on the London Eye. Matt has been a primary teacher, police officer and social researcher in London. He wrote this book while living in Buenos Aires.

www.curiocity.org.uk

OLD STREET

CURTAIN ROAD

NORTON FOLGATE

COCK HILL

GREAT EASTERN STRE

FINSBURY

CLERKENWELL ROAD

BELGR

BETHNAL GREEN ROAD

TOBACCO

E STREET

WAPPING WALL

BLACKWALL TUNNEL

WOOLWICH ROAD

CARDIGAN ROAD

GREENWICH HIGH ROAD

WAPPING HIGH

WEST HAM LANE

ROMFOR

DAVIES LANE